"With the increasing secularization of society and the current emphasis on multiculturalism—especially in matters religious—the massive impact that Christianity has had on civilization is often overlooked, obscured, or even denied. For this and many other reasons, a powerful response is long overdue, not only in the interests of defending the faith, but more urgently, to set the historical record straight. This book delivers that compelling response....

"No other religion, philosophy, teaching, nation, movement—whatever—has so changed the world for the better as Christianity has done. Its shortcomings, clearly conceded by this author, are nevertheless heavily outweighed by its benefits to all mankind. You will relish these pages as they unveil these benefits."

—Paul L. Maier
from the Foreword

It has become fashionable in "the academy" and "the public square" either to ignore or to deny the positive results of Christianity. Professor Schmidt's book instead offers a far more honest and realistic alternative. Reading this book is not only educational; it also is a fascinating inspirational experience.

—David O. Moberg, Ph.D.
Professor of Sociology Emeritus,
Marquette University

HOW CHRISTIANITY CHANGED the WORLD

A CHARITY HOSPITAL for children in London in the nineteenth century.
(Gustave Doré)

HOW
CHRISTIANITY
CHANGED
the WORLD

Formerly titled *Under the Influence*

ALVIN J. SCHMIDT

ZONDERVAN.com/
AUTHORTRACKER
follow your favorite authors

ZONDERVAN

How Christianity Changed the World
Copyright © 2001, 2004 by Alvin J. Schmidt

Requests for information should be addressed to:

Zondervan, *Grand Rapids, Michigan* 49530

Library of Congress Cataloging-in-Publication Data

Schmidt, Alvin J.
    [Under the influence]
    How Christianity changed the world: formerly titled Under the influence / Alvin J. Schmidt.
       p.   cm.
    Originally published: Under the influence. Grand Rapids, Mich.: Zondervan Publishing House,
© 2001.
    Includes bibliographical references and index.
    ISBN 978-0-310-26449-1 (softcover)
    1. Christianity—Influence. 2. Civilization, Christian. I. Title.
BR115.C5 S335 2004
270—dc22   2004023959

Interior design by Todd Sprague and Ruth Bandstra

Printed in the United States of America

HB 01.23.2018

To my cherished sons,
Timothy John and Mark Alvin.
May they and their descendants
continue steadfastly in the apostles' doctrine
as did so many of their Christian predecessors
since the time of Christ

CONTENTS

Summary Charts

ILLUSTRATIONS

FOREWORD

In what some have called this "post-Christian" era, new books on Jesus of Nazareth regularly appear in which there is less Christ and more caricature—all in the name of supposed scholarship. As for the Christianity Jesus founded, there is a similar tendency either to ignore its contributions to our world or to stress negative aspects of church history that also developed whenever believers belied their beliefs. It has become "politically correct" to fault Christianity for authoritarianism and repression, a faith that promoted fanaticism and religious warfare while impeding science and free inquiry.

With the increasing secularization of society and the current emphasis on multiculturalism—especially in matters religious—the massive impact that Christianity has had on civilization is often overlooked, obscured, or even denied. For this and many other reasons, a powerful response is long overdue, not only in the interests of defending the faith, but more urgently, to set the historical record straight. This book delivers that compelling response.

What If Jesus Had Never Been Born? by D. James Kennedy and Jerry Newcombe fired a fine opening salvo in the struggle to reclaim the massive heritage Christianity bequeathed civilization, but the present volume by Dr. Alvin J. Schmidt wins the battle. A now retired professor of sociology at Illinois College, Schmidt carefully documents how Christianity has dramatically improved our world across twenty centuries in so many varied facets of our culture.

Even knowledgeable believers will be amazed at how many of our present institutions and values reflect a Christian origin. Not only countless individual lives but civilization itself was transformed by Jesus Christ. In the ancient world, his teachings elevated brutish standards of morality, halted infanticide, enhanced human life, emancipated women, abolished slavery, inspired charities and relief organizations, created hospitals, established orphanages, and founded schools.

In medieval times, Christianity almost single-handedly kept classical culture alive through recopying manuscripts, building libraries, moderating warfare through truce days, and providing dispute arbitration. It was Christians who invented colleges and universities, dignified labor as a divine vocation, and extended the light of civilization to barbarians on the frontiers.

In the modern era, Christian teaching, properly expressed, advanced science, instilled concepts of political and social and economic freedom, fostered justice, and provided the greatest single source of inspiration for the magnificent achievements in art, architecture, music, and literature that we treasure to the present day.

These pages document it all, showing with meticulous care how so many of our current institutions originated and developed within the church, and how so many "greats" in all branches of human culture were Christian. The author carefully warns, however, that the current climate of secularism and pluralism is now fogging many of these facts. That is all the more reason for the reader to watch how this book dispels such mist in the name of historical truth.

Some moderns with no religious beliefs, of course, have high ethical standards and often show humanitarian concerns quite independent of Jesus' teachings. Professor Schmidt, however, tellingly shows how such secular morality could hardly have been possible without a prior Judeo-

Christian ethic that influenced generation after generation. Any "noble pagan" today recoils, for example, from the thought of killing babies, but "noble pagans" of antiquity prior to Christianity did *not* so recoil.

For years, Christian apologetics—defending the faith—has intrigued me, and I have used historical and archaeological tools to demonstrate how admirably the *sacred* evidence of Scripture correlates with purely *secular* evidence from the ancient world. Yet Professor Schmidt's brilliant study has convinced me that the faith can also be splendidly defended on another front: its record of being *the* most powerful agent in transforming society for the better across two thousand years since Jesus lived on the earth.

In a climate of multiculturalism and its mandate to "find the truths in all world religions," it is hardly politically correct to say this, yet, after reading this book, I must: No other religion, philosophy, teaching, nation, movement—whatever—has so changed the world for the better as Christianity has done. Its shortcomings, clearly conceded by this author, are nevertheless heavily outweighed by its benefits to all mankind. You will relish these pages as they unveil these benefits.

PAUL L. MAIER
The Russell H. Seibert
Professor of Ancient History
Western Michigan University
Author of *In the Fullness of Time*
and *The Flames of Rome: A
Novel*

INTRODUCTION

T his book is a survey of the vast, pervasive influence that Christianity has had for two thousand years on much of the world, especially in the West. Being a survey, the book does not pretend to provide a complete analysis or exhaustive discussion of the countless contributions that have resulted from Jesus Christ's life and teaching, effected through his followers. The book merely highlights some examples of the more prominent effects that Christ's profound influence has had on numerous components of human life. Thus, I am quite aware that in each chapter many additional examples could be cited. In fact, each chapter could be expanded into a book by itself.

Three compelling reasons prompted me to write this book. First, in December 1993, while researching for a Christmas sermon (I am a Lutheran clergyman who spent most his professional life as a professor of sociology), I discovered that there was a pronounced paucity of information extant and available regarding the influence and impact that Jesus Christ has had on the world for two thousand years. Yet, in a rather nebulous manner many of us "know" that much of our culture, especially in the Western world, bears prominent imprints of Christ's influence. Much of that influence is still with us even in the ever-growing secular and religiously pluralistic milieu of today. But when one looks for particular examples in books and articles regarding the influence that Christ exerted through his followers, there is very little that has been specifically delineated. In this regard there is a recent noteworthy exception, namely, the book *What If Jesus Had Never Been Born?* (Nelson, 1994), by D. James Kennedy and Jerry Newcombe. I reference this book a number of times, and to a degree, it provided me with some productive research leads for the present book. In earlier times Edward Ryan published *The History of the Effects of Religion on Mankind* (1802), a book that largely noted the moral contributions of Christianity; a similar emphasis is found in W. E. H. Lecky's *History of European Morals* (1911). The German scholar Gerhard Uhlhorn in 1883 wrote *Christian Charity in the Ancient Church;* and in 1907 C. Schmidt published *The Social Results of Early Christianity.* The latter two books accent only some of Christianity's social influences, and then only up to the Middle Ages. Thus, the present book adds to the historical literature by citing and discussing the multitude of influences and effects that Jesus Christ, through his followers, has had on the world, lifting civilization to the highest plateau ever known.

Apart from the five books just cited, one can also find occasional references in some history books that note the Christian influence on values, beliefs, and practices in Western culture, but such references are usually quite brief and tangential. Most history texts commonly ignore the Christian influence even where it would be very pertinent to cite. Thus, it took me several years to research and "mine" an extremely wide range of historical sources to find specific evidences of how Christ not only transformed the lives of countless people, but how his transformed followers turned an inveterate pagan world upside down. Hence the first chapter highlights the motivation of the early Christians, showing why they were so firmly committed to their Lord Jesus Christ, who had physically arisen from the dead. They knew that his resurrection was an empirical fact and that they were not worshiping a dead Jewish carpenter. This knowledge—not mere faith—gave them the courage and the stamina to counter the pagan forces that for three centuries fiercely opposed them and their existence, often persecuting them, torturing many of them with all sorts of barbarous acts of cruelty, and putting many of them to death.

The second reason for writing this book had to do with my having been a professor for more than three decades. As an educator I, like so many of my Christian predecessors, have always had a strong belief in the value of education and learning. Thus, I wanted to provide a one-volume resource by which the average reader could learn about the magnanimous influences that Jesus Christ, through his followers, has had for centuries on billions of people and social institutions to this very day. This educational objective is especially important today because Christianity is not only poorly under-stood, but also maligned, especially by many in the mass media.

Some media figures say their goal is to be "respectful" of Christianity's basic beliefs, as did Peter Jennings when he produced *Peter Jennings Reporting: The Search for Jesus* on June 26, 2000, in a Disney/ABC televi-sion special. But his respect faltered badly. For instance, by having given only a minimal role to one conservative biblical scholar in his two-hour pro-gram, as opposed to the prominence of liberal skeptics, he unwittingly revealed a disrespect for Christianity. This was particularly evident when he said that "most scholars we talked to think these stories [the miracles] were invented by the Gospel writers as advertisement for Christianity in its early years. Christianity, after all, was competing for followers with Judaism and with Greek and Roman pagan religions." It is not respectful to present Christianity as a story devised by con men, ignoring the historical fact that all of the apostles except John signed their testimony in blood, so to speak, by suffering the death of martyrdom for the veracity of what they preached and wrote. Con men do not die for stories they contrived.

Many today who disparage Christianity may not know or believe that, were it not for Christianity, they would not have the freedom that they presently enjoy. The very freedom of speech and expression that ironically permits them to castigate Christian values is largely a by-product of Christianity's influences that have been incorporated into the social fabric of the Western world, as chapter 10 documents. This freedom, similar to the freedom that Adam and Eve once had, ironically permits the possessors of freedom to dishonor the very source of their freedom. As Fernand Braudel has so eloquently stated, "Throughout the history of the West, Christianity has been at the heart of the civilization it inspires, even when it has allowed itself to be captured or deformed by it."[1]

On the basis of the historical evidence, I am fully persuaded that had Jesus Christ never walked the dusty paths of ancient Palestine, suffered, died, and risen from the dead, and never assembled around him a small group of disciples who spread out into the pagan world, the West would not have attained its high level of civilization, giving it the many human benefits it enjoys today. One only needs to look to sectors of the world where Christianity has had little or no presence to see the remarkable differences. This observation is not just the result of my Christian convictions, but also the opinion of many other reputable scholars, some of whom are or were not Christians. For instance, W. E. H. Lecky, although a critic of Christianity, in his voluminous writings frequently credits Christianity for the many civilized values and practices it gave to Western society.

In writing this book that accents Christianity's countless contributions, I am aware that often over the centuries many sins of omission and commission unfortunately were perpetrated by those who bore the name Christian. Where appropriate, I note some of those unfortunate occurrences. Yet, in spite of them God continued to furnish faithful followers of his Son Jesus Christ who, as a by-product of their faith in him, introduced and established immense improvements for two thousand years in virtually every human endeavor. As Thomas Cahill has expressed it, "We must consider that Christianity's 'initial thrust' has hurled 'acts and ideas' not only 'across centuries,' but also around the world."[2] That is what the following fifteen chapters portray.

NOTES

1. Fernand Braudel, *A History of Civilization,* trans. Richard Mayne (New York: Penguin Books, 1994), 333.

2. Thomas Cahill, *Desire of the Everlasting Hills: The World Before and After Jesus* (New York: Nan A. Talese, Doubleday, 1999), 311.

PEOPLE TRANSFORMED
by JESUS CHRIST

"Do not be conformed to this world, but be transformed...that you may prove what is that good and acceptable and perfect will of God."
St. Paul in Romans 12:2 NKJV

Jesus began his public ministry of preaching, teaching, and healing at about age thirty, using the town of Capernaum as his main base. Here, as in the two neighboring towns of Korazin and Bethsaida, he lamented the people's apathy and unbelief in spite of his having performed many miracles in their presence (Matthew 11:21–24). He healed the blind, the lame, the lepers, and the deaf. He miraculously fed five thousand with seven loaves and two fish. He never entertained an evil thought; he practiced no deceit, had no selfish desires, engaged in no false pretenses, harmed no one, and voiced no guile or hatred, even to those who maligned and mistreated him. He understood people like no other person did, and he spoke and taught as one "who had authority" (Matthew 7:29), a fact that even his critics admitted. Yet he received no honor or accolades. He had no home of his own. He once described his plight, saying, "Foxes have holes and birds of the air have nests, but the Son of Man has no place to lay his head" (Luke 9:58). To top it off, his own people crucified him.

This man's unique and exemplary life, and his suffering, death, and physical resurrection from the dead transformed his handpicked disciples as well as the lives of many others. As he once said, "I came that [you] may have life, and have it abundantly" (John 10:10 NRSV). The lives that he transformed in turn changed and transformed much of the world: its morals, ethics, health care, education, economics, science, law, the fine arts, and government. These changes, often not recognized, are still largely operative in the West, continuing to produce many positive effects that are also present in some non-Western areas of the world.

CHRIST TRANSFORMED HIS DISCIPLES

Jesus' disciples originally were plain, ordinary Jewish citizens. Several were fishermen, one came from the socially despised tax collectors, and the others similarly came from low-ranking occupations. They had different personalities and temperaments. One was overconfident, two craved special recognition, another was skeptical, and still another was a self-serving miser.

The evening before his trial and crucifixion, when Jesus went to the Garden of Gethsemane to pray, his disciples lacked the stamina to stay awake in order to support and comfort him. A few hours later one of them—the overconfident Peter—even denied knowing him. The next morning, as Jesus was crucified, all except John hid in fear. No one would have guessed at this time that these fear-stricken individuals and their associates would in a few years be accused by some of the Jews of having "turned the world upside down" (Acts 17:6 NKJV) by their preaching and teaching the message that Christ had entrusted to them.

When Pontius Pilate crucified Christ, it appeared to his disciples that everything had come to an end. Seeing the fate of their teacher and master, they feared for their lives. What they had been privileged to see and hear for three years now seemed to be a mistaken dream. Apparently, Jesus was just another man—and a badly mistaken one. They acted like sheep without a shepherd. Most surprising of all was their failure to remember what he had explicitly told them earlier, that "the Son of Man must suffer many things and be rejected by the elders, chief priests and teachers of the law, and he must be killed and on the third day be raised to life" (Luke 9:22).

The third day after Jesus had undergone the cruelest and most inhumane form of execution known to man, he physically rose from the dead.

Three female friends of the disciples went to the tomb early Sunday morning to anoint Jesus' dead body with spices. When they arrived at the tomb, they were shocked to find the stone rolled aside and the tomb empty. Only the linen cloths in which Jesus' body had been wrapped lay empty in the tomb. Luke says that the women ran to tell the disciples, but "they did not believe the women, because their words seemed to them like nonsense" (Luke 24:11). Nonetheless, Peter and John decided to go and see for themselves. Indeed, they too found the tomb empty.

As Peter and John returned home, Mary tarried at the tomb, weeping. An unknown man at the tomb asked why she was crying. Thinking the man was the gardener, she asked him where he had put Jesus' body. The man then called Mary by her name. At that moment she realized that she was talking not to the gardener but to the risen Christ. After this encounter, she again went to the disciples. This time she reported that she had not just seen the tomb empty, but that she had actually seen and spoken with the resurrected Jesus.

That Sunday evening, while ten of the fear-stricken disciples (Thomas being absent) were together in a tightly closed room, Jesus entered, locked doors notwithstanding. As he appeared, he said, "Peace be with you." Next he showed them his pierced hands and feet. This appearance brought joy to the disciples (John 20:19–20). It was the beginning of the transformation that would soon make them courageous proclaimers and defenders of his resurrection from the dead.

Soon after Christ appeared to his disciples, they told the formerly absent Thomas that the risen Lord had appeared to them behind locked doors. Thomas, however, refused to believe them, saying he needed to see and touch Christ's wounded hands and side before he would believe such a preposterous report. He was not about to accept their account on the basis of mere faith. He wanted concrete, empirical evidence. Eight days later Jesus gave Thomas the requested evidence when he again entered the same locked room. This time Thomas was present, and Jesus asked him to touch his pierced hands and side. Upon confronting the empirical evidence of the risen Christ's body, Thomas exclaimed, "My Lord and my God!" (John 20:28). His confession, the most significant one in the entire Bible, declared that this risen Jesus was not just a man but also God.

Encountering the physically resurrected body of Christ transformed Thomas from a skeptic to a believer. However, his fearful, doubting companions, who already had experienced great joy a week earlier, still needed more assurance. Jesus recognized their need. Thus, between the time of his resurrection on Easter and his ascension to heaven (a period of forty days), he made at least ten specific post-resurrection appearances. Twenty years or so after Christ's resurrection, Paul, the onetime persecutor of Christians, defended the historical fact of Christ's physical resurrection by telling some of the skeptics in Corinth that the risen Christ had appeared to some five hundred people on one occasion (1 Corinthians 15:6). Many of these individuals, said Paul, were still alive. Skeptics could ask them, if they did not want to believe the eyewitness accounts by him and the disciples.

In order to get the disciples to dismiss the thought that he might merely be a spirit, Jesus asked them on one occasion (similar to his encounter with Thomas) to touch his wounded hands and feet. Then he added, "A ghost does not have flesh and bones, as you see I have." To give them even more certainty, he supported this statement with further empirical evidence by asking if they had any food to eat. In response they handed him a piece of broiled fish, which he ate in their presence (Luke 24:37–43). These appearances fortified the disciples' first joyful experience, and they now became fully convinced that he had indeed risen from the dead.

The appearances of Christ's physically resurrected body not only transformed the disciples from fear and doubt, but it also enabled them to understand what Jesus had told them before his crucifixion. He said, " I am the resurrection and the life. He who believes in me will live, even though he dies; and whoever lives and believes in me will never die" (John 11:25–26), and also, "everyone who looks to the Son and believes in him shall have eternal life, and I will raise him up at the last day" (John 6:40). They finally understood that he would someday also raise them from the dead and that they, as believers in him and his resurrection, would live forever.

Now that they understood the full meaning of Christ's suffering, death, and resurrection, they were not only transformed, but they were also motivated to proclaim that message in various parts of the world without fear. Thus, not many years later, when threatened by the Roman authorities, Peter and John said fearlessly, "We cannot help speaking about what we have seen and heard" (Acts 4:20). Another time Peter told his fellow Christians, "We did not follow cleverly invented stories when we told you about the power and coming of our Lord Jesus Christ, but we were eyewitnesses of his majesty" (2 Peter 1:16). They knew Christ's physical resurrection was a historical fact, similar to all other facts in history. Unlike many modern liberal theologians, such as those who are part of the current "Jesus Seminar," who say that most of the words and acts of Jesus in the New Testament did not happen but are merely the words of his disciples and not of Jesus himself—unlike these, the apostles and disciples of Jesus knew (not just believed) that what they reported had empirically transpired.

So convinced and motivated were they that, according to well-attested tradition, all except the Apostle John signed their testimony in blood by dying for what they preached and wrote. Tradition and legends say that Matthew was killed by a sword in Ethiopia; Mark died after being dragged by horses through the streets of Alexandria, Egypt; Luke was hanged in Greece; Peter was crucified upside down; James the Just (half brother of Jesus) was clubbed to death in Jerusalem; James the son of Zebedee was beheaded by Herod Agrippa I in Jerusalem; Bartholomew was beaten to death in Turkey; Andrew was crucified on an X-shaped cross in Greece; Thomas was reportedly stabbed to death in India; Jude was killed with arrows; Matthias, successor to Judas, was stoned and then beheaded; Barnabas was stoned to death; Paul was beheaded under Nero in Rome.[1] As stated in the introduction, men do not die for stories they contrive.

More People Transformed

The power of Christ's gospel to transform individuals did not begin and end with his handpicked disciples. It also transformed countless others, and these individuals in various ways left their mark in history. They were individuals found in Jerusalem, Antioch, Alexandria, Rome, and other places throughout the world.

Stephen, the First Martyr

The English word *martyr* comes from the Greek *martyr,* meaning a witness, a word that early in the church's life came to mean more than witnessing. It soon referred to Christians who in times of persecution died as witnesses to the Christian faith. The word also became a verb as historians wrote about Christians being "martyred." Thus, every time we hear the word *martyr* today, it takes us back to the countless transformed followers of Christ who suffered some of the most severe, barbaric persecutions known to humankind for their Christian beliefs.

The first Christian martyr was Stephen, a deacon who preached to the Hellenistic Jews in one of Jerusalem's many synagogues. Luke, the writer of the book of Acts, says that Stephen was "full of God's grace and power, [and] did great wonders and miraculous signs among the people" (Acts 6:8). The number of Christians in Jerusalem increased rapidly. However, some of Stephen's fellow Jews despised his message and its effects, so they brought him before a religious council. In his own defense Stephen briefly

"MARTYRDOM OF ST. STEPHEN" depicts the stoning of Stephen that occurred in about A.D. 35 in Jerusalem. Stephen became the first Christian martyr. *(Gustave Doré)*

delineated the Hebrew history from Abraham to Jesus and then told his accusers that they, like many of their ancestors, were "stiff-necked" in resisting God's Holy Spirit, specifically by rejecting Jesus as the promised Messiah. Many of Stephen's fellow Jews did not take kindly to this message, so they falsely accused him of blasphemy and took him outside the limits of Jerusalem, where they stoned him to death. Before he died under an avalanche of stones, he fell down on his knees and cried out, "Lord, do not hold this sin against them." These words and his firm faith show that, like Jesus' disciples, he had been transformed by the power of the resurrected Christ. Upon finishing these words, he "fell asleep," becoming in about A.D. 35, only a few short years after Christ's resurrection and ascension, the first Christian martyr (Acts 7:59–60).

James, the Brother of Jesus, Another Martyr

While the biblical details concerning Jesus' immediate kin are sparse, most biblical scholars believe that he had four half brothers, one of whom was James. It appears that Jesus' brothers, like the multitudes around him, at first did not see him as the promised Messiah, the Son of God. One of the four Gospels notes that early in Jesus' ministry his family thought he was "out of his mind" (Mark 3:21). It is commonly assumed that James was one of the family's skeptics. But the resurrection of Christ changed him from a skeptic to a believer. Paul specifically notes that Jesus after his resurrection appeared to his brother James (1 Corinthians 15:7).

Since James lived a pious and upright life, spurning the secular values of his pagan Roman contemporaries, he received the name of James the Just. Eusebius, the fourth-century church historian, says the apostles had chosen James to be bishop of the church in Jerusalem. As a bishop, he reportedly prayed so much and so often in the Jerusalem temple that he developed calluses on his knees.[2] His piety and preaching led many of his fellow Jews to become Christians. This angered the Sadducees and Pharisees, so to stop this evangelizing, they asked him, the pillar of the church in Jerusalem, to deny his faith in Christ. Instead, he boldly and loudly confessed that Jesus was the Son of God. This provoked his opponents even more, so they stoned and clubbed him to death just outside the temple in Jerusalem. As he was physically assaulted with stones, he prayed, like Stephen, echoing the words of Christ on the cross: "O Lord, God and Father, forgive them for they know not what they do."[3] The risen Christ had transformed him too.

These and other early persecutions brought about consequences that were neither intended nor planned. Persecutions diminished neither the number nor the spirit of Christ's followers. The more Christians were persecuted, the more they grew in number and the more they spread to various parts of the Roman Empire. Immediately following the stoning of Stephen, we read that "those who had been scattered preached the word wherever they went" (Acts 8:4).

Saul (Paul)

When Stephen was executed, Saul, a fanatical persecutor of Christians, had given "approval to his death" (Acts 8:1). Soon after Stephen's death, Saul continued to seek out men and women who were followers of Christ and have them imprisoned. One day as he traveled to Damascus in pursuit of more Christians, a bright light from heaven literally struck him blind, and he fell to the ground. Accompanying the light, a voice said to him, "Saul, Saul, why do you persecute me?" When Saul asked, "Who are you, Lord?" the reply was, "I am Jesus, whom you are persecuting." Upon asking what he was to do, the voice (Jesus) directed him to go to Damascus and meet Ananias, who was a disciple of the Way, the name for Christians at this time (Acts 9:1–6).

In Damascus Ananias laid his hands on Saul, he regained his sight, and he was baptized. After being with some of Christ's followers in Damascus for a while, Saul began preaching to gain Christian converts just like the ones he had until recently been hunting down and imprisoning. Soon opponents of the Christian message plotted to kill him, prompting Christians in Damascus to hide Paul and help him escape by lowering him in a basket through an opening in the city wall (Acts 9:25).

Transformed by encountering the risen Christ, Paul, like the disciples and Stephen, was motivated to spread the news and spiritual benefits of Christ's resurrection. For this he suffered and endured much. In his second letter to the Corinthian Christians, he lists some of his sufferings. They included a number of imprisonments, five whippings with thirty-nine stripes each time, three beatings with a rod, and one stoning that left him as dead. He was shipwrecked, endangered by robbers, imperiled by false brethren; he endured hunger and thirst, and experienced cold and nakedness. As a missionary, he traveled back and forth to Jerusalem, crisscrossed Asia Minor, and visited cities such as Corinth, Ephesus, Antioch, Caesarea, and Rome. Everywhere he went, he preached and taught Christ crucified and risen, always trying not only to gain more converts for eternal salvation but also to build up those who already believed. Then in A.D. 67 he was imprisoned in Rome, where the mentally crazed Nero had him beheaded. While awaiting his execution, he wrote from prison to his spiritual son Timothy, assuring him that he had "kept the faith" and that he was ready to depart to go to his Lord. But before he closed his epistle, he added the wish that God would not hold it against those who did him harm or who deserted him when he came face-to-face with his persecutors (2 Timothy 4:16). Paul, once called Saul, had also been transformed.

An Army of Martyrs

Following the examples of Stephen, James, and Paul, first hundreds and then thousands of Christians suffered severe persecution that often led to their being imprisoned, tortured, and often executed during the church's first three hundred years. I say "thousands" because some skeptics have stated that the number of Christians martyred in the church's first three hundred years was relatively small. For example, Rodney Stark, a sociologist, believes less than a thousand were killed in the three centuries of persecution.[4] He rejects the multiple thousands figure first cited by Eusebius in the fourth century, apparently because Eusebius was a Christian historian. If a writer's religious orientation is the criterion for rejecting his reports, then of course one must ask why readers should accept Stark's low estimate, given that he reportedly is not a Christian. Moreover, it should be noted that "it would be false to judge the terror of the persecutions only by the number of those who were executed. When a Christian escaped with his life, it did not mean that he suffered nothing at all from persecution. Exile, painful tortures, flight, confiscation of property or at least business losses, the separation of families—something or other of this sort was experienced by very many Christians, if not by the majority."[5]

While the exact number of martyrs will never be known, it is quite evident from the writings of the early church fathers that the number of Christians who suffered martyrdom was far in excess of Stark's estimate. When one only counts the individual martyrs mentioned by name in the writings of the church fathers and other early Christian literature, that number alone runs into the hundreds. Moreover, in his *Ecclesiastical History*, Eusebius states, "Sometimes ten or more, sometimes over twenty were put to death, at other times at least thirty, and at yet others not far short of sixty; and there were occasions when on a single day a hundred men as well as women and little children were killed."[6] During the rule of Diocletian (284–305, W) and his coemperor Maximian (286–310, E)—a pronounced reign of terror against Christians—all the residents, including women and children, in a Phrygian town (probably Eumeneia) were persecuted and destroyed by fire. This incident was part of what historians call "the Great Persecution." Eusebius says this town's "inhabitants were all Christians."[7] And in Thebais, according to Eusebius, so many Christians were executed that "the murderous axe was dulled...while the executioners themselves grew utterly weary and took turns to succeed one another."[8]

The large number of persecutions cited by Eusebius seems to be corroborated by the pagan Tacitus (A.D. 55–120), a Roman historian and magistrate under Emperor Trajan's rule (98–117). Long before the empire-wide persecutions during the reign of Decius (249–51) and those during the rule of the coemperors Diocletian and Maximian, Tacitus wrote that "an immense multitude" *(multitudo ingens)* of Christians were persecuted by Nero.[9] Many modern scholars lend support to the reports of Eusebius and Tacitus. Even W. H. C. Frend, although hesitant to accept Eusebius's figures without some reservation, says that the "martyrdoms in Egypt [alone] could easily have run into four figures."[10] He concedes that the total number of Christians executed during all the persecutions was probably about thirty-five hundred.[11]

While some Christians (the less committed ones) in every persecution capitulated under the Roman threats and demands to honor the pagan gods and to declare the emperor as Lord, the martyrs who did not succumb undoubtedly remembered Christ's warning: "All men will hate you because of me, but he who stands firm to the end will be saved" (Matthew 10:22). Or surely they recalled Christ's other words: "Do not be afraid of those who kill the body but cannot kill the soul. Rather, be afraid of the One who can destroy both body and soul in hell" (Matthew 10:28).

Most of the early Christians had not personally seen the risen Christ, but they firmly believed the empirical reports of those such as Matthew, Peter, John, and Paul, who in fact had seen him after his resurrection. The apostles' message was strengthened by the miracles that many Christians saw performed. These miracles ("wonders and signs," as Luke calls them in the book of Acts) frequently moved many men and women to become believers. For example, on the day of Pentecost, the apostles, without knowledge of foreign languages, miraculously preached the gospel in various foreign tongues, resulting in three thousand new believers (Acts 2:41); in the town of Lydda, Peter healed Aeneas, a man bedridden for eight years, and all who saw it "turned to the Lord" (Acts 9:35); and in Joppa, Peter raised Dorcas from the dead, and "many people believed in the Lord" (Acts 9:42). Instances similar to these occurred frequently in the life of the early church.

The apostles' preaching, often accompanied by miracles, persuaded many pagans and Jews to become Christians, changing their lives spiritually and morally. Spiritually, they firmly believed that Christ was the only true and saving God, remembering his words: "I am the way and the truth and the life. No one comes to the Father except through me" (John 14:6). And they accepted Peter's reinforcement of these words when he declared, "Salvation is found in no one else, for there is no other name under heaven given to men by which we must be saved" (Acts 4:12).

Theirs was not a superficial faith, but one that moved them to live consistently with Jesus' words, namely, "If you love me, you will obey what I command" (John 14:15). They had no interest in reverting to their non-Christian past for, in the words of Peter, "[we] have spent enough time in the past doing what pagans choose to do—living in debauchery, lust, drunkenness, orgies, carousing and detestable idolatry" (1 Peter 4:3).

The spiritual and moral convictions of the early Christians soon produced consequences throughout the empire. The Romans were a syncretistic people who saw value in all religious beliefs; they wanted to be "inclusive," as multiculturalists would say today. They were proud of the Pantheon in Rome that displayed and honored all gods. They would gladly have welcomed the addition of Jesus Christ to the Pantheon if the Christians would only have agreed to give at least some obeisance to the Roman gods. To do this, however, would have been idolatrous, unthinkable to the early Christians, who unequivocally held to God's commandment: "You shall have no other gods before me" (Exodus 20:3). Thus, given their firm conviction that Christ was God and their only means of salvation, and given their desire to live a God-pleasing moral life, they were destined for inevitable conflict with the pagan society of Rome.

Conflict was not long in coming. Christians refused to perform the common libations, such as pouring some wine or oil on an object, altar, or victim, in honor of a pagan god or goddess. Rejecting libations, together with their refusing to call the emperor, who in the eyes of the Romans was a god ("Lord"), prompted the Romans to call the Christians "atheists." To prove that they were not atheists, they were often asked to denounce Jesus Christ and thereby honor the Roman gods. Declining to do so frequently meant imprisonment, torture, or death. Pliny the Younger, an advisor to Emperor Trajan in about A.D. 111, reported to the emperor that he personally "ordered them [Christians] to be executed"[12] because they refused to denounce Christ.

The first intensive, widespread persecution of Christians by the Romans began with Nero in A.D. 64. The earlier persecutions that resulted in the stoning of Stephen, the execution of James (one of the twelve disciples), and the dispersion of numerous Christians from Jerusalem into various parts of the Roman Empire were instigated by zealous Jews. But now, a generation later, the Romans were the ones who persecuted them, and Nero was the first Roman emperor to lead the attack.

Even tyrants try to justify their treacherous acts. So did Nero. The uncompromising religious and moral posture of the Christians prompted him to annul Christianity's status as *religio licita* (legal religion), a status it had shared with Judaism.[13] Before A.D. 64 the Romans did not distinguish between Christians and Jews. They were seen as a Jewish sect and hence were tolerated along with the Jews. But during Nero's tyrannical rule, Christians were increasingly distinguished from the Jews and thus became a nontolerated, illegal religious group. Some historians believe that the Romans, at about the time of Nero, began distinguishing Christians from Jews because Christians, wanting to commemorate Christ's resurrection, assembled for worship on Sunday before dawn. These predawn gatherings were seen as secretive and contrary to one of the Roman laws in the Twelve Tables.[14] On the other hand, the Younger Pliny, some forty years after Nero's time, refers to the predawn services of the Christians but does not say that those activities were a reason for persecuting them.

Exactly how many Christians were imprisoned and executed during Nero's persecution is not known. As previously noted, Tacitus, a Roman praetor and friend of Emperor Trajan (98–117), said that "an immense multitude" was persecuted by Nero. What comprised an "immense multitude" in this instance is not known. Some historians believe the term indicates at least hundreds; others, especially the skeptics, think it means numbers much smaller. The words "immense multitude," however, cannot simply be dismissed as an overstatement, because Tacitus, a pagan, had no love for Christians and hence no reason to exaggerate their numbers. An exaggeration would only have reflected positively on Christianity, for it would have implied that the population of Christians was so large that it was possible to persecute an "immense multitude." Moreover, a large Christian population would also have implied that the pagan gods did not meet people's spiritual needs.

While we may never know the total number of Christians martyred by Nero, we do know what methods he employed. Tacitus described the emperor's sadistic persecution in graphic terms: "Mockery of every sort was added to their deaths. Covered with skins of beasts, they were torn by dogs and perished, or were nailed to crosses, or were doomed to the flames and burnt to serve as nightly illumination....Nero offered his gardens for the spectacle."[15] Indeed, as Christians experienced Nero's cruelties and the numerous persecutions that followed for nearly three centuries, the words of Jesus, "I have chosen you out of the world. That is why the world hates you" (John 15:19 NKJV), proved to be remarkably true.

Christians were persecuted not only for not honoring the pagan gods and for refusing to call the emperor "Lord" but also because they lived morally upright lives, which was as offensive to the morally licentious Romans as was the religious exclusivity of the Christians. The high morality of the Christians is documented by non-Christian writers. In the words of Pliny's report to Emperor Trajan, the Christians "bound themselves by a solemn oath not to do any wicked deeds, never to commit any fraud, theft or adultery, never to falsify their word, nor deny a trust when they should be called upon to deliver it up."[16] Another pagan observer, the Greek physician Galen, in about A.D. 126 described the Christians as practicing "self-discipline and self-control in matters of food and drink, and in their pursuit of justice [attaining] a pitch not inferior to that of genuine philosophers."[17]

When people live a noticeably higher moral lifestyle, it often angers those who do not; such behavior casts them in a negative light. But the higher moral values of the Christians had another effect. It meant that some of Rome's favorite institutionalized practices and customs received no support from Christians, and the Romans resented this. Note the complaint of the Romans, as recorded by the early Christian apologist Minucius Felix: "You do not attend our shows; you take no part in the processions; you are not present at our public banquets; you abhor the sacred [gladiatorial] games."[18]

Christians also (as the next two chapters show) practiced a morality that condemned the common Roman practices of abortion, infanticide, abandoning infants, suicide, homosexual sex, *patria potestas,* and the degradation of women. Their moral posture was one of many reasons why they were harassed, hated, despised, and often imprisoned, tortured, or killed. The Romans made them into an army of martyrs.

The early Christians were persecuted for nearly three hundred years with intermittent periods of toleration. The persecutions varied with given Roman emperors and with governors in different geographic regions of the empire. To most of the Roman emperors and to much of the Roman populace, human life was cheap and expendable. Killing or harming people physically commonly failed to stir the conscience. For instance, Nero (at less than thirty years of age) killed two of his wives, one of whom was Poppaea, whom he kicked to death while she was pregnant. He also killed his stepbrother, sexually molested boys, and forced many Romans to commit suicide. In disguise he roamed the streets at night with his friends, mugging women; and with his thieving cohorts he also stole from shops. So why would killing Christians arouse any feelings of guilt within him? Indeed, one of his methods was to cover Christians with pitch and set them on fire at night so they would serve as torches to illuminate his beloved circus games.[19]

After Nero's suicide in A.D. 68, Christians experienced a respite of about seventeen years that ended with Emperor Domitian's rule (81–96), who called himself *dominus et deus* (Lord and God). He resumed the persecutions, particularly during the last two years of his reign. It was during this time that the Apostle John, one of Jesus' twelve disciples, was exiled and imprisoned on the Isle of Patmos, where he reportedly wrote the book of Revelation. Eusebius, the fourth-century church historian, wrote that Domitian was second to Nero in cruelty toward Christians: "At Rome great numbers of men distinguished by birth and attainments were executed without a fair trial, and countless other eminent men were, for no reason at all, banished from the country and their property confiscated."[20]

The army of martyrs grew as Emperor Trajan (98–117) extended the persecution beyond Europe. While his persecution was less intense than under Nero and Domitian, it nevertheless took the lives of many professing Christians. It was under Trajan's rule that Ignatius of Antioch in 107 was thrown to wild beasts in the Colosseum. The emperor Hadrian (117–138), who put to death many of his perceived enemies, ironically, executed relatively few Christians. He even protected them from the public mobs who often molested and murdered them. And while Hadrian's successor, Antonius Pius (138–161), was less severe than Nero, a number of Christians were still executed during his rule. One noteworthy Christian who was martyred in about 155 under Antonius Pius was Polycarp, bishop of Smyrna and once a student of the Apostle John. Forced into the stadium, Polycarp was asked by the Roman proconsul to swear by the genius of the emperor and to curse Christ. He replied, "Eighty and six years have I served Him, and He never did me any injury: how can I blaspheme my King and my Saviour?"[21] Before the day was over, he was burned at the stake. Like the martyrs before him and the multitudes after him, he had been transformed by the gospel of Jesus Christ.

It was during the reign of Antonius Pius that Christians were first persecuted simply for bearing the name *Christian*. Earlier, Christians were primarily persecuted for what they did,[22] for instance, refusing to call the emperor "Lord," not participating in pagan sacrifices, women for not honoring their pagan husbands' household gods and frequently for converting their pagan husbands. But with Antonius Pius, being known as a Christian

PERPETUA, a young mother in her early twenties, was martyred near Carthage (near present-day Tunis) in A.D. 202 during the reign of Emperor Septimius Severus. (Mansell Collection)

was added to the list of reasons for hatred and persecution. This undoubtedly reminded Christians of Jesus' words: "And you will be hated by all for My name's sake" (Matthew 10:22 NKJV).

After Pius came Emperor Marcus Aurelius (161–180). He revived the persecutions and on a rather wide scale. It was under his reign that Justin Martyr, once a pagan philosopher, who after his conversion devoted the rest of his life to defending Christianity in his teachings and writings, was executed in 166. It was also during Aurelius's tenure that in 177 Christians were brutally tortured and slaughtered in Lyons and in Vienne, two towns on the Rhone River in France. Throngs of people rushed into the homes of Christians, dragging them into the marketplace "with every kind of maltreatment" and with "every torment that bloodthirsty imagination could devise," says one historian.[23] At Lyons the ninety-year-old bishop Pothinus was slain along with numerous others. Eusebius reports that the many Christians martyred at Lyons were burned and their ashes cast into the Rhone River, thereby ridiculing the Christian belief in the resurrection of the body.[24]

Although after the reign of Aurelius, which ended in A.D. 180, the persecutions largely subsided, they did not come to an end. For instance, Perpetua, the twenty-two-year-old martyr, had her infant child taken from her as she was cast to wild beasts in the amphitheater at Carthage during the reign of Septimius Severus (193–211). In 250 Emperor Decius issued an empire-wide edict commanding all provincial governors to require all Christians to sacrifice to the pagan gods and to the genius of the emperor.[25] Those who refused were tortured and executed. Some capitulated to the emperor's demands by denying that Christ was their Lord, either audibly or by performing libations to some pagan god. Church historian Kenneth Latourette says that Decius's persecutions had a positive effect on the church in that it purged many of its lukewarm members.[26] Evidently, when lulls in persecutions occurred, some joined the church who had not been transformed by Christ's gospel. These members were known as "bread Christians"—adherents out of convenience rather than conviction.

Two years after Decius's reign, Valerian became emperor and ruled in 253–260. Like Decius, he lashed out against the Christians. In 257 he issued an edict that barred Christians from worshiping, and the next year he issued a second edict calling for the execution of bishops, priests, and deacons who did not comply. He also tried to eradicate Christians from the upper echelons of Roman society. Property and possessions of Christian senators and knights were confiscated. If, after these punitive acts, they still retained their Christian convictions, they were executed.[27]

Although a relative calm existed during the reign of Gallienus (260–268), some isolated incidents of persecution erupted here and there. However, a long series of violent persecutions arose under Emperor Diocletian's reign between the years of 284 and 305. Two years after he took office, he was compelled to share power with Maximian, the man who helped intensify the persecutions during the latter years (303–305) of Diocletian's tenure and for several years after. Several empire-wide edicts were issued. In 303 one edict dictated that all churches and copies of the Scriptures be destroyed.[28] The clergy, deacons, and readers were commonly tortured until they surrendered their copies to the flames.[29] A second decree during this persecution commanded that all leaders of the church be imprisoned. Herbert Workman states that in Carthage (Northern Africa) Diocletian so filled the dungeons with bishops, presbyters, deacons, and readers that no room was available for real criminals.[30] A third edict said that imprisoned clergy were to undergo torture if they refused to offer sacrifices to the Roman gods. And the fourth edict in 304 demanded that all Christians offer sacrifices or be put to death.

These brief references indicate that the several edicts during the Diocletian–Maximian–Galerian reign (284–311) resulted in persecutions that were comprehensive and brutally intense, the most severe of all Roman

EMPEROR DECIUS reigned for only two years (249–51), but was the first Roman emperor to initiate an empire-wide persecution of Christians. *(Bust in the Capitoline, Rome)*

EMPEROR DIOCLETIAN, who ruled from 284 to 305, unleashed the most severe campaign against Christians, known as "the Great Persecution."

persecutions. They were only less intense in some regions where given governors lacked the zeal to carry out the edicts as dictated. The severity was not mitigated by Diocletian's own behavior, for one day he personally drove his sword through a Christian in the presence of the praetorian court.[31] In Asia Minor, one town in which Christians were a majority was completely wiped out.[32]

In 305 Galerius, who previously as caesar (second in command) had aided Emperor Diocletian in persecuting Christians, became the new co-emperor with Maximian. Both of these emperors continued and renewed the persecutions until 311, causing the blood of Christians to flow profusely. According to one historian, "in some towns the streets were strewn with fragments of corpses."[33]

Writing about fifteen years after 311, Eusebius, who lived through this horrific first decade of the fourth century, provides a portrait of that persecution. The Christians suffered all sorts of cruelties. Some had their legs broken or torn apart; some had their noses and ears cut off and their eyes gouged out; others had their ankles cauterized and were then sent to the mines; still others were thrown to beasts in amphitheaters; some had their genitals mutilated; others had molten lead poured down their backs;

women were cast into brothels to suffer shame before being executed.[34] The gruesome list of the different methods goes on. According to Eusebius, judges often tried to outdo one another by devising and assigning new forms of punishment and execution.[35]

Ironically, the more the Christians were persecuted, the more their numbers grew. Tertullian had it right when he said, "The blood of the martyrs is the seed of the church." A renowned church historian corroborates Tertullian's claim, saying, "Many pagans became Christians only after seeing the death of the martyrs."[36] Obviously, the many desperate attempts to stamp out Christianity did not work. The persecuting emperors and their abettors—all of them pagans—failed to understand that they were persecuting a group of people who had been transformed by the man from Galilee, whom the Roman governor Pontius Pilate and his sycophants unwittingly made the model for all persecuted Christians to emulate. In pagan blindness, the persecutors refused to believe the Christians who, by their words and actions, made it very clear that in worshiping Jesus Christ they were not honoring a man-made deity (like the Greeks and Romans did), but someone who offered them eternal life, demonstrated through his own death and physical resurrection from the dead.

As noted earlier, many persecuted Christians surely recalled Christ's words that they were not to fear those who could kill the body. Undoubtedly, these words in many instances played a major role in their refusal to offer libations or to make sacrifices to the Roman gods. They were a people transformed, but the spiritually blind pagans refused to believe that it was the gospel of Jesus Christ that had transformed them. However, their adherence to the gospel often converted pagan onlookers, sometimes even those who were engaged in carrying out the acts of persecution. For instance, Maurice, a pagan military commander of the Roman army in 286, was so impressed by Christians not capitulating that he refused to carry out an order to execute Christians, an act that led to his own execution.

The frequent inhumane sufferings endured by the persecuted Christians led the Romans to remark cynically, "These imbeciles are persuaded that they are absolutely immortal and that they will live forever."[37] Similarly, the emperor Diocletian said, "As a rule the Christians are only too happy to die."[38] They imitated the many martyred Christians who preceded them and whose faith was unlike anything any Roman had ever witnessed. Paganism contained no promise that said "He who believes in me will live, even though he dies" (John 11:25). Paganism had no transforming spiritual power. None of their gods had risen from the dead; instead, their gods possessed all of the frailties and weaknesses of human beings.

In spite of the numerous persecutions, as Robin Lane Fox has noted, for virtually three centuries Christians were "not known to have attacked their pagan enemies; they shed no innocent blood, except their own."[39] As transformed people, they, in the words of Jesus, turned the other cheek. They evidently also remembered St. Paul's words that told the Christians that "everyone must submit himself to the governing authorities" (Romans 13:1).

As previously noted, the persecutions did not deter the growth of Christianity. Rodney Stark estimates that the church had a 40 percent growth rate during the first three hundred years. Thus, by the time Constantine legalized Christianity in 313, the Christians numbered between five and seven million, or at least about 10 percent of the empire's sixty million population.[40] Other estimates say they amounted to about ten million at this time.

SOME EMPERORS TRANSFORMED (?)

The Christian beliefs were already made clear to Emperor Hadrian (117–138) by Aristides, the second-century Christian apologist. He wrote a lengthy defense, addressed to Hadrian, explaining why Christians rejected the pagan gods of the Greeks and Romans. These gods, said he, were man-made and thus not gods at all; moreover, they were given to all of the weaknesses and sins common to mankind. Some of the gods, according to Roman mythology, committed adultery, murder, sodomy, and theft; others were envious, greedy, and passionate; still others had physical impediments; some had even died. But Christians, said Aristides, worship and honor God who is neither male nor female, whom "the heavens do not contain...but the heavens and all things visible and invisible are contained in Him."[41] He further explained:

> The Christians, then, reckon the beginning of their religion from Jesus Christ, who is named the Son of God most High; [who] came down from heaven, and from a Hebrew virgin took and clad Himself with flesh, and in a daughter of man there dwelt the Son of God. This Jesus, then, was born of the tribe of Hebrews....
> He was pierced by the Jews; and He died and was buried; and they say that after three days He rose and ascended to heaven; and then twelve disciples went forth into the known parts of the world, and taught concerning His greatness with all humility and sobriety; and on this account those also who today believe in this preaching are called Christians, who are well known.[42]

For three hundred years, more than forty emperors, from Nero (d. A.D. 68) to Maximinus Daia (d. A.D. 313), lived in constant danger of being assassinated by friend or foe; only a handful died a natural death. The remainder were either stabbed to death, poisoned, or committed suicide. Their knowing that the Christians believed in a resurrected life beyond the grave, which made them "happy to die," as Diocletian said, did not prompt a single emperor to ask: Given the ever-present likelihood of death by assassination, how might I learn from the Christians who do not fear death but see it as the entrance to eternal life?

The allegiance of the emperors to paganism finally broke with the co-emperor Galerius, the man who once aided and assisted Diocletian in persecuting Christians and who, after 305, inflicted a considerable amount of tortures and executions on Christians. In 310 he was stricken with the same disease that took the life of Herod the Great three hundred years earlier in 4 B.C. This disease ulcerated the emperor's genitals and spread to his intestines; it spawned worms and released an extremely obnoxious odor—so powerful that many physicians could not stand treating him. In apparent Christian repentance, he issued the Edict of Toleration in 311 on his deathbed. It granted the Christians the right to exist, to worship, and even to build church buildings. The edict was also signed by coemperors Constantine and Licinius. Maximinus Daia, ruler of Egypt and Syria, however, refused to cosign.[43]

What prompted Galerius's repentance is not known. It may have been partly the result of repeatedly seeing and hearing the courageous, unfaltering testimony of many Christians whom he and his subordinates imprisoned, tortured, or executed. It may have also been because his wife Valeria was a known Christian. Seeing him face eternity as he lay dying, she may very well have urged him to repent and believe in Jesus Christ so that he would inherit eternal life. She may have recalled the words that St. Paul spoke to the trembling Philippian jailer who, after he asked what he must do to be saved, heard Paul say, "Believe in the Lord Jesus, and you will be saved" (Acts 16:31). In any case, the edict of 311 apparently was the fruit of Galerius's repentance. Eusebius reports that Galerius died soon after the edict's proclamation.[44]

The second Christian transformation of an emperor, and a more noteworthy example, occurred in Constantine the Great. Having put on the purple in 307 as emperor of the West and cosigned the Edict of Toleration in 311 with Galerius, he defeated the usurper Maxentius at the Milvian

Bridge near Rome in 312. Unlike his foe, who was sacrificing to the gods to gain their favor, Constantine prayed to God for help in his upcoming battle. His prayers, he said, were answered by a vision of the Christian cross in the sky. The cross was formed by the Greek letters *chi* (C) and *rho* (R), one letter overlaid on the other. This cross also symbolized Christ in that both letters are the first two letters in the Greek name for Christ. The vision also revealed the inscription *"in hoc signo vinces"* (by this sign conquer). According to the emperor, the vision was confirmed in a dream in which God told him to make a likeness of the sign and use it as his military standard. His soldiers painted the *Chi-Rho* cross on their shields.

Constantine's army was marching to Rome, where he expected to do battle with Maxentius behind well-buttressed fortresses. But Maxentius, who consulted the Sibylline books, "found an enigmatic prophecy that an enemy of the Romans would perish."[45] Assuming the enemy was Constantine, he and his army left the city of Rome in October 312 to find and defeat him. He met Constantine and his forces by crossing the Tiber River at Milvian Bridge. Despite being significantly smaller in number, Constantine's army defeated Maxentius by driving him and his men back to the Tiber, where in retreating chaos, Maxentius drowned. Constantine then proceeded to Rome to be sole emperor of the West. The victory confirmed Constantine's faith in the new Christian symbol, the *Chi-Rho* cross. He believed that God had indeed helped him win, and he now "considered himself God's agent whose divine job it was to spread Christianity throughout the empire."[46]

One year later, in 313, Constantine (emperor in the West) and Licinius (emperor in the East) joined hands to issue what came to be known as the Edict of Milan; however, it was only an agreement between Constantine and Licinius saying they and the regional governors would no longer persecute Christians. This edict granted full freedom of worship to all, Christians and pagans, throughout the Roman Empire. The document also restored confiscated church buildings and lands without delay or expense. Gibbon says that the carefully worded declaration explained "every ambiguous word, remove[d] every exception, and exact[ed] from the governors of the provinces a strict obedience to the true and simple meaning of an edict."[47]

Although the Edict of Milan had been issued, it did not bring all persecutions to an abrupt end. Soon after Licinius had cosigned the edict with Constantine, he tried to wrest the empire from Constantine. One way of countering Constantine was to continue persecuting Christians in the eastern part of the empire. He prohibited Christians from attending divine services in their churches, and if Christian civil servants refused to honor the pagan gods, they lost their positions. A number of bishops were executed, and forty soldiers were martyred at Sebaste in 320 for refusing to renounce their faith in Christ. The persecutions finally ended in 324 when Constantine defeated Licinius in the battles of Hadrianopolis and Chrysopolis and banished him to Thessalonica, where he was executed.[48]

Had the gospel of Christ transformed Constantine at the time of his vision in 312? Was his influence in issuing the Edict of Milan one year later the result of his now being a Christian? Were his other acts (for example, imprinting the Christian cross on Roman coins begun in 314, granting clergy exemption from military service, declaring Sunday a religious holiday in 321, presiding over about three hundred bishops at the Council of Nicaea in 325, financing the building of numerous churches in the empire) proof that he, like so many others before him, had been transformed by the Christian message? Or, as the skeptics have asked, was he primarily a shrewd politician who saw it to his advantage to legalize Christianity?

This question is not totally without foundation if we remember that Constantine once was a pagan who worshiped the sun god, Apollo. Moreover, in 326 he had his son Crispus executed because he suspected him of conspiring to overthrow him as emperor, and he had Fausta, his wife and stepmother of Crispus, drowned because he believed she was having an affair with Crispus.[49] Furthermore, he was not baptized until the eve of his death in 337.

On the other hand, we must remember that Constantine's mother Helena was a devout Christian, and it is likely that through her words and example he may already have been a Christian, at least in an embryonic sense, when he cosigned the Edict of Toleration in 311. After all, why did he pray to God rather than sacrifice to the pagan gods before his battle with Maxentius in 312? Moreover, while still a catechumen, he became terminally ill in the spring of 337, and while ill, he chided some of his generals who prayed for his recovery. Reportedly, he "rebuked them and said that he was prepared to meet God."[50] He died a day later, on Pentecost.

Even if Constantine was a flawed Christian during much of his reign, the gospel of Christ and the lives of countless Christians nevertheless had a transforming effect on him in terms of the many sociopolitical changes he implemented over a span of twenty-five years. Will Durant describes him well: "He was impressed by the comparative order and morality of Christian conduct, the bloodless beauty of the Christian ritual, the obedience of

Christians to their clergy, their humble acceptance of life's inequalities in the hope of happiness beyond the grave."[51] It was the latter that transformed Christ's disciples and those who followed in their footsteps. From all indications, Constantine too joined that throng. That is why some historians call him the first Christian emperor.

After the death of Constantine in 337, the peace and calm that Christians had so much desired before his rule continued except for a two-year interruption (361–363) under Julian the Apostate, who had become emperor in 361. Julian, a nephew of Constantine the Great and once a Christian lector in his young adult years, renounced his Christian faith and became an inveterate pagan. He restored many pagan temples and tried to revive the worship of the paganism by purifying it and making it less superstitious. In so doing, he unwittingly revealed his onetime Christian influences. Even his negative treatment of Christians appears to have been tempered by his once having been a Christian. It is generally believed that he did not imprison or execute Christians. Instead, he abrogated the civil and religious rights that they had attained during the last fifty years by depriving them of state-held jobs and making them pay for the restoration of pagan temples.[52] He also loved to vex Christians by calling them "Galileans." So adamant was he in calling them Galileans that, even as he lay dying of battle wounds in Persia, he said, *"vicisti Galilaee"* (You Galileans have conquered). By this statement he admitted that the gospel of Jesus Christ had transformed countless individuals and that Christianity had changed the Roman Empire. Julian's statement was reminiscent of what the enemies of Christ had said some three hundred years earlier when Paul and his fellow Christians in Thessalonica were accused of having "turned the world upside down" (Acts 17:6 RSV).

Julian the Apostate, the last pagan emperor, was succeeded by Valentinian I (364–375), a professing Christian. As noted in chapter 2, Valentinian continued on a path that promoted the effects of the Christian transformation by criminalizing abortion and infanticide, two widely accepted barbaric practices in the Greco-Roman world. In 380 Emperor Theodosius, another transformed follower of Christ, made Christianity the official religion of the Roman Empire.

As an institution, the Christian church prospered after the Edict of Milan in 313 even though not all of the emperors were necessarily devout believers, although "all of them outwardly conformed to the faith."[53] The mere outward conforming to the Christian faith, rather than being spiritually transformed, became all too frequent in the life of the church. It often impeded the spiritual transformations that were, for the most part, so vibrant and effective during the church's first three hundred years. Even worse were the many contradictions that surfaced in some of the teachings and life of the organized church: tolerating clergy corruption, often on the highest level; condoning slavery; burning false teachers at the stake; and incorporating secular theories into doctrines and then defending them as biblically correct—for instance, defending the Ptolemaic (geocentric) theory in the sixteenth century.

Yet, in spite of the many harmful errors that the church's leaders condoned and sometimes even taught, the message of Christ crucified and risen still made its way through the tangled web of human sin and error over the centuries so that countless individuals continued to be transformed. The following are but a few noteworthy individuals who were transformed in the post–New Testament era: Polycarp, Irenaeus, Tertullian, Origen, St. Helena, St. Ambrose, Fabiolo, St. Chrysostom, St. Augustine, St. Olaf, Savonarola, John Hus, Martin Luther, Johann Sebastian Bach, William Wilberforce, David Livingstone, Dietrich Bonhoeffer, C. S. Lewis, and Richard Wurmbrand. The transformed lives of these devout and dedicated individuals, like those of their predecessors, effected monumental changes in the world at large. Yet many people today may not know, or may even try to deny, the many contributions that the transformed followers of Christ for two thousand years helped to bring about. These Christ-inspired individuals took the words of Jesus to heart: "Let your light shine before men, that they may see your good deeds and praise your Father in heaven"

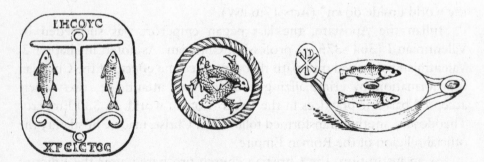

FISH SYMBOLS were found in frescoes in the catacombs in Italy. The fish became a common early Christian symbol because the Greek word for "fish"(IXΘΥΣ) forms the acrostic of "Jesus Christ God's Son Savior."

(Matthew 5:16). And because of them, the world became a more humane and civilized place.

It must also be noted that the early Christians, who were persecuted for three centuries, never set out to change the world. The changes largely occurred as a by-product of their transformed lives—lives that compelled them not only to spurn the pagan gods but also to reject the immoral lifestyles of the Greco-Romans (as discussed in the next two chapters). They knew that Christ had never promised his followers an easy, pain-free world; they also knew he had predicted that they would be hated and despised for his name's sake. "They will treat you this way because of my name" (John 15:21). The Roman persecutors fulfilled Christ's predictions to the nth degree.

By refusing to make sacrifices to pagan gods and by firmly resisting the order to call the emperor "Lord," the Christians did indeed look foolish to the Romans. They seemed to suffer needlessly. But ironically, it was their foolish behavior that eventually turned the empire culturally upside down. And so when the Emperor Julian the Apostate in 363 said, *"vicisti Galilaee"* (You Galileans have conquered), he unwittingly demonstrated the truthfulness of St. Paul's words that "the foolishness of God is wiser than man's wisdom" (1 Corinthians 1:25).

SOME TWENTIETH-CENTURY TRANSFORMATIONS

One Christian editor recently wrote, "You and I would not and could not hold faith in Christ today, if many of the early Christians had not marched into the arena or toiled in the mines, unbent and uncompromised." This editor continued, "Each time you and I meet a Christian, we are viewing a monument to the unknown early Christian martyrs."[54] True! Not only are present-day Christians monuments to the early Christian martyrs, but many still continue in their footsteps of martyrdom. One report in 1979 estimated that more Christians were martyred in the twentieth century than in the previous centuries combined.[55] Here are but a few examples of modern Christian martyrs.

In January 1956, *Life* magazine reported the brutal murdering of five American missionaries by the Auca Indians in Ecuador.[56] One month after the killings, the wife of one of the victims and the sister of another courageously went to live with the tribe. These women let the light of Christ shine while they lived with the natives. Before long, six of the murderers became Christians, and some even went as missionaries to an enemy tribe

Early Christianity Under Roman Emperors

Dates	Roman Emperors	Christian History
27 B.C.–A.D. 14	Caesar Augustus	Birth of Jesus Christ, ca. 4–6 B.C.
14–37	Tiberius	Jesus begins his ministry, ca. A.D. 27/28; crucifixion and resurrection of Jesus, ca. 30/31; Christ's resurrection transforms his disciples; Stephen stoned to death and becomes first martyr, ca. 35; Christians pushed out of Jerusalem into Samaria and other parts, ca. 35; Saul (Paul) becomes a Christian, ca. 37
37–41	Caligula	Christians suffer no Roman persecutions
41–54	Claudius	James, one of the twelve disciples, executed by Herod Agrippa I (grandson of Herod the Great), ca. 42; first church council meets in Jerusalem, ca. 50
54–68	Nero	James, half brother of Jesus and bishop of Jerusalem, martyred, ca. 62–66; an "immense multitude" of Christians, including Paul and Peter, are executed in Rome, 64–67
68–69	Galba, Otho, Vitellius	Christians not persecuted
69–79	Vespasian	Jude, the brother of James, crucified at Edessa, ca. 72
79–81	Titus	Christians live in relative peace
81–96	Domitian	Severe persecution of Christians, 92–96; John the Apostle exiled to Isle of Patmos; Luke, the writer of the Gospel, reportedly hanged in Athens, 93
96–98	Nerva	John writes the book of Revelation; Timothy martyred in Ephesus, 97
98–117	Trajan	Ignatius thrown to wild beasts, 107; Trajan's legate, Pliny the Younger, persecutes and executes some Christians for not denouncing Christ, ca. 111

Dates	Roman Emperors	Christian History
117–38	Hadrian	Golgotha (hill of Christ's crucifixion) leveled in Jerusalem; Eustachius, a Roman army commander, and his family martyred; many other Christians also suffer persecution
138–61	Antonius Pius	Christians persecuted for bearing the name Christian; Polycarp, bishop of Smyrna, burned at the stake, ca. 155
161–80	Marcus Aurelius	Justin Martyr, Christian philosopher and educator, and eleven other Christians executed in 166; numerous Christians tortured and slaughtered in Lyons, 177; additional Christians martyred elsewhere
180–192	Commodus	No apparent persecutions of Christians
193–211	Septimius Severus	Severus persecutes African Christians in 197–98; implements systematic persecutions in 202–3 in which Perpetua and Felicitas are tossed to wild beasts in arena, 202; Tertullian writes in defense of Christians
211–17	Caracalla	Some sporadic persecutions in 215; Tertullian continues defending Christians to the Romans
218–22	Elagabalus	Christians experience relative calm and peace
222–35	Alexander Severus	Christians experience more relative calm and peace
235–38	Maximinus Thrax	Two bishops of Rome (Pontianus and Anteros) martyred; some other Christians also martyred, including Hippolytus, ca. 237
238–44	Gordian I and II (238); Pupienus and Balbinus (238); Gordian III (238–244)	No Christians apparently persecuted
244–49	Philip the Arab	Christians again enjoy relative calm and peace; Origen writes Christian defense: *Against Celsus*, 246–48

Dates	Roman Emperors	Christian History
249–51	Decius	Edict of 250 commands all Christians to sacrifice to pagan gods; first empire-wide persecution; property confiscated from Christians who do not comply with edict; certificates *(libelli)* issued to Christians who recant and perform pagan sacrifices
253–60	Valerian	One edict bars Christian worship in catacombs; another orders bishops, priests, and deacons to make pagan sacrifices under pain of death; property confiscated from many Christians; many Christians maimed and sent to the mines; Bishop Sixtus and his deacons, St. Cyprian, St. Aemilian, Bishop Saturinus, and St. Lawrence all executed
260–84	Ten emperors	Emperor Aurelian decrees *Natali sol invictus* (birth of the unconquerable sun) in 274, evidently to counter Christians in Egypt honoring the birth of Jesus Christ
284–305	Diocletian (East) and Maximian (West), coemperors	All soldiers ordered in 298 to sacrifice to pagan gods; Christian soldiers who refused are discharged. Four edicts issued: (1) 303: order to destroy all churches and sacred Scriptures throughout empire; (2) imprison Christian leaders; (3) torture clergy and laity who refuse to sacrifice to pagan gods; (4) 304: order all Christians to offer pagan sacrifices under pain of death
305–10	Galerius and Maximinus Daia	Persecution of Diocletian and Maximian is extended
311	Galerius and Constantine	Edict of Toleration grants Christians freedom from persecution; Galerius decrees that Christian churches be built

Dates	Roman Emperors	Christian History
312	Constantine and Maxentius	Constantine with the sign of the Christian cross (Chi-Rho) conquers Maxentius at Milvian Bridge
313	Constantine (West) and Licinius (East)	Both emperors sign Edict of Milan giving Christianity legal status
320–24	Licinius in the East	Licinius resumes persecution of Christians in the East; many Christians and Christian soldiers martyred; Constantine defeats Licinius, 324 and becomes sole ruler
325–37	Constantine (sole emperor)	Emperor presides at Council of Nicaea, 325; introduces moral reforms: outlaws crucifixion and branding of slaves; he and mother Helena build numerous Christian churches in empire; Constantine dies day after his baptism on Pentecost Day, 337
337–61	Constantius II	Emperor implements additional moral reforms: segregates men from women in prisons
361–63	Julian the Apostate	As last pagan emperor Julian tries to stamp out Christianity, but dies of battle wounds in Persia, 363; his last words: *"vicisti Galilaee"* (You Galileans [Christians] have conquered)
378–95	Theodosius I	Emperor declares Christianity as official religion of empire, 380; second ecumenical council convened in Constantinople, 381; Bishop Ambrose has Theodosius do penance for killing innocent people in Thessalonica riot, 390
395–423	Honorius	Augustine becomes bishop of Hippo, northern Africa, 396; Honorius outlaws gladiatorial contests in East and West; Augustine begins writing *The City of God*, 413; Augustine dies, 430

down the river. Later two of the killers agreed to attend the World Evangelism Congress in Berlin. Another toured the United States, relating his conversion experience.[57] Today, the Auca village of Tiwaeno is peaceful with a church in its midst.

The Voice of the Martyrs, a Christian magazine that reports on the persecutions of Christians in various parts of the world, furnishes numerous instances of Christians today who, as transformed believers, refuse to deny their faith even at the cost of imprisonment or death. For instance, in November 1998, one hundred house-church Christians were arrested by the Communist government in China; in Sudan, the Islamic government burned down a church with Christians praying inside, and only one person survived; in Egypt, an eleven-year-old boy was hung upside down from an electric fan and tortured to death, young girls were raped, and mothers were forced to lay their babies on the floor in a police station and watch the police beat them with sticks; in Indonesia, Muslim extremists destroyed over five hundred church buildings, killing many Christians as well; and in Cuba, in 1996 more than three thousand house churches were ordered to close, though most did not comply.[58]

CONCLUSION

The countless number of people transformed by the life, death, and resurrection of Jesus Christ in the early years of Christianity was nothing short of phenomenal. The effects of those transformations were equally phenomenal. Christ's followers produced revolutionary changes—socially, politically, economically, and culturally. As George Sarton has said, "The birth of Christianity changed forever the face of the Western world."[59] Christ's transformed followers, especially during the first few centuries, effected that change because Christ's life and teachings challenged "almost everything for which the Roman world had stood."[60] And what Christianity changed, says Christopher Dawes, marked "the beginning of a new era in world history."[61] Or, in the words of Nathan Söderblom, without Christ's resurrection "the entire history of the world since the coming of Christ would have to be fundamentally altered."[62]

A British theologian recently said, "The oddest thing about Christianity is that it got going at all."[63] There were ten or more messianic movements in Palestine that failed within about one hundred years before and after Christ. One was the movement of Judas the Galilean, who led a revolt around the time of Christ's birth. In A.D. 66–70, Menachem, a leader of the Sicarii and seen as a messiah, was killed by a group of rival Jews. Following him, Eleazar assumed Menachem's leadership. He and his adherents, marooned on the Masada rock, committed suicide in A.D. 72 rather than let the Romans capture them.[64] Then about one hundred years after Christ's crucifixion and resurrection, Simeon ben-Kosiba (Bar Kokhba), also seen by many as a messiah, led a revolution. His movement ended with his execution. It was the end of another failed messianic group, but not so with the followers of Christ.

Unlike the leaders of these and other religious movements, Jesus was no political figure; he had no connection with Herod or the Sanhedrin; he took no political action; his disciples were relatively uneducated. Yet he changed millions more than Alexander the Great, Mohammed, and Napoleon put together.[65] It all happened because his message and his physical resurrection transformed his early followers, who did not pick up the sword to defend themselves even during brutal persecutions, but rather they went about spreading his love and the need for his forgiveness by word and deed to all—regardless of race, sex, ethnicity, poverty, or wealth. They did so because they believed with all their heart, soul, and might the words of Jesus: "I am the way and the truth and the life. No one comes to the Father except through me" (John 14:6). They echoed the conviction of Peter's words spoken to his fellow Jews: "Salvation is found in no one else, for there is no other name under heaven given to men by which we must be saved" (Acts 4:12).

They took this stance because they *knew* that Jesus Christ, who was crucified under Pontius Pilate, did in fact physically and empirically rise from the dead. They knew that it was not their faith that validated Christ's resurrection, as many of today's modern theologians teach and preach, but that it was his physical resurrection that validated their faith.

NOTES

1. Grant Jeffery, *The Signature of God: Astonishing Biblical Discoveries* (Toronto: Frontier Publications, 1996), 255–56.

2. Eusebius, *The Ecclesiastical History,* trans. Kirsopp Lake (New York: G. P. Putnam's Sons, 1926), 1:171.

3. Ibid., 175.

4. Rodney Stark, *The Rise of Christianity: A Sociologist Reconsiders History* (Princeton: Princeton University Press, 1996), 164.

5. Ludwig Hertling and Englebert Kirschbaum, *The Roman Catacombs and Their Martyrs,* trans. M. Joseph Costelloe (Milwaukee: Bruce Publishing, 1956), 107.

6. Eusebius, *Ecclesiastical History,* 2:277.

7. Ibid., 287.

8. Ibid., 277.

9. Cornelius Tacitus, *Annals of Tacitus*, trans. Alfred John Church and William Jackson Brodribb (New York: Macmillan, 1921), 305.

10. W. H. C. Frend, *Martyrdom and Persecution in the Early Church* (New York: New York University Press, 1967), 394.

11. Ibid.

12. *Pliny Letters*, trans. William Melmoth and rev. by W. M. L. Hutchinson (New York: Macmillan, 1915), 401.

13. Herbert Workman, *Persecution in the Early Church* (New York: Oxford University Press, [1906], 1980), 22.

14. *Remains of Old Latin*, ed. and trans. E. H. Warmington (Cambridge: Harvard University Press, 1938), 493.

15. Tacitus, *Annals,* 305.

16. *Pliny Letters*, 403.

17. Cited in Stephen Benko, *Pagan Rome and the Early Christians* (Bloomington: Indiana University Press, 1984), 142.

18. Minucius Felix, *Octavius* 12.

19. Chris Scarre, *Chronicle of the Roman Emperors* (New York: Thames and Hudson, 1995), 54.

20. Eusebius, *The History of the Church from Christ to Constantine*, trans. G. A. Williamson (New York: Dorset Press, 1965), 125.

21. "Concerning the Martyrdom of the Holy Polycarp" in *The Ante-Nicene Fathers,* ed. Alexander Roberts and James Donaldson (Grand Rapids: W. B. Eerdmans, 1981), 1:41.

22. William Ramsay, *The Church in the Roman Empire Before the Year A.D. 170* (New York: G. P. Putnam's Sons, 1893), 236.

23. Hans Lietzmann, "The Christian Church in the West," *Cambridge Ancient History* (Cambridge: Cambridge University Press, 1939), 12:519.

24. Eusebius, *Ecclesiastical History*, 1:437.

25. Henry Bettenson, ed., *Documents of the Christian Church* (New York: Oxford University Press, 1960), 19.

26. Kenneth Scott Latourette, *A History of Christianity* (New York: Harper and Brothers, 1953), 88.

27. George C. Brauer, *The Age of the Soldier Emperors: Imperial Rome, A.D. 244–284* (Park Ridge, Ill.: Noyes Press, 1975), 113.

28. E. R. Boak, *A History of Rome to 565 A.D.* (New York: Macmillan, 1943), 427.

29. Workman, *Persecution in the Early Church,* 108.

30. Ibid., 117.

31. Brauer, *The Age of the Soldier Emperors,* 262.

32. Workman, *Persecution in the Early Church,* 108.

33. Ibid.

34. Eusebius, *Ecclesiastical History*, 2:287.

35. Ibid., 291.

36. C. Schmidt, *The Social Results of Early Christianity*, trans. R. W. Dale (London: Wm. Isbister, 1889), 322.

37. Workman, *Persecution in the Early Church,* 134.

38. Ibid.

39. Robin Fox, *Pagans and Christians* (San Francisco: Perennial Library, 1988), 422.

40. Stark, *The Rise of Christianity,* 13.

41. Aristides, *The Apology of Aristides on Behalf of the Christians,* trans. J. Rendel Harris (Cambridge: Cambridge University Press, 1891), 36.

42. Ibid., 37.

43. See *Edict of Toleration* in Bettenson, *Documents of the Christian Church,* 22.

44. Eusebius, *Ecclesiastical History*, 2:323.

45. Robert M. Grant, *Augustus to Constantine* (New York: Harper and Row, 1970), 236.

46. Otto W. Neuhaus, "Constantine I and the Nicene Creed," *Lutheran Journal* (1993): 16.

47. Edward Gibbon, *The Decline and Fall of the Roman Empire* (Chicago: William Benton Publishers, The University of Chicago, 1952), 1:291.

48. Scarre, *Chronicle of the Roman Emperors, 215.*
49. Neuhaus, "Constantine I and the Nicene Creed," 16.
50. Ibid.
51. Will Durant, *Caesar and Christ* (New York: Simon and Schuster [1944], 1972), 656.
52. Gibbon, *The Decline and Fall,* 1:895.
53. Latourette, *A History of Christianity,* 95.
54. Kevin A. Miller, "Tomb of the Unknown Christians," *Christian History* 9, no. 27 (1990): 2.
55. James and Marti Hefley, *By Their Blood: Christian Martyrs of the Twentieth Century* (Grand Rapids: Baker, 1996), 637.
56. "'Go Ye and Preach the Gospel': Five Do and Die," *Life,* 30 January 1956, 10f.
57. Ibid., 17–21.
58. *The Voice of the Martyrs* (January 1999): 7–9.
59. George Sarton, *Introduction to the History of Science* (Baltimore: Williams and Wilkins, 1927), 236.
60. Elwood P. Cubberly, *A Brief History of Education* (Boston: Houghton Mifflin, 1922), 47.
61. Christopher Dawes, *Religion and the Rise of Western Culture* (London: Sheed and Ward, 1950), 25.
62. Nathan Söderblom, "A Pastoral Letter," in Frederick Schumacher, ed., *For All the Saints: A Prayer Book for and by the Church* (Delhi, N.Y.: American Lutheran Publicity Bureau, 1996), 4:388.
63. Tom Wright, *The Original Jesus: The Life and Vision of a Revolutionary* (Grand Rapids: Eerdmans, 1996), 68.
64. Ibid., 68–70.
65. Philip Schaff, *The Person of Christ: The Miracle of History* (Boston: American Tract Society, 1865), 40–49.

The SANCTIFICATION
of HUMAN LIFE

"I have come that they may have life."
Jesus Christ in John 10:10

Whaen in Rome, do as the Romans do." So goes an old saying. But when the early Christians arrived in Rome from Jerusalem and parts of Asia Minor, they did not do as the pagan Romans did. They defied the entire system of Rome's morality. The low view of human life among the Romans was one of their pagan depravities: "The individual was regarded as of value only if he was a part of the political fabric and able to contribute to its uses, as though it were the end of his being to aggrandize the State."[1] Moreover, the pagan gods taught the people no morals, as St. Augustine, a former pagan himself, knew from personal experience (*The City of God* 2.4). This too did not enhance the value of human life.

The low value of life among the Romans was a shocking affront to the early Christians, who came to Rome with an exalted view of human life. Like their Jewish ancestors, they saw human beings as the crown of God's creation; they believed that man was made in the image of God (Genesis 1:27). Although that image was tarnished by man's fall into sin, they nevertheless believed the words of the psalmist to be true: "You made him [man] a little lower than the heavenly beings and crowned him with glory and honor" (Psalm 8:5). They also knew that God so honored human life that he himself assumed it by becoming incarnate in the person of Jesus Christ, his only begotten Son (John 1:14). Thus, unlike the Romans, Christians did not hold human life to be cheap and expendable. It was to be honored and protected at all costs, regardless of its form or quality. By doing so, they countered many depravities that depreciated human life.

COUNTERING THE DEPRAVITY OF INFANTICIDE

One way that Christianity underscored the sanctity of human life was its consistent and active opposition to the widespread pagan practice of infanticide—killing newborn infants, usually soon after birth. Frederic Farrar has noted that "infanticide was infamously universal" among the Greeks and Romans during the early years of Christianity.[2] Infants were killed for various reasons. Those born deformed or physically frail were especially prone to being willfully killed, often by drowning. Some were killed more brutally. For instance, Plutarch (ca. A.D. 46–120) mentions the Carthaginians, who, he says, "offered up their own children, and those who had no children would buy little ones from poor people and cut their throats as if they were so many lambs or young birds; meanwhile the mother stood by without a tear or moan" (*Moralia* 2.171D). Cicero (106–43 B.C.) justified infanticide, at least for the deformed, by citing the ancient Twelve Tables of Roman law when he says that "deformed infants shall be killed" (*De Legibus* 3.8). Even Seneca (4 B.C.?–A.D. 65), whose moral philosophy was on a higher plane than that of his culture, said, "We drown children who at birth are weakly and abnormal" (*De Ira* 1.15). So common was infanticide that Polybius (205?–118 B.C.) blamed the population decline of ancient Greece on it (*Histories* 6). Large families were rare in Greco-Roman society in part because of infanticide.[3] Infant girls were especially vulnerable. For instance, in ancient Greece it was rare for even a wealthy family to raise more than one daughter. An inscription at Delphi reveals that one second-century sample of six hundred families had only one percent who raised two daughters.[4]

Historical research shows that infanticide was common not only in the Greco-Roman culture but in many other cultures of the world as well. Susan Scrimshaw notes that it was common in India, China, Japan, and the Brazilian jungles as well as among the Eskimos.[5] Writing in the 1890s, James Dennis shows in his *Social Evils of the Non-Christian World* that infanticide was also practiced in many parts of pagan Africa. He further states that infanticide was

FISHERMEN retrieve castaway infants from the Tiber River in Italy. (Artist unknown; courtesy of l'Hôpital du Saint-Esprit, Paris)

also "well known among the Indians of North and South America,"[6] that is, before the European settlers, who reflected Christian values, outlawed it.

As with abortion (discussed below), the early Christians called the Greco-Roman practice of infanticide murder. To them infants were creatures of God, redeemed by Christ. Moreover, they knew of Christ's high regard for little children, for he once said, "Let the little children come to me, and do not hinder them" (Matthew 19:14). He spoke these words in response to his disciples, who thought he should not be bothered with people bringing small children to him. Having been reared as Jews, who saw children as a blessing, the disciples oddly enough reflected an opinion of children that was inconsistent with their Jewish heritage. One wonders whether the prevailing Greco-Roman culture's low view of children had to some degree influenced the disciples' remarks.

Early Christian literature repeatedly condemned infanticide. The *Didache* (written between ca. 85 and 110) enjoins Christians, "[T]hou shalt not...commit infanticide."[7] One finds infanticide also condemned in the *Epistle of Barnabas* (ca.130) as it comments on the *Didache's* opposition to this immoral practice.[8] Callistus of Rome (d. ca. 222), a onetime slave who later became bishop of Rome, was equally appalled at this common method of disposing of unwanted infants.

The Christian opposition to infanticide was not only prompted by their seeking to honor one of God's commandments, "You shall not kill [murder]," but also by their remembering St. Paul's words, written to them in Rome shortly before Nero had him executed: "Do not conform any longer to the pattern of this world, but be *transformed* by the renewing of your mind. Then you will be able to test and approve what God's will is—his good, pleasing and perfect will" (Romans 12:2). There was no way that they would conform to the ungodly practice of infanticide; to do so would have violated their belief in sanctity of human life.

"Infanticide," said the highly regarded historian W. E. H. Lecky, "was one of the deepest stains of the ancient civilizations."[9] It was this moral practice that the early Christians continually opposed wherever they encountered it. And it was this depravity that they sought to eliminate. Before the Edict of Milan in 313, Christian opposition to infanticide obviously was not able to influence the pagan emperors to outlaw it. But only a half century after Christianity attained legal status, Valentinian, a Christian emperor who was sufficiently influenced by Bishop Basil of Caesarea in Cappadocia, formally outlawed infanticide in 374 (*Codex Theodosius* 9.41.1). He was the first Roman emperor to do so.

Total elimination of infanticide never became a reality, however, largely because not everyone converted to Christianity and because some who joined the church were only nominal Christians who still retained some pagan values and did not take seriously the church's stand on infanticide. Thus, evidence shows that many unwanted infants in many parts of Europe in the Middle Ages and after continued to have their lives snuffed out by their parents. But throughout the centuries the Christian church never wavered in its condemnation of infanticide. And as geographical states developed on the continent of Europe after the fall of the Roman Empire, the Christian influence that prompted Valentinian to outlaw the killing of infants became the norm throughout the West, and anti-infanticide laws (with the exception of today's partial-birth abortion) remain in effect in much of the world today. It is one of Christianity's great legacies.

COUNTERING THE DEPRAVITY OF ABANDONING INFANTS

When the Christians arrived in Rome and its vicinity, they encountered another culturally depraved practice that showed its low regard for human life. If unwanted infants in the Greco-Roman world were not directly killed, they were frequently abandoned—tossed away, so to speak. In the city of Rome, for instance, undesirable infants were abandoned at the base of the *Columna Lactaria*,[10] so named because this was the place the state provided for wet nurses to feed some of the abandoned children. Child abandonment had even become a part of Roman mythology. The city of Rome, according to mythology, was reputedly founded by Romulus and Remus, two infant boys who had been tossed into the Tiber River in the eighth century B.C. They both survived and were reportedly reared by wolves. This mythological account is one of many that reveal the Roman practice of abandoning undesired children, or *exposti*, as they were called.

Sometimes, according to Suetonius (A.D. ca. 69–ca. 140), the biographer of Roman caesars, infants were also abandoned in a symbolic ritual of grief, for instance, when people in A.D. 41 grieved the assassination of Emperor Caligula.[11] This supports the observation that "the 'exposure' of children was a part of the standard litany of Roman depravities."[12]

The Greeks too practiced child abandonment. Like the Romans, they had their cultural myths that related tales of child exposure. For instance, the well-known Greek play *Oedipus Rex* revolves around Oedipus, who, abandoned as a three-day-old infant by his father King Laius of Thebes, was found by a shepherd of King Polybus of Corinth and his wife Merope, who reared the boy. Similarly, Ion, the founder of Ionia, was abandoned as an infant by his mother, as were other noteworthy Greek characters, such as Poseidon, Aesculapius, and Hephaistos, according to ancient literature. Greek mythology also depicts Paris, who started the Trojan War, as an abandoned child. And Euripides, Greek poet of the fifth century B.C., mentions infants being thrown into rivers and manure piles, exposed on roadsides, and given for prey to birds and beasts.[13] In Sparta when a child was born, it was taken before the elders of the tribe, and they decided whether the child would be kept or abandoned.[14]

In neither Greek nor Roman literature can one find any feelings of guilt related to abandoning children. One could argue that there might have been at least a scintilla of subconscious guilt, however, for many of the

Greco-Roman stage plays and mythologies revolve around famous characters and heroes who were abandoned as children. These plays may unwittingly have soothed guilty consciences in that they permitted the audience to infer that their abandoned children really did not die but instead became cultural heroes.

As with infanticide, Christians opposed and condemned the culturally imbedded custom of child abandonment. Clement of Alexandria, a highly influential church father in Egypt in the latter part of the second century, condemned the Romans for saving and protecting young birds and other creatures while lacking moral compunctions about abandoning their own children.[15] Similarly, the African church father Tertullian (ca. 200) strongly denounced this practice.[16] Lactantius, the church father who tutored one of the sons of Constantine the Great, opposed child abandonment, saying, "It is as wicked to expose as it is to kill" (*Divine Institutes* 1.6). A sixth-century canon of the church called parents who abandoned children "murderers" (*Patri Graeco-Latina* 88:1933).

Christians, however, did more than just condemn child abandonment. They frequently took such human castaways into their homes and adopted them. Callistus of Rome gave refuge to abandoned children by placing them in Christian homes. Benignus of Dijon (late second century), who like his spiritual mentor Polycarp was martyred, provided protection and nourishment for abandoned children, some of whom were deformed as a result of failed abortions. Afra of Augsburg (late third century) was a prostitute in her pagan life, but after her conversion to Christianity she "developed a ministry to abandoned children of prisoners, thieves, smugglers, pirates, runaway slaves, and brigands."[17] Christian writings are replete with examples of Christians adopting throw-away children.

In spite of the many severe persecutions that Christians endured for three centuries, they did not relent in promoting the sanctity of human life. They saw child abandonment as a form of murder, and their tenacious efforts eventually produced results. When Emperor Valentinian outlawed infanticide in 374, he also criminalized child abandonment (*Code of Justinian* 8.52.2). Following him, Honorius and Theodosius II (both emperors in the fifth century) ruled that a foundling child had to be announced to people in the church, and if no one claimed it, the finder could keep it.[18] By the eleventh century, King Haroldsson (St. Olaf) of Norway fined parents who exposed a child; his successor, King Magnus, tightened the exposure law by charging such parents with murder.[19]

Although laws were enacted outlawing child abandonment in much of Europe, where Christianity was prominent, the practice did not come to a complete end. As with infanticide, many people did not internalize the moral and ethical teachings of Christianity. As Jesus said in one of his parables, some seed falls on good ground, some on stones, and some among thorns (Matthew 13:3–9). The "thorns" in the early church were those who never really converted to Christianity. Some joined the church, especially after the persecutions ended, because it was socially or materially advantageous. They had not really disavowed the pagan customs. Hence, one account in the sixteenth century reveals a priest lamenting that "the latrines resound with the cries of children who had been plunged into them."[20]

The Christian opposition to child abandonment, which resulted in laws outlawing this practice throughout Europe, along with outlawing infanticide, had the wholesome effect of morally and legally ascribing to newborn infants the sanctity of life. That sanctity is in part atrophying today as many people support abortion on demand and even favor partial-birth abortion (the modern way of practicing infanticide).

Yet some of Christianity's high accent on human life is still operative even among the advocates of partial-birth abortions, because they believe that abandoning an unwanted child in a back alley or in a garbage can is a heinously criminal act. But apparently the belief in the sanctity of human life of newborn children is changing, as indicated by the recent rise in the abandonment of newborn infants in parts of the Western world. The city of Hamburg, Germany, recently established "Project Findelbaby" for foundling babies by providing a "baby flap" (resembling a large mailbox slot) at some buildings where unwanted infants may be dropped off without legal jeopardy.[21] The problem is not confined to Germany. In the United States, billboards along highways in Texas have recently posted the plea: "Don't Abandon Your Baby."[22] And in the spring of 2000, twenty-two state legislatures in the United States were seriously thinking about imitating the Hamburg practice.

However unfortunate the present-day baby-flap boxes might be, they ironically reflect Christianity's influence with regard to saving the life of abandoned infants. Rescuing infants in this manner is in part a revival of what the Christian church did in the Middle Ages. In the ninth century the Council of Rouen (France) asked women who had "secretly borne children to place them at the door of the church and provided for them if they were not reclaimed."[23]

COUNTERING THE DEPRAVITY OF ABORTION

The low view of human life among the Greco-Romans also showed itself in widespread abortion practices. Ignoring this factor, historians and anthropologists tend to cite poverty or food shortage as the primary reason for their prevalence. However, historical data indicate that poverty was not the primary cause for the high abortion rates among the Romans in the century preceding and during the early Christian era. At this time in history the Roman honor and respect for marriage had virtually become extinct (see chapter 4). Roman "marriage, deprived of all moral character," as one historian has noted, "was no longer a sacred bond, and alliance of souls."[24] Juvenal apparently was not exaggerating when he said that a chaste wife was almost nonexistent (*Satire* 6.161). And Seneca, the Roman moralist, called unchastity "the greatest evil of our time" (*De Consolatione ad Helviam* 15.3). In light of this pronounced deterioration of marriage, countless Roman women engaged in adulterous sex, and when they became pregnant, they destroyed the evidence of their sexual indiscretions, thus adding to Rome's widespread abortions.

There was still another Roman motive—a rather unusual one—for aborting pregnancies, namely, the desire to be childless. Seneca said, "Childlessness bestows more influence than it takes away, and the loneliness that used to be a detriment to old age, now leads to so much power that some old men pretend to hate their sons and disown their children, and by their act make themselves childless" (*De Consolatione ad Marciam* 19.2). Why? Unmarried or childless persons were assiduously courted and given undue attention by fortune hunters who hoped to cash in on their "friends'" wills. Historian Will Durant says that "a large number of Romans relished this esurient courtesy."[25] So pronounced was this phenomenon that the Roman poet Horace (65–8 B.C.) showed his contempt by satirically telling would-be fortune hunters how to be successful in their pursuit of childless couples (*Satires* 2.5). Thus, a ghoulish desire for other people's fortunes added to the prolificacy of Rome's abortions.

Long before the birth of Christ, faithful Jews, contrary to the pagan societies around them, held to the sanctity of human life, including life in the womb. Flavius Josephus, the first-century Jewish historian, said that the biblical law (the Pentateuch) "forbids women from either to cause abortion or to make away with the fetus." He further stated that a woman who aborts her child "destroys a soul and diminishes the race."[26] First-century

Christians, being predominantly former Jews, similarly valued human life in the womb.

The popular Greco-Roman view, however, was remarkably different. Human life (as noted above) was cheap and expendable, particularly the life of the unborn. Long before the birth of Christ, some of the philosophers—such as Plato, Aristotle, Celsus, and others well into the fourth century after Christ—had no compunctions about taking the life of an unborn child. Plato argued that it was the prerogative of the city-state to have a woman submit to an abortion so that the state would not become too populous (*Republic* 5.461). Similarly, Aristotle, once a student of Plato, contended that there was a "limit fixed to the procreation of offspring," and when that limit was not heeded, "abortion must be practiced " (*Politics* 7.14).

The opinions of Plato and Aristotle and others like them prevailed among the people in ancient Greece. To be sure, there were some opposing views. For example, as early as the fifth century B.C. the Pythagoreans frowned upon free and easy abortions, as did the Greek physician Galen (137–200) and the gynecologist Soranus of Ephesus (ca. 98–138). Similarly, the Hippocratic Oath of the fifth century B.C. said, "I will not give to a woman a pessary to produce abortion."[27] These opposing positions, however, carried little or no weight among the general populace or its political leaders, no matter who uttered them.

The Romans essentially followed the Greeks. Abortion was common and widespread among them too. There was some opposition, but it also meant little or nothing because the Roman populace had an extremely low view of human life. Moreover, the few who saw abortion as wrong usually did so on pragmatic grounds rather than for moral reasons. Thus, the verbally eloquent Cicero (106–43 B.C.) argued that abortion was wrong because it threatened to destroy the family's name and its right of inheritance; it was an offense against the father (*pater*); and it deprived the Republic of a future citizen.[28] Another opposing voice was that of the Roman philosopher-statesman Seneca, a onetime teacher of Emperor Nero. The well-known Roman poet Ovid (43 B.C.–A.D. 17) said in his *Amores* that women who had abortions were worthy of death.[29] And the Roman writer Juvenal (ca. A.D. 60–140) said the abortionist was "paid to murder mankind within the womb" (*Satires* 7).

While a few poets and philosophers opposed abortion, the Roman populace received adequate support from its morally decadent culture and from its morally depraved emperors, who had no qualms about taking human life—young or old, prenatal or postnatal. Emperor Tiberius, who ruled from A.D. 14 to 37, and under whose reign Christ was crucified, loved to see tortured humans thrown into the sea. Emperor Caligula (A.D. 37–41), the crazed tyrant who succeeded Tiberius, arbitrarily killed all who once served in his palace. He enjoyed seeing human beings dragged through the streets with their bowels hanging out, and he forced parents to witness the executions of their sons. Claudius, the successor of Caligula, treasured seeing the blood and gore of men brutally disemboweled in the Colosseum. Nero (A.D. 54–68), who severely persecuted and executed hundreds of Christians and who had St. Paul and St. Peter executed, forced Seneca, his former teacher, to commit suicide. Emperor Vitellius, a successor to Nero, who ruled only for one year, said that the smell of dead enemy soldiers was sweet, and the death of fellow citizens sweeter yet. Emperor Domitian (A.D. 81–96) killed four vestal virgins, executed senators who opposed his policies, and killed his niece's husband.[30] And as shown in chapter 1, he severely persecuted Christians during his rule of terror. Bloody acts of other emperors could also be cited. Given this culture of killing, abortion was by no means an anomaly in the eyes of the populace.

Some have argued that the Bible nowhere specifically prohibits abortion. However, there are at least two biblical references that cast considerable doubt on this argument. Writing to the Christians in Galatia about A.D. 55, St. Paul issued a catalogue of sins (Galatians 5:20). One of the sins mentioned is *pharmakeia*, the making and administering of potions. This word has commonly been translated as "sorcery" (NRSV) or "witchcraft"(NIV) because potions were often made in a context of sorcery. However, it is quite likely that when Paul used the word *pharmakeia* in Galatians, he meant the practice of abortion, because administering medicinal potions was a common way of inducing abortions among the Greco-Romans. There is additional evidence in the New Testament in support of this argument. In Revelation 21:8, where the Apostle John condemns "sexual immorality," these two words are immediately followed by the plural word *pharmakois*, evidently because sexual immorality often resulted in unwanted pregnancies being aborted.

That *pharmakeia (pharmakon)*, as used by St. Paul in his letter to the Galatians and St. John in the book of Revelation, apparently refers to the practice of abortion has added support in extrabiblical literature, both pagan and Christian. Plutarch (A.D. 46–120), a pagan, uses *pharmakeia* to note that it was especially used for contraception and abortion purposes (*Romulus* 22 of his *Parallel Lives*). An early Christian document, the *Didache*, says that abortion is forbidden, and in so arguing, it uses the words *ou pharmakeuseis* (you shall not use potions). These words are immediately followed by "*ou phoneuseis teknon en phthora*" (you shall not kill a child by abortion).[31] Thus, this passage seems to link potions (drugs) with the killing of an unborn child. Clement of Alexandria (155–213), an early influential church father, identifies *pharmakeia* as an abortifacient. In criticizing women who conceal their sexual sin, he links abortion (*phthora)* with the taking of potions (*pharmakois)*.[32] About the same time (around 190), Minucius Felix, a Christian lawyer, declared, "There are women who, by medicinal draughts, extinguish in the womb and commit infanticide upon the offspring yet unborn."[33] About two hundred years later (in 375), Bishop Ambrose wrote that potions were used by well-to-do women to snuff out the fruit of their womb.[34] Similarly, St. Jerome in about 384 lamented that many women practiced abortion by using "drugs."[35] And in the latter part of the fifth century, Caesarius of Arles, in one of his sermons, said, "No woman should take any drug to procure an abortion."[36] In another sermon he again condemns abortion, and here too he links it with the taking of a pharmaceutical mixture (*potiones* in Latin).[37] Basil of Caesarea, a bishop in the latter half of the fourth century, asserted, "Women. . .who administer drugs to cause abortion, as well as those who take poisons to destroy unborn children are murderesses."[38]

Whether abortion was performed by using some type of potion or by some other means, prominent Christian leaders unequivocally condemned it. For instance, Athenagoras, a Christian philosopher and layman writing in about A.D. 177 to Emperor Marcus Aurelius, defended his fellow Christians against the preposterous charge of cannibalism that stemmed from Christians believing they received the body and blood of Christ in the Lord's Supper. He forcefully responded, "What reason would we [Christians] have to commit murder when we say that women who induce abortions are murderesses?"[39] Tertullian (d. ca. 220), the Latin church father in northern Africa, stated the Christian position in opposition to abortion by saying, "We may not destroy even the foetus in the womb." And he continued, "Nor does it matter whether you take away the life that is born or destroy one that is coming to birth" (*Apology* 9).

By the beginning of the early fourth century, Christian opposition to abortion was no longer voiced only by individual theologians but also by the church collectively. For instance, the church in the West not only condemned abortion in the Synod of Elvira, Spain (ca. 305 or 306), but it also excommunicated women who had abortions and did not accept repentance for their acts until their final hour of life.[40] In the East, the Council of Ancyra (now modern Turkey) took its stand against abortion in 314. The Canons of St. Basil, formulated by Basil of Caesarea (d. 379) and accepted by the Eastern church in the mid-fourth century, opposed abortion and the guild of abortionists (the *sagae*). This guild provided abortifacients and surgical devices for abortion. Its members also sold aborted bodies to the manufacturers of beauty creams.[41] Basil mobilized Christians to help minister to women who were facing unwanted pregnancies. At times he helped stage public protests against abortion. His efforts reportedly inspired Emperor Valentinian to outlaw abortion, along with infanticide and child abandonment, in 374.

Antiabortion laws did not put an end to all abortions, however. Pagans, of course, continued practicing it, as did some "so-called Christians," as Origen called them. So the church passed more canons (rules) proscribing it. Thus, in 524 the Synod of Lerida (Spain) condemned abortions, as had the Synod of Elvira two hundred years earlier. In the twelfth century Ivo Chartes and Gratian noted that from the fourth century to their day, over four thousand canons had been issued affirming the sanctity of life.[42] Nor did the pro-life affirmations end with the twelfth century. After the Reformation in the sixteenth century, Protestants joined the Catholics in condemning abortion. Martin Luther, for example, asserted that "those who pay no attention to pregnant women and do not spare the tender fetus are murderers and parricides."[43] John Calvin said, "The unborn child... though enclosed in the womb of its mother, is already a human being... and should not be robbed of the life which it has not yet begun to enjoy."[44]

Christian opposition to abortion, which resulted in antiabortion laws, continued uninterruptedly well into the twentieth century. In 1945 Dietrich Bonhoeffer, the German Lutheran pastor whom Hitler executed a month before the end of World War II, reflected the view of the Christian church's long-standing opposition to abortion. Said he: "Destruction of the embryo in the mother's womb is a violation of the right to live which God has bestowed upon this nascent life."[45] Bonhoeffer's statement was rather typical of Christian theologians and formal church positions up to the 1960s.

As is well known, abortion on demand has become widely accepted today in Western societies, and as indicated above, liberal theology and secularism have greatly contributed to its acceptance. Even most mainline Protestant churches, most of them influenced by liberal theology, have come to accept abortion on demand and have thereby largely rejected

Christianity's long-standing adherence to the sanctity of human life, at least in regard to abortion. Only a few of the larger denominations, such as the Christian Reformed Church in North America, the Lutheran Church–Missouri Synod, the Wisconsin Evangelical Lutheran Synod, the Southern Baptist Convention, and Wesleyan Methodists, continue to walk the path of their Christian ancestors, reaching back to the pristine church. And of course the Roman Catholic Church continues to be firmly opposed to abortion. But even within these denominations, in contrast to the early church, there is really no Christian admonition or discipline regarding abortion when some of their members—for instance, legislators—promote pro-abortion laws.

The early church's opposition to abortion, along with its condemnation of infanticide and child abandonment, was a major factor in institutionalizing the sanctity of human life in the Western world. As historian W. E. H. Lecky has observed, "the value and sanctity of infant life...broadly distinguishe[d] Christian from Pagan societies."[46] The sanctity of life, with the exception of abortion, is still largely present today. Thus, the words of another historian are fitting: "The intrinsic worth of each individual man and woman as a child of God and an immortal soul was introduced by Christianity."[47]

As already indicated, until about the mid-twentieth century Christianity's opposition to abortion was accepted virtually by everyone, even by those who had little or no identification with the church. For instance, in the latter part of the nineteenth century even the feminist leaders such as Elizabeth Cady Stanton, Susan B. Anthony, and Matilda Gage strongly opposed abortion. Anthony said, "I deplore the horrible crime of child murder [abortion]...No matter what motive, love of ease, or a desire to save from suffering the unborn innocent, the woman is awfully guilty who commits the deed;...but oh! thrice guilty is he who for selfish gratification...drove her to the desperation which impelled her to the crime."[48] Today, however, most feminists favor and support the pro-abortion stance. The sanctity of human life, so zealously proclaimed and defended by the early Christians and their followers for nearly two millennia, has in the last several decades been significantly undermined by pro-abortion advocates, commonly outside the context of the church but sometimes also within sectors of the organized church itself.

COUNTERING THE DEPRAVITY OF GLADIATORIAL SHOWS

According to Ausonius, the Roman writer, gladiatorial games were begun in Rome in 264 B.C. by Marcius and Decius Brutus, who introduced them at their father's obsequies. Thus, by the time Christians arrived in

"THUMBS DOWN ON GLADIATORS" depicts a once-common scene at the cruel Roman gladiatorial contests that existed during the early Christian era. (Wilhelm Peters)

Rome, the Romans had watched hundreds of thousands of gladiators mauled, mangled, and gored to death for at least three hundred years. These games, as one historian has noted, "illustrate completely the pitiless spirit and carelessness of human life lurking behind the pomp, glitter, and cultural pretensions of the great imperial age."[49] Like infanticide, child abandonment, and abortion, the games underscore Rome's low regard for human life.

Gladiators were usually slaves, condemned criminals, or prisoners of war, all of whom were considered expendable.[50] Each gladiator was seen as "crude, loathsome, doomed, lost. . .a man utterly debased by fortune, a slave, a man altogether without worth and dignity, almost without humanity."[51] Sometimes freemen (nonslaves) became gladiators to earn money or because they enjoyed the applause of the spectators. Only on rare occasions were there women gladiators. The gladiators were physically trained in advance of the contests so that they would be able to put forth a strenuous fight, thus pleasing the crowds that always included senators, emperors, praetorians, vestal virgins, pagan priests, and other prominent Romans.

Gladiatorial contests occurred irregularly and only by an emperor's decree. They were usually announced unexpectedly, thus intensifying the public's interest.[52] These barbaric spectacles often lasted for months, especially during the second century.[53] Sometimes a hundred or more gladiators fought on a given day. Before the games began, carriages drove the gladiators, dressed in purple chlamyses embroidered with gold, in a parade to the Colosseum in Rome or to an amphitheater in other cities. Upon entering the arena, each gladiator turned to the emperor and saluted with his right hand extended, saying, "Hail, Emperor, those who are about to die salute thee."[54]

Each contest required men to fight men, commonly with the aim of killing the opponents with a sword (*gladius*). It was the crowd that largely decided the fate of a weakened, gasping gladiator. A turned-thumb signal, usually given by women spectators, instructed the victor to go for the final blow. Often it was also the women who praised gladiators "with the largest wounds or fell with the greatest calm."[55] The barbaric cruelty, the agonizing screams of the victims, and the flow of human blood stirred no conscience in the crowds of the gladiatorial events. To the contrary, "the inability or unwillingness of the gladiator to go eagerly to his slaughter filled the audience with disgust and wrath and deprived the gladiator of his glory."[56] The Roman writer Seneca in the first century gives us a glimpse of the depraved enjoyment people had in seeing the gladiators brutally annihilated. He cites the spectators shouting, "Kill him! Lash him! Brand him! Why does he meet the sword in so cowardly a way? Why does he strike so feebly? Why doesn't he die game? Whip him to meet his wounds!" (*Ad Lucilium Epistulae Morales* 7.5). To see a gladiator stab and slice his opponent to death was top-ranked amusement.

Occasionally, gladiators fought wild beasts that often gored them to death. Whether fighting beasts or men, thousands upon thousands of gladiators were slaughtered during the seven centuries of this cruel institution. For instance, Emperor Trajan (98–117) celebrated his conquest of Dacia by holding gladiatorial shows lasting four months in which ten thousand gladiators participated, and ten thousand wild and domestic beasts were killed.[57] Of the ten thousand gladiators, at least half of them died on the sands of the amphitheater's floor, and many more expired later as a result of the wounds they had incurred. When Emperor Titus inaugurated the Colosseum in Rome in A.D. 80, five thousand wild animals were killed in one day, along with the numerous gladiators whose blood saturated the sand of the amphitheater.[58]

As indicated above, these "games" were not confined to the city of Rome. They were also held in other locations of the empire. Theodor Mommsen, a historian of ancient Rome, notes that these contests were also very popular in Asia Minor, Syria, and Greece.[59]

Christians were appalled by the gladiatorial games because they reflected the nadir of human morality: gambling with human lives. They saw these shows, like the moral depravities of infanticide, child abandonment, and abortion, as flagrant violations of God's commandment: "You shall not murder" (Exodus 20:13). Thus, they condemned and boycotted these bloody contests, and their opposition did not go unnoticed. Minucius Felix cites a Roman pagan who strongly criticized the Christians for their anti-gladiatorial posture: "You do not go to our shows; you take no part in our processions...you shrink in horror from our sacred [gladiatorial] games."[60]

The church's leaders enjoined their members not to attend any of these Roman events. The church father Tertullian (d. ca. 220), in his book *de Spectaculis* (Concerning Shows), devotes an entire chapter to admonishing Christians not to attend gladiatorial contests. In another of his writings, he condemns the gladiatorial shows for shedding human blood and reveals that at these events "the entrails of the very bears, loaded with as yet undigested human viscera, are in great request."[61]

Today the mere thought of the barbaric nature of the gladiatorial games and the fact that for hundreds of years people saw them as highly desired entertainment makes the average human recoil in horror. Such a reaction is powerful proof of Christianity's great humanitarian influence on the world at large. Most people now recoil at the inhuman features of the gladiatorial shows because they have absorbed Christianity's view of the sacredness of human life and rejected the pagan philosophy of Stoicism that was so prevalent among the Romans. Stoicism had no compassion for the weak and the oppressed. This view of human beings sheds considerable light on why abortion, infanticide, child abandonment, and delight in seeing helpless gladiators mangled to death were such an integral part of Roman culture.

Christianity's high view of human life and its concern for the weak and oppressed, together with its continual growth and influence, in time moved Christian emperors to ban the gladiatorial contests. Jerome Carcopino says that "the butcheries of the arena were stopped at the command of Christian emperors."[62] Similarly, W. E. H. Lecky states, "There is scarcely any single reform so important in the moral history of mankind as the suppression of the gladiatorial shows, a feat that must be almost exclusively ascribed to the Christian church."[63] In short, it was Christianity's high value of human life, together with its belief that God had sent his Son, Jesus Christ, so that people might have life more abundantly both here and hereafter, that slowly undermined the gladiatorial contests. Under the reign of the Christian emperor Theodosius I (378–395), gladiatorial contests were terminated in the East, and his son Honorius ended them in 404 in the West.

Some might think that the Roman enjoyment of the gladiatorial contests was no worse than what millions of Americans enjoy on television. Without defending the American penchant for violent programs, there is nevertheless a significant difference between the Roman gladiatorial contests and violent television scenes. The violence on television is contrived—it does not maim or kill people—whereas the Roman gladiatorial events were real; they brutalized human beings and took the lives of the contestants as well. Even modern boxing matches, whose violence is real, do not permit a knocked-down boxer to be further pursued by his opponent to the kill, as was required in the gladiatorial contests. When the downed boxer is seriously hurt, the referee terminates the match. On the other hand, as one observer has rightly noted, "To become a gladiator was to embrace, with vengeance, cosmic cruelty."[64] Disgusting as violent television programs are, they are substantially different from the violence of the gladiatorial events.

Allowing individuals to be deliberately killed for people's enjoyment has not again been permitted in Western societies since the Christian emperors

THE EMPEROR CONSTANTINE THE GREAT (Constantinus Maximus) did much for Christianity, including issuing in 313 (with coemperor Licinius) the Edict of Milan, which legalized Christianity, and he presided at the first ecumenical council of the Christian church at Nicaea in 325. (From the Musée de Sculpture by M. Clarac)

outlawed the gladiator contests. It seems appropriate to note that the frequent concern over violence on television that is often expressed by many Americans and other Westerners is a clear reflection of Christianity's accent on the sanctity of human life.

THE MORAL LAWS OF CONSTANTINE AND CONSTANTIUS

Along with the many changes that brought sanctity to human life during the first four centuries of Christianity, other humanitarian laws were instituted by the state. For instance, Constantine the Great (306–337), who issued the Edict of Milan in 313 that formally let the Christians live in peace, in 315 outlawed the branding of the faces of criminals condemned to serve in the mines or as gladiators. Seeing the human face as "the image of celestial beauty," he outlawed the branding of slaves. He also ordered speedy trials because he saw it as wrong to treat a person as guilty before being convicted. And given his high regard for the Christian cross, he outlawed crucifixion, the most cruel form of human execution.[65]

Other reforms followed. Constantine's son, Constantius (337–361), ordered the segregation of jailed male and female prisoners.[66] To most people today the segregation of male and female prisoners seems rather obvious. But it should be remembered that the pagan Romans had little or no regard for the welfare of women (see chapter 4), especially for women who were no longer under the *manus* (controlling hand) of their husbands. And since it was quite acceptable to have sexual relations with such women, the Romans had no moral qualms about housing men and women in the same prison quarters.

The salutary and humane acts by Constantine and Constantius are clear indications that the Christian values regarding the sanctity of human life had powerful influence on both of them. Constantine has often been criticized for having sided with the Christians out of mere political expedience. The acts just cited suggest that his critics have overstated their case.

COUNTERING THE DEPRAVITY OF HUMAN SACRIFICES

When paganism rules, it is not uncommon to see human beings sacrificed to pagan gods. Child sacrifices were common rituals of the Canaanite Baal worshipers in Palestine during the ninth century B.C. It was this practice that caused the prophet Elijah, with God's approval, to condemn and destroy 450 prophets of Baal on Mount Carmel (1 Kings 18:16–40). Near

Mount Carmel on the site of the ancient city of Meggido, archaeologists have discovered the remains of infants who, under the corrupt rule of the Israelite King Ahab and Queen Jezebel in the ninth century B.C., had been sacrificed in a temple of Ashtoreth, the goddess of Baal.[67] In the eighth century B.C. the corrupt King Ahaz of ancient Israel turned his back on God and sacrificed (by burning) his own son to the Canaanite god Molech (2 Kings 16:3). Not too long after Ahaz, another spiritually fallen king of Israel, King Manasseh, sacrificed his son (also by burning) in the Valley of Hinnon (2 Kings 21:6). And during the latter part of the seventh century B.C., the prophet Jeremiah condemned numerous Israelites for sacrificing "their sons and daughters in the fire" (Jeremiah 7:31).

Sacrificing human beings for religious reasons was not confined to the pagan Canaanites and the spiritually fallen Hebrew kings. For example, the Irish, before St. Patrick had brought the Christian gospel to them, "sacrificed prisoners of war to war gods and newborns to the harvest gods."[68] Sacrificing humans was also a common practice among the pagan Prussians and Lithuanians even until the thirteenth and fourteenth centuries. The British author Edward Ryan noted in 1802 that these people "would have done so to this day were it not for Christianity."[69]

Another place where widespread human sacrifices occurred was in what is now Mexico. Here the Aztec Indians, a warlike people, frequently fought in order to acquire prisoners whom they used for human sacrifices. Their prisoners were commonly led up the stairs through thick clouds of incense to the top of the Great Pyramid. Here the victims were laid on a sacrificial block, their chests were cut open, and each prisoner's heart was torn out while he was still alive. According to Richard Townsend, "Streams of blood [from the many sacrificed prisoners] poured down the stairway and sides of the monument [pyramid], forming huge pools on the white stucco pavement." The heads of the victims were commonly "strung up on the skull rack as public trophies, while the captor-warriors were presented with a severed arm or thigh." With great rejoicing, the severed body parts were taken home, where they were made into stew for special Aztec meals. The eating of human flesh was a ceremonial form of cannibalism.[70]

Very similar to the human sacrifices of the Aztecs were those of the Mayans. Howard La Fay describes their brutality: "A priest ripped open the victim's breast with an obsidian knife and tore out the still-beating heart." The priests also drew blood from the victim's genitals. La Fay continues, "Priests and pious individuals cut holes in their [prisoners'] tongues and drew rope festooned with thorns through the wound to collect blood offerings."[71]

Given the Christian precedence of having condemned abortion, infanticide, and gladiatorial contests of the Romans, it is not surprising that the European explorers in Mexico condemned the human sacrifices of the Aztec and Maya Indians. Referring to the gruesome religiously based human sacrifices of the Aztec and the Maya Indians, Hernando Cortes, the leader of the Conquistadors, said that it was "the most terrible and frightful thing [he and his men] have ever witnessed."[72] Bernal Diaz del Castillo, one of Cortes's surviving soldiers, wrote that as part of the sacrifices the Indians ate the flesh of the captured soldiers "with a sauce of peppers and tomatoes. They sacrificed all our men in this way, eating their legs and arms, offering their hearts and blood to their idols."[73] Cortes and his men had, of course, encountered unbridled paganism, and they engaged in war to eliminate its bloodcurdling abominations.

Castillo's shocking descriptions show that the Conquistadors—often correctly seen as ruthless, and who undoubtedly killed more of the enemy than was necessary (a phenomenon common in war, even though morally wrong)—nevertheless, still retained enough Christian values to be appalled by what they saw in the pagan sacrifices of the Aztec and Maya Indians. Cortes, says Castillo, had as his mission "putting a stop to human sacrifices, injustices, and idolatrous worship."[74] Only a consistent cultural relativist or zealous multiculturalist would find fault with Cortes's men conquering the Mayas and Aztecs and thereby abolishing their inhumane rituals. It was another step in spreading Christianity's doctrine that human life is sacred, this time bringing it to the New World.

COUNTERING THE DEPRAVITY OF SUICIDE

Before and during the time of Christ, the low view of human life among the Romans, largely influenced by the pagan philosophy of Stoicism, was not confined to the widespread practice of abortion, infanticide, child abandonment, and gladiatorial shows. It also affected how Romans viewed their own lives. Death was not an evil, so they "regarded the power of self-destruction as an inestimable privilege."[75] To take one's own life was an act of self-glory. Hence, it is not surprising to find that suicide was widely practiced on all levels of society. Famous Roman philosophers and writers—most of them of Stoic persuasion—not only spoke well of suicide, but many committed suicide themselves. The younger Cato, Seneca, Petronius, and some of the emperors are but a few examples.

"Open your veins" was a familiar pagan refrain among the Romans. It was the command that Nero gave to his victims, one of whom was his former teacher Seneca. Later, the Emperor Domitian (A.D. 81–96) gave similar orders to those whom he considered a threat to his rule. Seneca said, "Nothing but the will need postpone death." And he added, "If you do not lack the courage, you will not lack the cleverness to die" (*Epistle of Seneca* 70.21, 24). The Younger Pliny relates the story of Arria plunging a dagger into her breast and then giving it to her husband. Given her husband Paetus's terminal illness and her young son's recent death, she no longer cared to live. Pliny describes Arria's suicide, quoting her admiringly: "It does not hurt, Paetus." He called Arria's words "immortal, almost divine" (*Letters and Panegyricus* 3.16). Yet there was a certain ambivalence in Seneca regarding death, for in another context he said that when one approaches death, "one turns to flight, trembles, and laments" (*Epistle of Seneca* 77.11). This statement by Seneca shows that even he, the great advocate of suicide, was not without doubts regarding self-destruction.

Whether it was human life as a fetus, an infant, or an adult, the early Christians saw God as the creator of all human life, and thus it was God's exclusive prerogative to end an individual's life. Given their adherence to the Old Testament Scriptures, their views were consistent with the words of Job, who in the greatest depths of woe, having lost all of his many possessions, including his children, and been stricken with a horrible illness, did not, like the Stoics, think that he had the right to end his life. Instead, he said, "The LORD gave, and the LORD has taken away; may the name of the LORD be praised" (Job 1:21).

Critics of Christianity have sometimes called the nonresistant submission on the part of the persecuted Christian martyrs a form of suicide. While there were a few Christians who went out of their way to be martyred—for instance, Ignatius (d. A.D. 107), who willingly agreed to walk a thousand miles to his martyrdom—the vast majority of Christians who died in the persecutions were by no means suicidal.

A few of the early Christians, under the stress of persecution, did commit suicide. They apparently did not understand the Christian position on the sanctity of human life and God's role in giving and taking it. Eusebius cites one such case. A Christian mother and her two daughters who knew that their persecutors were about to molest them sexually and then execute them requested permission to go to the river to wash. As they approached the river, they threw themselves into the water and drowned.[76] There were other instances, but none of these cases received the approval of any corporate Christian community. Moreover, the lack of resistance to one's persecutors that was so apparent with many martyred Christians (as with Ignatius in 107) made their deaths no more suicidal than did Christ's lack of resistance make his crucifixion a suicidal act.

The Christian church as a body issued no formal statements regarding the sinfulness of suicide until the early fourth century. This occurred at the Synod of Elvira (ca. 305 or 306) when it condemned the acts of some Christians who apparently went out of their way to be martyred. The church's silence regarding suicide before this time is not difficult to understand when one remembers that for three centuries it had to fight for its life during the years of persecution. All of its energies were needed to survive.

Clement of Alexandria (d. 213), Lactantius (d. ca. 330), and Gregory of Nazianus (d. 374) were some early Christian opponents of suicide, along with Eusebius (d. 339), the church historian, who saw suicide so incompatible with Christianity's sanctity of human life that, when he referred to Emperor Maximian's taking his own life, he did not use the word "suicide" but instead called it a "most shameful death" (*Ecclesiastical History* 8.13.15).

The strongest opposition, however, came from St. Augustine in the early fifth century. He wrote in opposition to the Donatists, members of a heretical schismatic group within the church from northern Africa. Many of their members committed suicide en masse, primarily because they believed that there was no forgiveness of sin after baptism. Thus, right after baptism many of them took their lives. Augustine argued that suicide violated the commandment "You shall not murder." He further said that if suicide were an acceptable option, Christ would not have told his disciples to flee in times of persecution. He also contended that not a single case of suicide occurred among the patriarchs and prophets in the Old Testament or among the New Testament apostles.[77]

Although, as noted above, the church corporately condemned suicide at the Synod of Elvira, it did not address the matter again until the Council of Arles in 452 declared that suicide was the result of demonic forces. The Council of Orleans in 533 asserted that oblations (offerings) were not allowed for those who committed suicide.[78] A generation later, in 563, the Synod of Braga banned the singing of psalms at the funeral of a suicide and said that the body of a suicide could not be brought into the church building as part of the burial ceremony.[79] The Synod of Auxerre in 585 reiterated this position. In 693 the Synod of Toledo barred individuals who had attempted suicide from receiving the Lord's Supper for two months, during which time they were expected to repent of their sin.[80] The Council of Troyes in Süderköping in 878, and the Council of Nimes in 1184, denied suicides burial in church cemeteries. In 1441 the Synod of Sweden restated the decision of Nimes and added that the burial of a suicide would pollute the cemetery. This practice continued in many Roman Catholic and Protestant churches even into the twentieth century. If one visits rural cemeteries in Canada and the United States today, one can still find, outside the cemetery's fence line, the graves of individuals who committed suicide.

Following the condemnation of suicide by church councils, Thomas Aquinas in the thirteenth century said that taking one's life was morally wrong because it was a sin against nature: Everyone naturally loves himself; suicide also injured the community of which man is an integral part; it was a sin against God's gift of life; and, finally, it was an act of which one could not repent.[81]

Christian opposition to suicide over the centuries influenced and prompted Western nations to outlaw it. The recent desire for physician-assisted suicides in the United States—for example, Oregon's Death with Dignity Act (assisted-suicide law), first passed in 1994 and reapproved by voters in 1997—is not only a rejection of Christianity's historic opposition to suicide but also a repudiation of its doctrine that human life is sacred and only to be terminated by God, who gave it in the first place.

BURYING, NOT CREMATING, THE DEAD

To the early Christians the sanctity of life and the human body did not come to an end when a person died. Believing Christ's promise that he would raise them and all the dead on Judgment Day, they buried their deceased rather than cremate them as the Romans commonly did. The Christians strongly opposed cremation. Similar to their Hebrew ancestors, they saw it as a pagan custom, and given the sanctity they assigned to the human body (alive or dead), they also rejected it for is violence and cruelty, according to Tertullian (ca. 160–ca. 220). With specific reference to cremation, he faulted the Romans, saying, "What pity is that which mocks its victims with cruelty?" (*On the Resurrection of the Flesh* 1). But Christians most prominently opposed cremation because they saw it as contrary to their firm faith in the resurrection of the body, a faith that their Roman persecutors (as noted in chapter 1) sometimes mocked by defiantly burning

MORES OF HUMAN LIFE

	Greco-Roman Culture	Other Cultures	Christianity
Infanticide	Once approved by many pagan philosophers and practiced long before and after Christianity entered Greco-Roman society	Once approved and practiced in the pagan societies of China, India, Japan, Brazil, American Indians, Eskimos, African tribes, and many others	Condemned by Christians, whose influence prompted Roman emperors to outlaw infanticide in the middle fourth century
Child Abandonment	Condoned and practiced for centuries without guilt or remorse; extolled by Greco-Roman mythologies	Condoned and practiced for centuries in Persia, Africa, and many other pagan societies before and after the birth of Christ	Condemned by Christians, who rescued and adopted many castaway Greco-Roman children
Abortion	Condoned, advocated by philosophers, and widely practiced long before and after Christianity entered Greco-Roman society	Practiced for centuries in virtually all pagan cultures before and after the birth of Christ	Condemned by the church fathers and by the church councils—e.g., Council of Elvira (Spain), A.D. 305
Human Sacrifices	Roman gladiatorial shows sacrificed multitudes of human beings for public entertainment before and after Christ	The Canaanites, some deviant Hebrews, and virtually all ancient societies sacrificed children, often to pagan deities; Aztec and Maya Indians sacrificed captive warriors in their religious rites	Christian emperors outlawed gladiatorial games in the East in the 390s and in the West in 404
Suicide	Generally condoned, often advocated, and sometimes extolled by the poets and philosophers; committed by the elite and the populace	Permitted by the Japanese and by some religions such as Hinduism and Jainism	Seen as a violation of the Commandment: "You shall not murder." Formally condemned by many church fathers and church councils

the bodies of executed martyrs. When the latter happened, surviving Christians "tried to gather the fragments of their brethren who had been martyred in the flames."[82] They wanted their deceased to "sleep in peace," an expression found on many epitaphs in the Christian catacombs (subterranean cemeteries) near Rome. As one historian of the catacombs has said, they believed that "the body was only consigned to the earth for a while, as a sacred deposit which could be reclaimed at some future time when the sea and the earth shall give up their dead."[83]

So strong was the Christians' belief that the dead were "asleep," waiting to be resurrected, that they called every burial place a *koimeterion*, a word borrowed from the Greek that meant a dormitory where people slumbered.[84] *Koimeterion* became "cemetery" in the English language. Thus, every time people use the word *cemetery* they are using a term that harks back to the early Christians and their belief that the dead are merely slumbering until the day of their resurrection.

One Roman history scholar writes that while cremation was still the general practice, for example, among the Romans in the city of Ostia, burial was introduced in various parts of the empire during Emperor Hadrian's reign (A.D. 117–138).[85] Whether this change was prompted by Christianity's opposition to cremation cannot be determined with certainty; some think it came too early in the life of the church to be thus caused. However, as A. D. Nock has shown, cremation became increasingly rare by the third century, and by the fourth it had "almost disappeared."[86] While it may be arguable whether Christianity influenced many of the Romans to bury their dead in the second century under Hadrian's reign, it does seem plausible that when cremation virtually disappeared in the fourth century, it apparently was largely the result of Christian influence. We need only recall that the aura of Christian values was so pervasive already in the early fourth century that Constantine the Great not only issued the Edict of Milan to legalize Christianity, but he and other Christian emperors were moved to implement numerous other laws and customs (noted earlier) that supported Christian beliefs and practices.

The practice of burying people continued, and in the eighth century Charlemagne the Great, who was strongly supportive of Christian doctrine, made cremation a capital crime. Burial had become the only acceptable way of disposing of the dead throughout the Holy Roman Empire. Not until the nineteenth century was cremation brought back into Western countries, and then only by freethinkers, many of whom, similar to the Romans, denied the biblical doctrine of the resurrection of the human body.

So consistent and influential did the Christian practice of burying their dead become over the centuries that today even American Indians have come to believe that inhumation is the only proper way to dispose of their dead, as has been shown by their insistence on burying recently repatriated human skeletons from museums, for instance. However, when the Europeans arrived on American soil in the sixteenth and seventeenth centuries, most American Indians did not bury their dead. The Indians in the Northern Plains, in the Mackenzie subarctic region, and in many other locations did not inhume their dead, but placed them on elevated scaffolds. In parts of the Yukon, California, and the Great Basin area, some tribes cremated the dead. The Choctaws skeletonized their deceased and then stored the bones in bone houses; some of the Pueblo buried their dead in refuse mounds. In still other parts of North America, Indians left their dead to be eaten by dogs or wolves. And the Teton Dakotas wrapped their dead in cloth and then placed them in forked trees.[87]

Today, contrary to centuries of Christian opposition, more and more Christian denominations, even some conservative ones, are permitting their members to cremate the deceased bodies of their loved ones. However, before 1930 in the United States, cremation was considered "bizarre."[88] In 1996 about 22 percent of the dead in the United States were cremated, and it is estimated that by 2010 the number will climb to 40 percent.[89] With the growing practice of cremation, many no longer see it as bizarre, but a new kind of bizarreness is now often present, especially with regard to how many survivors dispose of the ashes. Some have shot the ashes into space. Sometimes they are cast on the ocean, as in the case of John Kennedy Jr. in 1999. Frequently they are sprinkled on flower gardens. One firm in California mixes the ashes with gun powder and packs them in fireworks; an Iowa firm will, upon request, put the ashes into shotgun shells.[90]

What accounts for the recent increase in cremation practices? Among many Christians it probably reflects ignorance about how strongly the early Christians felt in rejecting the custom. Among non-Christians it likely indicates a denial of the resurrection. And, as noted above, it also reflects a permissive church posture. For instance, the Roman Catholic Church, which once strongly condemned it, in 1963 made an about-face regarding cremation by not only accepting it but also producing an order of worship for the practice. In 1969 the Church of England also accepted it. Many other church bodies, with the exception of the Eastern Orthodox Church, are imitating the Catholics and the Church of England. This change, similar to churches tolerating or accepting abortion on demand, indicates that some of the once-powerful influences that the church exerted in society for two millennia are slowly eroding.

Nowhere is there any evidence that the early Christians and their descendants believed that an omnipotent God could not, or would not, resurrect cremated individuals. That was never a question. They had other reasons for spurning cremation. Along with their belief in the resurrection of the body, they wanted to be faithful to the long-standing biblical practice of placing the dead person back into the earth from which God created him. In doing so, they, like their Jewish forbears, were mindful of the words of Moses that when man's life is over, he would "return to the ground" (Genesis 3:19). This is corroborated by the church historian Eusebius. Quoting the Christians, who saw many of their fellow believers martyred and burned by the pagans in Lyons in 177, he has them saying, "but in our circle great grief obtained because we could not bury the bodies in the earth" (*Ecclesiastical History* 1:437). Centuries later, Johann Heermann (1558–1647), the hymn writer, captured this Christian sentiment in his hymn "O God, Thou Faithful God." In one stanza he wrote:

> *And let my body have*
> *A quiet resting-place*
> *Within a Christian grave;*
> *And let it sleep in peace.*

The early Christians were mindful of Christ's promise: "For a time is coming when all who are in the *graves* will hear his voice and come out— those who have done good will rise to live, and those who have done evil will rise to be condemned" (John 5:28–29). They heard him say "graves," not "urns." But even with the rise in cremation practices, the majority of the deceased in Western societies are still being buried, yet another sign of Christianity's pervasive, two-thousand-year influence.

CONCLUSION

People who today see murder and mass atrocities as immoral may not realize that their beliefs in this regard are largely the result of their having internalized the Christian ethic that holds human life to be sacred. There is no indication that the wanton taking of human life was morally revolting to the ancient Romans. One finds no evidence in Roman literature that indicates that incidents such as the ethnic cleansing atrocities in the former

Yugoslavia during the 1990s or the Columbine High School massacre in Colorado in 1999, for example, would have been morally abhorrent to the ancient leaders of Rome or to its populace. One need only remember how both the Roman populace and its emperors enjoyed seeing gladiators massacred in the arenas. These events and other massive atrocities evoked no sympathy or moral outrage. It was part of the stoic culture of pagan Rome.

The low view of life and its accompanying lack of moral outrage is also seen in the behavior of many Roman emperors. The Roman view that life was cheap, including that of the emperors, easily fostered paranoia in many emperors, leading them to kill large numbers of people whom they perceived as possible enemies or traitors, within or without the imperial court. Suetonius, the biographer of emperors, says that under Tiberias (A.D. 14–37) "not a day passed without an execution."[91] Caligula (A.D. 37–41) enjoyed killing individuals, and sometimes he would shut down granaries so that people would starve to death. And from 27 B.C. to A.D. 324, only thirteen (26 percent) of the fifty emperors who reigned during that period died a natural death; the other thirty-seven were either assassinated or committed suicide. Given the low value of life, it mattered little whose life was extinguished. Whether it was executing Christian martyrs, encouraging or committing suicide, assassinating emperors, or slaughtering gladiators, the Roman conscience was not stirred. Thus, the moral revulsion in regard to the taking of innocent life of humans, on a large or small scale, came about largely as the result of Christianity's doctrine human life is sacred.

Significant as the influence of Christianity has been in giving sanctity to human life, recent trends indicate that its salutary value is diminishing. For instance, it is well known that since 1976, each year in the United States alone one-third of pregnancies have been aborted, amounting to more than one million per year.[92] The Alan Gutmacher Institute reports that 13,000 partial-birth abortions are occurring annually in the United States.[93] In 1991, sixty-five babies were abandoned in the United States, a figure that grew to 105 in 1998. Thirteen infants were abandoned in Houston, Texas, alone during a ten-month period in 1999.[94]

Christianity's high view of human life is also diminishing as some people seriously begin to argue that human life is not more valuable than the life of animals. Media executive Ted Turner was heard to remark in a speech that Christianity was to blame for having taught that humans are of higher value than animals.[95] A related argument appeared in an editorial of *Wild Earth* magazine. The writer suggested that every problem on earth, whether social or environmental, is caused by humans, and he concluded, "No matter what you're doing to improve life on Earth, I think you'll find that phasing out the human race will increase your chances for success."[95]

If the decline with respect to the sanctity of human life continues and becomes even more common, the following story may no longer have much significance. During World War II on a remote island in the Pacific, an American soldier met a native who could read, and the native was carrying a Bible. Upon seeing the Bible, the soldier said, "We educated people no longer put much faith in that book." The native, from a tribe of former cannibals, replied, "Well, it's good that we do, or you would be eaten by my people today."[97] This is only one illustration of how Christ's magnanimous influence has taught people that human life is sacred. It is one of Christianity's outstanding legacies.

NOTES

1. Richard Frothingham, *The Rise of the Republic of the United States* (Boston: Little, Brown, 1910), 6.

2. Frederic Farrar, *The Early Days of Christianity* (New York: A. L. Burt Publishers, 1882), 71.

3. Charles Merivale, *History of the Romans Under the Empire* (New York: D. Appleton, 1866), 166.

4. Jack Lindsay, *The Ancient World* (New York: G. P. Putnam's Sons, 1968), 168.

5. Susan C. M. Scrimshaw, "Infanticide in Human Populations: Societal and Individual Concerns," in *Infanticide: Comparative and Evolutionary Perspectives,* ed. Glenn Hausfater and Sarah Hrdy (New York: Aldine Publishing, 1984), 439.

6. James S. Dennis, *Social Evils of the Non-Christian World* (New York: Fleming H. Revell, 1898), 69–70.

7. *The Didache,* in *The Apostolic Fathers,* trans. Kirsopp Lake (Cambridge: Harvard University Press, 1955), 1:319.

8. *The Epistle of Barnabas,* in *The Apostolic Fathers,* trans. Kirsopp Lake (Cambridge: Harvard University Press, 1955), 1:402.

9. W. E. H. Lecky, *History of European Morals: From Augustus to Charlemagne* (New York: Vanguard Press, 1927), 2:24.

10. Will Durant, *Caesar and Christ: A History of Roman Civilization and of Christianity from Their Beginning to A.D. 325* (New York: MJF Books, 1944), 364.

11. Suetonius, "Caligula," *Lives of the Caesars,* trans. J. C. Rolfe (New York: William Heinemann, 1914), 1: .

12. John Boswell, *The Kindness of Strangers: The Abandonment of Children in Western Europe from the Late Antiquity to the Renaissance* (New York: Pantheon Books, 1988), 4.

13. Euripides, *Ion,* trans. Arthur S. Way (New York: William Heinemann, 1919), 51.

14. Kenneth J. Freeman, *Schools of Hellas* (London: Macmillan, 1922), 13.

15. Clement of Alexandria, *The Instructor,* in *The Ante-Nicene Fathers,* ed. Alexander Roberts and James Donaldson (Grand Rapids: Wm. B. Eerdmans, 1982–83), 2:279.

16. Tertullian, *Apology,* in *The Ante-Nicene Fathers,* 3:24–25.

17. These three examples are cited in George Grant, *The Third Time Around: A History of the Pro-Life Movement from the First Century to the Present* (Brentwood, Tenn.: Wolgemuth and Hyatt, 1991), 249–51.

18. Gerhard Uhlhorn, *Christian Charity in the Ancient Church* (New York: Charles Scribner's Sons, 1883), 386.

19. L. W. Larson, *The Earliest Norwegian Laws* (New York: Morningside Heights, 1935), 50.

20. Richard Trexler, "Infanticide in Florence," *History of Childhood Quarterly: The Journal of Psychohistory* (Fall 1973): 99.

21. Lucian Kim, "In Hamburg, A Warm, Safe Spot for Abandoned Babies," *Christian Science Monitor,* 4 April 2000, 70.

22. Warren Cohen, "Keeping the Nation's Newborns Safe," *U.S. News and World Report,* 28 February 2000, 32.

23. Lecky, *History of European Morals,* 2:32.

24. C. Schmidt, *The Social Results of Early Christianity,* trans. R. W. Dale (London: Wm. Isbister, 1889), 48.

25. Will Durant, *Caesar and Christ,* 222.

26. Flavius Josephus, *Against Apion,* trans. H. St. J. Thackeray (New York: G. P. Putnam's Sons, 1926), 375.

27. *Hippocrates,* trans. W. H. S. Jones (New York: G. P. Putnam's Sons, 1923), 299.

28. Cicero, "Pro Cluentio," in *Cicero: The Speeches,* trans. H. Grose Hodge (New York: G. P. Putnam's Sons, 1927), 255.

29. *Ovid: Heroides and Amores,* trans. Grant Showerman (New York: Macmillan, 1914), 427.

30. Chris Scarre, *Chronicle of the Roman Emperors* (New York: Thames and Hudson, 1995), 77-83.

31. *The Didache,* in *The Apostolic Fathers,* 319.

32. Clement of Alexandria, "Paedagogus," in *Clementis Alexandrini Opera,* ed. Guliemi Dindorfii (Oxonii: E Typographeo Clarendoniano, 1859), 1:296.

33. *Minucius Felix,* "Octavius," trans. Gerald H. Rendall (New York: G. P. Putnam's Sons, 1931), 401.

34. Ambrose, Hexameron, *Liber V,* in *Patrologiae Latinae,* ed. J. P. Migne (Paris: Jean-Jacques Rousseau, 1882), vol. 14, col. 245.

35. *Select Letters of St. Jerome: Letter XXII,* trans. F. A. Wright (New York: G. P. Putnam's Sons, 1933), 79.

36. Caesarius of Arles, "Sermo I," in *Corpus Christianorum,* ed. D. Germani Morin (Turnholti: Typographi Brepolis Editores Pontificii, 1953), 103:9.

37. Ibid., 91.

38. Basil of Caesarea, *The Treatise De Spiritu Sancto,* trans. Bloomfield Jackson, in *Nicene and Post-Nicene Fathers of the Christian Church* (Grand Rapids: Wm. B. Eerdmans, 1984), 227.

39. Athenagoras, "A Plea for the Christians," in *The Ante-Nicene Fathers,* 2:147.

40. Synod of Elvira, Canon 68, in Charles Joseph Hefele, ed., *A History of the Christian Councils,* trans. William R. Clarke (Edinburgh: T and T Clark, 1894), 1:67.

41. George Grant, *The Third Time Around: A History of the Pro-Life Movement from the First Century to the Present* (Brentwood, Tenn.: Wolgemuth Publishing, 1991), 19.

42. Ibid., 40.

43. Martin Luther, "Lectures on Genesis, Chapters 26–30," *Luther's Works,* eds. Jaroslav Pelikan and Walter A. Hansen (St. Louis: Concordia Publishing House, 1968), 5:382.

44. John Calvin, *Calvin's Commentaries,* trans. Charles Bingham (Grand Rapids: Baker, 1981), 3:42.

45. Cited in Grant, *Third Time Around,* 133.

46. Lecky, *History of European Morals,* 2:23.

47. Ferdinand Schenck, *Christian Evidence and Ethics* (New York: YMCA Press, 1910), 92.

48. Susan B. Anthony, "Marriage and Family," *The Revolution,* 8 July 1869, 4.

49. William Stearns Davis, *A Day in Old Rome* (Boston: Allyn and Bacon, 1925), 389.

50. Antony Kamm, *The Romans* (London: Routledge, 1995), 126.

51. Carlin A. Barton, *The Sorrows of the Ancient Romans* (Princeton: Princeton University Press, 1993), 12.

52. Jerome Carcopino, *Daily Life in Ancient Rome,* trans. E. O. Lorimer (New Haven: Yale University Press, 1940), 239.

53. Ibid.

54. Ibid.

55. C. Schmidt, *The Social Results of Early Christianity,* 93.

56. Barton, *Sorrows of the Ancient Romans,* 22.

57. Davis, *A Day in Old Rome,* 375.

58. Carcopino, *Daily Life in Ancient Rome,* 239.

59. Theodor Mommsen, *The History of Rome,* trans. William P. Dickson (New York: Charles Scribner's Sons, 1887), 1:295.

60. Minucius Felix, *The Octavius of Minucius Felix*, in *The Ante-Nicene Fathers*, 4:179.

61. Tertullian, *Apology*, in *The Ante-Nicene Fathers*, 3:25.

62. Carcopino, *Daily Life in Ancient Rome*, 247.

63. W. E. H. Lecky, *History of European Morals*, 73.

64. Barton, *Sorrows of the Ancient Romans*, 47.

65. Julien Ries, "Cross," in *The Encyclopedia of Religion* (New York: Macmillan, 1987), 4:161–62.

66. C. Schmidt, *The Social Results of Early Christianity*, 441–42.

67. H. H. Halley, *Halley's Bible Handbook* (Grand Rapids: Zondervan, 1965), 198, 206.

68. Thomas Cahill, "Ending Human Sacrifice," *Christian History* 60 (1998): 16.

69. Edward Ryan, *The History of the Effects of Religion on Mankind: In Countries Ancient and Modern, Barbarous and Civilized* (Dublin: T. M. Bates, 1802), 267.

70. Richard Townsend, *The Aztecs* (London: Hudson and Hudson, 1992), 100.

71. Howard La Fay, "The Maya: Children of Time," *National Geographic* (December 1975): 738.

72. Hernando Cortes, *Letters from Mexico*, trans. and ed. Anthony Pagden (New Haven: Yale University Press, 1986), 35.

73. Bernal Diaz del Castillo, *The Conquest of New Spain*, trans. J. M. Cohen (New York: Penguin Books, 1963), 387.

74. Bernal Diaz del Castillo, *The True History of the Conquest of Mexico*, trans. Maurice Keating (New York: National Travel Club, 1938), 87.

75. J. B. Bury, *A History of the Later Roman Empire* (New York: American Book Company [1889], 1958), 575.

76. Eusebius, *The Ecclesiastical History*, trans. J. E. L. Oulton (New York: G. P. Putnam's Sons, 1932), 2:289–90.

77. See Matthew 10:5–15, and also see Augustine, *The City of God Against the Pagans*, trans. George E. McCracken (Cambridge: Harvard University Press, 1957), 99.

78. Carl Joseph Hefele, *A History of the Councils of the Church from the Original Documents*, trans. William Clark (Edinburgh: T and T Clark, 1895), 3:171.

79. Ibid., 4:187.

80. Carl Joseph Hefele, *Concilien Geschichte* (Freiburg im Breisgau: Herder'sche Verlags-Handlung, 1873), 3:15.

81. Thomas Aquinas, *Summa Theologica*, trans. Fathers of the English Dominican Province (Westminster, Md.: Christian Classics, 1948), 2:1463.

82. Adolf Harnack, *The Mission and the Expansion of Christianity in the First Three Centuries*, trans. James Moffat (New York: G. P. Putnam's Sons, 1908), 1:166.

83. Spencer Northcote, *Epitaphs of the Catacombs During the First Four Centuries* (London: Longmans, Green, 1878), 79.

84. "Cemetery," in *The Oxford English Dictionary* (Oxford: Clarendon Press, 1978), 2:217.

85. Russell Meiggs, *Roman Ostia* (Oxford: Clarendon Press, 1973), 464.

86. A. D. Nock, "Cremation and Burial in the Roman Empire," *Harvard Theological Review* (October 1932): 326.

87. For additional information on how Indians disposed of their dead, see Paul S. Martin et al., *Indians Before Columbus* (Chicago: University of Chicago Press, 1947); Thomas Morton, *The New English Canaan* (1632; reprint, New York: Burt Franklin, 1883).

88. William G. Flanagan, "The New (and More Convenient) American Way of Death," *Forbes*, 21 October 1996, 324.

89. Ibid.

90. Ibid.

91. Suetonius, *Lives of the Caesars*, 1:353.

92. *Statistical Abstracts of the United States: 1999* (Washington, D.C.: U.S. Census Bureau, 1999), 87.

93. "The Facts About Partial-Birth Abortions" (Washington, D.C.: National Right to Life Committee, Office of Congressman Charles Canady, Family Research Council, and the *Washington Post*, 2000), one-page leaflet.

94. Cohen, "Keeping the Nation's Newborns Safe," 32.

95. Cited by Marvin Olasky, "Mess in Miami," *National Review*, 8 June 1992, 26.

96. Les U. Knight, "The Answer to All Our Problems: Voluntary Human Extinction," *Wild Earth* (Summer 1991): 72.

97. Cited by James Hefley, *What's So Great About the Bible?* (Elgin, Ill.: David C. Cook, 1966), 76.

CHRISTIANITY ELEVATES
SEXUAL MORALITY

*"It is God's will that you should be sanctified:
that you should avoid sexual immorality."*

St. Paul in 1 Thessalonians 4:3

In the previous chapter we saw that when the early Christians came to Rome, they encountered an extremely low regard for human life. But that was not the only moral depravity that confronted them. Depraved sexual relations were everywhere; they were an integral part of the pagan culture. Christians stepped into a culture that had indeed "exchanged the truth of God for a lie, and worshiped and served created things rather than the Creator," and because of this, "God gave them over to shameful lusts" (Romans 1:25–26). That is how St. Paul described the Greco-Roman rejection of the natural/moral law to the Christians a few years before Nero had him decapitated in A.D. 64.

THE REJECTION OF PROMISCUOUS HETEROSEXUAL SEX

Roman literature, written by its own authors such as Juvenal, Ovid, Martial, and Catullus, indicates that sexual activity between men and women had become highly promiscuous and essentially depraved before and during the time that the Christians appeared in Roman society. The British historian Edward Gibbon says in his *History of the Decline and Fall of the Roman Empire* that the breakdown in sexual morality began after the Punic Wars ended in 146 B.C. By the first and second centuries after Christ, undefiled sexual intercourse, along with marital faithfulness, had essentially disappeared. Not only were adultery and fornication common, but people engaged in all sorts of sexual methods, many of them obscene. These sexual practices were shamelessly illustrated on household items such as oil lamps, bowls, cups, and vases. The aftermath of the Punic Wars broke down the onetime Roman modesty, in part because that is when the Romans first combined the Greek gymnasiums with their public baths. Before this time, the Romans, unlike the Greeks, did not believe it proper to exercise or bathe publicly in the nude.[1] One must assume that there once was a similar modesty regarding the open portrayal of various human sexual acts.

The widespread, licentious sex practices threatened the institution of marriage, so Caesar Augustus in 18 B.C. enacted *lex Julia de adulteriis,* a law that tried to curb the people's addiction to widespread illicit sex. This law had little effect, however, perhaps because it only punished the married woman in an adulterous act. Roman marriages had greatly deteriorated; they had become a "loose and voluntary compact [and] religious and civil rites were no longer essential."[2] Marriage was "detested as a disagreeable necessity."[3] Since people had become obsessed with sex, marital unions were very short-lived.

The second-century Latin orator and satirist Juvenal said his society had lost Chastity (the goddess) by its widespread addiction to promiscuous and prurient sex. In *Satire* 6, he portrayed the sexually loose morals of women who lecherously gave themselves to gladiators, actors, comedians, and others who were in the public spotlight. This sensuous behavior is also mentioned and condemned by the early Latin church father Tertullian in his *De Spectaculis* (Concerning Shows). Ovid, another Roman writer, in his *Ars Amatoria* (The Art of Making Love), notes that male/female sex relations had become sadistic and masochistic. In his *Amores* he reveals how for many, heterosexual love had turned into a type of sport. Catullus, a Roman poet, refers to his fellow Romans practicing group sex (*Palatine Anthology* 5.49). And Martial's *Epigrams* of the late first century also reflect the defilement of sexual life common in his day.

The depraved sexual practices that accompanied heterosexual sex in Roman life were not common only among the populace but were also very

"ADULTEROUS WOMAN" illustrates the woman forgiven by Jesus (John 8:1–11). She was subject to a double standard of sexual morality. *(Julius Schnorr)*

prevalent in the lives of the Roman emperors. Hence, the Roman saying: *"Qualis rex, talis grex"* (like king, like people). For example, the Roman biographer of emperors, Suetonius, reports that Emperor Tiberius (A.D. 14–37) often had nude women wait on the tables at which he dined (*Tiberius* 42). He also had male and female prostitutes openly engage in group sex as entertainment for his pleasure (*Tiberius* 43). Emperor Caligula (A.D. 37–41), Tiberius's successor, lived a licentious sex life and was given to habitual incest with all of his sisters (*Gaius Caligula* 24). He loved to engage in sex while he ate, and he often had people tortured during his many sexual escapades (*Gaius Caligula* 32). Titus (A.D. 79–81) liked to surround himself with catamites and eunuchs, apparently for sexual enjoyment. Titus's successor, Emperor Domitian, like Caligula, also engaged in incestuous relations.[4] Emperor Commodus (A.D.180–92) had a harem of three hundred concubines with whom he lived a life of sexual debauchery.[5]

The debasement of heterosexual sex in Roman society is empirically corroborated by archeological findings. A recent book by John Clarke, *Looking at Lovemaking: The Constructions of Sexuality in Roman Art, 100 B.C.—A.D. 250*,[6] depicts numerous relief portraits of heterosexual sex acts embossed on ceramic items, mosaics, drawings, and other artifacts. They depict oral and group sex as well as two men and one woman, and two men and two women copulating. These sexual graphics were not camouflaged, nor did Roman parents shield their children from seeing sexual portrayals on household items.[7] As one historian has noted, "There was nothing in which they [the Romans] did not indulge or which they thought a disgrace."[8]

Sexual immorality was so pronounced that a chaste wife was seen as a rarity, says the early second-century historian Tacitus (*Annals* 3.34). Many married women of high-ranking families asked to have "their names entered amongst the public prostitutes in order that they might not be punished for adultery."[9] Among the Greco-Romans, adultery was exclusively defined in terms of a woman's marital status, not the man's. A man, married or single, could only commit adultery with another man's wife, because she was his property and adultery was a property offense. The man, however, was never a woman's property. Thus, if he sexually consorted with an unmarried woman or a prostitute, he could not commit adultery. But if a married woman had sex with a single or married man, she was always guilty of adultery. So when a married woman registered as a prostitute, she was no longer seen as exclusively belonging to her husband, meaning that legally she could not be accused of adultery and thus could incur no punishment—which under *patria potestas* made her subject to the death penalty (see chapter 4).

Some stage plays focused on incestuous behavior and some on physical mutilation. In *Procne and Tereus* the tongue of Philomela is cut out to keep her from telling others that she had been raped by her brother-in-law Tereus. And "the bestial Pasiphae, in the play of that name, offered herself to a bull in the Cretan labyrinth."[10] "These shocking dumb shows," says Jerome Carcopino, "threw women into ecstasy. Lascivious gestures moved them."[11] Decadent plays such as this one were common during the reigns of Nero (54–68) and Trajan (early second century).

Into this immoral sexual environment came the Christians with a radically different sexual ethic and lifestyle, one which held that sex between an unmarried man and woman was sinful and contrary to one of God's Ten Commandments ("You shall not commit adultery"—Exodus 20:14). Only sex between a married man and woman was God-pleasing. The Christians took seriously the words of the Epistle to the Hebrews in the New Testament that said, "Marriage should be honored by all, and the marriage bed kept pure, for God will judge the adulterer and all the sexually immoral" (Hebrews 13:4).

To Christians, sex between husband and wife was an expression of mutual love and respect, not of self-serving, lustful gratification. St. Paul told the Corinthian Christians: "The husband should fulfill his marital duty to his wife, and likewise the wife to her husband" (1 Corinthians 7:3). A Christian man and wife were obligated to "submit to one another out of reverence for Christ" (Ephesians 5:21). Similarly, St. Peter told husbands, "Be considerate as you live with your wives, and treat them with respect" (1 Peter 3:7).

Not only did the Christians contend that sexual relations had to be confined to marriage, but they also believed that the sex act made the couple "one flesh" (Ephesians 5:31), a very radical tenet. This was a belief they had acquired from their Jewish ancestors, which was also affirmed by Jesus (Matthew 19:5–6). For when God instituted marriage at the time of creation, he told Adam and Eve that the sex act made a husband and wife one flesh (Genesis 2:24). The one-flesh concept required the married couple to be totally faithful to each other. Contrary to the pagan Roman view, Christians saw sex outside of marriage as sinful and wrong. Extramarital sex was not just unfaithfulness to one's spouse and to God's command not to commit adultery, but it also violated the one-flesh concept.

A second-century document describes how the early Christians differed from the pagan Romans by confining their sexual behavior to married life: "They [Christians] marry as do all; they beget children. . . . They have a common table, but not a common bed" (*Epistle to Diognetus*). By rejecting adultery and fornication they instituted a new sexual morality, one that received positive comments even from some of the pagan observers. Galen, a Greek physician of the second century, was impressed with the upright sexual behavior of Christians. He said they were "so far advanced in self-discipline and...intense desire to attain moral excellence that they are in no way inferior to true philosophers."[12] In this context it is noteworthy to observe that the early Christians also believed that the sex act was not to be performed openly or graphically portrayed on various household items for others to see, as the Romans did. Sex was a gift of God. So powerful was the Christian doctrine and practice of marriage that Edward Gibbon says, "The dignity of marriage was restored by the Christians."[13]

Christianity brought this dignity and honor to marriage in the pagan world of the Romans by confining heterosexual sex to a married man and woman and by spurning the deviant sex of the pagans. But given that Christians were also *in* the world, they sometimes faltered by mimicking the world's sinful standards. Thus, early in the fourth century the church in some regions went along with the Roman *lex Julia de adulteriis* (noted above), which defined adultery on the basis of the marital status of the woman. A married man was not guilty of adultery if he had sex with a single woman, whereas a married woman was guilty if she had sex with either a single or a married man. The church's Council of Arles (A.D. 314) in France essentially upheld this old definition. One of its canons "did not regard the connection of a married man with an unmarried woman as adultery."[14] This church council apparently forgot Christ's words: "I tell you that anyone who looks at a woman lustfully has already committed adultery with her in his heart" (Matthew 5:28), and that Christ did not set one standard for men and another for women.

There were, however, some Christian theologians who had not forgotten Christ's words. St. Gregory of Nazianzus (d. 389), for example, argued that adultery could also be committed by the man (*Oration* 37.6). Unfortunately, it took another half-century after Gregory's argument for the voice of Jesus to get through when the church declared in 449 that the sin of adultery applied to the husband as well as to the wife.[15] The wife was now able to divorce her adulterous husband, something that had never occurred before in the ancient world. Edward Westermarck, the renowned scholar of the history of marriage, says that a woman being able to divorce her husband on grounds of adultery or sodomy is "an innovation [that reveals] the influence of Christian ideas."[16] In other words, even though the church did not always get it right, the teachings of Jesus did eventually get through, despite his error-prone followers, thus changing and improving the way much of the world viewed sex and marriage.

Westermarck credits Christianity not only with equalizing the sin of adultery but also with having brought dignity and beauty to the formal wedding ceremony.[17] We do not know what dignity, if any, a Roman wedding once had, but whatever it had was largely lost by the first century. The

Roman poet Catullus reveals that the wedding ritual in his day was a face-tious mockery, apparently because of the low regard the Roman culture had developed for marriage as a whole. Depicting a wedding scene, he cites the singing of an obscene song: "Raise aloft the torches, boys. I see the wed-ding veil coming. Go on, sing in measure, Io Hymen Hymenaeus, Io Hymen Hymenaeus!.... Today and yesterday you disdained the country wives...Wretched, ah! wretched lover, throw the nuts!" (*Catullus* 61). Regarding this disrespectful view of the wedding ceremony and its accom-panying low view of marriage, Susan Treggiari, in her analysis of the Roman wedding, says: "Constantine [fourth-century emperor] revolutionized the state's view of marriage in order to bring it more into line with Christian ideas."[18] Thus, every time we see the dignity, beauty, and solemnity that accompanies the average wedding ceremony today, even in an era of high divorce rates, we would do well to remember that this is the result of Christianity's influence. Moreover, the belief that marriage is a divine insti-tution, still widely held by many in Western societies, also stems from Christianity.[19]

The dignity and sanctity of marriage that Christianity brought to Roman culture were mostly due to the early Christian women. As already noted, they appreciated the dignity and worth that Christ's teachings accorded them, and seeing themselves as God's redeemed children, they, more so than men, understood the seriousness of their biological role as bearers of children in God's created order. Thus, the wedding rite, the pre-cursor to the fulfillment of that role, needed to be conducted with solem-nity and reverence. This conclusion is not mere speculation. We need only recall what the pagan Libanius said when he lauded the Christian women's high level of commitment and dedication to their role as wives and moth-ers: "What women these Christians have!"[20]

THE REJECTION OF HOMOSEXUALITY

In addition to the depraved heterosexual sex acts of the Romans, and the uninhibited portrayal of those acts, there was the widespread depravity of homosexual sex. The latter went well beyond two adult males or females sexually cohabiting with one another.

PEDERASTY (PEDOPHILIA)

Many people today know that the Greeks were notorious for their homo-sexual behavior. But often they do not know that Greek homosexual sex was primarily pederasty or pedophilia, that is, an adult man having sex with a young boy who commonly was between twelve and sixteen years old. The Romans practiced the same perversity. Roman literature both before and after the birth of Christ has numerous references, similar to Greek writings, showing that this kind of homosexual behavior was widespread and common.

That Roman homosexuality was largely pederastic is underscored by its own poet Martial. He is rather explicit and unembarrassed in referring to it. To Phaedrus, he writes, "You sleep with well-endowed boys" (*Epigrams* 3.72). To another he says, "You do it with long-haired boys whom you have procured for yourself with your wife's dowry" (*Epigrams* 7.97). So explicit are Martial's writings that he even notes one man was unable to sodomize his boy lover who had diarrhea (*Epigrams* 11.88). Florence Dupont, a modern historian, writes that the Romans were so obsessed with pederasty that "beardless youths had to be prohibited from taking part in Saturnalia [a festival in honor of Saturn, the harvest god] in order to protect their virtue."[21] And according to Martial, young boys were not only sodomized by adult men but also by women (*Philaenis* 7.67).

The acceptance of pedophilia among the Roman populace is not just evident in the literature of its poets and philosophers; it is also illustrated on archaeological artifacts. Clarke's book (cited above) shows many plates of Roman relief portraits of man-boy couples engaged in sex. These pictures depict behavior that today, even in an increasingly secular and anti-Christian society, is regarded as morally abhorrent and thus legally classified as child molestation.

As with the heterosexual customs, the sexual depravities were not confined to the Roman public, but were also practiced by society's upper echelon. Thus, we find pederastic sex as common behavior among many Roman emperors. Legends say that Tiberius, the emperor under whose rule Christ was crucified, often surrounded himself with young boys whom he used sexually.[22] Nero had at least two boys, Sporus and Pythagoras, with whom he engaged in sexual acts. Sporus was castrated so he could assume the role of "wife" for Nero, and with Pythagoras, Nero himself assumed the role of "wife."[23] Emperor Galba, who succeeded Nero, had at least one male lover, and Titus loved to party with his catamites and eunuchs.[24] Hadrian (117–38), the emperor who built Hadrian's Wall across northern England, not only had numerous affairs with women, but he also had a young lad, Antinous, as his sexual companion.[25] Emperor Commodus, along with three hundred concubines, also had three hundred young boys to satisfy his sexual appetite. Emperor Elagabalus (218–22) had many homosexual liaisons. He often went about town at night playing the part of a male prostitute. Still another emperor, Carus (282–83), used boys sexually.[26] These emperors, given to the perversity of pederasty or pedophilia, were commonly bisexual. As one Roman historian has noted, Rome's sexual sensuality in its most degrading forms pervaded all classes and was "the opprobrium of history."[27]

Whether it was the craving to have sex with boys or to have sex with all sorts of women, the conscience of the Roman populace and its emperors was dead as stone. The pagan gods whom the Romans worshiped did not set high moral standards, nor did they ask for contrition or repentance—that was foreign to Greco-Roman paganism. Instead, as one historian says, the pagan gods "were often seen as the First Cause [sic] of the spiral of desire."[28]

Today's outlawing of pedophilia, that is, an adult having sex with someone who is a juvenile, is the result of Christianity's influence. Had Christianity not entered the pagan culture of the Greeks and Romans, where pederasty was common, widespread, and accepted, it is doubtful that there would now be laws against child molestation.

It can also be argued that if Christian values and influence continue to deteriorate, the resistance to pederasty will weaken and decline. It is no secret that Christian values have recently declined rather precipitously in many Western countries and that along with this decline there has been a weakening of the condemnation of pederasty. For instance, in England in 1994, the age at which homosexual sex was legal was reduced from age twenty-one to eighteen, and in July, 1998, the British Parliament again reduced such acts to age sixteen.[29] In Denmark, where Christianity also has lost much of its presence, the age for homosexual sex has in recent years been lowered to age fourteen.

Lowering the legal age for homosexual sex has strong advocates. For example, in the United States the North American Man/Boy Love Association (NAMBLA) with one million members seeks to remove all present legal restrictions in regard to sex between adult males and boys. In 1991 the *Journal of Homosexuality* devoted an entire issue to man/boy homosexuality, and not one article condemned such behavior. One article even questioned the American assumption that sexual contact with an adult is harmful and traumatic to a boy. It also tried to distinguish between child sexual abuse and pedophilia, implying that the two should not be equated.[30] And in 1998 the *Psychological Bulletin,* a publication of the American Psychological Association, published a lengthy article that questioned the unqualified cultural belief that adult/adolescent sex is necessarily harmful. The article further stated that "adult-adolescent sex has been commonplace cross-culturally and historically, often in socially sanctioned forms, and may fall within the 'normal' range of sexual behaviors."[31] This statement clearly implies that if the American culture took a similar stance, pedophilia would not be abnormal or wrong.

The Christian rejection of pederasty (pedophilia) among the Greco-Romans, fortunately, is still with us. Whether it is in the United States or in other civilized countries, there is a pronounced public abhorrence of the sexual molestation of a child. Few are not outraged when an adult—male or female—is found having sexual relations with a minor. All fifty states of the United States classify sex with a minor as a felonious offense, subject to prison if convicted. This abhorrence is a direct result of Christianity having brought a moral perspective to human sexual behavior.

If the current trend of rejecting Christianity's two-thousand-year influence on sexual morality continues, as is now occurring with regard to the acceptance of adult homosexuality, the abhorrence of man/boy sex may someday also change to toleration and even to acceptance as it had among the Greco-Romans. The following could be a signal of what is to come. On June 21, 2000, *South Park,* an animated show produced by Comedy Central, portrayed a character named Eric who unknowingly came in contact with a real pedophile group, the North American Man/Boy Love Association (mentioned above). One scene has a NAMBLA member blasphemously saying, "Thank you, Jesus," for sending a boy who is presumed to want sex with adult men. In a similar manner, another scene refers to another boy as a "gift from God," also assuming he is present to have sex with grown men.[32] In addition, there are influential groups such as the National Education Association (NEA) that are advocating programs that present homosexuality as an alternative lifestyle to children in grade schools.[33] In 1996 the Women's Educational Media of San Francisco, California, produced a video titled *It's Elementary: Talking About Gay Issues in Schools.* This video promotes the acceptance of homosexuality, and during the last several years it has been shown to many grade-school teachers in various parts of the United States with the goal of communicating the acceptance of homosexual behavior to young pupils.

ADULT MALE HOMOSEXUALITY

Christian abhorrence of homosexuality was not confined to pederasty, however. Sex between two adult males was also considered abhorrent. For instance, St. Paul condemned men's "indecent acts with other men" (Romans 1:27). He did not differentiate between pedophilia and adult homosexual acts; both were sinful sexual perversions in God's eyes.

It seems that wherever pagan values reign, as in the Greco-Roman culture, there one finds widespread homosexuality. For instance, homosexuality was common among numerous American Indian tribes. Walter L. Williams, in a book that focuses on homosexuality among American Indians, sympathetically notes that the Kwakiutl Indians of British Columbia, the Crows, the Klamaths, the Hopi, the Sioux, the Navajo, the Zuni, the Yokuts, and other tribes in the United States all practiced homosexuality before contact with Westerners. Sometimes homosexual acts were intertwined with the religious ceremonies performed by shamans. Williams not only conveys a great deal of empathy for the homosexual customs of the American Indians but also throws frequent punches at Christianity for having influenced most American Indians to believe that homosexual behavior is morally bad.[34]

The biblical condemnation and rejection of homosexuality was not a novel idea introduced by St. Paul. Jude, the writer of the New Testament book that bears his name, told his readers that sexual immorality led God to destroy the cities of Sodom and Gomorrah (Jude 7). And it may be that Jesus also had this sin in mind when he referred to God annihilating these two ancient cities (Matthew 11:23).

Had Christ never been born, and had his followers not been transformed by his spirit, the homosexual behavior of the ancient Romans would likely never have been outlawed in the Western world. In addition to laws prohibiting homosexual acts for individuals underage, there also are still laws against adult homosexual sex. For instance, in 1999 more than twenty of the fifty American states still had statutes on their law books outlawing homosexual behavior. This fact is not widely known because the mass media give the impression that homosexuality is a free and legal option (an "alternative lifestyle") and that there are no longer any laws against homosexual practices. It is also worth noting that these state laws were upheld by the U.S. Supreme Court in Bowers v. Hardwick (1986). In other words, when many in the mass media, as well as others, advocate that homosexual behavior should be tolerated, and even accepted, they often are really abetting criminal behavior.

LESBIANISM

In addition to some women sodomizing young boys, Roman women also engaged in homosexual activities with other women. The Roman poet Juvenal talks about women taking turns in riding each other (*Satire* 6). As with male homosexual sex, there was no guilt, shame, or inhibition. Homosexual graphics, similar to the heterosexual depictions, were openly portrayed on household items such as frescos, lamps, bowls, and cups.[35] Commenting on this Roman way of life, Clarke says, "Imagine drinking from an elegant sliver cup with scenes of male-to-male intercourse on it... or visiting someone's house and seeing fresco paintings depicting sexual activity on the walls of the best room."[36]

Extrapolating from twentieth-century research studies of homosexuality, which commonly indicate that female homosexuality is significantly less prevalent than among men, we can assume that this difference was also true of the Romans. That, however, did not make this behavior any less depraved in the eyes of the early Christians. To the Christians in Rome, both male and female homosexual acts were a clear violation of the natural/moral law as well as an affront to God's divine law set forth by Moses some fourteen hundred years before the birth of Christ. Leviticus 20:13 warned: "If a man lies with a man as one lies with a woman, both of them have done what is detestable. They must be put to death." And in the New Testament, as noted earlier, St. Paul unequivocally condemned both male and female homosexuality.

THE REJECTION OF BESTIALITY

Many Romans even engaged in sex with animals. Apuleius, the second-century Latin author, tells of wealthy Romans having sex with donkeys and of a woman named Pasiphae sexually consorting with a bull (*Metamorphoses* 10.19). How widespread bestiality was among the Romans is difficult to ascertain, but that it was a part of their degenerate, depraved sexual life is beyond debate. Barton states that "Roman 'bestiality' formed part of the extended repertoire of pleasures."[37] Pierre Wuilleumier and Amable Audin in their book on Roman medallions depict a scene on a medallion from the Rhone River Valley in France of a woman arched forward with her buttocks extended toward a rearing stallion that is ready to penetrate her sexually.[38] As with homosexuality, such behavior was an unmitigated abomination to the Christians, who honored the natural/moral law and God's divine law as stated in Leviticus 20:15–16. Thus, St. Paul, writing to the Christians in Rome, condemned the sexual behavior of women who "exchanged natural relations for unnatural ones" (Romans 1:26).

CHRISTIANITY'S IMPACT ON SEX AND MARRIAGE

Christian opposition to the opprobrious sex of the Romans has left its salutary mark to this very day. The Christian ethic not only condemned adultery, fornication, and the public portrayal of sexual activity, but in time brought noteworthy, wholesome changes to how people in a civilized society viewed human sexual behavior.

MARRIAGE IS DIGNIFIED

Christians believed that the sex act was not to be enjoyed lustfully at will, that is, by engaging in it whenever it was available or by deriving vicarious satisfaction from its visual portrayals on various artifacts in people's homes. As already noted, to Christians sexual intercourse belonged exclusively to a married man and woman within the bonds of marriage: "Marriage should be honored by all, and the marriage bed kept pure, for God will judge the adulterer and all the sexually immoral" (Hebrews 13:4). Sexual intercourse was a private act between a husband and wife, performed in mutual love, rather than a self-serving act of passion. It was to be governed by the standard that St. Paul delineated: "Husbands, love your wives, just as Christ loved the church and gave himself up for her" (Ephesians 5:25). Marriage, instituted by God when Adam and Eve were brought together, was a sacred institution. It was this view of marriage and sex among Christians that brought honor and dignity to it.

MARITAL PRIVACY

Another major impact that Christianity had on sex and marriage was its advocacy of privacy in marital sexual relations. As noted above, the shameless, promiscuous practice of sexual acts by Rome's emperors and by much of its populace, often performed in public, was a reflection not only of the Roman culture having had an extremely low level of sexual morality, but also of its having no institutionalized concept of sexual privacy, not even for married men and women. In contrast to this Roman depravity, the Christians made much of the biblical doctrine that sexual intimacy between a husband and a wife was a hallowed gift of God. It was only to be engaged in in the context of their marital privacy and never outside the domain of a married couple's private bedchamber. Neither was this gift of God to be visually portrayed on household artifacts (such as bowls, lamps, vases, or pictures, as was common in Roman culture); nor was it to be engaged in in public, similar to the behavior of animals.

The Christian concern for the privacy of the marital sex act essentially led to the institutionalization of privacy. Richard Hixson reminds Westerners that privacy has strong Christian roots.[39] Another scholar has

THE MORALITY OF SEX AND MARRIAGE

Activity	Greco-Romans	Early Christians
Marriage	A man-made custom devised for the good of the state	A lifelong holy estate instituted by God
Sexual Intercourse	Need not be confined to marriage	Only acceptable and pleasing to God in marriage
Adultery	A double standard: a husband having sex with an unmarried woman or prostitute was not guilty of adultery; a wife having sex with any man (married or single) was always adultery	Adopted Christ's single standard; the man was as responsible as the woman (Matthew 5:27–28); sex outside of marriage by husband or wife constituted adultery
Fornication	No religious, moral, social, or cultural stigma pertained to premarital sexual intercourse	Sinful and wrong, condemned by God; equal to the sin of adultery (1 Corinthians 6:9)
Prostitution	No religious, moral, social, or cultural stigma; male and female prostitution taken for granted; legal and widely practiced	Condemned by God; pollutes the temple of the Holy Spirit, the Christian's body (1 Corinthians 6:16–19)
Homosexuality	No religious, moral, social, or cultural stigma; legal and widely practiced	Sinful, unnatural, morally wrong, and condemned by God (Romans 1:24–27);not tolerated in Christian circles
Pederasty (pedophilia)	No religious, moral, social, or cultural stigma; legal and widely practiced; most homosexual acts were pederastic	Sinful, unnatural, morally wrong, and condemned by God; not tolerated in Christian circles
Lesbianism	Similar to homosexuality and pederasty; not seen as morally wrong; its practice carried no stigma	Sinful, unnatural, morally wrong, and condemned by God; not tolerated in Christian circles
Group Sex	Practiced by many, including some emperors; graphically portrayed on various artifacts	Sinful, morally wrong, and condemned by God; unthinkable to Christians
Bestiality	No religious, moral, or cultural stigma; portrayed on various artifacts; practiced but its extent is unknown	"Anyone who has sexual relations with an animal must be put to death" (Exodus 22:19); this precept made it unthinkable to Christians

argued that "our [Western] approach to privacy is a function of the ways of thinking that are initially identified with Christianity."[40] Similarly, still another observer says that there is a marked relationship between the rise of Christianity and the rise of privacy.[41]

To be sure, the concept of privacy has been and continues to be abused by many, especially by those who ignore or reject Christianity's biblical morality with regard to promiscuous sexual relations and related shameful behavior. The early Christians did not use privacy to hide illicit or extra-marital sex such as fornication, adultery, or homosexuality. They knew that a sin committed in a private setting was still a sin. They had no interest in using the concept of privacy to evade personal accountability before God or man, as is often done today.

CONCLUSION

Edward Gibbon, the famous historian of the Roman Empire, said that the Romans were the masters of the world. Ironically, however, as this chapter has shown, they were incapable of mastering their sexual lusts and passions. Their pagan religious beliefs imposed no constraints on sensual pleasures. In fact, sometimes religious practices were intertwined with sex, as in the pagan institution of temple prostitutes.

When the early Christians spurned the immoral sexual activities of the Romans, they were motivated by the love of Christ their Lord, whose words told them: "If you love me, you will obey what I command" (John 14:15). One of God's commandments told them, "You shall not commit adultery." In addition, they knew from St. Paul's words that "neither the sexually immoral nor idolaters nor adulterers...nor homosexual offenders... [would] inherit the kingdom of God" (1 Corinthians 6:9–10). And they also believed the words that followed this admonition: "The body is not meant for sexual immorality, but for the Lord, and the Lord for the body" (1 Corinthians 6:13). They also knew from St. Paul that their body was "a temple of the Holy Spirit" (1 Corinthians 6:19). It was inconceivable for them to pollute their bodies with sexual depravities. So they rejected all sexual immoralities. In time, the Christian moral posture prompted the Western world to condemn and outlaw adultery, pedophilia, adult homosexual behavior, and bestiality. Again, the moral teachings of Jesus Christ made a significant and salutary difference, this time by elevating sexual behavior to a level far above paganism.

Obviously, the Christians were not admired for rejecting the sexual immoralities of the Romans. St. Augustine in the early part of the fifth century said that the Romans despised Christians because they opposed their unrestrained sexual lifestyles (*The City of God* 1.30). Tertullian said that the Romans so despised the Christians that they hated the name "Christian" (*Apology* 3). One finds a similar hatred directed toward Christians today. Given that biblically minded Christians oppose the currently growing sexual immoralities, such as sex outside of marriage and homosexuality, they are negatively referred to as "the religious right" or as "bigots." Similar to the Romans, these critics do not like it when sensually lustful behavior is morally questioned and called sinful. The hateful attitudes that once were directed against the early Christians seem to be returning, and for similar reasons, despite the current attention given to toleration. Increasingly, Christians are hated by many who advocate "hate crime" laws. In large measure, they are hated because they seek to honor God and his laws rather than "redefine God as our future selves," as Richard Rorty, a self-proclaimed leftist, believes ought to be modern man's concept of God.[42]

When individuals redefine God as their future selves, they no longer fear God, and so they practice whatever behavior pleases them. One is reminded of St. Paul's words that described the sexual perversions of the ancient Romans:

> Therefore God gave them over in the sinful desires of their hearts to sexual impurity for the degrading of their bodies with one another....God gave them over to shameful lusts. Even their women exchanged natural relations with unnatural ones. In the same way the men also abandoned natural relations with women and were inflamed with lust for one another. Men committed indecent acts with other men, and received in themselves the due penalty for their perversion (Romans 1:24, 26–27).

Such behavior was contrary to God's natural/moral law and repugnant to all God-fearing Christians.

By opposing the Greco-Roman sexual decadence, whether it was adultery, fornication, homosexuality, child molestation, or bestiality, and by introducing God-pleasing sexual standards, Christianity greatly elevated the world's sexual morality. It was one of its many major contributions to civilization, a contribution that too many Christians today (who nominally comprise about 83 percent of the American population) no longer seem to appreciate, much less defend, as feverish efforts are underway to bring back the sexual debauchery of ancient paganism. If the Apostle John were here today, he would undoubtedly say what he said to the Christians in Laodicea: "Because you are lukewarm—neither hot nor cold—I am about to spit you out of my mouth" (Revelation 3:16).

NOTES

1. Fikret Yegül, *Baths and Bathing in Classical Antiquity* (Cambridge: MIT Press, 1992), 34.
2. Edward Gibbon, *The History of the Decline and Fall of the Roman Empire* (reprint, London: Penguin Books, 1994), 2:813.
3. Frederic W. Farrar, *The Early Days of Christianity* (New York: A. L. Burt Publishers, 1882), 71.
4. Chris Scarre, *Chronicle of the Roman Emperors* (New York: Thames and Hudson, 1995), 83.
5. Ibid., 125.
6. John R. Clarke, *Looking at Lovemaking: Construction of Sexuality in Roman Art 100 B.C–A.D. 250* (Berkeley: University of California Press, 1998), passim.
7. Ibid., 276.
8. C. Schmidt, *The Social Results of Early Christianity,* trans. R. W. Dale (London: Wm. Isbister, 1889), 47.
9. Ibid.
10. Jerome Carcopino, *Daily Life in Ancient Rome* (New Haven: Yale University Press, 1940), 228.
11. Ibid.
12. Cited in Will Durant, *Caesar and Christ: A History of Roman Civilization and of Christianity from Their Beginnings to A.D. 325* (New York: MJF Books, 1971), 599.
13. Gibbon, *Decline and Fall,* 813.
14. Carl J. von Hefele, *A History of the Christian Councils* (Edinburgh: T and T Clark, 1894), 1:170.
15. Ibid.
16. Edward Westermarck, *The History of Marriage* (New York: Allerton Book Company, 1922), 326.
17. Ibid., 2:576.
18. Susan Treggiari, "Roman Marriage," in *Civilization of the Ancient Mediterranean: Greece and Rome,* ed. Michael Grant and Rachel Kitzinger (New York: Charles Scribner's Sons, 1988), 1343.
19. Westermarck, *History of Marriage,* 2:577.
20. Cited in L. Millar, *Christian Education in the First Four Centuries* (London: Faith Press, 1946), 54.
21. Florence Dupont, *Daily Life in Ancient Rome,* trans. Christopher Woodall (Cambridge: Blackwell Publishing, 1989), 206.
22. Scarre, *Chronicle of the Roman Emperors,* 35.
23. Ibid., 54.
24. Ibid., 73.
25. Ibid., 101.
26. Ibid., 151.
27. Charles Merivale, *History of the Romans* (New York: D. Appleton, 1866), 227.
28. Carlin A. Barton, *The Sorrows of the Ancient Romans: The Gladiator and the Monster* (Princeton: Princeton University Press, 1993), 69.
29. Andrew Grice and Christopher Morgan, "Blair's Gay Vote Dismays Bishops," *Sunday Times* (London), 21 June 1998, 14.
30. Gerald P. Jones, "The Study of Intergenerational Intimacy in North America: Beyond Politics and Pedophilia," *Journal of Homosexuality* 20 (1991): 275–95.
31. Bruce Rind, Philip Tromovitch, and Robert Bauserman, "A Meta-Analytic Examination of Assumed Properties of Child Sexual Abuse Using College Samples," *Psychological Bulletin* (July 1998): 46.
32. "South Park Hits New Low With Pedophilia, Abortion Themes," *American Family Association Journal* (August 2000): 8.
33. "Gay and Lesbian Caucus Targets Youth: First Graders Must Be Taught Tolerance," *Education Reporter* (August 1994): 1.
34. Walter L. Williams, *The Spirit and the Flesh* (Boston: Beacon Press, 1986).
35. Clarke, *Looking at Lovemaking,* plates 1–16.
36. Ibid., 1.
37. Barton, *Sorrows of the Ancient Romans,* 68.
38. Pierre Wuilleumier and Amable Audin, *Les medaillons d' applique gallo-romains de la vallee du Rhone* (Paris: Societe D'Edition Les Belles Letteres, 1952), 136.
39. Richard Hixson, *Privacy in a Public Society* (New York: Oxford University Press, 1987), 5–6.
40. Larry Peterman, "Privacy's Background," *Review of Politics* (Spring 1993): 244.
41. Hannah Arendt, *The Human Condition* (Chicago: University of Chicago Press, 1958), 35, 60.
42. Richard Rorty, *Achieving Our Country: Leftist Thought in Twentieth Century America* (Cambridge: Harvard University Press, 1998), 22.

Two ARTISTS' concepts of the account of the woman confronted by Jesus at the well in Sychar (John 4): (top) "The Woman of Samaria" *(William Dyce from C. Birmingham Art Gallery);* (bottom) "Jesus and the Woman of Samaria" *(Gustave Doré).*

WOMEN RECEIVE FREEDOM
and DIGNITY

*"There is neither...male nor female, for you are
all one in Christ Jesus."*

St. Paul in Galatians 3:28

W hat would be the status of women in the Western world today had Jesus Christ never entered the human arena? One way to answer this question is to look at the status of women in most present-day Islamic countries. Here women are still denied many rights that are available to men, and when they appear in public, they must be veiled. In Saudi Arabia, for instance, women are even barred from driving an automobile. In the summer of 1999, news reports revealed that women in Iran are forbidden to wear lipstick, and if they do, they can be arrested and jailed.[1] Whether in Saudi Arabia or in many other Arab countries where the Islamic religion is adhered to strongly, a man has the right to beat and sexually desert his wife, all with the full support of the Koran, which says, "Men stand superior to women. . . .But those whose perverseness ye fear, admonish them and remove them into bedchambers and beat them; but if they submit to you then do not seek a way against them" (Sura 4:34). This command is the polar opposite of what the New Testament says regarding a man's relationship with his wife. St. Paul told the Christians in Ephesus, "Husbands, love your wives, just as Christ loved the church and gave himself up for her." And he added, "He who loves his wife loves himself" (Ephesians 5:25, 28).

The high and honorable marital ethic set forth in Ephesians, which stems from Christ's interactions with women, cannot be found in the pagan literature of the Greco-Romans or in the cultures of other societies. The civil and humane behavior that is expected between husband and wife today, even by secularly minded people, reflects the sea change effect Christ has had on the lives of women and on marriage, especially in the West.

One scholar of ancient Rome has aptly said that "the conversion of the Roman world to Christianity [brought] a great change in woman's status."[2] Another has expressed it even more succinctly: "The birth of Jesus was the turning point in the history of woman."[3] To understand more fully how Christ's teachings and actions began the process of improving the status of women, we need to take a brief look at the abjectly low status they had in his day. We go first to ancient Greece.

THE LOW STATUS OF GREEK WOMEN

Many Americans and Europeans are unaware of the extremely low status that women, especially wives, had among the ancient Athenians of Greece. A respectable Athenian woman was not permitted to leave her house unless she was accompanied by a trustworthy male escort, commonly a slave appointed by her husband.[4] When the husband's male guests were present in his home, she was not permitted to eat or interact with them. She had to retire to her woman's quarters (*gynaeceum*).[5] The only woman who had some freedom was the *hetaera*, or mistress, who often accompanied a married man when he attended events outside his home. The *hetaera* was the man's companion and sexual partner.[6]

The Greek wife had virtually no freedom. Even in Sparta, where women had more freedom than in Athens, men kept their wives "under lock and key," according to Plutarch, the second-century Greek biographer and essayist (*Lycurgus* 15.8). The poet Aristophanes has Calonice say in one of his plays, "We women can't go out just when we like. We have to wait upon our men" (*Lysistrata* 16–19). The average Athenian woman had the social status of a slave.[7] And according to Euripides' tragedy *Medea*, the wife could not divorce her husband, whereas he could divorce her anytime. Small wonder that Medea in Euripides' play lamented, "Surely, of all creatures that have life and wit, we women are of all unhappiest" (*Medea* 231–32).

Greek discrimination against women began early in a woman's life cycle. Nonslave boys in Athens were sent to school, "taught to read and write, and educated in poetry, music and gymnastics; girls did not go to school at all," says one Greek scholar.[8] Throughout a woman's entire life she was not permitted to speak in public. Sophocles wrote, "O woman, silence is an adornment to woman" (*Ajax* 293); Euripides asserted, "Silence and discretion are most beautiful in woman, and remaining quiet within the house" (*Heraclitus* 476); and the philosopher Aristotle said, "Silence gives grace to woman" (*Politics* 1.1260a). But long before the days of Euripides, Sophocles, and Aristophanes, the writer Homer portrayed Telemachus rebuking his mother Penelope for speaking in the presence of men. Dogmatically, he tells her that "speech shall be for men" (*Odyssey* 1.359).

The Athenian woman was also deemed inferior to man. Given this cultural perception, the Greek poets were fond of equating her with evil. Euripides (480–406 B.C.) has Hippolytus ask, "Why hast thou given a home beneath the sun, Zeus, unto woman, specious curse to man?" (*Hippolytus* 616–17). Aeschylus (525?–456 B.C.) has a chorus declare, "Evil of mind are they [women], and guileful of purpose, with impure hearts" (*Suppliant Maidens* 748–49). Another Greek poet, Aristophanes, has the chorus in his play *Lysistrata* say, "For women are a shameless set, the vilest of creatures going" (368–69). The great epic writer Homer has Agamemnon declare, "One cannot trust women" (*Odyssey* 11). And, of course, it was the Greek myth of Pandora's jar that blamed woman for introducing evil into the world.

The extremely low status of the Athenian woman extended far beyond her not being allowed to have a meaningful social life in public or in the presence of men even in private life. Beginning with childhood, her life had little or no social value. For instance, as I have already mentioned, female infanticide far exceeded that of males. Baby girls were expendable. The words of Hilarion come to mind. He told his wife, when she was about to give birth, that if the infant was born a male to let it live, but if it was a female to "cast it out."[9] One Greek scholar writes that a male child was of vital importance, even to the wife. A male offspring was "her principal source of prestige and validation," whereas a female child was "an economic liability, a social burden."[10]

THE LOW STATUS OF ROMAN WOMEN

The status of women was also exceedingly low in Roman society. It revealed itself in many ways, one of them being the higher rate of female infanticide. Like the Greeks, the Romans valued baby girls significantly less, so they accounted for most of the infanticides.[11] However, the early Christians (as noted in chapter 2) consistently opposed infanticide, not just for boys but also for girls. They saw Christ as having redeemed both male and female. They remembered St. Paul's words: "There is neither...male nor female, for you are all one in Christ Jesus" (Galatians 3:28).

Although the Roman woman at the time of Christ and his apostles had somewhat more freedom than her Greek counterpart, she had essentially none of the rights and privileges that men enjoyed. While many upper-class girls informally received some education in grammar and reading, a Roman wife, like her Athenian counterpart, was not allowed to be present with her husband's guests at a meal.[12] There were numerous other restrictions on women as well. For instance, a married woman was commonly under the Roman law of *manus,* which placed her under the absolute control of her husband, who had ownership of her and all her possessions.[13] He could divorce her if she merely went out in public without a veil, according to Plutarch (*Romulus* 22.3). Although a husband could divorce his wife, she could never divorce him. Cato notes that the wife even lacked the right to tell her husband's slave what to do (*Aulus Gellius Noctium Gellius* 17.6). According to *lex Voconia* (a law enacted in 169 B.C.) a woman under *manus* was legally prohibited from inheriting property. This law was still in force in the early part of the fifth century and received strong criticism from Augustine, the Christian bishop of Hippo in northern Africa.

The most severe deprivation of a Roman woman's freedom and rights had its roots in table 4 of the Twelve Tables of Roman law that originated in the fifth century B.C. Table 4 spelled out the law of *patria potestas,* which conferred rights of *paterfamilias* on the married man. In his role as *paterfamilias,* the man had supreme, absolute power over his children even when grown, including grandchildren. He alone had the power to divorce his wife, and he also possessed the power to execute his children. He could even execute his married daughter if she committed adultery in his or in her husband's house.[14] This latter right was reinforced by Caesar Augustus when he issued *lex Julia de adulteriis* in 18 B.C. A man's wife was also subject to her husband's power of life and death.[15] He had "full authority to chastise his wife and, in some cases, even to kill her, in the same way as he might chastise or kill his child."[16] To kill his wife for a nonadulterous offense, the husband ordinarily required the consent of an extended family tribunal, but in the case of adultery no such consent was necessary.[17]

Compared with the modern woman in today's Western society, the Roman woman had little or no property rights. Goods or money that she could inherit were legally limited. She was not even allowed to leave money to her children if they were under her husband's *patria potestas*.[18] *Patria potestas* and its corollary *paterfamilias* prohibited women from speaking in public. Rome's city councils, senate, legal courts, and other civic entities were all governed by men. Roman men, like their Greek counterparts, had no tolerance for women speaking in public settings. A number of Roman records corroborate this posture. One prominent example reveals that in 215 B.C. a group of women assembled in the Roman Forum, which was not open to them. Nevertheless, a number of women entered the Forum to protest and to ask for repeal of the Oppian Law. This law had made it illegal for women to don multicolored robes, to wear more than one ounce of gold, and to ride in the *carpentum* (a covered carriage). In response to their public gathering and protesting, the statesman and philosopher Cato asked, "Could you not have asked your own husbands the same thing at home?" (Livy, *The Founding Fathers of the City* 34.10). In short, women were to be silent. If they had any questions, they were to convey them to their husbands, who would then take them to the appropriate public setting for consideration. The imposition of silence on a woman meant that she could not speak in court.[19]

In addition to depriving women of basic freedoms, Roman culture also had an extremely low regard for women. This is expressed by Tacitus (ca. A.D. 55–ca. 120), who in his *Annuals* argued that women were domineering and cruel. The philosopher and statesman Seneca saw human anger as a womanish and childish trait (*De Ira* 1.190), and the satirist Juvenal said, "There is nothing a woman will not permit herself to do" (*Satires* 6.457). Given this prejudice, one sees why it was a cultural taboo for a woman to appear on public stage. If she did, she was labeled *infamia*.[20] Nor was the situation much better if she left her husband's house, even for religious reasons: "Women's journeys from the house for religious purposes were regarded by the elegists and satirists with grave suspicion."[21]

The low regard for women also showed itself in how they were used sexually. "The virtue of chastity, in our Christian sense, was almost unknown among the heathens. Woman was essentially a slave of man's lower passions."[22] And given that sensuality in its most degrading forms pervaded all classes, as we have seen in chapter 3, we find that promiscuous women were often part of the pagan temple worship, for instance, in the Temple of Aphrodite. In the Roman and Greek temples sex was a common religious activity. The pagan gods of the Romans or Greeks set no precepts with regard to moral behavior.

THE LOW STATUS OF HEBREW WOMEN

Although it did not use women sexually in religious activities, the Hebrew culture was in some other ways as badly biased against women as was the culture of the Greco-Romans. This was particularly true during the rabbinic era (ca. 400 B.C. to ca. A.D. 300). The rabbinic oral law (now essentially recorded in the Talmud and Midrash), like the customs of the Greeks and Romans, barred women from testifying in court (*Yoma* 43b). And like the Athenians, the Jews barred women from public speaking. The oral law taught that "out of respect of the congregation, the woman should not read [out loud] in the Law [Torah]" (*Megillah* 23a). Another rabbinic teaching proclaimed that it was "shameful" to hear a woman's voice in public among men (*Berakhoth* 24a). Still another taught, "Let the words of the Law [Torah] be burned rather than committed to a woman...If a man teaches his daughter the Law, it is as though he taught her lechery" (*Sotah* 3.4). Josephus, the first-century Jewish historian, who was also a Pharisee, corroborated this posture when he said that women were not to speak because the Law of Moses proscribed it (*Jewish Antiquities* 4.8.15).

Given the belief that a woman's voice should not be heard among men in public, synagogue worship consisted entirely of male participants. Women, if present, were passive listeners, separated from men by a *michetza* (partition). Sometimes they were "secluded in an adjoining room or gallery ...[and] they were never to raise their voices."[23] Only men did the singing or chanting. Raphael Patai says that Jewish women were not permitted to sing in a synagogue until the Enlightenment (late 1700s) and then only in the Reformed (liberal) synagogues or temples.[24]

CHRIST ACCORDS WOMEN FREEDOM AND DIGNITY

The extremely low status that the Greek, Roman, and Jewish woman had for centuries was radically affected by the appearance of Jesus Christ. His actions and teachings raised the status of women to new heights, often to the consternation and dismay of his friends and enemies. By word and deed, he went against the ancient, taken-for-granted beliefs and practices that defined woman as socially, intellectually, and spiritually inferior. True to his own words, he once said, "I have come that [you] may have life, and have it to the full" (John 10:10). If any group of human beings was in need of a more abundant life, spiritually and socially, it was the women of his day.

THE SAMARITAN WOMAN

The humane and respectful way Jesus treated and responded to the Samaritan woman (as recorded in John 4:5–29) may not appear unusual to readers in today's Western culture. Yet what he did was extremely unusual, even radical. He ignored the Jewish anti-Samaritan prejudices along with the prevailing view that saw women as inferior beings.

Meeting a Samaritan woman at Jacob's Well, Jesus asked her for a drink. Shocked, she asked, "You are a Jew and I am a Samaritan woman. How can you ask me for a drink?"(John 4:9). His speaking to her, a woman, was part of her shock. She might merely have asked, "How is it that you, a Jew, ask a drink of me, a Samaritan?" But instead she said, "I am a Samaritan woman." To speak to a Samaritan was bad enough, but Jesus also ignored the extant rabbinic belief that a self-respecting man did not speak to a woman in public. The rabbinic oral law was quite explicit: "He who talks with a woman [in public] brings evil upon himself" (*Aboth* 1.5). Another rabbinic teaching prominent in Jesus' day taught, "One is not so much as to greet a woman" (*Berakhoth* 43b).

The Samaritan woman account says that the disciples, as faithful Jews, "were surprised to find him talking with a woman" (John 4:27). They were not amazed because he talked with a Samaritan, but because he spoke to a woman in public.

THE MARY-MARTHA INCIDENT

Luke's Gospel reports that a woman named Martha invited Jesus into her home (Luke 10:38–42). Martha assumed the traditional female role of preparing a meal for Jesus, her guest, while her sister Mary did what only men would do, namely, learn from Jesus' teachings. Mary was the cultural deviant, but so was Jesus, because he violated the rabbinic law of his day. Moreover, when Martha chided Mary for not helping her, Jesus did not side with Martha but rather commended Mary for her behavior.

By teaching Mary theological verities, Jesus again violated the rabbinic oral law. Recall the words of *Sotah* 3.4 quoted above: "Let the words of the

Law [Torah] be burned rather than taught to women. . . . If a man teaches his daughter the Law, it is as though he taught her lechery."

Jesus Taught Martha

On another occasion Jesus told Martha, "I am the resurrection and the life. He who believes in me will live, even though he dies; and whoever lives and believes in me will never die. Do you believe this?" (John 11:25–26). These words, which contain the heart of the Christian gospel, are only recorded once in the four Gospels. And to whom were they spoken? To a woman! To teach a woman was bad enough, but Jesus did more than that. He called for a verbal response from Martha. Once more, he went against the socioreligious custom by teaching a woman and by having her publicly respond to him, a man.

Jesus Appeared to Women After His Resurrection

That Jesus consistently accorded women equal rights, sometimes even exclusively selecting women to spread his message, is especially evident in his appearance to the several women who came to his open tomb on Easter Sunday morning. He chose these women to tell his disciples that he had indeed risen from the dead. Said he, "Do not be afraid. Go and tell my brothers to go to Galilee; there they will see me" (Matthew 28:10).

Why did Jesus not tell Peter and John, who also had come to the tomb, to tell the other disciples what had happened? Why did he want the women to tell the men? He often came to the defense and assistance of the deprived and neglected. Women were indeed socially and religiously neglected. His action here brings to mind the words that he spoke on another occasion: "There are those who are last who will be first, and first who will be last" (Luke 13:30).

Women Followed Jesus

All three of the Synoptic Gospels note that women followed Jesus, a highly unusual phenomenon in first-century Palestine. Mark, for instance, states that "many other women who had come up with him to Jerusalem were also there" (Mark 15:41). Luke mentions by name some women who went with him (Luke 8:1–3). This behavior may not seem unusual today, but in Jesus' day it was highly unusual. Scholars note that in the prevailing culture only prostitutes and women of very low repute would follow a man without a male escort.[25] So comforting was Christ's message that honorable women defied conventional social norms in order to follow him, and he uttered no words of reproof. On another occasion, a woman with an issue of blood came up from behind him to touch the hem of his garment so that she would be healed of her physical infirmity (Mark 5:25–34). Jesus' response? He healed her and told her to go in peace.

Lest modern readers conclude that Jesus started a woman's movement, it needs to be said that he did not. Christ came to change the hearts and minds of people rather than to implement social or political movements. Yet his giving women respect and status equal to men meant that he not only broke with the antifemale culture of his era, but he set a standard for his followers to emulate.

THE APOSTOLIC CHURCH WELCOMED WOMEN

The culturally defying acceptance that Jesus accorded women was not lost on the early apostolic church. Following Christ's precedent, the early Christians ignored the confining, restrictive cultural norms to which women were subjected in their society. Soon after Christ's physical resurrection, his followers regularly assembled on the first day of the week (Sunday) to renew their joy of this unique miracle. They commonly assembled in synagogues or in their private homes, known as house churches. In the latter, women were often very prominent, not just as worshipers but also as leaders. St. Paul notes that Apphia, "our sister," was a leader in a house church in the city of Colossae (Philemon 2). In Laodicea, there was Nympha, who had a "church in her house" (Colossians 4:15). In Ephesus, Priscilla, with her husband Aquila, had a church that met "at their house" (1 Corinthians 16:19). And Paul states that Priscilla was one of his "fellow workers" (Romans 16:3) in advancing the Great Commission of Christ that told his followers to go into all the world to make disciples of all nations (Matthew 28:19).

Another key female leader in the apostolic church was Phoebe. In Romans 16:1–2 Paul refers to her by the male title of *diakonos* (deacon), a position she held in the church at Cenchreae. Paul did not use any feminine form of the word, but the word is rendered "deaconess" in many translations. That word did not come into existence until the latter part of fourth century. In addition to calling her a deacon, Paul referred to her as a *prostatis,* or "leading officer." In ancient Greek literature the word *prostatis* meant "preside in the sense of to lead, conduct, direct, govern," according to Bo Reicke.[26] Another scholar observes that Phoebe had a "position of

THIS MOSAIC SHOWS HELENA (254–ca. 330), the mother of Constantine the Great, who was reportedly a Christian before her son issued the Edict of Milan and who with his assistance built many Christian churches throughout the Roman Empire.

authority in the churches."[27] She was so highly regarded as a leader that scholars believe Paul even chose her to deliver the Epistle to the Romans for him from Corinth to Rome, a distance of 400 miles. This was no mean accomplishment in those days. Even Origen (A.D. 185–254), who was hardly pro-woman, saw Phoebe as having apostolic authority (*Commentarium in Epistolam B. Pauli ad Romanos* 10.1278).

According to Acts 16, Paul and Silas met Lydia, a Jewish woman in Philippi who sold and traded purple goods, articles highly sought after by individuals in the upper socioeconomic ranks. Soon after she met Paul and Silas, she became a convert to Christianity and had her entire household (family and servants) baptized. The Greco-Roman and Judeo cultural mores did not support the notion of a woman engaged in business activities. However, Lydia's cultural deviancy did not deter Paul from befriending her in order to promote the Christian gospel. He ignored the ancient prejudices and discriminations that barred women from leadership roles.

In his letter to the Christians in Philippi, Paul says that two women, Euodia and Syntyche, "contended at my side in the cause of the gospel, along with Clement and the rest of my fellow workers" (Philippians 4:2–3). By calling these two women "fellow workers," Paul equates their roles with those of Priscilla and Aquila noted above. Robin Scroggs says that "Paul esteemed women as his peers. They helped gather and lead the church; they prayed and prophesied in public assemblies."[28] Paul followed Christ, rather than the pagan culture, by honoring women as co-workers. That is apparently why he told the Galatian Christians, "There is neither Jew nor Greek, slave nor free, male nor female, for you are all one in Christ Jesus" (Galatians 3:28).

Jesus, Paul, and the early church broke the ancient bonds that kept women secluded and silent (as in the Athenian society), subservient (as under the Roman law of *patria potestas* and *manus*), and silent and segregated in public worship (as in the Jewish culture). The freedom and dignity that the early Christians gave to women is also evident by their having access equal with men to baptism and the Lord's Supper.

CHRISTIANITY'S APPEAL TO WOMEN

As already noted, neither Christ nor his apostles promoted or organized a woman's movement. Yet Christ's message of repentance and salvation proclaimed by the apostles had revolutionary effects on the lives of women. The early Christians not only included women in the life of the church, but they also gave them freedom and dignity unknown in the Greco-Roman and Judaic cultures.

The acceptance that women had in Christian circles was not an end in itself. It moved them to become ardent evangelists and missionaries, as we saw earlier with Phoebe and Priscilla. The work and zeal of faithful Christian women was a powerful force in the early church's spiritual and numerical growth and geographic expansion. As every church historian knows, women commonly were more active in the early church than were men. Helena, the mother of Constantine the Great (noted in chapter 2), built many churches throughout the empire, one of them being the Church of the Nativity in Bethlehem. St. Chrysostom (late fourth century) corroborates this by saying, "The women of those days [early apostolic church] were more spirited than men." The historian W. E. H. Lecky credits women "in the great conversion of the Roman empire," and adds, "In the ages of persecution female figures occupy many of the foremost places and ranks of martyrdom."[29] Leopold Zscharnack says, "Christendom dare not forget that it was primarily the female sex that for the greater part brought about its rapid growth. It was the evangelistic zeal of women in the early years of the church, and later, which won the weak and the mighty."[30]

While Zscharnack's observation is correct with regard to evangelism, it must also be noted that Christianity's growth was also, to no small degree, the result of Christian women not practicing abortion or infanticide, both of which were extremely common among the Greco-Romans. Unlike the pagans, the Christians valued baby girls as much as boys. This added to the church's membership. Moreover, when Christian women married pagan husbands, "the overwhelming majority of children from these 'mixed marriages' were raised within the church."[31]

Not only were women a major force in the growth of Christianity, but they also outnumbered the men in the early church. Does this mean that there were not enough Christian men available for Christian women to marry? Apparently so, because women in the early church soon outnumbered men to such a degree that there simply were not enough Christian men available for marriage. Rodney Stark estimates that the early Christian community "may well have been 60 percent female."[32] By the fourth century some Christian women even married pagan priests.[33] The unbalanced sex ratio in the early church is also evident from what Celsus, the second-century pagan critic of Christianity, said concerning Christians. He ridiculed them by saying Christianity was a religion that attracted women.[34] To him and to many other Romans, this was a sign of weakness and low repute.

The high proportion of women in the early church (low sex ratio, as demographers call it) in many respects is also true of the church today. A 1998 Gallup survey reported that the percentage of "unchurched" Americans is considerably higher for men than for women. This survey found that 39 percent of women were unchurched, but 50 percent of men were.[35] Sociological research has known this phenomenon to be true for many years.

Given the Roman culture's negative posture toward women, Christianity, in providing women freedom and dignity, was seen as a threat to domestic tranquility. The conversion of women to Christianity affected the society's family life. As soon as the Roman wife married, the culture expected her to honor the ancestral gods of her husband's family. The first-century Roman writer Plutarch said, "It is becoming for a wife to worship and to know only the gods that her husband believes in, and to shut the door tightly upon all queer rituals and outlandish superstitions" (*Coniugalia Praecepta* 140 D). It was also her duty to keep the family hearth (sacred fire) from dying out.[36] Thus, when a married woman converted to Christianity, she no longer revered her husband's gods, and the flames of the sacred fire in her husband's home became extinct. Roman men saw this as a threat to the stability of their society, since they believed the family was the microcosm of the nation.[37] A wife's conversion to Christianity therefore provoked the husband's wrath against her and her new religion. The Latin church father Tertullian, in the early third century, describes the anger of some such Roman husbands whose wives became Christians: they "preferred to be the husbands of she-wolves than of Christian women: they could commit themselves to a perverse abuse of nature, but they could not permit their wives to be reformed for the better!" (*Ad Nationes* 1.4).

Yet, in spite of the anger and rejection that many women received from their husbands and from society at large, the gospel of Christ kept drawing them. They fulfilled Christ's words: "If you hold to my teaching, you are really my disciples. Then you will know the truth, and the truth will set you free" (John 8:31–32).

SOME ANOMALIES

With the end of the apostolic church era (after about A.D. 150), some of the church's leaders, many of whom had either come from a pagan background or had been deeply steeped in the pagan literature of the time, unfortunately reverted to some former practices of the Greco-Romans. They often contradicted the spirit and actions of Christ, his disciples, and the pristine church with regard to women in the church. As the well-known German sociologist Max Weber observed in his analysis of early Christianity, women were slowly excluded from leadership roles as the church routinized its activities.[38] He might have added that it was also the influence of the antifeminine values and beliefs of the Greco-Roman and Judeo cultures that resulted in women being excluded in some aspects of the life and structure of the church. The ancient prejudices against women that Jesus and his early followers rejected began to enter the church in the latter part of the second century.[39] By the third, fourth, and fifth centuries the antifeminine views of the ancient Greeks, Romans, and Judaizers (Christians who believed they had to follow Jewish laws and customs) were even more widely incorporated into the church's theology and practice by prominent church fathers. Many of them had studied and unwittingly absorbed some of the teachings of the Greco-Roman poets and philosophers as well as the rabbinic oral law, which espoused numerous negative teachings regarding women. Some of them were influenced by the antiwomen prejudices of the Greco-Roman literature, and some by the Judaic oral law taught by the rabbis.

Clement of Alexandria (d. 215) believed and taught that every woman should blush because she is a woman (*Instructor* 3.11). Tertullian (d. ca. 220) said, "You [Eve] are the devil's gateway. . . . You destroyed so easily God's image, man. On account of your desert, that is death, even the Son of God had to die" (*On the Apparel of Women* 1.1). Cyril of Jerusalem (d. 368), a bishop, argued that women were to pray in church by only moving their lips. He wrote, "Let her pray, and her lips move, but let not her voice be heard" (*Procatechesis* 14). Jerome, the monk (d. 420), who studied under some rabbis, was even opposed to women singing in the company of men in congregations (*Against the Pelagians* 1.25). Augustine (d. 430) expressed belief that a woman's image of God was inferior to that of the man's. He asserted that apart from her husband, a woman did not possess the image of God (*On the Trinity* 12.10). Somewhat similarly, Thomas Aquinas (thirteenth century) thought the image of God was different in woman than in man (*Summa Theologiae* 1a, 93.5).

Many similar statements by some of the church's leaders could be cited. Such unfortunate statements were uttered on occasion for more than a thousand years, extending well beyond the Protestant Reformation era. All too many clergy and theologians had apparently forgotten how differently Jesus and the apostles viewed women. These critics of women often talked and acted more like the pagan Greco-Romans and the rabbis of the oral law period than like Christ or Paul.[40]

CHRIST'S WAY PREVAILS

Although after the apostolic era the Christian women within the organized church were for centuries often viewed and treated contrary to the way Christ and his apostles related to them, they nevertheless still had considerably more freedom than their pagan counterparts had in the Greco-Roman and Judeo cultures before and during the time of Christ. In numerous ways the church has always treated woman as man's equal. For instance, before becoming a member of the church, she received the same catechetical instruction as did a man, she was baptized like a man, she participated equally with men in receiving the Lord's Supper, and she prayed and sang with men in the same worship settings.

A NEW FAMILY STANDARD

The new ethic that Christ introduced in his interaction with women had significant side effects with regard to family life. Cognizant that Christ treated women equal to men, St. Paul commanded the husband to love his wife as Christ loved the church (Ephesians 5:25). He also told the fathers, "Do not exasperate your children; instead, bring them up in the training and instruction of the Lord" (Ephesians 6:4). Such directives were in direct conflict with the Roman institution of *patria potestas* discussed above.

Did Christian men, as husbands and fathers, heed Paul's command? There is no evidence to suggest they ignored Paul's words. In fact, it seems that they followed Paul's admonition so well that this new family ethic eventually undermined *patria potestas* and its unjust patriarchal by-products.

Thus, a half-century after the legalization of Christianity in A.D. 313, the teachings and examples of Christ with regard to women that St. Paul so clearly mandated for married men moved Emperor Valentinian I in the year 374 to repeal the one-thousand-year-old *patria potestas*.[41] A sea change indeed! The pagan husband had lost the power of life and death over his family, including his wife.

With the abrogation of *patria potestas*, the accompanying cultural mores of *manus* and *coemptio* became defunct too. As noted earlier, *manus* placed the married woman under her husband's absolute rule, and *coemptio* gave the Roman father the right to sell his daughter to her husband. With the outlawing of *patria potestas*, the validity of marriage without the consent of the father began to be recognized.[42] Soon this practice was widely accepted with support of the church's theologians. But apparently because *patria potestas* had been entrenched for centuries, the practice of getting married without the father's consent required periodic reinforcement.

Not only did the mores of *manus* and *coemptio* become extinct, but "women were [also] granted substantially the same rights as men in control of their property; and they were no longer compelled to be subject to tutors."[43] They also received the right of guardianship over their children, who previously were the sole possession of men.[44]

BRIDAL FREEDOM

Men in ancient societies, whether in Babylon, Assyria, Greece, or Rome, commonly married child brides, often as young as eleven or twelve years of age and hence before menarche. The men were considerably older, often in their early twenties or older. In his *Parallel Lives of Illustrious Greeks and Romans*, Plutarch says the Roman fathers gave their daughters into marriage at age twelve or younger. Justinian's *Institutes* corroborate Plutarch's observation. The ancient practice of marrying prepubertal brides, however, became less and less common with the influence of Christianity.

Research shows that Christian women married later than their pagan Roman counterparts.[45] They not only used their freedom to marry later, but they also, by not conforming to the Roman institution of *patria potestas*, had a choice as to whom they married. Under *patria potestas* the Roman woman had no such choice. Her father made that decision, not she. Although the Roman woman had a little more freedom than her Greek counterpart, the words of Medea in one of Euripides' tragedies describe not only the Greek but also the Roman woman: "We [women] may not even reject a suitor" (*Medea* 237).

The Christian woman's freedom to marry at a more mature age some-one whom she wanted to marry was complemented by the apparent change that had occurred in many Christian men. The husband, on the basis of Paul's teaching as noted above, saw his wife as a partner, spiritually and otherwise. Given this model of marriage, it is reasonable to conclude that Christian men were far less likely to compel young women, or older ones, to marry someone against their will. This marital deference to women was another affront to the pagan Roman culture, and it did not make Christians popular.

The greater marital freedom that Christianity gave to women in time gained wide appeal. Thus, today a woman in the Western world is no longer compelled to marry someone she does not want; nor can she legally be married as a child bride. Lest we forget, in some countries where Christianity has little or no presence, child brides are still compelled to marry older, unwanted men. Reuters News Agency reported in January 1999 that the Maasai tribe in Kenya, an African country, still has the father give his twelve- or thirteen-year-old daughter in marriage to a man who is often old enough to be her grandfather.[46] Although it is theoretically illegal, in Bangladesh, where daughters are seen as a financial burden, young girls in their early teens are frequently given to much older men in marriage. The law that formally bans child marriages is regularly circumvented by parents falsifying their daughter's age.[47] China currently also has a large market for child brides. "Some girls as young as 12 are recruited by traveling agents who promise impoverished parents that they will find their daughters a factory job in the big city. Too often there is no factory job and the girls are instead forced to marry a peasant farmer in circumstances where escape is virtually impossible."[48] And in Mauritania, Africa, it is common in isolated villages to find brides as young as ten or eleven years of age.[49]

REMOVAL OF THE VEIL

When Christianity came on the scene, the veiling of women was wide-spread in many cultures. Alfred Jeremias, in his noteworthy study *Der Schleier von Sumer Bis Heute* (*The Veil from Sumer to Today*, 1931), has shown that women at the time of Christ were veiled by the Sumerians, Assyrians, Babylonians, Egyptians, Greeks, Hebrews, Chinese, and Romans. In some instances a man divorced his wife if she left his house unveiled. The Roman divorce of Sulpicius Gallus is one such case.[50] After marriage the Greek woman always wore a veil, a practice similar to the wife wearing a wedding ring in Western society today, says Q. M. Adams.[51] Among the Hebrews, the oral law of the rabbis in Jesus' day taught that "it is a godless man who sees his wife go out with her head uncovered. He is duty bound to divorce her" (*Kethuboth* 2). Only single women, prostitutes, and women in the lower classes were not required to be veiled in ancient societies.

As already noted, the freedom that Christ and the apostles made available to women, ironically, was not always fully accepted and adopted by some church leaders. Just as some of the church's leaders (mostly church fathers, cited above) tried to keep women silent in public settings, so there were also some who wanted them to remain veiled, in keeping with ancient cultural customs. Clement of Alexandria (A.D. 150–215) argued that when a woman attended church with her face veiled, it would protect her "from being gazed at. And she will never fall. . .nor will she invite another to fall into sin by covering her face" (*Instructor* 8.11). Tertullian, a contemporary of Clement, chided women who came to church unveiled: "Why do you denude [unveil] before God [in church] what you cover before men? Will you be more modest in public than in the church?" (*On Prayer* 22). St. Chrysostom in his *Homilies on I Corinthians* (fourth century) even contended that women were to be veiled on a continual basis. And St. Augustine (early fifth century) linked the veiling of women to their lacking the image of God. Said he, "Have women not this renewal of the mind which is the image of God? Who would say this? But in the sex of their body they do not signify this; therefore they are bidden to be veiled" (*Of the Works of Monks* 32). Unbeknownst to these men, the pagan culture sometimes led them to forget Christ's liberating view of women.

The church fathers were not alone in commanding women to wear a veil. At least two synods (official regional assemblies) of the church did so too. In the mid-fifth century an Irish synod, led by St. Patrick, announced in its fourth canon that the wife of a priest "must be veiled when she goes out of doors."[52] And in 585 the Synod of Auxerre in France demanded in its forty-second canon that women attending the Lord's Supper be veiled.[53] As late as 866 Pope Nikolaus I declared *ex cathedra*, "The women must be veiled in church services."[54]

Pope Nikolaus's declaration appears to be the last formal announcement regarding the veiling of women. Apparently the practice of veiling women in the church disappeared by the end of the first millennium. How consistent and widespread veiling was in the church for the first thousand years is difficult to say. St. Paul did urge the women in the Corinthian church to

"WOMEN AT THE POLLS IN NEW JERSEY" illustrates women exercising their right to vote between 1790 and 1807—reputed to be the earliest instance of voting by women in the English-speaking world, more than a hundred years before the ratification of the Nineteenth Amendment in 1920. *(Originally published in Harper's New Monthly Magazine, November 12, 1880)*

cover their heads (1 Corinthians 11:5–16). But did he mean that women also were to cover their faces? It appears that he did not. Yet many of the church's leaders who commanded women to be veiled apparently did so on the basis of this Pauline reference. They failed to note that Paul, in his first letter to Timothy, in which he tells women to dress in modest apparel and not to braid their hair, makes no mention that they need to be veiled (1 Timothy 2:8–9). In this instance, he does not even tell them to cover their heads.

Evidently it was the lack of any specific reference by the New Testament writers, plus the freedom introduced by Christ, that increasingly prompted women in congregations during the second millennium not to veil themselves. This pattern continued. By the time of the Protestant Reformation in the sixteenth century, the matter of a woman not veiling herself was no longer an issue. Christ's free and open interaction with women, which made no mention of their having to be veiled, could not be held back forever by even some of the church's misguided leaders. In due time Christ's will came to prevail.

POLYGYNY NULLIFIED

Although Greek and Roman men had their mistresses, their culture did not permit them to have polygynous marriages. However, among other ancient societies, especially in the Middle East, such marriages were common. Numerous polygynous marriages, for instance, are found in the Old Testament. Biblical heroes such as Abraham, Jacob, Elkanah, David, Solomon, and others had multiple wives. In referring to the time of Christ and before, Josephus, the Jewish historian and friend of the Romans, said, "It is the ancient practice among us [Jews] to have many wives at the same time" (*Jewish Antiquities* 17.1, 2, 15).

It was this polygynous culture that Jesus entered. But he never lent any support to polygyny. Whenever he spoke about marriage or used a marriage illustration, it was always in the context of monogamy. He said, "The two [not three or four] will become one flesh" (Matthew 19:5). Another time he said that if anyone wished to follow him, he would have to choose him over his brothers, sisters, mother, and his wife (Luke 14:26). He did not say "wives."

Christ's view of marriage as monogamous complemented his high regard for women in that polygyny invariably demeaned women. Additional support for monogamous marriages for Christians came from St. Paul when he enjoined bishops (overseers) of the church to be "the husband of but one wife" (1 Timothy 3:1–2). And it should be noted that whenever marriage or married life is mentioned in the New Testament, monogamy is the only form of marriage assumed. Thus, as Christianity spread and gained ascendancy, monogamy became the marriage norm in all countries where the church became prominent. For example, when Utah applied to become a state within the United States in the 1890s, the Mormons, who dominated the state, were compelled to outlaw all polygynous marriages before the state would be accepted into the Union. The Christian value of what constitutes a marriage had once more permeated the secular law, as it had previously in other Western societies.

As a result of Jesus Christ and his teachings, women in much of the world today, especially in the West, enjoy more privileges and rights than at any other time in history. It takes only a cursory trip to an Arab nation or to a Third World country, to see how little freedom women have in countries where Christianity has had little or no presence. Today radical feminists, many of whom express a strong hatred for Christianity, seem not to recognize that had it not been for Jesus Christ's influence on his followers, women would likely have no more freedom in the West than the Islamic women have today in the Middle East. Freedom indeed has its ironies. It allows its beneficiaries to deny and despise the source of their freedom, in this instance, Jesus Christ's salutary influence in the life of women.

WIDOWS HONORED, NOT BURNED ALIVE

For hundreds of years India's cultural custom of *suttee* (or *sati*), the burning alive of widows, was an integral part of India's Hindu-oriented culture. When a woman's husband died, she, as a good and faithful wife, was expected voluntarily to mount her husband's funeral pyre and be cremated with him. If she refused, she was often put there by force, even by her son(s). If she managed to elude this pagan institution, her life in society was ruined. She was treated as a nonperson—not just because she evaded the pyre, but also because among the Hindus in India a widow's life was culturally and religiously despised. A widow could only eat one meal per day, perform only menial tasks, and wear the dowdiest of clothes; she could no longer sleep in a bed; her head had to be shaved monthly so that she was conspicuous and undesirable to promiscuous men; religious ceremonies and weddings were off limits to her; she could not be seen by a pregnant woman because her glance might bring a curse.[55] Not infrequently, as a result of India's child-bride custom, a widow was burned while she was still a child between the ages of five and fifteen.[56] In some instances when widows were not burned alive, they were buried alive with their husbands.[57]

Nor was pagan India alone in burning widows. History shows that widows were once also burned in pre-Christian Scandinavia, among the Chinese, the Finns, and the Maori in New Zealand, and by some American Indians before Columbus arrived.[58]

How refreshingly different and humane is the Christian view of widows in the New Testament! Jesus had compassion on the widow of Nain, whose son he raised from the dead (Luke 7:11–15). Another time he chided the Pharisees for taking financial advantage of widows (Mark 12:40), and he commended the widow who, although poor, gave two mites in her offering (Luke 21:2–3). Writing to Timothy, St. Paul urged him to have the Ephesian Christians, especially the children and grandchildren, honor their widowed mothers (1 Timothy 5:3–4). Similarly, the Epistle of James reminded the Christians, "Religion that God our Father accepts as pure and faultless is this: to look after...widows in their distress" (James 1:27).

After the New Testament era, the concern for widows in the church continued. In the early second century, Ignatius, bishop of Antioch, wrote to Polycarp, "Let not the widows be neglected. Be thou, after the Lord, their protector and friend."[59] Later, in the fourth century, Constantine the Great gave special recognition to widows by giving them the honorary Roman rank of *tagma*, and still later they were often chosen as deaconesses by the church, especially in the East.

Given Christianity's respect for women and concern for widows, the British authorities in 1829, under the suasion of Governor-General William Bentinck, outlawed the practice of *suttee*. When the ban went into effect, many "cried that the foundations of Hindu society would be shaken if widows were not burnt alive."[60] Others argued that the ban violated Article 25 of India's constitution that gave the people freedom of religion.[61] But the British were not deterred, for in 1856 Indian widows were granted another humane right, the right to remarry.[62]

The legal ban on *suttee* is still in effect today, although numerous violations of the ban occurred, especially in the mid-1800s. One report notes that during the 1990s there were additional attempts to revive the custom; for instance, in Rajasthan, India, there have been acts of "open revival and glorification of *sati* widow burning."[63] Some widows were also burned in the 1980s, one of which was reported in *Time* magazine in 1987. An eighteen-year-old widow in the Indian village of Deorala voluntarily mounted the pyre; then, holding her husband's head in her lap, she asked for the pyre to be ignited.[64] A throng of cheering women supported her act of immolation. After she was cremated, thousands of women came to receive "blessings" from this dead widow, who in their eyes was a goddess. Evidently the supporting women still believed the Hindu saying: "If her husband is happy, she should be happy; if he is sad, she should be sad; and if he is dead, she should also die."[65] The *Time* article noted that the construction of a shrine was being planned, for which $160,000 had already been donated by devotees, to honor the cremated widow.[66]

In light of the current, almost worldwide promotion of multiculturalism, which argues that all cultures and religious beliefs are essentially equal, the desire and efforts to bring back India's pagan custom of *suttee* may gain momentum in the future. If that were to happen, one of the relatively few but vitally important freedoms that Indian women have gained during the past one and a half centuries, much to the credit of Christianity's influence,[67] would be greatly threatened and perhaps even lost.

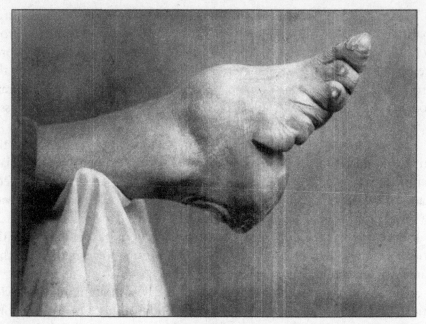

THIS CHINESE WOMAN'S BOUND FOOT shows the cruelty inflicted on countless little girls during a thousand years before Christian influence led to its banning. Note the break in the foot and the curled-under toes. *(Peabody and Essex Museum, Salem, MA)*

CHINESE FOOT BINDING ABOLISHED

To the east of India lies China, where small girls, usually at about five years of age, had their feet bound, a practice that existed for at least a thousand years. A long cotton bandage several inches wide was tightly wrapped around both feet, forcing the four smaller toes of each foot under and up against the fleshly part of the foot. In time the toes stopped growing and became stunted. In the process the heel was forced down, pushing the instep outward, all of which made the foot like a clenched fist. The big toe, says Harrison Forman, was left free, but it was forced into the front part of a small shoe.[68] Foot binding frequently caused severe infection. As one missionary described it, "The flesh often became putrescent during the binding and portions sloughed off from the sole; sometimes one or more toes dropped off."[69] Frequently gangrene set in, leading to leg amputation or even death.

Why did this cruel custom exist? There is only one answer: to please men. It made a woman, with her feet bound in an arch, walk tiptoe and sway seductively. Moreover, a woman whose feet were not small by not having been bound was "disgraced and it was impossible to get a desirable husband for her," according the Yale University historian Kenneth Scott Latourette, who once served as a missionary in China.[70] Cruel customs are often highly valued in some societies even by those who have to endure the cruelty. So it was with foot binding. When some Christian missionaries in the nineteenth century tried to have girls unbind their feet, their Chinese mothers would rebind them as soon as the missionaries were out of sight. The social pressures to conform to this cruel cultural custom were immense, all at the expense of young, helpless girls.[71]

In spite of the longstanding practice of foot binding, it was Christianity's influence that eventually led the Chinese government to outlaw this dehumanizing practice in 1912. Lin Yutang has shown that Christian missionaries led the crusade to abolish foot binding.[72] And as Christians worked on abolishing this cruel custom, the Chinese government often condemned Christian missionary women who interfered with foot binding.[73] Even after it became illegal in 1912, the practice lingered for at least another decade as many girls still had their feet bound in the 1920s.[74]

Today the feet of Chinese women are no longer bound and mutilated. Although the world, including the Chinese, may not know it, had it not been for the presence of Christianity, Chinese girls today might still have their feet bound and deformed. As in many other instances, the freedom and dignity that women enjoy in much of today's world is largely the result of the valiant efforts of Christians who, little by little, made life in a fallen world more humane.

CLITORIDECTOMY BANNED

In recent years, much as been written about the practice of female clitoridectomy in many African countries. To some degree, it is also practiced in Europe and even in America by many recent African immigrants. Countries such as Canada, France, Sweden, England, and some American states have recently outlawed the practice.

Clitoridectomy (often but erroneously called female circumcision) is an age-old cultural practice. One recent source indicates that it is performed in twenty-six African countries. Depending on the country and region, 5 to 99 percent of the girls are subjected to this barbaric ritual.[75] Minimally, clitoridectomy involves the removal of a young girl's clitoris. Frequently, however, the procedure also includes removing the inner and outer labia,

THE ROLE AND STATUS OF WOMEN

Non-Christian Practices (Past or Present)	Christian Practices (Past or Present)
Gynaeceum: segregated quarters for the wife in her husband's home in ancient Athens	No segregated quarters for wife in her home; she shared with her husband at all times
Athenian wife was confined to her quarters when men guests were present	Women (Mary and Martha) hosted Jesus in their home
Hetaera: man's legal mistress in ancient Greece	No mistresses for men allowed
Veil: worn publicly by married women in Greco-Roman times and most other ancient societies	Veiling of women discontinued after ninth century
Patria potestas: father's absolute power over family members	Father possessed no absolute family power
Manus: Roman husband's absolute power over his wife	Husbands and wives: "Submit to one another out of reverence for Christ" (Ephesians 5:21)
Infamia: label for a disobedient Roman woman	No cultural label for a disobedient woman
Coemptio: Roman father sells daughter to her husband	Father not permitted to sell his daughter to her husband
Adultery: based on woman's marital status; a double standard of sexual behavior	Based on marital status of a man or woman; a single standard of sexual behavior
Female babies valued less than male babies	Female and male babies valued equally.
Infanticide: once widely practiced in pagan countries; victims are commonly female infants	Condemned and outlawed in countries with Christian influence.

Polygyny: man may legally have multiple wives	Monogamy: the only acceptable marriage
Michetza: ancient synagogue partition for women	No church partitions for women
Child brides: prepuberty girls given in marriage; still practiced in China, India, and some African countries	Child bride marriages not permitted in countries with Christian influence
Suttee (sati): Hindus burning husband's widow in India; practiced for many centuries	Banned in India by the British under Christian influence in 1829
Foot binding of young girls: once common in China for centuries	Condemned by Christian missionaries; Christian influence led to China's outlawing female foot binding in 1912
Clitoridectomy: female genital mutilation, still common in Muslim countries in Africa and Middle East	Unequivocally condemned and outlawed in countries with Christian influence

and sometimes "almost all of the girl's genitalia are cut away and the remaining flesh from the outer labia is sewn together, or infibulated, and the girl's legs are bound from ankle to waist for several weeks while scar tissue closes up the vagina almost completely."[76] One physician says that even in its mildest form the operation "is anatomically equivalent to amputation of the penis."[77]

The act commonly forces a young girl to submit by tying her down. One author notes that American viewers cringe when shown this operation on a video. Often it is done by one of the parents using a razor blade.[78] Sometimes, especially in America, immigrant mothers want their daughters to have the operation because they believe it will make them less desirous of having sex in their teenage years.

Why have Western countries, as they have recently received immigrants from Africa, where clitoridectomy is widespread, outlawed this cruel practice? And why is it still widely practiced in twenty-six African countries? The answer is relatively simple: Western countries, in spite of growing secularism, still retain sufficient Christian values that make civilized people recoil at this gruesome custom. On the other hand, in many African countries, where Christianity is a minority religion with little or no influence, clitoridectomy is an acceptable and institutionalized part of the cultural fabric.

CONCLUSION

"The birth of Jesus," said one observer, "was the turning point in the history of woman."[79] Another has noted, "Whatever else our Lord did, He immeasurably exalted womanhood."[80] Yet neither Christ nor the early Christians ever preached an outright revolution.[81] Rather, it was his example that his followers reflected in their relationships with women, raising their dignity, freedom, and rights to a level previously unknown in any culture. One only needs to remember how badly women were once treated by the Greeks, Romans, Hindus, and Chinese and by many other societies where paganism prevailed. Before Christianity arrived, century upon century had brought little or no freedom or dignity to women in any pagan culture. In short, where else do women have more freedom, opportunity, and human worth than in countries that have been highly influenced by the Christian ethic?

NOTES

1. Farzaneh Milani, "Lipstick Politics in Iran," *New York Times,* 19 August 1999, A21.

2. J. P. V. D. Balsdon, *Roman Women: Their History and Habits* (New York: John Day, 1963), 283.

3. L. F. Cervantes, "Woman," *New Catholic Encyclopedia* (New York: McGraw-Hill, 1967), 14:991.

4. Charles Albert Savage, *The Athenian Family: A Sociological and Legal Study* (Baltimore: n.p., 1907), 29.

5. C. M. Bowra, *Classical Greece* (Chicago: Ime, Inc., 1965), 85.

6. Verena Zinserling, *Women in Greece and Rome* (New York: Abner Schram, 1972), 39.

7. F. A. Wright, *Feminism in Greek Literature: From Homer to Aristotle* (Port Washington, N.Y.: Kennikat Press, [1923], 1969), 1.

8. H .D. F. Kitto, *The Greeks* (Chicago: Aldine Publishing, 1964), 231.

9. A. Deissmann, *Light from the Ancient East* (New York: George H. Doran, 1927), 168.

10. Philip Slater, *The Glory of Hera: Greek Mythology and Greek Family* (Boston: Beacon Press, 1968), 29.

11. John Boswell, *The Kindness of Strangers: The Abandonment of Children in Western Europe from Late Antiquity to the Renaissance* (New York: Pantheon Books, 1988), 4.

12. Balsdon, *Roman Women,* 272.

13. Ibid., 276.

14. Jane Gardner, *Women in Roman Law and Society* (Bloomington: Indiana University Press, 1986), 7. See also J. A. C. Thomas, *The Institutes of Justinian* (Oxford: North-Holland Publishing, 1975), 335.

15. Rudolph Sohm, *The Institutes of Roman Law,* trans. James Crawford Ledlie (Oxford: Clarendon Press, 1892), 389.

16. Ibid., 365.

17. W. A. Becker, *Gallus* (London: Longmans, Green, 1920), 156.

18. O. A. W. Dilke, *The Ancient Romans: How They Lived and Worked* (New York: Dufour Editions, 1975), 49.

19. Ibid.

20. William Smith, *A Dictionary of Greek and Roman Antiquities* (New York: n.p., 1871), 635.
21. Balsdon, *Roman Women*, 278.
22. Philip Schaff, *The Person of Christ: The Miracle of History* (Boston: American Tract Society, 1865), 210.
23. Raphael Patai, *The Jewish Mind* (New York: Charles Scribner's Sons, 1977), 365.
24. Ibid., 366.
25. Balsdon, *Roman Women*, 278.
26. Bo Reicke, "Proistemi," in *Theological Dictionary of the New Testament*, ed. and trans. Geoffrey Bromiley (Grand Rapids: Wm. B. Eerdmans, 1968), 700.
27. E. A. Judge, "Early Christians as a Scholastic Community," *Journal of Religious History* 1 (1960–61): 128.
28. Robin Scroggs, "Paul: Chauvinist or Liberationist?" *Christian Century*, 15 March 1972, 308.
29. W. E. H. Lecky, *History of European Morals from Augustine to Charlemagne* (New York: D. Appleton, 1870), 385.
30. Leopold Zscharnack, *Der Dienst der Frau in den ersten Jahrhunderten der christliche Kirche* (Gottingen: n.p., 1902), 19.
31. Rodney Stark, *The Rise of Christianity: A Sociologist Reconsiders History* (Princeton: Princeton University Press, 1996), 127.
32. Ibid., 126.
33. Shirley Jackson Case, *The Social Triumph of the Ancient Church* (New York: Harper and Brothers, 1933), 124.
34. Origen, *Origen Against Celsus*, in *The Ante-Nicene Fathers*, ed. Alexander Roberts and James Donaldson (Grand Rapids: Wm. B. Eerdmans, 1982), 4:484, 486.
35. Gallup Survey, "Percentage of 'Unchurched' Americans Has Changed Little in Last 20 Years," *Emerging Trends* (October 1998): 1.
36. Fustel de Coulanges, *The Ancient City* (Boston: Lee and Shephard, 1882), 128.
37. Hugh J. Schonfield, *Those Incredible Christians* (New York: Bantam Books, 1969), 6.
38. Max Weber, *Sociology of Religion* (Boston: Beacon Press, 1957), 104.
39. A. C. Headlam, "Prisca or Priscilla," *Dictionary of the Bible* (New York: Charles Scribner's Sons, 1911), 102–3.
40. Thomas Boslooper, *The Image of Women* (New York: Rose Sharon Press, 1980), 147.
41. William C. Morey, *Outlines of Roman Law* (New York: G. P. Putnam's Sons, 1894), 150.
42. Jean-Louis Flandrin, *Families in Former Times*, trans. Richard Southern (Cambridge: Cambridge University Press, 1979), 131.
43. Morey, *Outlines of Roman Law*, 151.
44. Ibid.
45. Keith Hopkins, "The Age of Roman Girls at Marriage," *Population Studies* (1965): 315, 320.
46. "Kenya School Saves Girls from Early Marriage," Reuters (Kajiado, Kenya), 27 January 1999 (obtained from Lexis-Nexis Internet Service).
47. Tabibul Islam, "Bangladesh-Health: Despite Laws, Many Brides Are Mere Girls," *Inter Press Service English News Wire* (Dhaka, Bangladesh), 8 October 1996 (obtained from Lexis-Nexis Internet Service).
48. Damien McElroy, "Focus Brides for Sale," *Sunday Telegraph* (Beijing), 22 November 1998 (obtained from Lexis-Nexis Internet Service).
49. Nicholas Phythian, "Moslem Mauritania to Stop Child Brides," Reuters (Nouakchott, Mauritania), 28 October 1996 (obtained from Lexis-Nexis Internet Service).
50. James Donaldson, *Woman: Her Position and Influence in Ancient Greece and Rome and Among Early Christians* (New York: Longmans, Green, 1907), 88.
51. Q. M. Adams, *Neither Male Nor Female* (Devon, England: Arthur Stockwell, 1973), 192.
52. Carl Joseph Hefele, *A History of the Councils of the Church* (Edinburgh: T and T Clark, 1895), 4:9.
53. Carl Joseph Hefele, *Conciliengeschichte* (Freiburg: Herder'sche Verlag, 1877), 3:46.
54. Ibid., 4:349.
55. Katherine Mayo, *Mother India* (New York: Blue Ribbon Books, 1927), 73.
56. Monica Felton, *A Child Widow's Story* (New York: Harcourt, Brace and World, 1966), 69.
57. H. G. Rawlinson, *India: A Short Cultural History* (New York: Frederick A. Praeger, 1952), 279.
58. Dorothy K. Stein, "Women to Burn: Suttee as a Normative Institution," *Signs: Journal of Women Culture and Society* (Winter 1978), 253.

59. Ignatius, "The Epistle of Ignatius to Polycarp," in *The Ante-Nicene Fathers*, 1:94.
60. Rawlinson, *India: A Short Cultural History*, 279.
61. Sakuntala Narasimhan, *Sati: Widow Burning in India* (New York: Anchor Books, 1990), 4.
62. Stanley Wolpert, *A New History of India* (New York: Oxford University Press, 2000), 233.
63. Ibid.
64. "Fire and Faith," *Time* (September 28, 1987), 41.
65. Narasimhan, *Sati*, 27.
66. "Fire and Faith," 41.
67. Vincent A. Smith, *The Oxford Dictionary of India* (Oxford: Clarendon Press, 1967), 725.
68. Harrison Forman, *Changing China* (New York: Crown Publishers, 1948), 199.
69. Howard S. Levy, *Chinese Foot Binding: The History of a Curious Erotic Custom* (New York: W. Rauls, 1966), 26.
70. Kenneth Scott Latourette, *The Chinese: Their History and Culture* (New York: Macmillan, 1964), 576.
71. M. E. Burton, *Notable Women of Modern China* (New York: Fleming H. Revell, 1912), 20, 163.
72. Lin Yutang, *My Country and My People* (New York: Halcyon House, 1935), 168.
73. M. G. Guiness, *The Story of China* (London: n.p., 1894), 298.
74. C. P. Fitzgerald, *History of China* (New York: American Heritage Publishing, 1969), 152.
75. Nabid Toubia, "Female Circumcision as a Public Health Issue," *New England Journal of Medicine* 15 (15 September 1994): 712.
76. Linda Burstyn, "Female Circumcision Comes to America," *Atlantic Monthly* (October 1995): 32.
77. Toubia, "Female Circumcision as a Public Health Issue," 712.
78. Burstyn, "Female Circumcision Comes to America," 33.
79. Cervantes, "Woman," 14:993.
80. George H. Morrison, *Christ in Shakespeare* (London: James Clarke, 1928), 58.
81. Robin Fox, *Pagans and Christians* (San Francisco: Perennial Library, 1988), 21.

CHARITY and COMPASSION:
their CHRISTIAN CONNECTION

"Where charity is not, justice cannot be."

St. Augustine

For I was hungry and you gave me something to eat, I was thirsty and you gave me something to drink, I was a stranger and you invited me in, I needed clothes and you clothed me, I was sick and you looked after me, I was in prison and you came to visit me" (Matthew 25:35–36). These words of Christ, along with the parable of the Good Samaritan (Luke 10:30–37), the almsgiving practiced in many Hebrew synagogues, and the Old Testament precedent allowing the poor to glean fields, all made a profound impression on the minds of the early Christians, and they diligently sought to emulate these practices.

Tertullian (d. ca. 220), the Latin church father in northern Africa, informs us that the early Christians had a common fund to which they gave voluntarily, without any compulsion, on a given day of the month or whenever they wished to contribute (*Apology* 39). This fund supported widows, the physically disabled, needy orphans, the sick, prisoners incarcerated for their Christian faith, and teachers requiring help; it provided burials for poor people and sometimes funds for the release of slaves.[1] Historian W. E. H. Lecky says that every Christian was expected to give one-tenth of his income to charity.[2] How many gave 10 percent is not known, but it is known that they gave generously.

CHRISTIAN CHARITY VERSUS GRECO-ROMAN GIVING

Christian charity differed profoundly from that of the Greco-Romans. The early Christians practiced *caritas,* as opposed to the *liberalitas* of the Romans. *Caritas* meant giving to relieve the recipient's economic or physical distress without expecting anything in return, whereas *liberalitas* meant giving to please the recipient, who later would bestow a favor on the giver. For centuries the Roman pagans practiced *liberalitas,* not *caritas.*[3] Only in extremely rare instances did some of the Romans give without expecting something in return. It was usually the most honorable, those who really did not need help, who received "all or most of the charity dispensed."[4]

The charity (*caritas*) of Christians also differed with regard to the motive for giving. Rome's pagan religions provided no motive for charity. In the pagan religious practices, people were mere spectators at temple sacrifices, where they passively watched the priests perform. Some attenders gave *stips* (coins) to some god or goddess or for the erection of a statue (*stip collata*). Christians, on the other hand, were active participants in their divine services; they heard and shared with one another God's gracious, redemptive act of love in Jesus Christ that motivated them to help and give to those in need.[5] Their giving reflected the Apostle John's words: "This is love: not that we loved God, but that he loved us and sent his Son as an atoning sacrifice for our sins. Dear friends, since God so loved us, we also ought to love one another"(1 John 4:10–11). They also heeded the Apostle Paul's writings to the Christians in Philippi: "Each of you should look not only to your own interests, but also to the interests of others" (Philippians 2:4).

These New Testament words provided the motive and direction for Christian charity, whether it was collecting money for the poor and starving or nursing the sick and dying. Thus Cyril, the bishop of Jerusalem (fifth century), "sold treasures and ornaments of the church for the relief of a starving people, [and] Ethelwold, bishop of Winchester [tenth century] sold all of the gold and silver vessels of his cathedral to relieve the poor who were starving during a famine."[6] In doing so, he said, "There is no reason the temples of God should abound in riches, while the living temples of the Holy Ghost starve for hunger."[7] Christopher Dawson, speaking of early Christianity, writes: "Every church had its *matriculum,* or list of persons in receipt of relief, and enormous sums were spent in every kind of charitable work."[8]

There was still another difference between the pagans and the Christians with regard to charity. The Christians helped and gave to everyone in need. St. Paul's admonition to the church in Philipi (noted above) made it clear that charity was to be given to all, Christians and pagans alike. A late first-century Christian document, the *Didache,* urged: "Give to everyone who asks thee, and do not refuse." Similarly, *The Shepherd of Hermas,* an early second-century epistle, enjoins all Christians: "Give simply to all without asking doubtfully to whom thou givest, but give to all." Giving to all often meant bringing food to Christians who were imprisoned during the persecutions, an act of charity that often had to be done in defiance of the law. Eusebius, the early church historian, reports that Emperor Licinius (early fourth century) had decreed that persecuted Christians in prison were not to receive help or humane treatment (*Ecclesiastical History* 10.8.11).

Finally, Christian charity was completely voluntary. According to the Roman culture of that era, such behavior defied common sense; it was seen as a sign of weakness and was viewed with suspicion. There was nothing to be gained by expending time and energy, even if voluntary, with people who could not contribute to Roman valor and to the strength of the state. The prevalence of Stoic philosophy also made it disrespectful to associate with the weak, the poor, and the downtrodden. To Christians, however, the individual, regardless of his social or economic status, was valuable because he possessed a soul redeemed by Jesus Christ. Thus, the differences between Christian and Roman charity in regard to motivation and practice were profound.

To extend charity to the poor, the ailing, and the dying was not a pagan practice. There was, of course, the odd exception. Tacitus (A.D. 55–120), the Roman historian, notes one occasion where, in Fidena (near Rome) in A.D. 27, the wealthy opened their homes to help victims of the collapsed amphitheater (*Annals* 4.63). And early in the second century Pliny, in one of his letters to Emperor Trajan, refers to some mutual benefit groups, wondering whether such groups should be allowed to exist (*Epistolae,* or *The Letters of Pliny* 10.92). But for the most part, the few Roman acts of relief and assistance were isolated state activities, "dictated much more by policy than by benevolence."[9] The Roman "habit of selling young children, the innumerable expositions, the readiness of the poor to enroll themselves as gladiators, and the frequent famines, show how large was the measure of unrelieved distress."[10] It is also helpful to recall the observation of La Bleterie, a historian of ancient society, that before Christianity arrived, some pagans did perform some isolated humanitarian acts. However, such behavior was not motivated by pagan cultural values or religion, but rather was an exception to them on the part of some individuals. As he expressed it, "Pagans had a morality, but Paganism had none."[11]

What did the pagan philosophers, who were commonly seen as individuals holding to higher values, write with regard to charity? Their concern regarding charity was minimal, but a few isolated references can be found. For instance, Aristotle, Demosthenes, Cicero, and Seneca suggest that conferring a benefit on someone should not be done with the intent of receiving something in return.[12] These comments, however, were rarely heeded; and other noteworthy philosophers contradicted them, as shown below in the discussion regarding compassion. Thus, as W. E. H. Lecky, who was not a friend of Christianity, once said: "The active, habitual, and detailed charity of private persons, which is such a conspicuous feature in all Christian societies, was scarcely known in antiquity."[13] And when one considers the remarks by Seneca (d. A.D. 65), who spoke about giving to people "who would be grateful and mindful of the benefit," it can be argued that his comments may have been influenced by the practice of Christian charity that was widely practiced for at least three decades before Nero ordered him to commit suicide.

COMPASSION: A CHRISTIAN INNOVATION

The gospels of Matthew and Mark speak in several instances about Jesus having compassion for the people, particularly for those who were sick. For example: "He had compassion on them and healed their sick " (Matthew 14:14). So it was with the early Christians when they saw the sick and dying. Their compassion was *caritas* driven. Knowing of Christ's compassionate love for the sick, they sought to heed his admonition.

Human compassion, especially with regard to the sick and dying, among the ancients was rare, notably among the Greco-Romans. As with the practice of charity, such behavior was contrary to their cultural ethos and to the teachings of the pagan philosophers. For instance, Plato (427–347 B.C.) said that a poor man (usually a slave) who was no longer able to work because of sickness should be left to die. He even praised Aesculapius,

"St. Francis Teaches Charity" acknowledges the role of St. Francis of Assisi (1182–1226) in continuing the longstanding tradition of Christian charity. *(Carving by Augustin Querol, 19th cent.)*

the famous Greek physician, for not prescribing medicine to those he knew were preoccupied with their illness (*Republic* 3.406d–410a). The Roman philosopher Plautus (254–184 B.C.) argued, "You do a beggar bad service by giving him food and drink; you lose what you give and prolong his life for more misery" (*Trinummus* 2.338–39). Thucydides (ca. 460–400 B.C.), the honored historian of ancient Greece, cites an example of the plague that struck Athens during the Peloponnesian War in 430 B.C. Many of the sick and dying Athenians were deserted by their fellow residents, who feared that they too would catch the plague (*Peloponnesian War* 2.51). Similarly, the Romans panicked and fled from a contagious plague in Alexandria during the fourth century A.D., leaving behind their friends and next of kin.[14] Such behavior prompted Emperor Julian the Apostate (who reigned from 361 to 363), to lament that the Christians, whom he detested, showed love and compassion, whereas his pagan countrymen did not. Said he: "The impious Galileans [his word for the Christians] relieve both their own poor and ours." And, he continued, "It is shameful that ours should be so destitute of our assistance" (*Epistles of Julian* 49). Finally, one need only recall the utter lack of compassion that was so pronounced in the great delight that the Roman spectators took at seeing gladiators mauled or stabbed to death in the arenas (discussed in chapter 2), a practice that had been institutionalized for over six hundred years. Similarly, there was no compassion in many of the Roman emperors, who often had people killed for no just reason or cause whatsoever.

It was this callous, compassionless culture that the Christians entered. Unlike the pagans, they showed compassion in caring for the weak, the sick, the downtrodden, and the dying, often risking their own lives in the process. One historian writes that the Christians "in the midst of manifold and malignant pestilences...did not hesitate to devote their services, and too often their lives to the sick."[15] By putting their lives in jeopardy, they took seriously Christ's command to visit and care for the sick. They understood what Jesus meant when he said, "Whatever you did not do for one of the least of these, you did not do for me" (Matthew 25:45). They also understood another of Christ's teachings: "Greater love has no one than this, that he lay down his life for his friends" (John 15:13).

History records the account of Pachomius, a pagan soldier in Emperor Constantine's army. Pachomius was profoundly moved when he saw Christians bringing food to his fellow soldiers who were afflicted with famine and disease. "He learned that they were people of a special religion and were called Christians. Curious to understand a doctrine which inspired them with so much humanity, he studied it, and that was the beginning of his conversion."[16] Incidents such as the one witnessed by Pachomius were a major reason that the early church grew in spite of the numerous persecutions.

Why were Pachomius and others moved by the compassionate acts of the Christians? The answer lies in the fact that the Greco-Roman culture did not see the hungry, the sick, and the dying as worthy of humane assistance. The worth of a human being was determined by external and accidental circumstances in proportion to the position he held in the community or state. A human being only had value as a citizen, but very few people qualified as citizens.[17] The physically ailing, the poor, and the lower classes (slaves, artisans, and other manual workers) for whom the Christians had compassion, were not citizens in the eyes of the Greeks and Romans who were freemen. Noncitizens were defined as having no purpose and hence not worthy to be helped when their lives were in jeopardy. In their dire condition they received no food or physical protection.[18] The attitude of Plautus, the Roman, and Plato, the Greek, cited above, was still very much the cultural norm at the time of early Christianity.

The virtual lack of compassion for the sick and stricken among the Greco-Romans has been noted by many medical historians. Fielding

Garrison, a physician and historian, says that before the birth of Christ "the spirit toward sickness and misfortune was not one of compassion, and the credit of ministering to human suffering on an extended scale belongs to Christianity."[19] The German historian Gerhard Uhlhorn states, "The idea of humanity was wanting in the old world."[20]

Nor were the Greeks and Romans the only people who had little or no compassion for the indigent. Before the compassionate, humanitarian values of Christianity spread to different parts of the world, the ancient Japanese culture, for instance, resembled that of the Greco-Romans: "The bonzas or Japanese priests, by maintaining that the sick and needy were odious to the gods, prevented the rich from relieving them."[21]

When modern secularists show compassion today upon seeing or hearing of some human tragedy—for example, massive starvation, earthquake disasters, mass murders—they show that they have unknowingly internalized Christianity's concept of compassion. Even so-called objective news reporters often find it difficult to hide their emotions when they report major calamities on radio or television. But had these reporters not grown up under the two-thousand-year-old umbrella of Christianity's compassionate influence, they would probably be without much compassion, similar to the ancient Greeks, Romans, and others. As Josiah Stamp has said, "Christian ideals have permeated society until non-Christians, who claim to live a 'decent life' without religion, have forgotten the origin of the very content and context of their 'decency.'"[22]

CHARITY AND COMPASSION FOR ORPHANS

I have already mentioned that the early Christians in Roman society rescued abandoned children by taking them into their homes and rearing them as their own. Early Christian literature frequently commanded Christians to care not only for the widows, the sick, the disabled, and the poor, but also for the orphans. Life expectancy at the time of Christ and for centuries thereafter was relatively short, only about thirty years. Many parents died, leaving their children parentless.

The Christian concern for orphans stemmed from the biblical teachings that every human being was precious in the sight of God. For instance, a number of Old Testament books (for example, Exodus, Psalms, Zechariah) clearly state that fatherless children, like widows, were to be honored, protected, and cared for. And similarly in the New Testament, James writes, "Religion that God our Father accepts as pure and faultless is this: to look after orphans..." (James 1:27).

Very early in the church, Justin Martyr (ca. 100–166), an early defender of Christianity, reveals that collections were taken during church services to help the orphans (*Apology* 67). Another church father, Tertullian, reports that the church in Carthage, Africa, had a common treasury "to aid the boys and girls who have neither fortune nor parents" (*Apology* 39). In the latter part of the fourth century, *The Apostolic Constitutions* speak about how the Christian bishops solicited help for orphans. And in the sixth, seventh, and eighth centuries, the Italian bishops and clergy "zealously defended widows and orphans."[23]

Before the legalization of Christianity in A.D. 313, orphans were reared in family homes. After 313, Christians also cared for many child orphans in *orphanotrophia* (orphans + *trophos* = rearer, nourisher). Infant orphans or newborn foundlings were nurtured and cared for in *brephotrophia* (*brephos* = child). Both of these institutions mark the formal beginning of orphanages, later to become common, especially in the West. In time the *brephotrophia* were absorbed by *orphanotrophia*, institutional structures that took parentless children from infancy on up. In some instances the exceptionally poor children were separately cared for in *ptochotrophia* (*ptochos* = poor) institutions. By the middle and latter part of the fourth century, St. Basil of Caesarea and St. Chrysostom of Constantinople urged the construction of *orphanotrophia*. They were commonly built in the shadow of cathedrals, sometimes along with other hospices.[24] In the twelfth century some of the religious orders that arose during the Crusades provided hospices for abandoned and orphaned children. The Order of the Holy Ghost was one such group.[25] By the end of the thirteenth century, this order operated more than eight hundred houses for orphans. Many monasteries also cared for orphans during the Middle Ages.[26]

Over the centuries orphanages supported by Christian charity continued to spread throughout Europe. Many orphanages were founded and operated by individual Christians. One such person was A. H. Francke, a Lutheran pastor and professor at Halle University in Germany. One of Franke's students, George Müller, who converted to Christianity while a university student, was greatly impressed with his orphanage. In 1829 he went to England as a missionary to the Jews. In 1836, when he could not come to terms with the London Jews Society, he founded a home in the city of Bristol for thirty orphaned girls. He believed they needed Christian love and education. His work soon spread to other British cities. By the time he died

JULIAN THE APOSTATE, a Roman emperor (361–63), tried to restore a revised form of paganism. Although a pagan, he envied Christian charity. *(Louvre, Paris)*

in 1898, more than eight thousand children were being cared for and educated in numerous orphanages.[27] His strong belief in the Bible, his faith, and his many prayers for the success of the orphanages bore abundant fruit.

Before Christians built and operated orphanages, they had already shown their concern for potential orphans by requiring godparents at a child's baptism. Since human life expectancy was only about thirty years during the early centuries of Christianity, it was not uncommon for small children to have one or both parents die. Thus, should the child lose his or her parents, the baptismal rite required the godparents to promise that they would provide for the child, both spiritually and materially.

Orphans, like the poor, were seen as redeemed creatures of God and therefore worthy of human love and attention. Placing them in orphanages was one way of demonstrating that belief. Orphanages did not "warehouse" children but rather gave them both a home and usually a rudimentary education.

Not all orphans or neglected children in the Middle Ages and after ended up in orphanages, however. Some became vagrants. It was this situation that motivated Charles Loring Brace, an American clergyman of the Congregational Church, to found an organization in 1853 that would help vagrant urban boys and girls. It was called the Children's Aid Society. Brace and his newly formed organization believed that vagrant orphans and abandoned children would be best served if they could live with an American farm family. Here they would experience normal family living and receive plenty of fresh air, good food, disciplined guidance, and wholesome family interaction. They would also learn the value of meaningful, productive work. To accomplish this objective, hundreds of homeless orphans were placed on trains ("orphan trains") and sent to farm families in upstate New York, Connecticut, New Jersey, and the Midwestern states. Some weeks before being taken to the various farms, the children were taught the Lord's Prayer, the Ten Commandments, some Psalms, some parables of Jesus, and other portions of the Bible. They were also taught Christian hymns and anthems. Later, when they embarked on the train, they were given a short speech and a divine blessing.[28] The entire orphan train philosophy was prompted by Christian charity and compassion.

The establishment of orphanages, the custom of requiring godparents at baptism, and orphan trains were all Christian innovations. The Greeks and the Romans would never have entertained such a posture, for it would have contradicted their cultural practices of infanticide and child abandonment. Thousands upon thousands of unwanted infants (as noted in chapter 2) were rescued by the early Christians and given the chance to attain a normal life, all because Jesus Christ had inspired his followers to heed his words: "I was as stranger and you invited me in" (Matthew 25:35) and "Let the little children come to me, and do not hinder them, for the kingdom of God belongs to such as these" (Mark 10:14).

CHARITY FOR THE AGED

As already stated, life expectancy before the birth of Christ and for centuries later was relatively short. There are a number of reasons for the brief life span: Medical knowledge and medicines were primitive; childbirth took the lives of many women in their prime years; infant mortality rates were extremely high; nutrition was commonly poor; diseases, famines, and plagues

"JOHN POUNDS' SCHOOL FOR RAGGED CHILDREN AT PORTSMOUTH" shows poor children in Portsmouth, England, being cared for out of Christian charity. *(Edward H. Wehnert)*

made frequent appearances. Yet there were always some men and women who became septuagenarians and even octogenarians. Thus, we find that at the time of Emperor Justinian (483–565), churches were operating homes for the aged called *gerontocomia* (*geras* = aged + *comeo* = take care of).

Beginning with the Christian era, homes for the aged spread throughout Europe and North America. Most were organized and operated by churches. One finds no evidence of homes for the aged in the years preceding Christianity. Given the absence of such homes, it is sometimes argued that homes for the aged were not needed in ancient times or in preliterate societies because the aged were highly respected and adequately cared for by their respective families. But whether this was ever really so is doubtful. As Richard Posner has shown, "The social status of the old has varied bewilderingly across different cultures and eras, and even within them."[29] Moreover, even when the elderly have relatively high status, as for instance among the Herero of Botswana, it does not necessarily result in their being adequately cared for when they are alone, frail, or ailing.[30] And it needs to be remembered that some research shows that "the poorer a society is, the more likely it will be to kill or let die its oldest members."[31]

Here the onetime practice of the Eskimos letting their aged slowly freeze to death comes to mind—further evidence that the aged do not necessarily fare well in nonindustrial societies.

Very little is known in regard to the social and economic conditions that led Christians to establish *gerontocomia* in the fifth century. That there was a need for them is not debatable, but one must remember that the presence of need does not necessarily translate into appropriate solutions. The need for hospitals existed for centuries, but that need was not met until Christianity introduced them in the fourth century. Whatever the specific needs of the aged were during the early years of Christianity, the Christians, moved by compassion, sought to meet them by establishing homes for the aged. By so doing, Christianity introduced a method of human compassion that in time became a major social institution.

Today homes for the aged, operated by both churches and secular organizations, are widely prevalent and indispensable in modern technological societies. In the United States, Canada, England, and other Western countries there are retirement homes in which older people live in apartment-like units, often in relatively large complexes. Besides retirement homes, there are countless nursing homes for older individuals who often are too frail physically to live without assistance or some form of nursing care. People today take these facilities for granted. Yet they all bear the compassionate marks of Jesus Christ, who moved his early followers to practice compassion motivated by *caritas*.

CHRISTIAN CHARITY VIA VOLUNTARY ASSOCIATIONS

From its inception, Christian charity was voluntary. The aid and assistance that the early Christians gave, whether nursing the sick and dying, feeding the poor and starving, or rescuing abandoned children, was all done voluntarily. In light of the church being outlawed and persecuted, even membership in the church was completely voluntary. Thus, each individual had to make a deliberate decision whether to join it or not, whether such membership was worth potential persecution, imprisonment, or perhaps even death.

Although the early Christians never fought back individually or collectively when they were physically persecuted, Emperor Trajan (98–117) nevertheless saw voluntary associations (*collegia, soladitates,* or *factionis*) of Christians as dangerous, so he, like previous emperors, outlawed them.[32] Such associations were still illegal at the time of Tertullian in the early third century when he defended his fellow Christians for assembling in their congregations (voluntary associations). He explained that in their assemblies they prayed and read the sacred Scriptures and that they had a "treasure chest" to which members contributed funds. These funds were not spent on feasts or drinking bouts but were used to support the poor, supply the wants of parentless boys and girls, and assist confined old people (*Apology* 39). Thus, Christian congregations were types of *collegia* that functioned in part as vehicles for dispensing charity. Now two thousand years later, countless voluntary associations, church-related and nonchurch-related, dispense a wide variety of charity, particularly in democratic countries where people are free to form and join voluntary organizations.

In the United States the spirit of charity in voluntary associations is greater among church members than among those who are not, according to a nationwide study conducted in 1987. Those belonging to Christian churches also give more financially to nonchurch charities, and they give a higher proportion of their income to such charities.[33] Given the long-standing importance that charity has had in Christianity, these findings should not be surprising. If they are, it is probably because the general public has received very little information regarding charitable activities of American Christians, a fault that some social scientists say lies with their colleagues who have done too little research studying the influences that Christian beliefs have on people's motivations to give to charity and to participate in volunteer activities.[34]

AMERICAN CHARITY

Christian aid to the poor did not end with the early church or the Middle Ages. Churches continue to aid the poor to this very day. In the United States, for example, most Christian denominations collect funds to give clothing, food, and medical relief for the poor far beyond their country's boundaries. And as is well known, the worldwide work done by the Salvation Army in alleviating the plight of the poor is both commendatory and significant. This Christian organization, founded by William Booth, a devout Christian, in London in 1865, is still an excellent example of Christian charity.

The earliest examples of American charity, as Marvin Olasky has shown, occurred among the Pilgrims in Plymouth, Massachusetts, by the colonists governed by William Bradford. When deadly sickness greatly reduced the group, Bradford said that the people willingly toiled to aid the stricken with wood, food, and clean clothes, risking their own health.[35] Later, Congregational, Presbyterian, Anglican, and Methodist sermons urged church members to help the poor and the sick, reminding them that without compassion their faith was dead.[36]

With these early American precedents, it is not surprising that astute foreign observers have noted that the United States has, virtually from its inception, been a shining example of a charity-minded country. Fifty years after the nation came into being, when Alexis de Tocqueville visited the United States in 1831, he astutely observed: "If an accident happens on the highway, everybody hastens to help the sufferer; if some great and sudden calamity befalls a family, the purses of a thousand strangers are at once willingly opened and small but numerous donations pour in to relieve their distress."[37]

A hundred years later in the 1940s, Gunnar Myrdal, another foreign observer, remarked: "No country has so many cheerful givers as America."[38] He attributed this cheerful giving, or "Christian neighborliness," as he called it, to the "influence from the churches."[39] Americans continue to be cheerful givers. For example, the amount that they gave to the poor and needy in 1991 amounted to $650 per American household.[40] And in 1998 American church members contributed more than $24 billion, amounting to $407 per member.[41]

In the 1890s Amos Warner observed that much of America's giving was the product of the nation's churches. He said that the church, as a voluntary association, was "the most powerful agent in inducing people to give."[42] That still seems to be true. For instance, in 1994 religious donations in the United States totaled $59 billion. This amounted to 45 percent of all voluntary giving by individuals and organizations.[43] In North America, but mostly in the United States, there are currently 750 Protestant mission agencies that receive and dispense $2 billion annually.[44] Complementing this action, there are at least 500 rescue missions in the United States that are supported through charitable giving.[45] And Americans also give liberally for the construction of new churches and other religious buildings. In 1998 they spent over $6 billion in church-related construction.[46] Charity-minded Christians, however, have not confined their charity efforts to their respective congregations. Back in 1887, a number of Christian religious leaders met in Denver, Colorado, and founded the Charity Organizations Society. This was the beginning of the United Way, a charitable organization that every American knows. After its inception, the organization planned and coordinated local services and conducted a fund-raising campaign for twenty-two charitable agencies. In 1888 the first United Way campaign raised over $21,000.[47]

Today the United Way gathers an immense amount of money each year that is distributed to various charitable agencies across the nation. In 1998–99 the United Way organization raised $3.58 billion, an increase of 5 percent from the previous year.[48] This commendable organization is another example of Christ's abiding influence—an influence that initially moved a number of Christian men in Denver over a hundred years ago to practice Christian charity in an organized manner that now has grown far beyond the confines of churches.

FRATERNAL BENEFIT SOCIETIES

A great deal of charity in America has been, and still is, practiced by fraternal organizations, especially fraternal benefit societies. From the mid–1800s to the mid–1900s fraternal organizations were in superabundance. One estimate said that in 1927 there were 800 different fraternal associations in the United States. In 1920, when the country had 60 million people, about half of them belonged to at least one fraternal society.[49]

Fraternal benefit groups have provided various forms of charity and mutual aid to their members in times of adversity. In the past, relief for widows and orphans, burial assistance, and life insurance were common forms of aid. Some also operated hospitals. Almost all of the fraternal groups were organized by Christians from various denominations, and their names often reflected denominational ties: Baptist Life Association, Catholic Workmen, Greek Catholic Union, Lutheran Brotherhood, Presbyterian Beneficial Union, and so on. Some organizations had ethnic identities (Sons of Norway, Sons of Poland, Danish Sisterhood, Ukrainian National Association, etc.), but these too were commonly begun by concerned Christians.

While many of the fraternal benefit associations became extinct in time, especially the smaller ones, some have grown extensively and are thriving entities. These survivors today are mainly fraternal insurance organizations. A few have more than a million members, and they commonly fund educational scholarships, promote volunteer activities, encourage new educational programs, support the physically handicapped, and so forth. These charitable efforts are supported by each organization's surplus monies that accrue from the members' life insurance contracts.

Along with the fraternal benefit societies there are also numerous fraternal secret orders, most of which have in recent years experienced notable membership declines. These groups usually have rather elaborate rituals, initiation oaths, and secret passwords. Freemasonry, Independent Order of Odd Fellows, Knights of Pythias, Rebekah Assemblies, Order of the Eastern Star, and Shriners are some of the better known groups. While these fraternal organizations are not really benefit-oriented or church-related, some—for example, the Shriners—have become renowned for their many hospitals that provide free medical assistance to burn-injured patients and crippled children. The Loyal Order of Moose is known for its home in Mooseheart, Illinois, that houses and educates in a village-like atmosphere children who have lost one or both parents.

All of the fraternal benefit societies, and even some of the fraternal secret groups, were primarily founded to provide charitable aid to individuals stricken with misfortune. To be sure, in most instances the aid went to their own members or their children. Yet the fact remains that these organizations were all touched by the tradition of Christian compassion.

SERVICE CLUBS

In the early 1900s, the heyday of voluntary associations, several service clubs arose in the United States, and before long they became international organizations. The most prominent and widely known are the Kiwanis Club, Lions Club, Optimist Club, and Rotary Club. These clubs, which draw their members from the professional and business classes, exist to provide various humanitarian services to their local communities, the nation, and other nations. Many of the services they provide are charity endeavors. For example, the Lions Club donates money and services to the blind and the deaf. In 1994–95 the International Rotary Club received contributions of $60 million for its foundation that underwrites most of the society's charitable programs.

These service organizations, and many lesser-known ones, were founded by Americans, whom Myrdal dubbed "cheerful givers." They, like the founders of the fraternal benefit societies, were largely influenced by the spirit of Christian charity.

YOUNG MEN'S CHRISTIAN ASSOCIATION (YMCA)

In the early 1840s George Williams, an Englishman, said he would give his life to Jesus Christ. He soon found a way to channel his commitment as he began helping young men who came to London from the rural areas to find work in the big city. Often these young men turned to the lowest sensual activities. So Williams and a dozen other young men formed a purely religious organization that sought "to improve the spiritual condition of young men engaged in the drapery and other trades." They called it The Draper's Evangelical Union. In 1844 it was renamed Young Men's Christian Association. Its objective was "the winning of young men to Jesus Christ, and the building in them of Christian character."[50] In order to achieve this goal, the organization invited young men to join its fellowship, which offered them the opportunity for prayer, Bible reading, and social and recreational activities. By 1851 the YMCA had crossed the Atlantic to Boston and Montreal. Its membership requirement stated: "Any young man who is a member in regular standing of an evangelical church may become a member."[51] The YMCA grew rapidly and flourished most notably in North America. It soon broadened its objectives and activities, which among other things included making available inexpensive temporary lodging in YMCA hotels to young men while they searched for jobs or while they were en route from one city to another. Many major American cities had such "Y" hotels. During World War II the organization raised millions of dollars to aid prisoners of war and helped found the United Service Organization (USO),[52] a civilian group dedicated to bolstering the morale of the armed forces.

YOUNG WOMEN'S CHRISTIAN ASSOCIATION (YWCA)

Although young women were eligible to join the YMCA early in the organization's existence, women nevertheless organized their own group, also in London, in 1855. Initially, the organization's major goal was to find housing for female nurses who returned from the Crimean War. Its American counterpart, first known as the Ladies' Christian Association, was formed in the city of New York in 1858, but in 1866 it chose the name of Young Women's Christian Association. In the United States the YWCA did much of its work, which accented leadership training, on college and university campuses. And in the 1890s the organization sent its secretary to India for foreign service.

Both the YMCA and the YWCA began as Christian associations, seeking to integrate Christian values and beliefs in the everyday lives of young men and women, who often stood on the threshold of social disorganization, during the early years of the Industrial Revolution. Both organizations were charity minded; neither sought any financial gain for themselves. They began with the spirit of Christ, which they believed would not only help young men and young women to live better lives but would also enable them to glorify God. Today both groups still have "Christian" in their official names, but neither group is a Christian organization, nor does either group require its members to be affiliated with a Christian church, as was true when the organizations came into being. Nevertheless, Christianity deserves the credit for the initial appearance of these associations. Founding them was just another way that Christianity extended its arms of charity, and the world became a better place because of it.

CHILD LABOR LAWS

At times in the history of Christianity many of its professed adherents were like the seed that fell among thorns in Jesus' parable; they cared too much for this world, and as a result they choked the spirit of Christ and became unfruitful (Matthew 13:22). This parable is an apt picture of numerous people who, during the early years of the Industrial Revolution of the 1800s in Western Europe, nominally identified with Christ but ignored his precepts with regard to compassion. England was one such country.

A major tragedy of this era in England was the widespread exploitation of child laborers. Boys and girls from ages seven to fourteen years worked in cold, wet, and dangerous coal mines, often crawling on their hands and knees in narrow, low tunnels to fill carts with coal. Frequently they had only tattered clothes; many, including young girls, were more naked than clothed; and the clothes they did have were wet from the drippings off the shaft. They often lacked food as well. One report said, "Two boys were drawn up from the pit...and water actually kept dripping from them and they looked as wretched as drowned rats."[53] In other instances, small boys were forced to climb up inside chimneys to clean them for the chimney sweeps who employed them. Examples like these were commonplace in industrial England.

The deplorable conditions of child labor prompted men of compassion to fight against their callous countrymen to enact laws in the British Parliament that would outlaw child labor under a given age. Although there were men like William Wilberforce, Charles Dickens, and Thomas Carlyle who worked to improve child labor conditions, the most indefatigable proponent of child labor laws was Anthony Ashley Cooper, Lord Shaftesbury (1801–85), who served a number of years as a member of England's Parliament. This determined man

"FLOWER GIRL" depicts a poor, barefoot girl in London in 1869. *(Gustave Doré Gallery, London)*

was spurred on by his Christian compassion. At age twenty-six he wrote, "I want nothing but usefulness to God and my country."[54] Charles Spurgeon, the renowned preacher, said of Shaftesbury, his contemporary, "A man so firm in the Gospel of Jesus Christ, so intensely active in the cause of God and man, I have never known."[55] With Shaftesbury's years of intensive pleadings, countless speeches, personal sacrifices, and dogged persistence, he was able to get Parliament to pass a number of bills that vastly improved child labor conditions. The Factory Act of 1833 was the first noteworthy bill to pass. It limited the number of hours to forty-eight per week for children under thirteen years. Other bills were passed in the 1840s; three Factory Acts became law in 1864, 1867, and in 1871; and in 1875 the Chimney Sweeps Act went into effect, all as a result of Shaftesbury's untiring efforts. These new laws were giant steps forward, even though inadequate because they still permitted children to work in substandard settings.

The laws continued to improve, and eventually they banned all child labor in factories, mills, and mines. Countries like the United States, Germany, and France took their cue from England and also enacted laws to improve the child labor problem. The United States, for instance, still refined its child labor laws as late as 1938 in its Fair Labor Standards Act.

While child labor in the Western countries today has effectively been outlawed, it continues to be widespread and common in many non-Western countries. In China, Thailand, Bangladesh, West Africa, Mexico, and other locations, children as young as seven are still today working in factories, garment industries, and vegetable fields. In 1997 UNICEF estimated that two to four million children worked in various sectors of Mexico's economy.[56]

When Westerners express surprise and shock upon hearing that child labor is still widespread and common in so many non-Western countries, they are unwittingly reflecting Christian compassion that was the moving force in the life and work of Shaftesbury. It was he, not Karl Marx (as is sometimes reported), who aroused the British social conscience with regard to the tragedies of child labor. When England's Factory Act was passed in 1833 at the prodding of Shaftesbury, Karl Marx was only fifteen years old. In short, as a result of Shaftesbury's efforts, the credit for improving and eventually outlawing child labor goes to him, who was influenced by Christianity, and not to Marx, the atheist.

FROM CHRISTIAN CHARITY TO STATE WELFARE

From the earliest years of Christianity to the ninth century, charity needs in the West were regularly provided for by the church. After the death of Charlemagne in 814, and the arrival of feudalism with its complexity, church-dispensed charity declined sharply. Feudal lords were to take care of the poor on their lands, but they often did so inadequately. By the sixteenth century charity had become largely secularized. Charity now shifted from the poor man as brother to the poor man as citizen.[57] England's sixteenth-century Poor Laws, which authorized parishes (similar to counties) to levy taxes in order to relieve the poor when ecclesiastical charity fell short, further weakened the church's charity efforts.

As time progressed, particularly by the twentieth century, state welfare payments replaced much of the churches' charity. Today, millions who receive state welfare payments in the Western world probably know little or nothing about the fact that the payments they receive are largely the result of Christianity's influence. Robert Banks says it well: "The whole approach to [governmental] social welfare that has developed in the West, and more recently in the East as well, is debtor to the Christian contribution and has been profoundly influenced by it."[58] Another has said, "It is difficult to understand the great influence that charity exerted on the acts of man unless one realizes how religion, especially Christianity, has reinforced by its teachings the instinct of sympathy and altruism."[59]

While it is indisputably true that modern state welfare is largely the outgrowth of Christianity's centuries-old charity practices, it needs to be noted that there are several reasons why state welfare programs cannot be equated with Christian charity. State welfare today corresponds more to the pagan *liberalitis* of Rome than to Christian *caritas*. The latter, as noted earlier, was

DEVELOPMENT AND MAINTENANCE OF CHRISTIAN CHARITY AND COMPASSION

CHRISTIANS:

- Created a *diaconia* that cared for widows (Acts 6:1–7, about A.D. 37)

- Furnished *matricula* (church lists of needy persons)

- Established common treasuries to aid the needy (1 Corinthians 16:2; mid-1st cent.)

- Formed *collegia, soladitates,* or *factionis* (voluntary associations) to aid the unfortunate (2nd and 3rd cent.)

- Provided for orphans:

  —Godparents at baptism (care for their orphaned godchildren)

  —Help solicited by bishops (4th cent. and after)

  —*Orphanotrophia* introduced (buildings for orphans, 4th cent.)

  —*Brephotrophia* established (buildings for foundlings, 4th cent.)

  —Monasteries used for housing many orphans

- Introduced *morotrophia* (mental asylums, begun in A.D. 321)

- Established *nosocomia,* first institutions that served only the sick (late 4th cent.)

- Constructed *xenodochia* (buildings that housed strangers, travelers, and the sick, late 4th cent.)

- Operated *ptochia* (institutions for the poor, 4th cent.)

- Introduced *gerontocomia* (institutions for the aged, 5th cent.)

- Established *typholocomia* (institutions for the blind): first one established in Jerusalem (630)

- Provided medical care by Knights Hospitalers of St. John during the Crusades (12th cent.)

- Provided health care for lepers by Hospitalers of St. Lazarus during the Crusades (12th cent.)

- Maintained *Domus Sancti Spiritus* (House of the Holy Spirit): German hospitals (14th cent.)

- Maintained voluntary associations: primary and longstanding instruments of Christian charity and compassion (1st cent. to present) done out of selfless love, whereas the former was done with the objective of receiving some type of reciprocity. While a great deal of today's state welfare is provided to assist those in need, it lacks genuine love. State welfare programs operate on the basis of coercion; funds are involuntarily gathered by means of enforced taxation, and thus they violate the spirit and method of true Christian charity. Although governmental welfare programs help many of the unfortunate, and while they might be called charity, they are not Christian charity; nor are they Christian compassion.

State welfare programs are also at odds with Christian charity in that they often produce unintended harmful effects by unintentionally encouraging the loss of individual responsibility[60] and even rewarding it. One such effect has been the continued rise in the rates of children born out of wedlock, a trend that has steadily increased from the mid–1960s to 2000. In 1960 the out-of-wedlock birth rate was 5.3 percent of all births in the United States, while in 1998 it was 33 percent,[61] an increase of nearly 600 percent. Another unintended, harmful effect of state welfare has been the rewarding of the indolent, thus nullifying the Christian admonition: "If a man will not work, he shall not eat" (2 Thessalonians 3:10). Walter Benjamin refers to these effects as products of "imprudent charity."[62]

Another effect of governmental welfare programs at odds with Christian charity is that they often foster political demagoguery by pandering to the voters who are recipients of social welfare. Political demagoguery clearly violates Christian charity, not only because it uses lies and deception, but also because it benefits the selfish interests of the demagogues who, by presenting themselves as advocates of state welfare programs, reap political gain since those who are dependent on governmental handouts will vote for them in order to keep the handouts coming. Such politicians are practicing Roman *liberalitis*, not Christian *caritas*.

When the Swedish sociologist Gunnar Myrdal noted in the 1940s that Americans voluntarily were "cheerful givers," he credited their cheerful giving to Christianity's tradition of charity, and he further noted that their generous posture had at least three salutary effects: (1) it lightened the burdens of the poor and the unfortunate; (2) it kept the altruistic spirit alive; and (3) it delayed the socialistic encroachment of governmental welfare programs.[63] The latter two are not in tune with state welfare.

Christianity, as delineated in chapter 11, fosters freedom from all forms of slavery. State welfare, on the other hand, tends to create a permanently dependent class, really a new type of slavery. The essence of slavery is being dependent on someone or some entity for one's livelihood, and all forms of slavery demoralize human beings. Thus, enforced social welfare programs, which at first may appear altruistic and generous, are, in the long run, often detrimental. As George Gilder says, "Excessive welfare hurts its recipients, demoralizing them or reducing them to an addictive dependency that can ruin their lives."[64]

State welfare induces many people to think that government should pay for their needs that they feel they cannot afford. Apparently when the government pays for people's needs, it does not appear as though others are paying for them. Such thinking forgets that the government has no funds except those taken by means of compulsory taxation. And it is the latter that distinguishes state welfare programs from Christian charity, regardless of any resemblance.

The Austrian economist Wilhelm Röpke once said, "The welfare state is the favorite playground of a cheap sort of moralism," and he further remarked that "cheap morality is anything but moral."[65] Such morality is not Christian morality, nor is it Christian charity. It violates the spirit of Christ's example of the Good Samaritan, who gave, not because he was coerced, but because he had a heartfelt, voluntary desire to help someone in need. He practiced real *caritas;* government programs do not.

Finally, it must be noted that even though the present-day state welfare programs evolved out of Christian charity and compassion, they cannot be equated with Christian charity or compassion because Christ said that his followers were to give "a cup of water *in my name*" (Mark 9:41). State welfare programs are not offered in the name of Jesus Christ.

CONCLUSION

People who may think that current human charity and compassion in the Western world, whether it is state welfare or voluntary charity, developed on its own as a result of mere civilization, without the impetus and influence of Christianity are misinformed. As the German church historian C. Schmidt said a century ago, such thinking is "blind to the history of nations, and to the history of the human heart. Both proclaim loudly that charity cannot be the product of egoism, nor humility of pride; that without the intervention of God no new spirit could have regenerated individuals and the world."[66]

"From the wellsprings of Christian compassion," says Carlton Hayes, "our Western civilization has drawn its inspiration, and its sense of duty, for feeding the hungry, giving drink to the thirsty, looking after the homeless, clothing the naked, tending the sick, and visiting the prisoner."[67] Similarly, George Grant states, "As missionaries circled the globe [after Columbus]. . . . They established hospitals. They founded orphanages. They started rescue missions. They built almshouses. They opened soup kitchens. They incorporated charitable societies. They changed laws. They demonstrated love. They lived as if people mattered."[68]

In short, every time charity and compassion are seen in operation, the credit goes to Jesus Christ. It was he who inspired his early followers to give and to help the unfortunate, regardless of their race, religion, class, or nationality. Apostolic injunctions are repetitive in the New Testament. For instance, St. Paul enjoined the Christians at Colossae: "Therefore, as God's chosen people, holy and dearly loved, clothe yourselves with compassion. . ." (Colossians 3:12), and to the Ephesian Christians he wrote: "Be kind and compassionate to one another. . ." (Ephesians 4:32). Similarly, St. James reminded his hearers: "Religion that God our Father accepts as pure and faultless is this: to look after orphans and widows in their distress. . ." (James 1:27). These early Christians set a model for their descendants to follow, a model that today's modern secular societies seek to imitate, but without Christian motivation. Sympathy toward the poor is a concept that comes from Christianity, for the rich and well-to-do in Greece and Rome despised the poor.[69]

NOTES

1. Adolf Harnack, *The Mission and Expansion of Christianity in the First Three Centuries,* trans. James Moffat (New York: G. P. Putnam's Sons, 1908), 1:153.

2. W. E. H. Lecky, *History of European Morals: From Augustus to Charlegmagne* (New York: D. Appleton, 1927), 2:81.

3. Gerhard Uhlhorn, *Christian Charity in the Ancient Church* (New York: Charles Scribner's Sons, 1883), 7, 9.

4. Robert Banks, "The Early Church as a Caring Community," *Evangelical Review of Theology* (October 1983): 318.

5. Ibid., 319.

6. Edward Ryan, *The History of the Effects of Religion on Mankind: In Countries Ancient and Modern, Barbarous and Civilized* (Dublin: T. M. Bates, 1802), 132.

7. Cited in Ryan, *The History of the Effects of Religion,* 133.

8. Christopher Dawson, *Medieval Essays: A Study of Christian Culture* (Garden City, N.Y.: Image Books, 1959), 46.

9. Lecky, *History of European Morals,* 2:78.

10. Ibid.

11. Abbe De La Beterie's comment in *Select Works of the Emperor Julian and Some Pieces of the Sophist Libanius,* trans. John Duncombe (London: J. Nichols, 1784), 2:131.

12. A. R. Hands, *Charities and Social Aid in Greece and Rome* (Ithaca: Cornell University Press, 1968), 27–28.

13. Lecky, *History of European Morals,* 2:79.

14. Ibid., 82.

15. T. Clifford Allbutt, *Greek Medicine in Rome* (New York: Benjamin Blom, 1921), 402.

16. C. Schmidt, *The Social Results of Early Christianity,* trans. R. W. Dale (London: Wm. Isbister, 1889), 327.

17. Ibid., 17.

18. Ibid., 18.

19. Fielding H. Garrison, *An Introduction of the History of Medicine* (Philadelphia: W. B. Saunders, 1914), 118.

20. Uhlhorn, *Christian Charity in the Ancient Church,* 38.

21. Edward Ryan, *The History of the Effects of Religion on Mankind: In Countries Ancient and Modern, Barbarous and Civilized* (Dublin: T. M. Bates, 1802), 268.

22. Josiah Stamp, *Christianity and Economics* (New York: Macmillan, 1938), 69.

23. Ryan, *History of the Effects of Religion on Mankind,* 152–53.

24. J. Beaudry, "Orphans (in the Early Church)," *New Catholic Encyclopedia* (New York: McGraw-Hill, 1967), 10:785.

25. Daniel-Rops, *Cathedral and Crusade* (New York: E. P. Dutton, 1957), 255.

26. Schmidt, *The Social Results of Early Christianity,* 258.

27. Cyril J. Davey, "George Müller," in *Great Leaders of the Christian Church,* ed. John Woodbridge (Chicago: Moody Press, 1988), 320.

28. Matthew A. Crenson, *Building the Invisible Orphanage: A History of the American Welfare System* (Cambridge: Harvard University Press, 1998), 26.

29. Richard A. Posner, *Aging and Old Age* (Chicago: University of Chicago Press, 1995), 31.

30. Jennie Keith et al., *The Aging Experience: Diversity and Commonality Across Cultures* (Thousand Oaks, Calif.: Sage, 1994), 19, 21.

31. Posner, *Aging and Old Age,* 205.

32. W. M. Ramsay, *The Church and the Roman Empire Before A.D. 170* (London: Hodder and Stoughton, 1893), 358.

33. Robert Wuthnow and Virginia A. Hodgkinson, *Faith and Philanthropy in America* (San Francisco: Jossey-Bass, 1990), 102, 103.

34. Ibid., 113.

35. Marvin Olasky, *The Tragedy of American Compassion* (Washington, D.C.: Regnery Gateway, 1992), 6.

36. Ibid., 7.

37. Alexis de Tocqueville, *Democracy in America,* trans. Henry Reeve and rev. by Francis Bowen (New York: Vintage Books, 1945), 2:185.

38. Gunnar Myrdal, *An American Dilemma: The Negro Problem and Modern Democracy* (New York: Harper and Row, 1944), 11.

39. Ibid.

40. V. Hodgkinson and M. Weitzman, *Giving and Volunteering in the United States* (Washington, D.C.: Independent Sector, 1992), 1.

41. Eileen W. Lindner, *Yearbook of American and Canadian Churches, 1998* (Nashville: Abingdon Press, 1998), 14.

42. Amos Warner, *American Charities: A Study in Philosophy and Economics* (New York: Thomas C. Crowell, 1894), 316.

43. Dean R. Hoge, et al., "Giving in Five Denominations," in *Financing American Religion,* ed. Mark Chaves and Sharon L. Miller (Walnut Creek, Calif.: Altamira Press, 1999), 3.

44. Sharon L. Miller, "Financing Parachurch Organizations," in *Financing American Religion,* 120.

45. Ibid., 122.

46. "Religious Construction on the Rise," *World,* 12 June 1999, 19.

47. United Way of America, "United Way: A Brief Chronology" (1999).

48. Ibid.

49. Alvin J. Schmidt, *Fraternal Organizations* (Westport, Conn.: Greenwood Press, 1980), 3.

50. L. L. Doggett, *History of the Young Men's Christian Association* (New York: International Committee of Young Men's Christian Association, 1896), 47.

51. Ibid., 116.

52. Owen E. Pense, "Young Men's Christian Association," *The World Book Encyclopedia* (Chicago: Field Enterprises Educational Corporation, 1958), 18:8978.

53. Grace Abbott, *The Child and the State: Legal Status in the Family Apprenticeship and Child Labor* (Chicago: University of Chicago Press, 1938), 166.

54. J. Wesley Bready, *Lord Shaftesbury* (New York: Frank-Maurice, 1927), 23.

55. Cited in Bready, *Lord Shaftesbury,* 13.

56. S. L. Bachman, "Young Workers in Mexico's Economy," *U.S. News and World Report,* 1 September 1997, 42.

57. M. Scaduto, "Charity, Works of," *New Catholic Encyclopedia,* 3:491.

58. Banks, "The Early Church as a Caring Community," 319.

59. Frank Dekker Watson, *The Charity Organization Movement in The United States* (New York: Macmillan, 1922), 12.

60. Wilhelm Röpke, *Welfare, Freedom, and Inflation* (London: Pall National Press, 1957), 41.

61. *Statistical Abstract of the United States,* 1978, 1998, 65, 74.

62. Walter W. Benjamin, "Compassion That Kills: Is Mainline Christianity a Dangerous Samaritan?" *The World: Currents in Modern Thought* (May 1995): 400.

63. Crenson, *Building the Invisible Orphanage,* 26.

64. George Gilder, *Wealth and Poverty* (San Francisco: Institute for Contemporary Studies, 1993), 30.

65. Cited in Benjamin, "Compassion That Kills," 406.

66. Schmidt, *Social Results of Early Christianity,* 448.

67. Carlton J. H. Hayes, *Christianity and Western Civilization* (Stanford: Stanford University Press, 1954), 56.

68. George Grant, *The Last Crusade: The Untold Story of Christopher Columbus* (Wheaton, Ill.: Crossway Books, 1992), 127.

69. Schmidt, *Social Results of Early Christianity,* 69.

HOSPITALS and HEALTH CARE: THEIR CHRISTIAN ROOTS

*"Whatever you did not do for one of the least of these,
you did not do for me."*
Jesus Christ in Matthew 25:45

Christ was concerned not only with humanity's spiritual condition but also with its physical state. He told his disciples, "I was sick and you looked after me" (Matthew 25:36). These words did not go unheeded. History shows that early Christians not only opposed abortion, infanticide, and abandoning infants, but they also nurtured and cared for the sick, regardless of who they were. Christian or pagan, it made no difference to them.

JESUS, HEALER OF BODY AND SOUL

All four of the Gospels reveal that along with his teaching, Jesus had compassion for the sick. He healed many. Matthew states that "Jesus went throughout Galilee. . .healing every disease and sickness among the people" (Matthew 4:23). He healed the blind, the lame, the deaf, the palsied, and even the lepers, who were quarantined and considered social outcasts.

Moreover, his healing acts were never divorced from his concern for people's souls, their spiritual well-being. "For him no healing was complete which did not affect the soul."[1] Christ was a holistic healer!

The twofold focus (teaching and healing) of Jesus' acts was conveyed by the New Testament's writers, who often used the Greek word *soter* for both "savior" and "healer." The German word *Heiland* for the English word *savior,* for instance, also conveys the meaning that Christ is both a spiritual and physical healer.

As noted above, Jesus expected his disciples, along with their preaching and teaching, to heal: "He sent them [the twelve disciples] out to preach the kingdom of God and to heal the sick" (Luke 9:2). As he commissioned the seventy to enter towns, he gave them a similar message: "Heal the sick who are there" (Luke 10:9). And as the early Christians were dispersed throughout Asia Minor, largely as a result of being persecuted, we find them engaged in healing in addition to their preaching and teaching. The New Testament, especially the Acts of the Apostles, cites a number of instances where Peter, Paul, Stephen, Barnabas, Ananias, and other Christians healed people as part of their missionary activities.

THE PAGAN VOID

The world the Christians entered during the Greco-Roman era had a colossal void with respect to caring for the sick and dying, as indicated in chapter 5. Dionysius, a Christian bishop of the third century, described the existing behavior of the pagans toward their fellow sick human beings in an Alexandrian plague in about A.D. 250. The pagans, he said, "thrust aside anyone who began to be sick, and kept aloof even from their dearest friends, and cast the sufferers out upon the public roads half dead, and left them unburied, and treated them with utter contempt when they died" (*Works of Dionysius, Epistle* 12.5).

How different from the behavior of the Christians! Dionysius tells us that the Christians, when it came to caring for the sick and dying, ignored the danger to themselves:

[V]ery many of our brethren, while in their exceeding love and brotherly kindness, did not spare themselves, but kept by each other, and visited the sick without thought of their own peril, and ministered to them assiduously and treated them for their healing in Christ, died from time to time most joyfully...drawing upon themselves their neighbors' diseases, and willingly taking over to their own persons the burden of the sufferings of those around them. (*Works of Dionysius, Epistle* 12.4)

Lack of humanitarian behavior on the part of the Romans regarding the sick, in contrast with Christian compassion, was lamented by the pagan emperor, Julian, who ruled from 361 to 363. The contrast is also noted by modern historians. "When epidemics broke out," says Howard Haggard, the Romans "often fled in fear and left the sick to die without care."[2] Haggard further notes that the Romans saw helping a sick person as a sign of human weakness; whereas Christians, in light of what Jesus taught about helping the sick, believed they were not only serving the sick but also serving God. Thus, Christianity filled the pagan void that largely ignored the sick and dying, especially during pestilences. In so doing, it "established the principle that to help the sick and needy is a sign of strength not weakness."[3] This Christ-motivated humanitarian behavior, so admirably displayed by his early followers, also introduced "the notion that because God loves humanity, Christians cannot please God unless they love one another." This, as Rodney Stark puts it, was revolutionary.[4]

The early Christians unequivocally rejected the callous, inhumane culture of the Greco-Roman world. They saw each person as having a redeemable soul, and therefore it was God-pleasing to nurture and nurse any and every person, regardless of his or her social status. Because eternal life awaited all those who believed and died in Christ, life on earth was not the ultimate value. Even if one died while caring for the sick, a greater and better life lay ahead; moreover, if a sick or dying person came to see and accept Christ's forgiveness, another soul was gained for eternal life. That kind of behavior was totally foreign to pagan thought.

Very few of the early Christians who, out of love, risked their lives as a result of tending to the contagiously sick and dying have had their names recorded in history. But one name that *is* known is Benignus of Dijon, a second-century Christian who was martyred in Epagny because he "nursed, supported, and protected a number of deformed and crippled children that had been saved from death after failed abortions and exposures."[5] Saving physically frail, unwanted children was an affront to the Romans. It violated their cultural norms. Recall the words of Seneca, the first-century Roman philosopher: "We drown children who at birth are weakly and abnormal" (*De Ira* 1.15).

HOSPITALS(?) IN ANTIQUITY

Given the pervading fear the pagans had about caring for the sick and dying, together with their low view of the poor and of manual laborers, it is not surprising that before Christian compassion for the sick and indigent was practiced, there were no established medical institutions (hospitals) for nursing and ministering to the general populace. Some might ask whether the pre-Christian shrines or temples of the mythical Greek healing god Aesculapius, of which there reportedly were more than three hundred, were hospitals.[6] Historians of antiquity commonly contend that these shrines were not hospitals but places where people spent "only a single night and that for religious reasons."[7] Others argue that the sick came to these Greek shrines (*Aesculapia*), not for medical treatment, but to have Aesculapius, the Greek healing god, appear to them in their dreams and thereby reveal "to them the particular treatment which they ought to follow."[8] Near the temples or shrines of Aesculapius were some buildings that housed those who came to receive their dream revelations, but as Gerhard Uhlhorn, an expert on ancient Christian charity, contends, these houses were "only hospices for shelter, and not hospitals for care and attendance."[9]

Others might wonder whether the Greek *iatreia* functioned as hospitals. Research indicates that the *iatreia* were places where sick people went to have their ailments diagnosed by physicians who prescribed medicine for them, but they provided no nursing provisions.[10] Still others, like Ralph Johnson in his relatively recent book, *Doctors and Diseases in the Roman Empire* (1988), think that the Roman *valetudinaria* were hospitals. However, these facilities, as various historians have shown, treated only sick slaves, gladiators, and sometimes ailing soldiers; whereas the sick common people, manual laborers, and the poor "had no place of refuge."[11] Although Johnson argues that the *valetudinaria* (from *valetudo* = state of health) were hospitals, he talks only about Romans soldiers being treated in these facilities.[12] He makes no mention of whether these facilities existed as charity institutions to treat civilians. Thus, whether *Aesculapia, iatreia,* or *valetudinaria,* none of these really functioned as hospitals did later in the Christian era, providing a place of rest and healing.[13] One scholar, Henry Burdett, states that King Asoka of India issued an edict in the third century B.C. to establish hospitals. While there is some evidence of the edict, there is no evidence that hospitals were ever built, and if built, whom they served. Burdett notes that by the time the British occupied India in the eighteenth century, hospitals "for the poor and sick had entirely disappeared."[14] In trying to minimize the argument that hospitals are a Christian innovation, Burdett points to a purported hospital of the pre-Christian era, namely, one that he says was founded by Princess Macha in Ireland. This apparently was a building where wounded soldiers were treated.[15] A few historians believe that the Roman emperor Hadrian (117–38) built a military hospital in Jerusalem in the second century. Similarly, Alan Marty thinks the Romans had some facilities that approximated hospitals and that these even served a civilian population. One such building, he says, was erected to honor Aesculapius on Tiber Island near Rome by Antonius (A.D. 150 to 190), a senator.[16] Given that the island on the Tiber was a refuge for the sick and poor, it is thought that the building probably functioned as a hospital. In response to this argument, Smout admits there is a modicum of truth to the belief that the Greeks and Romans had some form of hospital before the Christians introduced them, but he asserts that the *Aesculapia* or *valetudinaria* were not places where the sick of the general public were housed and cared for out of charity.[17] They were at best only places for treating soldiers. Charity hospitals for the poor and indigent public did not exist until Christianity introduced them.[18] Moreover, it needs to be underscored that even if the Greco-Romans had some kind of hospitals that preceded Christian hospitals, none of them ever became institutionalized.

THE FIRST CHRISTIAN HOSPITALS

During the first three centuries of Christianity's existence, when its members were subjected to frequent and severe persecutions, the most that Christians could do was to care for the sick where they found them, in many instances by taking them into their own homes. But after the Edict of Milan in 313, and especially after Constantine defeated his coemperor Licinius in the East in 324, Christians were able to direct more attention and energy toward providing care for the sick and dying. Hence, the first ecumenical council of the Christian church at Nicaea in 325 directed bishops to establish a hospice in every city that had a cathedral.[19] Many of the early Christian hospitals or hospices were not what people understand by hospitals today. Although their most important function was to nurse and heal the sick, they also provided shelter for the poor and lodging for Christian pilgrims. These hospitals, known as *xenodochia*[20] (*xenos* = stranger + *dechesthai* = to receive) were prompted by Christ's command to care for the physically sick and by the early apostolic admonition that Christians be hospitable to strangers and travelers. With regard to the latter, the Apostle Peter told the recipients of his Epistle, "Offer hospitality to one another without grumbling" (1 Peter 4:9). Similarly, Paul told the bishops (overseers) that they were to be given to hospitality (1 Timothy 3:2 and Titus 1:8). These admonitions meant

"SCRIPTURE READER IN A NIGHT REFUGE" is a scene from the nineteenth century that recalls the charitable Christian institutions of *ptochia* and *xenodochia* that arose in the church some 1,500 years earlier. *(Gustave Doré)*

more than just being pleasant, but rather that Christians were expected to take strangers and itinerants into their homes as well as to care for and nurse the sick and the dying.

The first hospital was built by St. Basil in Caesarea in Cappadocia about A.D. 369. It was one of "a large number of buildings, with houses for physicians and nurses, workshops, and industrial schools."[21] Some historians believe that this hospital was not a *xenodochium*, but rather a *nosocomium* (*nosus* = disease + *komeo* = take care of) that ministered exclusively to the sick.[22] The rehabilitation unit and workshops gave those with no occupational skills opportunity to learn a trade while recuperating.[23] These units reveal additional humanitarian awareness, and it would be difficult to argue that this awareness had nothing to do with the spirit of Christ alive in St. Basil, the good bishop of Caesarea.

After St. Basil's hospital was built in the East and another in Edessa in 375, Fabiola, a wealthy widow and an associate of St. Jerome, built the first hospital in the West, a *nosocomium*, in the city of Rome in about 390. According to Jerome, Fabiola donated all of her wealth (which was considerable) to construct this hospital, to which she brought the sick from off the streets in Rome (*Letter to Oceanus* 5). In 398, Fabiola, together with Pammachius, founded another hospital in Ostia, about fifty miles south-west of Rome.[24] Although the *nosocomium* differed from the *xenodochium*, essentially all the hospitals were called *xenodochia* until the twelfth century, when "hospitale" became the common term.

The building of Christian hospitals continued. St. Chrysostom (d. 407), the patriarch of the Eastern church, had hospitals built in Constantinople in the late fourth and early fifth centuries, and St. Augustine (354–430), bishop of Hippo in northern Africa, was instrumental in adding hospitals in the West. By the sixth century, hospitals also had become a common part of monasteries.[25] Hence, by the middle of the sixth century in most of Christendom, in the East and the West, "hospitals were securely established."[26] Also in the sixth century, hospitals received an additional boost when the Council of Orleans (France) passed canons assuring their protection, and in the last quarter of this same century, Pope Gregory the Great did much to advance the importance of hospitals.[27]

It is important to note—and the evidence is quite decisive—that these Christian hospitals were the world's first voluntary charitable institutions. There is "no certain evidence," says one scholar, "of any medical institution supported by voluntary contributions...till we come to Christian days."[28] And it is these Christian hospitals that revolutionized the treatment of the poor, the sick, and the dying.

By 750 the growth of Christian hospitals, either as separate units or attached to monasteries, had spread from Continental Europe to England. About this time the city of Milan in Italy established a hospital that specialized in caring for foundlings.[29] During his reign in the eighth century, Charlemagne, emperor of the Holy Roman Empire and a strong defender of the sick and poor, constructed numerous hospitals. And by the mid–1500s there were 37,000 Benedictine monasteries that cared for the sick.[30]

Nearly four hundred years after the Christians began erecting hospitals, the practice drew the attention of the Arabs in the eighth century. Impressed with the humanitarian work of Christian hospitals, the Arab Muslims began constructing hospitals in Arab countries. Thus, Christ's influence, which moved his followers to build and operate hospitals, spilled over into the Arab-Islamic world, demonstrating once more that Christianity was a major catalyst in changing the world, even beyond the boundaries of the West. In this instance, it changed a world in which the sick were once largely left to fend for themselves, to one in which they were

Domus Sancti Spiritus (House of the Holy Spirit) was an example of small hospitals once common in Germany and other parts of Europe during the late Middle Ages. The building is now a restaurant in Nuremberg.

now given humanitarian medical care, a practice not known previously. Christ's parable of the Good Samaritan had become more than merely an interesting story.

Although the Crusaders have received an abundance of harsh and judgmental criticisms, some of them well deserved, not everything that they did during the two hundred years of the Crusades was a violation of Christian principles. One of their nobler acts was the construction of hospitals in Palestine and other Middle Eastern areas. Howard Haggard, who is sometimes quite critical of Christian acts in the context of medicine, nevertheless notes that hospitals received a big momentum during the Crusades.[31]

The Crusaders also founded healthcare orders, providing health care to all, Christians and Muslims alike.[32] The Order of Hospitallers recruited women for nursing the sick.[33] The Hospitallers of St. Lazarus, founded in the East in the twelfth century, devoted themselves primarily to nursing. This order spread to Europe, where it founded many more hospitals and treated people with various diseases.[34] The Knights of the Order of Hospitallers of Saint John of Jerusalem (Knights of Malta) not only operated and maintained hospitals, but also admitted the insane. They founded a Christian insane asylum in 1409 in Valencia, Spain.[35]

By the thirteenth century most hospitals in Europe were under the direction of Christian bishops, who often came from wealthy homes and who frequently used their financial resources to aid and assist hospitals. Many hospitals also cared for the poor and orphans and, on occasion, fed prisoners. Some provided medical training to monks who sometimes became competent physicians.[36]

Hospitals had become quite plentiful by the fourteenth century in Europe. For instance, England alone, with less than four million people, had six hundred hospitals; France, Germany, and Italy each had even more.[37] The British often referred to a hospital as "God's House."[38] The fourteenth century also saw the origin of the *Domus Sancti Spiritus* (House of the Holy Spirit), a small hospital located in many German towns. Vestiges of these hospitals can still be seen in a number of German cities today. Most of them have now been converted to other uses; for instance, the one in Nuremberg, Germany, is now a fashionable restaurant.

Although the average hospital today is no longer a charity institution, the precedent that the early Christian hospitals set not only alleviated human suffering but also extended the lives of multitudes of people, whether rich or poor. Moreover, these institutions reflected Christ's love for mankind. Today this innovative humanitarian contribution—the hospital—is unanimously appreciated throughout the world.

HOSPITALS IN THE NEW WORLD

With Columbus's discovery of America, the Christian concern for the sick and dying soon showed itself in the New World. Thus, in 1524 Hernando Cortes, the Conquistador, founded Jesus of Nazareth Hospital in Mexico City, which is still operative today.[39] A few years later, in 1541, Zumarraga established a hospital that cared for the poor who were afflicted with venereal diseases. Soon a hospital was built for Indians.[40] And by 1583 every principal town in the archdiocese of Mexico had a hospital, each with a priest who cared for the souls of the patients.[41]

While there already were numerous hospitals on the Continent and in England during the late Middle Ages and following, for some reason they did not spread very quickly to British Colonial America. Even after the American Colonies had gained their independence, the growth of hospitals in America was minimal during the first decade of the new nation. One study indicates that at the time of President Thomas Jefferson's inauguration in 1801 there were only two hospitals in the United States. One was located in Philadelphia, the other in New York.[42] The former was founded by the Quakers in the first half of the 1700s.

In the nineteenth century hospitals in the United States became more common, especially after the Civil War. As the growth of hospitals spread across the nation, it was predominantly local churches and Christian denominations that built them. This was evidenced by many of the hospitals' names. Most reflected their affiliation with a given Christian denomination or honored a Christian saint; hence, names such as Baptist Hospital, Lutheran Hospital, Methodist Hospital, and Presbyterian Hospital abound. Others were called St. John's, St. Luke's, St. Mary's, St. Joseph's, and so forth.

The Christian identity and background of many American hospitals is now being erased, however. In recent years, as health maintenance organizations (HMOs) have been purchasing more and more private Christian hospitals, their Christian names are being replaced. Thus, people, at least in America, will soon have no more symbolic reminders that the hospital(s) in their town or city had Christian origins.

MENTAL INSTITUTIONS

Compared with the service that the early Christians rendered to the physically sick and dying, we know much less about the treatment that the mentally disturbed received. This is true even though bishops and monks of the early Christian church "took charge of lunatics at a very early period, and gathered them together in houses specially assigned for that purpose."[43] Thus, even before hospitals came into being for the physically ill and dying in the second half of the fourth century, a mental asylum (*morotrophium*, that is, *moron* = fool + *trophos* = nourisher) was founded as early as A.D. 321.

During the early Middle Ages, the mentally disturbed were primarily cared for in the monasteries. But in the later Middle Ages, the earlier humane treatment of the mentally ill was slowly abandoned. However, it is known that in 1369 in London a hospital was founded "for poor priests and others, men and women, who in that city suddenly fell into a frenzy."[44] It is also known that in the early 1400s a well-known refuge for the mentally disordered existed in London. What kind of treatments were employed is not known.

The church, composed of sinners who often forgot that they professed to be Christians, did not always replicate the noble examples of its early predecessors. Commonly, the mentally disturbed were incarcerated in damp, filthy, dungeonlike asylums, where they were shackled because they were thought to be less than human. It was believed that they could be

DOROTHEA LYNDE DIX (1802–87) was an American who devoted her life's energies to making institutional care for people with mental problems more humane. *(Photograph by George M. Cushing, Boston)*

brought back to reason and sanity by physical punishment and chained confinement. Often they were treated like wild animals.

It was these inhuman practices that stunned Phillipe Pinel (1745–1826), a frail, timid French physician and onetime divinity student. Believing that the mentally disturbed were sick rather than criminal, he entered the asylum at Bicetre, France, defied the authorities, and cut loose the chains of some of the inmates, an act thought to be insane. He not only cut their chains, but also showed the inmates love and kindness. The response was amazingly civil and restrained.[45] As a Christian, Pinel showed compassion reminiscent of Jesus' acts toward the sick and ailing. The Frenchman's unusual behavior produced a real paradigm shift with respect to treating the mentally disturbed. His actions once again show the powerful impact that Christ, through his followers, has had upon the world.

Quite some time before Pinel, in 1709, the Association of Friends (Quakers) in the United States, erected a general hospital in Philadelphia that housed "lunaticks."[46] This was one of the two hospitals in the United

States, mentioned earlier. This Philadelphia hospital prospered, and in 1841 the Quakers opened a separate building just for the insane.[47] The next noteworthy development in treating the mentally disturbed in the United States came with Dorothea Dix (1802–87). An avowed Christian who had daily morning devotions, Dix authored *Meditations for Private Hours* in 1828 and later wrote to John Greenleaf Whittier (the poet), saying that he had given her a "deeper conviction of the truths of the gospel of our Lord and Savior Jesus Christ."[48] During the Civil War she went from one battlefield to another, directing nurses and assisting wounded and dying soldiers.

Motivated by the spirit of Christ, she traveled to many states in her efforts to obtain better care for the mentally disturbed. Like Pinel, she was appalled by the inhumane treatment the insane received. In one of her many appearances before state assemblies, she chided the Massachusetts State Legislature, which was reluctant to honor her requests for providing better facilities and care for the insane. Fearing rejection, she declared, "I dishonor you, divest you at once of Christianity."[49] She also traveled to England and Scotland, promoting the same goals abroad as at home. In addition to her focus on mental asylums, she also tried to get authorities to improve prisons and poorhouses. But her most persistent and successful efforts, in spite of being resented by many physicians and ignored by many intellectuals, were in improving conditions and treatment for the insane in many American states.

The name Dorothea Dix became synonymous with enlightened care for persons with mental disorders for much of the nineteenth century. She elevated the care of mental health to levels previously unknown in the United States. She was the Pinel of America. By leaving her Christian imprint in the field of mental health, she was a little Christ.

MEDICAL NURSING: A CHRISTIAN INNOVATION

Given the absence of hospitals in ancient Greece and Rome, and the cultural belief that the sick and dying, especially those who were slaves and laborers, were not worthy of humanitarian help, there was obviously no perceived need for medical nurses. As already noted, the Greeks and Romans had their *iatreia* to which patients who were not slaves or artisans came to be diagnosed, but they had no beds and no nurses.[50]

When Christians introduced hospitals, it was of course necessary that the sick be nursed. But little is known about those who performed the nursing role. Most of the evidence, although it is sparse, indicates that widows, deaconesses, and virgins commonly served as nurses in the early Christian hospitals. Paula (347–404), a female associate of St. Jerome, was essentially a nurse. So was Fabiola, a widow and another associate of Jerome's who served as a nurse in the hospital that she helped found in Rome in 390.

In the Middle Ages monks and nuns did much of the nursing, as was true at the monastery of Monte Cassino, Italy, founded in 528 by St. Benedict to care for the sick.[51] Its healthcare providers were called "infirmarians," a term that had already been used of hospital attendants in St. Basil's hospital in Caesarea.[52] In the twelfth century the Knights Hospitalers of St. John, a military order of the Crusaders, recruited women to serve as nurses in caring for leprosy patients in Jerusalem. Then in the thirteenth century, the order of Augustinian Nuns arose. This group is the oldest nursing order of sisters.[53]

The next significant change in nursing came with the efforts of Theodor Fliedner, a Lutheran pastor in Kaiserswerth, Germany. Fliedner's work of mercy first began by caring for one destitute prisoner, who was housed in the pastor's summer house in his backyard in 1833. The Christian spirit moved him to pen a hymn. One of its stanzas read:

> *Blessed fount of heavenly gladness*
> *Jesus, Thine are all our powers,*
> *Thee in sickness, want, and sadness*
> *To behold and serve is ours.*

Fliedner's work soon evolved into a hospital of one hundred beds. He also founded a Lutheran deaconesses order, composed primarily of peasant women, whom he trained as nurses. His hospital and nurses became known throughout Europe, attracting the attention of young Florence Nightingale, who desired to dedicate her life to nursing. She went to Kaiserswerth to observe its health care practices. The Christian spirit of Fliedner and the deaconesses greatly impressed her. Upon returning home to England, where her well-to-do parents expressed their disgust with her visit to Kaiserswerth and her nursing desires, she reported feeling "so brave as if nothing could vex me again."[54]

In 1854 Nightingale went to Crimea, on the shores of the Black Sea. Here she nursed British soldiers wounded in the Crimean War. Sometimes she spent twenty-four hours on her feet or eight hours a day on her knees dressing wounds. She comforted, consoled, and wrote letters for many; often she wrote mothers that their sons died holding her hand.[55] Like the early Christians who nursed the sick and dying without thought or fear for

ORIGIN AND DEVELOPMENT OF HOSPITALS

Greco-Roman Health Care Units Before Christ to Mid-4th Century A.D.	Health Care Rendered
Aesculapia shrines	Only prescribed treatment; no nursing provisions
Iatreia	Diagnosed ailments only; no nursing provisions
Valetudinaria	Apparently treated and housed soldiers; no civilians admitted

Christian Health Care Units From Mid-4th to 20th Century	Health Care Rendered
Morotrophia, built in A.D. 321	Housed mentally disturbed
Nosocomia, first built in 369 by St. Basil, built in 375, 390, 398, etc.	Housed and nursed the sick exclusively
Xenodochia, late 4th cent.	Housed strangers and also nursed the sick
Monastery at Monte Cassino, founded in 529	Cared for the sick; many monasteries followed suit; many also cared for mentally disturbed
Hospital in Milan, founded by Dateo, a priest, 8th cent.	Cared for foundlings only
Hospitals of Military Religious Orders: Knights Hospitaler of St. John, Teutonic Knights, Hospitalers of St. Lazarus, 12th cent.	Treated and cared for the wounded during the Crusades
Hospitalers of St. Lazarus, 12th cent.	Nursed lepers
Domus Sancti Spiritus, mostly in Germany, 14th cent.	Small hospitals; treated, housed, and nursed civilians; some housed mentally disturbed
Mental asylums, London, 15th cent.	Housed and nursed the mentally disturbed
Jesus of Nazareth Hospital, Mexico City, 1524	Nursed mostly Meso-American Indians
Many general and mental hospitals, combined from 17th–19th cent.	Nursed the physically ill and mentally disturbed
Units for mentally disturbed reformed and separated from general hospitals, late 19th and during 20th cent. by Pinel in France and Dix in America	Freed mental patients from chains and provided psychological care
20th cent., large growth in general hospitals, most named in honor of Christian saints, leaders, denominations	Increasingly provided specialized medical care

their own welfare, she exposed herself to deadly contagious diseases as she reflected the compassion of Jesus Christ.

"The Star of the East," as Nightingale was often called, returned to England after the war as a national heroine. Indeed, who has not heard of her! At home she devoted the remaining fifty years of her life to promoting hospital reform in administration and in nursing. In 1860 she founded a school of nursing at St. Thomas Hospital in London.[56] This humble, compassionate woman, who was propelled by her love for Christ to help the sick and dying, lifted the art of nursing to a level of dignity, honor, and medical expertise not previously known. Today there are thousands of nursing schools indebted to her principles. She accomplished what she did because she never doubted her own words: "The kingdom of heaven is within, but we must also make it so without."[57]

Before she departed this earthly life, she made a simple Christian request in her will. She asked that a plain cross be placed on her grave that would bear only her initials, not her name. Like so many Christian saints that preceded her, she willingly served without acclaim as Christ's instrument in a world that needed his love and his compassionate words put into practice. She nobly filled both of these roles as a medical nurse. And because of her efforts, nursing became an honorable profession both within and outside of the context of Christian hospitals.

THE RED CROSS

While Florence Nightingale worked to improve hospitals and hone the skills of nursing, another Christ-minded person labored to spread humanitarian aid to unfortunate victims. He was Jean Henri Dunant (1828–1910), the son of a wealthy Geneva banking family.

In 1859 Dunant witnessed the suffering of wounded soldiers at the Battle of Solferino in Italy's struggle for unification. "Never shall I be able to forget," said he, "the eyes of these victims who wished to kiss my hand."[58] Five years later (1864), he and four associates, together with twenty-four delegates from sixteen nations, formed the International Red Cross.[59]

Although Dunant was at times very critical of the organized church, he did not allow his criticisms to mitigate his desire to heed Christ's words in regard to caring for the sick and ailing. Nor did he let personal setbacks derail him, for life was not always kind to him. He lost his banking fortune, was expelled from his country, lost his good name, and lived as a virtual vagrant for many years in Paris. But God did not forsake him. A decade or so before he died, his native country Switzerland allowed him to return with honor and dignity, and in 1901 he received the first Nobel Peace Prize ever bestowed. What seemed to matter most to him was his faith in Jesus Christ. This is apparent from the words he spoke on his deathbed: "I am a disciple of Christ as in the first century, and nothing more."[60]

Dunant's Christian beliefs moved him to establish an organization that would console and bind up the wounds of battle-scarred soldiers. His faith apparently also led him to choose the Christian cross, the symbol of Christ's suffering and redemption, as the new organization's emblem. This symbol, a cross painted red, is recognized today by Christians and non-Christians alike as a symbol of mercy and love on or off the battlefield. "The significance of the symbol chosen (although it is essentially the Swiss flag in reverse)," say Kennedy and Newcombe, "should not be lost by anyone."[61] In 1876 the Muslim country of Turkey adopted the humanitarian idea of the Red Cross, and as it did, it changed the Christian symbol to the Red Crescent. Thus, the Red Crescent not only is the outgrowth of the Red Cross, but also indicates that "the Muslims inadvertently recognized the driving force behind one of the greatest humanitarian movements in history—Jesus Christ."[62]

In the United States, Clara Barton is often credited as one of the founders of the American Red Cross. Barton valiantly nursed soldiers in the American Civil War. She was known to say, "Follow the cannon." She risked her life on many occasions. At the Battle of Antietam a soldier was killed in her arms. In keeping with her Christian compassion, she visited prisoners from the Union Army at the notorious Confederate prison at Andersonville.[63] Although Barton is often credited as a key figure in having brought the Red Cross to America, it was not until six years after the Civil War (1871) that the organization was officially founded.

The humanitarian works and achievements of Dunant and Barton stand as ideal examples of what Christ meant when he said, "As you did it to one of the least of these My brethren, you did it to Me" (Matthew 25:40 NKJV). "Were it not for Christianity, there would be no Red Cross, nor for that matter, a Red Crescent."[64]

CONCLUSION

The physician and medical historian Fielding Garrison once remarked, "The chief glory of medieval medicine was undoubtedly in the organization of hospitals and sick nursing, which had its organization in the teachings of Christ."[65] Thus, whether it was establishing hospitals, creating mental institutions, professionalizing medical nursing, or founding the Red Cross, the teachings of Christ lie behind all of these humanitarian achievements.

It is an astonishing mystery that the Greeks, who built large temples in honor of their numerous gods and goddesses, fashioned statues of all sorts, and wrote a wide variety of illuminating literature, never built any hospitals. It is further astonishing when one remembers that while they had some *iatreia* that served as medical facilities to diagnose people's physical ailments, these units did not function as hospitals where the sick could be treated and get rest and recuperate. The situation was similar with the Romans, who were also great builders of temples, large arenas, impressive aqueducts, and the highly advanced Appian Way. While some historians, with extremely weak evidence, believe the Romans did have some type of hospitals for its soldiers, they, like the Greeks, did not have any hospitals for the general populace.

Perhaps the astonishment loses much of its mysteriousness when one recalls some of the observations made earlier in this chapter that showed the Greco-Romans really had no concept of charity and compassion, which are necessary values preceding the arrival of hospitals. While modern readers may find the ancient state of medical affairs almost incredible, it was nevertheless true. Thus, the American church historian Philip Schaff summed it up well when he said, "The old Roman world was a world without charity."[66]

NOTES

1. V. G. Dawe, "The Attitude of the Ancient Church Toward Sickness and Healing" (Th.D. thesis, Boston University School of Theology, 1955), 3.
2. Howard W. Haggard, *The Doctor in History* (New Haven: Yale University Press, 1934), 108.
3. Ibid., 137.
4. Rodney Stark, *The Rise of Early Christianity: A Sociologist Considers History* (Princeton: Princeton University Press, 1996), 86.
5. George Grant, *Third Time Around: A History of the Pro-Life Movement from the First Century to the Present* (Brentwood, Tenn.: Wolgemuth and Hyatt, 1991), 27.
6. A. C. Merriam, "The Treatment of Patients in the Temple of Aesculapius," *Boston Medical and Surgical Journal,* 26 March 1885, 305.
7. Haggard, *Doctor in History,* 78.
8. George E. Gask and John Todd, "The Origin of Hospitals," in *Science, Medicine, and History,* ed. E. Ashworth Underwood (New York: Arno Press, 1975), 122.
9. Gerhard Uhlhorn, *Christian Charity in the Ancient Church* (New York: Charles Scribner's Sons, 1883), 323.
10. David Riesman, *The Story of Medicine in the Middle Ages* (New York: Harper and Brothers, 1936), 355.
11. John Jefferson Davis, *Your Wealth in God's Word* (Phillipsburg, N.J.: Presbyterian and Reformed Publishing, 1984), 65.
12. Ralph Johnson, *Doctors and Diseases in the Roman Empire* (London: British Museum Press, 1988), 133–37.
13. Gask and Todd, "Origin of Hospitals," 123.
14. Henry C. Burdett, *Hospitals and Asylums of the World* (London: J. and A. Churchill, 1893), 3:8.

15. Ibid., 12.

16. Alan T. Marty, "The Pagan Roots of Western Hospitals," *Surgery, Gynecology, and Obstetrics* (December 1971): 1020.

17. C. F. V. Smout, *The Story of the Progress of Medicine* (Bristol: John Wright and Sons, 1964), 36.

18. Haggard, *Doctor in History*, 19.

19. Nathaniel W. Faxon, *The Hospital in Contemporary Life* (Cambridge: Harvard University Press, 1949), 7.

20. Roberto Margotta, *The Story of Medicine: Man's Struggle Against Disease—From Ancient Sorcery to Modern Miracles of Vaccines, Drugs, and Surgery* (New York: Golden Press, 1968), 102.

21. Fielding H. Garrison, *An Introduction to the History of Medicine* (Philadelphia: W. B. Saunders, 1914), 118.

22. Grant, *Third Time Around*, 19.

23. Gask and Todd, "Origin of Hospitals," 127.

24. Ibid., 129.

25. Riesman, *Story of Medicine in the Middle Ages*, 356.

26. Gask and Todd, "Origin of Hospitals," 130.

27. Ibid.

28. Garrison, *Introduction to the History of Medicine*, 118.

29. E. Nasalli-Rocca, "Hospitals, History of," *New Catholic Encyclopedia* (New York: McGraw-Hill, 1967), 3:160.

30. Smout, *Story of the Progress of Medicine*, 40.

31. Haggard, *Doctor in History*, 138.

32. Mary Risley, *House of Healing: The Story of the Hospital* (Garden City, N.Y.: Doubleday, 1961), 106.

33. Faxon, *Hospital in Contemporary Life*, 10.

34. Nasalli-Rocca, "Hospitals," 3:161.

35. W. E. H. Lecky, *History of European Morals* (New York: Vanguard Press, 1926), 81.

36. Kenneth Scott Latourette, *The Thousand Years of Uncertainty, A.D. 500–1500* (New York: Harper and Brothers, 1938), 364.

37. Ibid., 162.

38. Rotha Mary Clay, *The Medieval Hospitals of England* (London: Methuen, 1909), 32.

39. Margotta, *Story of Medicine*, 102.

40. Charles H. Lippy, Robert Choquette, and Stafford Poole, *Christianity Comes to the Americas, 1492–1776* (New York: Paragon House, 1992), 43.

41. Alexander C. Flick, *The Decline of the Medieval Church* (New York: Alfred A. Knopf, 1930), 303.

42. Charles E. Rosenberg, *The Care of Strangers: The Rise of America's Hospital System* (New York: Basic Books, 1987), 337.

43. Burdett, *Hospitals and Asylums*, 1:16.

44. Clay, *Medieval Hospitals of England*, 32.

45. Haggard, *Doctor in History*, 355–61.

46. Thomas G. Morton, *The History of the Pennsylvania Hospital* (New York: Arno Press, 1973), 4–5.

47. Ibid., 122.

48. Cited in Dorothy Clark Wilson, *Stranger and Traveler: The Story of Dorothea Dix* (Boston: Little, Brown, 1975), 337.

49. Cited in Morton, *History of the Pennsylvania Hospital*, 106.

50. Gask and Todd, "Origin of Hospitals," 122.

51. Smout, *Story of the Progress of Medicine*, 40.

52. C. M. Frank, "Nursing, History of," *New Catholic Encyclopedia* (San Francisco: McGraw-Hill, 1967), 10:581.

53. Ibid., 10:582.

54. Paul Chrastina, "Florence Nightingale Becomes a Nurse," *Old News* (1999): 12.

55. Cecil Wood-Smith, *Florence Nightingale, 1820–1910* (New York: McGraw-Hill, 1957), 143.

56. Rosenberg, *The Care of Strangers*, 264.

57. Cited in Rosenberg, *The Care of Strangers*, 124.

58. Cited in Martin Gumpert, *Dunant: The Story of the Red Cross* (New York: Oxford University Press, 1938), 63.

59. D. James Kennedy and Jerry Newcombe, *What If Jesus Had Never Been Born* (Nashville: Thomas Nelson, 1994), 152.
60. Cited in Gumpert, *Dunant*, 300.
61. Kennedy and Newcombe, *What If Jesus Had Never Been Born*, 152.
62. Ibid.
63. Gumpert, *Dunant*, 102–103.
64. Kennedy and Newcombe, *What If Jesus Had Never Been Born*, 152.
65. Garrison, *Introduction to the History of Medicine*, 118.
66. Philip Schaff, *History of the Christian Church* (New York: Charles Scribner's Sons, 1896), 2:373.

CHRISTIANITY'S IMPRINT
on EDUCATION

"The fear of the LORD is the beginning of knowledge."

Proverbs 1:7

F ew if any, would dispute the fact that Jesus was the greatest teacher the world has ever known. He employed words, parables, and human-life illustrations that stirred both friend and foe. When he spoke, "people were amazed at his teaching, because he taught them as one who had authority" (Mark 1:22). One observer has noted, "Had Christ left this world without making any provision for carrying on His work, He would still have been the greatest teacher of all time, and His life and example would have influenced profoundly the whole development of educational theory."[1]

Christ's teaching was not an end in itself. He taught so that those who followed him might teach others. Shortly before ascending to heaven, he told his disciples to "make disciples of all nations. . .teaching them to obey everything I have commanded you" (Matthew 28:19–20).

EARLY CHRISTIAN EDUCATION

The apostles took Jesus' command to teach others seriously, for beginning with Pentecost, Luke writes that "they never stopped teaching. . .that Jesus is the Christ" (Acts 5:42). Similarly, St. Paul in his epistles makes references to Christians teaching in Ephesus, Corinth, Rome, Thessalonica, and other places. Paul even told Timothy that one of the qualifications for being a bishop (spiritual overseer) was to be "able to teach" (1 Timothy 3:2).

The earliest Christians were primarily Jews who came from a long-standing tradition that valued formal education. Although this background was important, the early followers of Christ had a more compelling reason for their strong emphasis on teaching: it was a matter of heeding the Great Commission that Christ gave to his disciples and their successors (Matthew 28:19–20).

After the death of the apostles, the teaching continued. Thus, very early in the life of the church (A.D. 80–110), there appeared the *Didache*, which was essentially an instructional manual, primarily for new converts to Christianity. And in the first decade of the second century, Ignatius, a bishop of Antioch, urged that children be taught the Holy Scriptures and a skilled trade.[2] Learning a trade was a carryover from the Jews, who taught their sons a trade skill along with biblical and literary learning.

Obedient to Christ's command that the disciples and all Christians were to teach people "all things" that he commanded them, newcomers to the church were instructed as "catechumens"; that is, they were taught orally by the question-and-answer method in preparation for baptism and church membership. Both men and women were catechized, often over a period of two to three years. At first individuals were often instructed in the teacher's home.[3]

Catechetical instruction led to formal catechetical schools with a strong literary emphasis. Thus, by about A.D. 150, Justin Martyr, often called the first great scholar of the Christian church, established such catechetical schools, one in Ephesus and one in Rome. Soon these schools appeared in other regions. Some became well known. For example, the one in Alexandria, Egypt, was widely recognized for its literary qualities, where Athenagoras reportedly was its first head, though others believe it was Pantaenus. Clement (ca. 150–215), who later became bishop of Alexandria, succeeded Pantaenus. Clement's school developed an excellent reputation, which it retained for more than a century until the school at Caesarea in Palestine overshadowed it.

In most instances, catechetical schools soon provided the theological and literary foundation for future Christian leaders such as Origen (185–254), Athanasius (ca. 296–373), and others. Although the teaching of Christian doctrine was the primary focus of these schools, some, such as the school in Alexandria, also taught mathematics and medicine; and when Origen ("the prince of Christian learning") succeeded Clement at Alexandria, he added grammar classes to the curriculum.

The catechetical schools exerted a strong influence in Christian circles and also in Roman society at large. Their existence, says William Boyd, had far-reaching effects. Through them, "Christianity became for the first time a definite factor in the culture of the world."[4]

EDUCATION FOR BOTH SEXES

While Christians were not the first to engage in formal teaching activities in school-like settings, they appear to have been first to teach both sexes in the same setting. Given that Christianity from its beginning accepted both men and women into its fold and required that both learn the rudiments of the Christian faith, both men and women were catechized before being baptized and received into church membership. Furthermore, catechetical instruction commonly continued after baptism.

Instructing both men and women, as the early Christians did, was rather revolutionary. Although there is no unanimity among historians, many indicate that the Romans before the birth of Christ did not formally educate girls in literary skills. Their schools, says one educational historian, apparently only taught boys—and then only boys from the privileged class—in their *gymnasia*, while girls were excluded.[5] In light of this ancient practice, Tatian, once a student in one of Justin Martyr's catechetical schools, proclaimed that Christians taught everybody, including girls and women.[6]

Formally educating both sexes was also largely a Christian innovation. W. M. Ramsay states that Christianity's aim was "universal education, not education confined to the rich, as among the Greeks and Romans...and it [made] no distinction of sex."[7] This practice produced results, for by the early fifth century St. Augustine said that Christian women were often better informed in divine matters than the pagan male philosophers.

It is difficult to say much with certainty regarding the details of the early Christian education, especially with regard to children. Sometimes it appears that there was very little literary education outside of catechizing adults for church membership. One finds St. Chrysostom early in the fifth century writing about children attending school, but he gives no details.[8] We know more about Christians educating children (boys and girls) when we look at the cathedral and episcopal schools that existed from the fourth to the tenth century. Maintained by bishops, these schools taught not only Christian doctrine but commonly also the seven liberal arts, the *trivium* (grammar, rhetoric, and logic) and *quadrivium* (arithmetic, music, geometry, and astronomy). Although the episcopal schools (usually taught by bishops) primarily existed to train priests, they also enrolled others. Children

JUSTIN MARTYR (martyred in 166) was an early Christian philosopher who defended Christianity among the pagan Romans and who once operated a catechetical school.

of royalty and the higher social ranks often attended the cathedral schools, whose teachers were scholastics *(scholasticii)*, appointed by the bishop. Still other children were instructed in monasteries or nunneries, where girls predominated. Children who attended either the episcopal or monastic schools were encouraged to enter church vocations, but there was no formal requirement for them to do so. Many entered secular vocations.[9] By the ninth century, Christians also had parochial (parish) schools separate from the cathedral or monastery. These schools primarily taught doctrine; reading and writing were not ordinarily offered.[10]

Given that the early church from the very beginning catechized both sexes in preparation for membership and later provided more extensive education in its catechetical and episcopal schools, it might be asked whether both sexes were equally represented. In preparing individuals for church membership, men were not favored over women because the church never discriminated against women in terms of admitting them to baptism and membership. In fact, since more women than men were attracted to the early church as converts (noted in chapter 4), more women were catechized for

"KING ALFRED VISITING A MONASTERY SCHOOL," a scene from the ninth century, reflects the interest that Christianity instilled in leaders for education, much of which occurred in monastery schools of the Middle Ages. *(Etching from an anonymous print)*

baptism and membership than men. However, in the episcopal/cathedral schools, boys definitely outnumbered girls. Girls received their education mostly in the arts and letters in convents or nunneries, but even in these schools girls were underrepresented.

Although the church in all of its schools never taught boys only, it nevertheless paid more attention to boys than girls. Herein lies a good deal of irony, for from its very beginning, Christianity defied many ancient cultural practices of the Greco-Romans. One such defiance was its openness to receiving women; yet by having fewer girls than boys attend its schools, it had not overcome all of the ancient cultural biases that favored boys and men. Even in the nunneries there were comparatively fewer girls than boys in school. While the church baptized and received girls and women into membership without any discrimination, it apparently did not see education, outside of learning the basics of the Christian faith, so important for females. On occasion, however, some churchmen would draw attention to the imbalance of the sexes in education, as did Leonardo Bruni and Battista

Guarinao the Younger in the Renaissance era of the fifteenth century. Both men wanted more girls in the church's schools.[11]

In the 1330s an interesting report from a chronicler in Florence notes that his city had between eight and ten thousand children in school, and he specifically mentions girls along with boys as attending the city's grammar schools.[12] These girls likely were mostly from families in higher social positions. For instance, it is well known that Charlemagne (eighth century), the great advocate of education (who himself could read but not write), had his sons and daughters attend school. His palace school, run by Alcuin, who was imported from England, had girls other than the king's daughters in attendance. Similarly, a hundred years later, King Alfred of England had both his sons and daughters learn Latin and other subjects in school.[13]

While the sex ratio in education was decidedly tilted in favor of boys, some prominent and well-educated women nevertheless appeared throughout the Middle Ages. Here are but a few: Lioba (ca. 700–782) was a comissionary worker of St. Boniface (eighth century). Hrotsvitha of Gandersheim (932–1002) was a canoness and was well versed in the Latin classics and wrote plays, poems, legends, and epics. Hildegard of Bingen (1098–1179) founded her own monastery, wrote a mass, and corresponded with popes, emperors, and bishops. Brigitta of Sweden (1303–73) opposed high taxes and founded a religious order. Catherine of Siena (1347?–89), one of the most famous women in the medieval church, labored for peace and wrote letters of counsel to men in authority. Christine de Pizan (fourteenth century) authored a number of books. And as is well known, Spain's Queen Isabella (1451–1504) underwrote Columbus's trip to America.

Girls who received their education in the nunneries were usually schooled in the liberal arts. Some of these girls, who remained in the cloistered environment and became nuns, were as competent as the men (monks) in literary matters, for example, in the work they did in the *Scriptoria* of the monasteries. Here, along with the men, they transcribed copies of biblical manuscripts in Greek and Latin, and sometimes they also made copies of the ancient classics.[14]

In teaching both sexes, Christians took their cue from Jesus, who never had a problem teaching women along with men. Whether he taught publicly in his Sermon on the Mount or instructed Mary and Martha in their home, he taught men and women alike. Thus, even though the church often failed to practice coeducation consistently, it never totally neglected it. This is important to remember, for had the church reverted to the

Greco-Roman practice of excluding girls and women from the formal education process, it is unlikely that the practice of coeducation that is so widely accepted and practiced on all levels in Western societies and in many other regions of the world would be what it is today. Hence, coeducation appears to be another product of Jesus Christ's wholesome influence.

BEYOND CLASS AND ETHNICITY: UNIVERSAL EDUCATION

The historian Will Durant described early Christianity as offering itself "without reservation to all individuals, classes, and nations; it was not limited to one people, like Judaism, nor to the freedmen of one state, like the official cults of Greece and Rome."[15] This openness, of course, existed not just relative to those whom the church sought as members, but also in its educational activities. Unlike the Greek and Roman practice of teaching only boys from the privileged segment of society, Christians taught individuals from all social classes and ethnic backgrounds, especially in preparation for church membership. There was no ethnic or class bias. In fact, for the longest time, the poor and lower classes made up the majority of the church's members,[16] although there were always some who came from the upper echelon as well. The *Acts of Peter* (second century), for instance, lists some Roman senators, equestrians, and women of high social standing as members who reportedly belonged to the Apostle Peter's congregation.

The most significant move in the direction of universal education occurred with the Protestant Reformation in the sixteenth century. The early church catechized individuals from all social classes and ethnic backgrounds in preparation for membership. But this practice had greatly deteriorated by the time Luther hammered his Ninety-five Theses to the door of the Castle Church on the campus of Wittenberg University in 1517. In the fall of 1528 when he visited the churches of Saxony, to his dismay he found widespread ignorance. In order to improve this deplorable condition, he wrote his *Small Catechism* in 1529. In his catechism's preface, he notes that he found that common people had little or no knowledge of Christian teachings and that many pastors were incompetent to teach. Countless members of the church did not even know the Lord's Prayer, the Creed, or the Ten Commandments. He faulted the bishops and asked how they would someday answer for this lamentable state before Christ.[17]

Luther's concern for education did not stop with his writing the *Small Catechism*. He was not an esoteric theologian. Mark Noll notes that to Luther cultivating the human mind was absolutely essential "because people needed to understand both the word of Scripture and the nature of the world in which the word would take root."[18] He urged a state school system "to include vernacular primary schools for both sexes, Latin secondary schools, and universities."[19] He once said that parents who failed to teach their children were "shameful and despicable" and that he would write a book against such parents.[20]

Even though Luther sometimes mentioned only boys when he talked about teaching the youth, there were times when he specifically included girls in his discussion. For instance, he wanted mendicant houses "converted into good schools for boys and girls."[21] On another occasion, when he urged parents to send and keep their children in school, he also mentioned girls.[22] William Boyd is right when he notes that "Luther, in fact, wanted a system of education as free and unrestricted as the Gospel he preached [and] indifferent, like the Gospel, to distinctions of sex or of social class."[23] And although he never denied that one of the purposes of education was to train pastors for the church, he also wanted children to be educated as God-fearing and law-abiding lay citizens who would serve God and society in all stations of life. Schools, to him, were to train and prepare more than just clergy. He criticized the popes of the late Middle Ages for having done just that.

John Calvin, another leader in the Protestant Reformation, also advocated universal education. His Geneva plan included "a system of elementary education in the vernacular for all, including reading, writing, arithmetic, grammar, and religion, and the establishment of secondary schools for the purpose of training citizens for civil and ecclesiastical leadership."[24]

The examples of Luther and Calvin show that the desire to educate everyone is not the product of the modern secular world, but rather a concept that is the logical outgrowth of two of Christianity's biblical tenets, namely, that God is no respecter of persons (Acts 10:34) and that every individual is responsible for his or her own salvation (John 3:16). The latter teaching especially, says Gabriel Compayre, logically led to the conclusion that everyone needed to be educated.[25]

TAX-SUPPORTED PUBLIC SCHOOLS

Public schools are a common, widespread phenomenon today. As best as can be determined, this concept first came from the mind of Martin Luther. Before this time, education, especially on the elementary level, was supported and operated by the church in cathedral/episcopal schools along

CATHERINE OF SIENA (14th cent.) in her brief life of thirty-three years wrote Christian materials and spent much of her time caring for the sick and evangelizing prisoners. She has been declared a "doctor of the church."

with monasteries and nunneries. Luther had lost faith in those schools, and with good reason. Most people were illiterate, and he knew that most boys and girls really received no education when they stayed home. Most parents evidently were incapable of teaching, and others lacked interest. Lack of education, he believed, would eventually spell doom for the church and society. If the civic authorities could spend money on military arms, bridges, roads, dams, and so forth, then why could they not also spend money to educate the youth? In short, the country needed public schools, supported by funding from the public treasury.[26]

Philipp Melanchthon (1497–1560), Luther's principal co-worker, often called "the preceptor of Germany," helped further Luther's educational desires when he successfully persuaded the civic authorities to implement the first public school system in Germany.[27] The organization of these schools was largely the accomplishment of Johannes Bugenhagen, pastor of St. Mary's Church, where Luther attended and often preached. For his efforts, Bugenhagen has been called the father of the *deutsche Volkschule* (German public school).[28]

Fifty years after Melanchthon, John Comenius (1592–1670), a bishop of the Moravian Brethren, echoed Luther's idea of education for all children, especially for the poor, since the wealthy had the means to educate their children. He opened a school at Fulneck in Moravia. Here, as he had formally proposed to the Kingdom of Bohemia, he taught children about God, man, and nature. So convinced was he that children from all social classes should be educated, that failing to do so, he felt, was flouting God's purpose. He concluded his proposal to Bohemia with the words, "Have mercy, O Lord, on your heritage."[29]

Thus, the desire to have public tax-supported schools, whether wise or not, even in a society where Christian values predominate, has its roots in the thinking of prominent Christian reformers like Luther and Comenius. Although public schools have by now become totally secularized, especially in the United States, it is helpful to know that the idea of tax-supported schools originated with individuals who were motivated by the love of Jesus Christ, whom they wanted taught for people's spiritual and material benefit.

COMPULSORY EDUCATION

One historian of education said that Luther clearly "enunciated the most progressive ideas on education of the German Protestant reformers."[30] So certain was Luther regarding the value of education for all children that he told civic authorities they should *compel* children to attend school. Said he, "I hold that it is the duty of the temporal authority to compel its subjects to keep their children in school, especially the promising ones we mentioned above."[31] According to Harry Good and James Teller, Luther was "the first modern writer to urge compulsory [school] attendance and proposed that the state should pass such legislation and enforce it."[32]

According to James Bowen, Luther knew that civic leaders, and much of the German populace, harbored a "distrust of formal book learning."[33] This distrust stemmed in part from people's awareness of the long-standing papal corruption of the church and from the working man's belief that educated people had it too easy in life. To Luther, however, as noted earlier, the lack of education would bring ruination to the church and society, so every child, he told civic leaders, should be compelled to go to school—at least one hour per day for girls and two hours each day for boys.[34]

FRIEDRICH FROEBEL (1782–1852), born and raised in a Lutheran parsonage in Germany, pioneered kindergarten education, a concept that soon spread to other parts of the world. *(By Friedrich Unger in the State Museum, Heidecksburg)*

Luther's idea of compulsory education spread to other parts of Europe, although rather slowly. A hundred years later La Salle, a Roman Catholic priest, advocated it in France.[35] In Western societies today the idea that every child should attend school is an accepted norm encoded in law. Just as only a few people today, if any, can imagine that children should not attend school, similarly, probably only a few, if any, know that the present norm of compulsory school attendance was first advocated by Luther who, every informed church historian knows, saw Jesus Christ (*solus Christus,* as he would say) at center of everything in life.

GRADED EDUCATION

Johann Sturm (1507–89), a Lutheran layman, introduced graded levels of education, a system that he felt would motivate students to study because they would be rewarded by advancing to the next level.[36] Complementary to his idea of graded learning, he also introduced in 1538 in Strasbourg, France, the humanistic *gymnasium*, a secondary level of education that he headed for forty years. This system is still in use in Germany and some other European countries.[37]

Sturm was not a secular educational philosopher but an ardent believer in Christian values. He was persuaded that unless students were inculcated with these values, all educational efforts were wasted.[38] Today graded education is taken for granted on all levels—elementary, secondary, and higher education. While people in most countries know and value graded education, not many know that behind this system lies the thinking of an educator whose intellect was formed and shaped by his Savior, Jesus Christ.

THE KINDERGARTEN CONCEPT

Education for more children received additional support from Friedrich Froebel (1782–1852), originator of the kindergarten school. The son of a Lutheran pastor, Froebel was a devout Christian whose beliefs convinced him that the world of man and nature were connected by God. He felt this needed to be taught to children at an early age.[39]

As a child, young Froebel often had to help his father in the family garden. Unpredictably, this experience later had educational relevance. One day while walking in the mountains, he came upon the idea of a school that would allow young children to grow under the care of an expert gardener (a teacher) in a child's garden (*kindergarten*).[40]

In the United States, the first kindergarten school (taught in German) was begun by Mrs. Carl Schurz in Watertown, Wisconsin, in 1855. She was the wife of Carl Schurz, who later served in President Abraham Lincoln's cabinet. The first English-speaking kindergarten began as a private school in Boston in 1860, founded by Elizabeth Peabody.[41]

Froebel's religiously motivated innovation, the kindergarten school, has been borrowed by educators in Christian and secular schools alike. Today virtually all industrialized countries have kindergarten schools. The influence of Christ through Froebel, as in so many other instances, greatly changed and improved the world, this time in the realm of early childhood education.

EDUCATION FOR THE DEAF

Few, even those engaged in educating the deaf, know that the thought of formally teaching the deaf an inaudible language originated largely as a result of the strong Christian convictions of three individuals. They were Abbe Charles Michel de l'Epee, Thomas Gallaudet, and Laurent Clerc. Epee, an ordained priest, developed a sign language for school use in Paris in 1775. He was prompted by his desire for deaf people to hear the gospel of Jesus Christ.[42] Soon after Epee's groundbreaking innovation, Thomas Gallaudet and Laurent Clerc brought sign language to the United States from France.

In 1817 Gallaudet, a Congregational clergyman who never served a parish, opened the first school for the deaf in the United States in Hartford, Connecticut.[43] This man, who was physically frail but a mental giant, once said to a young deaf girl as he sailed for Europe to learn more about working with the deaf, "I hope when I come back to teach you much about the Bible, and about God, and Christ."[44]

Clerc, too, was a devoted Christian. In discussing the work of Gallaudet and Epee, Clerc wrote that both men were concerned about "saving the pupils' souls."[45]

Although Gallaudet could not heal the deaf, he did the next best thing. He taught them a sign language so they could read, write, and communicate—not only the three Rs, but also the fourth R, religion. Deaf children now were able to "hear" Christ's gospel. His determination led to founding a school for the deaf in 1817, noted above. He also established a college, known today as Gallaudet University in Washington, D.C.

While formal deaf education is mostly under secular auspices today, this brief survey shows that originally it arose as the product of Christian motivation. Epee, Gallaudet, and Clerc, dedicated Christians, played key roles in launching education for the deaf. Who knows when deaf education would have occurred had it not been for these foresighted Christian leaders?

LOUIS BRAILLE (1809–52), a Frenchman blind from early childhood, developed education for the blind and saw the need for devising a method of sight reading that is known today as the Braille system.

EDUCATION FOR THE BLIND

As we have already noted, human life in the Greco-Roman world was extremely cheap; people were expendable. This was especially true for infants born with physical defects such as blindness. Blind infants were commonly abandoned in the wilderness or taken to die in a mountain gorge. In Lacedaemonia (Greece), for instance, blind babies were cast into the sea. Boys who survived their blind infancy or who became blind later in childhood usually became galley slaves, and blind girls were commonly destined for a life of prostitution.[46]

Aside from the fact that Jesus in his ministry miraculously healed some blind individuals, very little is known about how the early Christians after Jesus' time related to the blind. We do know, however, that in the fourth century, Christians operated some asylums for the blind and that in 630 a *typholocomium* (*typholos* = blind + *komeo* = take care of) was built in Jerusalem.[47] In the thirteenth century Louis IX (St. Louis) built the famous Hospice des Qwuinze-Vingts for the blind in Paris.[48]

In the sixteenth century attempts were made to teach blind persons to read by means of using raised letters on wax or wood. But the greatest step forward in blind education came in the first half of the nineteenth century because of Louis Braille, a dedicated Christian. At the age of three, he lost his sight by accidentally puncturing his left eye with an awl in his father's harness shop in Coupvray, France. The injury was so severe that it infected his other eye, and he lost its sight as well. Highly influenced by the pious Christian demeanor of his father, who sometimes carved out leather images of Jesus in his shop for his son,[49] Louis attended mass every Sunday, and while still a teenager became a proficient church organist, a position that gave him great joy.[50] He also learned to read in Valentin Haüy's school for the blind in Paris.

Great inventions in history have rarely occurred without some previous attempt(s) that tried to meet a given human or societal need. This was also true with regard to Braille's invention. He came upon Charles Barbier's elevated dots, which were used to read military messages at night; however, they were cumbersome and inefficient. This motivated him to spend endless hours, usually at night, depriving himself of sleep, in pursuit of a better reading method. Inspired by Barbier's method, he developed his own system of pin-pricked raised dots. By 1834 he gave to the world of the blind six embossed dots, three high and two wide, for each letter of the alphabet; and in 1844 his six-dot system was officially recognized by the French government.[51]

At first blush, Braille's accomplishment may seem quite divorced from any influence of Christianity. But that would be a false conclusion, for he saw his work as a divine mission. When he lay on his deathbed, he said, "I am convinced that my mission is finished on earth; I tasted yesterday the supreme delight; God condescended to brighten my eyes with the splendor of eternal hope."[52] Thus, another great advance occurred in education, this time for the blind. And the advance, as in so many other instances in Western history, was prompted by the spirit of Jesus Christ, enabling millions of blind people to see with their fingers.

ROBERT RAIKES (1735–1811) encounters some of the poor children for whom he founded a school that met on Sunday, the one day of the week when the children were not work-ing—a development that rapidly grew into the Sunday school movement. *(Hare Lane, Gloucester, 1780)*

SUNDAY SCHOOLS

Although education for everyone was theoretically encouraged, especially since Luther's time during the Reformation, in practice it often failed to take place. The large number of poor and disadvantaged commonly did not learn to read or write. Various social and economic forces prevented them from getting a basic formal education. Sometimes the opportunity was indeed available, but agrarian or peasant-minded parents who had no education themselves saw no value in it, so their children were either not sent to school or, if they were sent, it was only for a minimal amount of time. Often the church was at fault too. For instance, during the eighteenth century the church in England greatly neglected the welfare and education of the poor. Little attention was paid to the widespread practice of child labor in British factories. Going to school was not a social norm, especially not for children of poor families. But as so often has happened in the history of the church, God again brought forth a leader to keep the spirit of Jesus Christ alive.

Robert Raikes of Scotland, a printer by trade, struck upon the idea that he would help the children of the poor by teaching them on Sundays. He chose Sundays because before the advent of child labor laws (discussed in chapter 5), whether on the farm or in the cities, children worked up to twelve hours per day, six days a week. But they were free on Sundays. He began his first school in 1780 in a rented kitchen and brought boys and girls from some of the poorest homes. The children were required to come with clean hands and faces, combed hair, and with the clothing they had. For some he provided shoes and clothing.[53] Classes were held Sunday mornings from ten to twelve. A committed Christian, Raikes's primary purpose was to teach the children the Bible, but he quickly discovered that most of the students could not read. So before he could teach them the Bible, he first had to teach them the skill of reading.[54]

Noble ideas and practices are often resisted and rejected. This was also true of Raikes's Sunday school idea. Many, including some misguided clergy, accused Raikes of engaging in demoralizing and dangerous behavior; some said he was an agent of the devil. Apparently the latter remark stemmed from the fact that he violated the sanctity of Sunday. But cooler heads soon came to Raikes's defense. Some of his defenders were individuals whom we, even as Americans, now know as famous: John Newton, Charles and John Wesley, William Cowper, John Howard, and others. Some ladies of high fashion also came to his support. And soon the queen summoned him to the palace to hear of his efforts from his own lips.[55]

The Sunday school movement grew rapidly. Soon it spread to North America. Although the nature of Sunday school is very different today, there is hardly a Christian congregation in North America that does not have one. Major denominations publish Sunday school literature for teachers and students on a regular basis. Few Christians today know that teaching children on Sunday is the outcome of a man who wanted all children, especially the poor, to know what Jesus meant when he said, "Let the little children come to me, and do not hinder them, for the kingdom of God belongs to such as these" (Mark 10:14).

THE CHRISTIAN ORIGIN OF UNIVERSITIES

Several hundred years before Christ, the ancient Greeks had their philosophers (Thales, Xenophanes, Parmenides, Zeno, Pythagoras, Democritus, Socrates, Plato, and Aristotle) and their poets (Euripides, Aeschylus, Aristophanes, and Sophocles). And to a lesser degree, the Romans also had their gifted thinkers (Seneca, Cicero, Plautus, Pliny the Elder, Lucretius, Tacitus, and others). All were learned men who functioned in the realm of what today is called higher education. Given this literary orientation, some historians have referred to the Greeks and Romans as having had the first "universities." But as Charles Haskins has noted, these brilliant men developed no permanent institutions. They had no libraries, they had no guild of scholars or students, and they certified no one.[56] Even more important, it can be argued, they tested no theories and engaged in no research; in fact, they ignored and even spurned the inductive method. Hence, it does not appear correct to assume, as is sometimes done, that the university of the twentieth century is a lineal descendant of the ancient Greek philosophers.[57] The best evidence indicates that universities grew out of the Christian monasteries.

MONASTERIES AS EMBRYONIC UNIVERSITIES

Regarding his disciples, Christ prayed to God, "My prayer is not that you take them out of the world but that you protect them from the evil one" (John 17:15). He did not want his followers to withdraw from the world as some like St. Anthony, who lived a hermitlike life for religious reasons, began doing in the third century. Christ wanted Christians to be *in* but not *of* the world. Thus, the founding of monasteries in a sense was inconsistent with his will. But because of the ever-present tension that exists between Christians and the world, some Christians, like the monks and nuns, physically separated themselves from the world. Nevertheless, God often makes good things come out of very flawed human efforts. This was true with regard to the medieval monasteries, for in many instances they became the seedbed of modern universities.

With regard to the early origin of universities, history points us to St. Benedict of Nursia (480–543?), who founded the Benedictine order's first monastery at Monte Cassino, Italy, in 528, and soon built monasteries in many other locations. Benedict's monasteries all placed great value on the literary treasures of antiquity and of Christianity. Daniel Boorstin says that St. Benedict has been called "the godfather of libraries."[58] The Benedictines originated an elaborate library system in their many monasteries; they collected books, copied manuscripts in the *scriptoria*, loaned books to other monasteries, and required monks to read books daily. Benedictine library holdings included the Holy Scriptures, writings of the church fathers, and biblical commentaries as well as secular books of Greek and Roman writers. So indispensable were libraries to this monastic order that the monks said a library was a monastery's armory, similar to the armory of a castle.[59]

186

The *scriptoria* and libraries in the Benedictine monasteries of Europe in the sixth and seventh centuries, however, were by no means full-fledged universities. These came later. With the academic footing provided by the Benedictine monasteries, the first universities arose in the twelfth and thirteenth centuries, although some suggest that the first university was the medical school in Salerno, Italy, in the tenth century. The evidence, however, is rather obscure for this claim.[60] Thus, the university commonly cited to be the first is the University of Bologna, Italy, founded in 1158, which has been credited to Emperor Frederick Barbarossa's efforts.[61] At least one scholar, however, argues that the university at Bologna was a descendant of the school of law founded by Emperor Theodosius II as early as the year 425 in Constantinople.[62] Theodosius's school reportedly had thirty-one professors who taught Latin, Greek, law, and philosophy.[63] Overlooking the dubious history of Theodosius's school, there is some evidence that points to Bologna's school having first appeared in the tenth century.[64] Regardless of its exact time of origin, the University of Bologna in 1158 specialized in the study of canon law. The next to appear was the University of Paris in 1200. Some credit Abelard for laying its foundations some sixty years before its formal founding in 1200.[65] Paris specialized in theology, and in 1270 it added the study of medicine.

Bologna became the mother of several universities in Italy, Spain, Scotland, Sweden, and Poland. The University of Paris became the mother of Oxford and of universities in Portugal, Germany, and Austria. Cambridge University, through its Emmanuel College, became the mother of Harvard in America.[66] With the establishment of the University of Bologna and the University of Paris and their numerous offspring, formal higher education had become permanently institutionalized. According to Haskins, the university of the twentieth century is "the lineal descendant of medieval Paris and Bologna."[67]

From their monastic roots and through the nineteenth century, all universities were founded as Christian institutions, regardless of whether they taught law, theology, or medicine. Until well into the nineteenth century, even with the growth of scientific studies, Western universities and colleges "almost always operated within theological boundaries."[68] The Christian stamp on colleges and universities was evidenced by their names. In England and the United States numerous colleges and universities were named in honor of Christian saints: St. Anne's, St. Anthony's, St. Mary's, St. Bernard's, St. Olafs, and others. Still other colleges received names like: Christ, Trinity, Emmanuel, King's, Magdalene, and so forth.

MILESTONES IN EDUCATION: CHRISTIANITY'S INFLUENCE

Educational Entity	Initial Advocate(s) and Time Period
The New Testament Gospels	Jesus commands his disciples: ""Teaching them" (Matthew 28:20)
The *Didache* (The Teaching of the Twelve)	Author unknown, ca. A.D. 85–110
Catechetical schools	Justin Martyr, ca. A.D. 150
Cathedral/episcopal schools	Founder unknown, 4th cent.
Monastery/nunnery schools	Founder unknown, 5th cent.
First university (Bologna, Italy)	Emperor Frederick Barbarossa, 1158
Public schools	Martin Luther, 1530s
Universal (education for all)	Martin Luther, 1530s / John Calvin, 1550s
Tax-supported education	Martin Luther and Philipp Melanchthon, 1530s
Compulsory education	Martin Luther, 1530s
Graded education	Johann Sturm, 1530s
First American college (Harvard)	New Towne (1636) renamed Harvard College after John Harvard (a clergyman) in 1639
Kindergarten schools	Friedrich Froebel, 1840s
Sunday schools	Robert Raikes, 1780
Deaf education (Europe)	Abbe Charles Michel de l'Epee, 1775
Deaf education (America)	Thomas Gallaudet, 1817
Blind education (France)	Founder unknown, 16th cent.
Blind education (Braille method)	Louis Braille, 1834

RESEARCH: ITS MONASTIC ROOTS

When people think of universities today, in contrast to colleges, they think of research. Were the universities at Bologna and Paris research institutions? The answer is a minimal yes. In the monasteries, where translations and copies of various biblical and nonbiblical books and manuscripts were made, the monks often compared and consulted the different sources from which they copied or translated. This is evident from the variant readings found in extant copies of Greek and Latin biblical texts, as well in the nonbiblical classical texts. These research-related activities continued in the universities, for now professors compiled lectures from the different library sources. This certainly was research, although not empirical research.

Not too long after the first universities arose, some schools engaged in empirical research. By 1300, for example, the University of Bologna (initially a law school) dissected human cadavers for forensic purposes to settle legal suits. The dissecting of human bodies soon spread to other universities that functioned as medical schools, for instance, Montpellier and Padua.[69] And by 1396, King Charles VI in France ordained that each year a cadaver of a criminal be delivered to the faculty at Montpellier for anatomical study.[70] The king's action was preceded by the University of Montpellier's statutes of 1340, which provided for dissection of human cadavers every two years.

That empirical research, at first confined to medical schools, occurred relatively early in the existence of the medieval universities should not come as a surprise if one remembers that it was the monks who were the university lecturers and who came from a long-standing tradition of doing both physical and intellectual work. Monks were used to getting dirt under their fingernails.[71] Doing empirical research was simply an extension of their physical work; it was the Christian way of combining manual and intellectual activity.

Before this time in history, with the minor exception of Archimedes (ca. 287–230 B.C.), who built a water screw and a device to study geometry, and Galen (A.D. 131–200), who dissected animals and some human cadavers, the great thinkers never tested their theories empirically. Educated Greeks and Romans saw all manual activity as only fit for slaves, and since empirical research required manual activity, the brilliant theories proposed by the ancient Greek philosophers were left untested. For instance, Pythagoras (ca. 560–489 B.C.) argued that the earth was spherical and that it revolved; Anaxagoras (ca.500–428 B.C.) theorized that the moon received its light from the sun and that moon's eclipses were the result of the earth's impeding a portion of the sun's light; Democritus (ca. 460–370 B.C.) espoused the view that the world consisted of an infinite number of atoms that moved in a void (vacuum); and Archimedes (ca. 287–212 B.C.) put forth the theory of a sun-centered (heliocentric) universe and thought that the earth revolved around the sun, which was stationary. Thus, the empirical research, which really first appeared in the medieval monasteries where intellectual and manual activities were not seen as incompatible, was a major innovation and revolutionary contribution to the world of learning, a contribution bequeathed to posterity, and one that today's universities, secular or church-related, could not do without. The world of knowledge would be greatly enhanced if scholars and scientists were to make this major legacy of Christianity known.

THE ORIGIN OF COLLEGES AND UNIVERSITIES IN AMERICA

Given the powerful influence that secularism now has on most Americans, they are probably not aware that "every collegiate institution founded in the colonies prior to the Revolutionary War—except the University of Pennsylvania—was established by some branch of the Christian church."[72] Nor are most Americans aware that in 1932, when Donald Tewksbury published *The Founding of American Colleges and Universities Before the Civil War,* 92 percent of the 182 colleges and universities were founded by Christian denominations.

Most colleges and universities that are well known today began as Christian schools. Harvard College, established in 1636, now known as Harvard University, was founded by the Congregational Church as a theological institution; the College of William and Mary started as an Episcopalian school, also primarily to train clergy; Yale University began mostly as a Congregational institution to "Educate Ministers in our Own Way."[73] The Methodists founded Northwestern University in Evanston, Illinois; Columbia University (first known as King's College) began as an Episcopalian venture; Princeton University started as a Presbyterian school; and Brown University had Baptist origins. Even some state universities, for example, the University of Kentucky, the University of California (Berkeley), and the University of Tennessee, had their origins as church schools. But today these institutions of higher learning have abandoned their onetime Christian foundations. Other colleges, which still have some tenuous ties to their founding denominations, also have largely deserted their Christian allegiance. However, in this latter group of colleges or universities, it is not unusual to see a college catalogue state that its college is a "Christian institution" although what is taught in its classrooms is commonly as secular as anything that is taught in state universities. Despite the massive departure of so many formerly Christian colleges from their original charters, the fact remains that many would not be in existence today had it not been for their Christian forbears. Similarly, most of the present state universities in Europe—for example, Oxford, Paris, Cambridge, Heidelberg, and Basel—had Christian origins.

CONCLUSION

Catechetical schools, cathedral schools, episcopal schools, monasteries, medieval universities, schools for the blind and deaf, Sunday schools, modern grade schools, secondary schools, modern colleges, universities, and universal education all have one thing in common: they are the products of Christianity. Thus, Kennedy and Newcombe are right when they write, "Every school you see—public or private, religious or secular—is a visible reminder of the religion of Jesus Christ. So is every college and university."[74] This statement, together with this chapter's brief survey, may be news to most people in our secular age. If so, there is a certain irony here. Individuals in Western societies spend many years in schools, colleges, or universities, but they have learned very little about the contributions Christianity has made to education, so highly treasured today. In the absence of this knowledge, it is not only Christianity that has been slighted, but Jesus Christ as well. Were it not for him and his teachings, who knows at what stage of development education would be today?

NOTES

1. L. Millar, *Christian Education in the First Four Centuries* (London: Faith Press, 1946), 10–11.

2. See "The Epistle of Ignatius to the Philadelphians," in *The Ante-Nicene Fathers*, ed. Alexander Roberts and James Donaldson (Grand Rapids: Wm. B. Eerdmans, 1981), 1:81.

3. Ibid., 1:39.

4. William Boyd, *The History of Western Education* (New York: Barnes and Noble, 1965), 84.

5. Kenneth J. Freeman, *Schools of Hellas* (London: Macmillan, 1922), 46.

6. Tatian, "Address of Tatian to the Greeks," in *The Ante-Nicene Fathers*, 2:78.

7. W. M. Ramsay, *The Church in the Roman Empire Before A.D. 170* (London: Hodder and Stoughton, 1893), 345.

8. Chrysostom, "Homilies of St. Chrysostom," in *Nicene and Post-Nicene Fathers of the Christian Church*, ed. Philip Schaff (Grand Rapids: Wm. B. Eerdmans, 1983), 13:278.

9. D. D. McGarry, "Medieval Education," *New Catholic Encyclopedia* (San Francisco: McGraw-Hill, 1967), 5:113.

10. F. V. N. Painter, *Luther on Education* (St. Louis: Concordia Publishing House [1889]), 78.

11. Ibid., 116.

12. David Herlihy, "Women and the Sources of Medieval History," in *Medieval Women and the Sources of Medieval History*, ed. Joel T. Rosenthal (Athens: University of Georgia Press, 1990), 134.

13. Ellwood P. Cubberley, *Readings in the History of Education* (Boston: Houghton Mifflin, 1920), 97.

14. Margaret Wade Labarge, *A Small Sound of the Trumpet* (Boston: Beacon Press, 1986), 10.

15. Will Durant, *Caesar and Christ: A History of Roman Civilization and of Christianity from Their Beginnings to A.D. 325* (New York: Simon and Schuster, 1972), 602.

16. Carl von Weizsacker, *The Apostolic Age of the Christian Church* (New York: G. P. Putnam's Sons, 1897), 306.

17. Martin Luther, "Preface," *Small Catechism,* in *The Book of Concord,* ed. Theodore G. Tappert (Philadelphia: Fortress Press, 1959), 338.

18. Mark Noll, *The Scandal of the Evangelical Mind* (Grand Rapids: Wm. B. Eerdmans, 1994), 37.

19. Lars P. Qualben, *A History of the Christian Church* (New York: Thomas Nelson and Sons, 1958), 241.

20. Martin Luther, "Introduction: A Sermon on Keeping Children in School," in *Luther's Works,* trans. Charles M. Jacobs, ed. Robert Schultz (Philadelphia: Fortress Press, 1967), 46:211.

21. Martin Luther, "Ordinances of a Common Chest," in *Luther's Works,* ed. Walther I. Brandt (Philadelphia: Muhlenberg Press, 1962), 45:175.

22. Martin Luther, "To The Councilmen Of All Cities In Germany That They Establish And Maintain Christian Schools," in *Luther's Works,* trans. Albert T. W. Steinhauser; ed. Robert Schultz (Philadelphia: Fortress Press, 1967), 45:344.

23. William Boyd, *The History of Western Education* (New York: Barnes and Noble, 1965), 189.

24. Qualben, *History of the Christian Church,* 270.

25. Gabriel Compayre, *The History of Pedagogy,* trans. W. H. Payne (Boston: D. C. Heath, 1896), 136.

26. Martin Luther, "To the Councilmen..." in *Luther's Works,* 45:350.

27. Douglas H. Shantz, "Philipp Melanchthon: The Church's Teacher, Luther's Colleague," *Christian Info News* (February 1997).

28. Qualben, *History of the Christian Church,* 241.

29. John Comenius, "A Brief Proposal Regarding the Renewal of Schools in the Kingdom of Bohemia," in *J. A. Comenius: Selection from His Works* (Prague: Statni Pedagogicke Nakladatelstvi, 1964), 28.

30. Ellwood P. Cubberly, *The History of Education* (Boston: Houghton Mifflin, 1948), 312.

31. Martin Luther, "A Sermon on Keeping Children in School," in *Luther's Works,* 46:256.

32. Harry Good and James D. Teller, *A History of Western Education* (London: Macmillan, 1969), 152.

33. James Bowen, *A History of Western Education* (New York: St. Martin's Press, 1975), 367.

34. Martin Luther, "To the Councilmen...," in *Luther's Works,* 45:370.

35. Compayre, *The History of Pedagogy,* 262.

36. Lewis Spitz and Barbara Sher Tinsley, *Johann Sturm on Education* (St. Louis: Concordia Publishing House, 1995), 85.

37. Good and Teller, *History of Western Education,* 153.

38. Spitz and Tinsley, *Johann Sturm,* 347.

39. Good and Teller, *History of Western Education,* 281.

40. Ibid., 285.

41. Ellwood P. Cubberley, *Public Education in the United States* (Boston: Houghton Mifflin, 1919), 319.

42. Harlan Lane, *When the Mind Hears* (New York: Random House, 1984), 58.

43. Richard A. Tennant and Marianne Gluszak Brown, *The American Sign Language Handshape Dictionary* (Washington, D.C.: Clerc Books/Gallaudet University Press, 1998), 10.

44. Lane, *When the Mind Hears,* 185.

45. Ibid., 229.

46. Ishbel Ross, *Journey into the Light* (New York: Appleton-Century-Crofts, 1951), 11.

47. R. M. McGuinness, "Blind and Visually Handicapped," *New Catholic Encyclopedia* (San Francisco: McGraw-Hill, 1967), 2:615.

48. Ibid.

49. Alvin Kugelmass, *Louis Braille: Windows for the Blind* (New York: Julian Messner, 1951), 14.

50. Ibid., 77.

51. Etta DeGering, *Seeing Fingers: The Story of Louis Braille* (New York: David McKay, 1962), 110.

52. Ibid., 121.

53. Edwin Wilbur Rice, *The Sunday-School Movement and the American Sunday-School Union* (Philadelphia: Union Press, 1917), 15.

54. Ibid., 18.

55. Ibid., 20–21.

56. Charles H. Haskins, *The Rise of Universities* (New York: Henry Holt, 1923), 3.

57. A. B. Cobban, *The Medieval Universities: Their Development and Organization* (Chatham, England: Methuen, 1975), 22.

58. Daniel J. Boorstin, *The Discoverers* (New York: Vintage Books, 1983), 491.

59. Ibid., 492–93.

60. Bowen, *History of Western Education,* 109.

61. Gabriel Compayre, *Abelard and the Origin of the Early History of Universities* (New York: Charles Scribner's Sons, 1899), 42.

62. Ibid., 56.

63. Millar, *Christian Education in the First Four Centuries,* 125.

64. Ibid., 110.

65. Compayre, *Abelard,* 14.

66. Cubberly, *History of Education,* 218.

67. Haskins, *Rise of Universities,* 5.

68. George M. Marsden, *The Outrageous Idea of Christian Scholarship* (New York: Oxford University Press, 1997), 15.

69. Cobban, *Medieval Universities,* 44.

70. Compayre, *Abelard,* 255.

71. Lynn White uses this expression in "The Significance of Medieval Christianity," in *The Vitality of the Christian Tradition,* ed. George F. Thomas (New York: Harper and Brothers, 1945), 93.

72. Paul Lee Tan, *Encyclopedia of 7700 Illustrations: Signs of the Times* (Rockville, Md.: Assurance Publishers, 1984), 157.

73. Thomas Clap: cited in Donald Tewksbury, *The Founding of American Colleges and Universities Before the Civil War* (New York: Teachers College Columbia University, 1932), 82.

74. D. James Kennedy and Jerry Newcombe, *What If Jesus Had Never Been Born?* (Nashville: Thomas Nelson, 1994), 40.

LABOR and ECONOMIC FREEDOM DIGNIFIED

"To work is to pray."
Benedictine Proverb

When Christ was born, the country of his birth was occupied by the Romans, who, like the Greeks, had an extremely low view of physical work. In their minds, manual labor was only suitable for slaves and the lower classes; it was demeaning for philosophers, theorists, and freemen. Plutarch (ca. 46–120) said that the philosopher Plato was incensed at two men (Endoxus and Archytas) for constructing an apparatus to solve geometry problems. Manually constructed devices, if made at all, were to be made by artisans, who were usually slaves, not by thinkers or freemen. Moreover, mechanical devices corrupted "the pure excellence of geometry" (*Plutarch's Lives* 5). The ancient mathematician Archimedes was ashamed for having built devices that aided his studies in geometry.[1] Among the Romans, Cicero (first century B.C.) said that working daily for a livelihood was "unbecoming to a gentleman" (freeborn man), and that "vulgar are the means of livelihood of all hired workman whom we pay for mere manual labor....

"BILLINGSGATE—LANDING THE FISH" depicts a scene of eighteenth-century England's laboring class. *(Gustave Doré)*

And all mechanics are engaged in vulgar trades" (*De Officiis* 1.150). And the Roman philosopher Seneca (d. A.D. 65), in his many *Moral Essays, Epistles,* and *Natural Questions,* never mentions labor as an honorable activity for freemen.

In ancient Athens at the time of the early church, one-third of the freemen sat daily in the court of the *Comitia* discussing the affairs of the state, while slaves performed all the manual labor that was loathed by the freemen.[2] Athens had "five times as many slaves as citizens."[3] The ratio was not much better in the Roman culture, where its nonslave population sought personal pleasure above everything else.[4] "In the classical tradition," says Lynn White, "there is scarcely a hint of the dignity of labor."[5] It was this anti-work cultural environment that the early Christians entered in the Greco-Roman world.

LABOR HONORED AND DIGNIFIED

As noted in the first three chapters, Christianity's beliefs and practices often clashed with the pagan values of the Greco-Roman culture. The Christian view of labor and work as honorable and God-pleasing was another of the value clashes.

The dignity and honor that Christians assigned to work stemmed from at least three sources. First, they had Jesus as a role model; they remembered that he grew up in a carpenter's home, where he worked until he began his ministry at about age thirty. Second, they had another excellent role model in St. Paul, who from his Hebrew heritage had learned a trade skill (tent making) along with his scholarship. This skill often helped him supplement his income while he was on his missionary journeys. And third, the early Christians were well aware of Paul's admonition to the Thessalonians: "If a man will not work, he shall not eat" (2 Thessalonians 3:10).

The view that all work is honorable set the early Christians apart not only in their rejecting the Greco-Roman attitude that despised manual work but also because they prospered economically as a result of their strong work ethic. Their prosperity was sometimes an additional reason that the Romans saw them as undesirable people, resulting in their persecution.[6]

When new values and ideas are introduced and applied to a specific social phenomenon, they commonly produce more than one effect. This was also true with regard to Christians giving dignity to work and labor. A noteworthy by-product of the dignity and honor given to labor was that it undermined slavery, as the historian Kenneth Latourette has pointed out.[7]

THE DIGNITY OF WORK REINFORCED

The Apostolic Constitutions (ca. A.D. 375), a collection of ecclesiastical precepts, reinforced Christianity's conviction regarding the honorableness of work by condemning slothfulness on the basis of St. Paul's statement to the Thessalonians. Book 2 of the *Constitutions* states that "the Lord our God hates the slothful." With the advent of the monasteries in the early Middle Ages, Christianity's high regard for work continued. For instance, the Benedictine monks (sixth century) saw labor as "an integral and spiritual part of their discipline [that] did much to increase the prestige of labor and the self-respect of the laborer."[8] Whether Benedictines or other monastic orders, they all honored work as they tilled the soil, tended herds, milked cows, crafted artifacts, and so forth.

Work was also a Christian antidote to the sin of laziness. St. Basil of Caesarea in the fourth century said, "Idleness is a great evil; work preserves us from evil thoughts." Similarly, St. Bernard in the twelfth century taught, "The handmaid of Christ ought always to pray, to read, to work, lest haply the spirit of uncleanness should lead astray the slothful mind. The delight of the flesh is overcome by labor."[9] So strong was the Christian concern in the Middle Ages regarding the willful avoidance of work that the church counted laziness (sloth) as one of the Seven Deadly Sins.

WORK AS A CALLING (*VOCATIO*)

The high value that Christianity assigned to work and manual labor received further support during the Reformation, especially from Martin Luther, who saw work not only as God-pleasing but also as a calling (*vocatio*) to serve God. Luther's concept of work, says Emil Brunner, had revolutionary consequences. It meant there was no low-status or high-status work, good work or bad work. It made no difference what kind work the Christian did so long as he performed it to the glory of God. This notion of work shifted the meaning from "what" and "how" to "why."[10] Work was not an end in itself but something the person did in everyday life to the glory of God and to the service of mankind. It was through work, especially the work of Christians, that God maintained and preserved the world and the people in it. Thus, all legitimate work was noble and God-pleasing. Work was a Christian duty.[11]

Luther saw work as the "mask of God" (*larvae Dei*), meaning that God is in it, although hidden. So hidden is God in one's work that unless the Christian thinks about it (and only the Christian, with the Spirit of God in him, can do so), he will have no awareness of God's presence in his work. Given that God is hidden in one's work, to the Christian all work is of equal value. Here Luther in part echoed Johann Tauler, a fourteenth-century monk who maintained that all work, no matter how low its status in society, was nevertheless providing a service to God and humankind.

THE LABORER IS WORTHY OF HIS WAGES

When Jesus said "the worker deserves his wages" (Luke 10:7), he paraphrased an Old Testament norm first spoken by Moses when he commanded the Israelites: "Do not muzzle an ox while it is treading out the grain" (Deuteronomy 25:4). Just as the ox treading out the grain needs to be rewarded for his work, so too the human laborer is worthy of his reward or wages. These biblical references not only made it mandatory that every worker be paid for his efforts, but they also underscored once more in the eyes of Christians the honorable role of work.

In today's world it is simply assumed by all that workers deserve a wage or salary for services performed. But this has not always been so. In pagan societies during the days of Moses, the Old Testament prophets, and early Christianity, it was quite common for societies to have the majority of their residents work as slaves. These slaves, who performed all manual labor, commonly received very little remuneration other than a meager subsistence allowance. This was given so that they would be able to perform additional work, not as a reward for their toil. It would be helpful if people today knew and appreciated that the current practice of compensating workers, undergirded by the belief that it is unjust to deprive them of fair remuneration, would not be in place today were it not for the fact that Christianity held up the norm that "a worker deserves his wages."

Two additional observations should be noted. First, had employers, many of whom identified themselves as being Christian, faithfully heeded the biblical admonition to pay their workers as they truly deserved, labor unions might never have needed to come into existence—assuming that workers also would not have made excessive demands. And second, the influence of the biblical admonition that the laborer is worthy of his hire undoubtedly lies behind today's institutionalized practice of unions negotiating contracts for their members. If there is any doubt regarding this claim, one need only ask: If it did not come from this biblical norm, from where did it come? It was not present in the Greco-Roman era, where slaves performed all of the manual labor. Thus, Christianity's two-thousand-year influence is more deeply ingrained and pervasive in Western economic values and practices than is often realized.

THE DIGNITY OF LABOR PRODUCES A MIDDLE CLASS

Before Christians brought dignity to work and labor, there was not much of a middle class in the Greek or Roman cultures. People were either rich or poor, and the poor were commonly slaves. The Christian emphasis on everyone being required to work and work being honorable and God-pleasing had the effect of producing a class between the patricians (the wealthy) and the plebes (the poor). People like the Christians, who were not given to living for "bread and games" (to use Cicero's expression), says Herbert Workman, "could not fail to prosper."[12] Hence, the economic phenomenon of a middle class arose, now present in all Western societies but unknown before the advent of Christianity.

The presence of a middle class in Western societies has rightly been credited with greatly reducing the extent of poverty and its concomitant by-product, disease. It has also been a potent variable in fostering and maintaining political and economic freedom.

THE PROTESTANT (CHRISTIAN) WORK ETHIC

In 1905 the German sociologist Max Weber published his renowned work, *The Protestant Ethic and the Spirit of Capitalism*. He noted that "business leaders and owners of capital, as well as the higher grades of skilled labor, and even more the higher technically and commercially trained personnel of modern enterprises, [were] overwhelmingly Protestant."[13] He further argued that Protestantism, which held to Luther's and Calvin's teachings that work for the Christian in his community was a calling (*vocatio*), gave a strong emphasis to a work ethic. In the case of Calvin, Weber further argued that the work ethic was supplemented by Calvin's teaching that it was acceptable and not sinful for Christians to receive interest income from loans.

Weber's observation is correct. For Calvin argued that the Bible's anti-usury position meant that only the poor were not to be charged interest money, and that "reason does not suffer us to admit that all usury is to be condemned without exception."[14] The prohibition of usury, he believed, was a part of the ancient Hebrew political constitution. "Hence it follows," Calvin said, "that usury is not now unlawful, except in so far as it contravenes equity and brotherly union."[15] He also stated, "Nor will that subtle argument of Aristotle avail, that usury is unnatural, because money is barren."[16] Calvin's position clearly contravened what numerous church councils had called sin for more than a thousand years.

Weber also contended that by giving approval to taking interest money, Calvin's followers, many of whom were Puritans, functioned as inner-worldly ascetics, as opposed to other-worldly ascetics. The latter withdrew from the world to the monastery in order to deny themselves worldly pleasures, whereas the inner-worldly ascetics were Christians who remained in society[17] but denied themselves pleasures by working hard, saving, and practicing thrift in order to attain future prosperity and wealth, both of which they saw as a sign of divine blessing, and as being of God's elect. Here the

MAX WEBER (1864–1920) was a German sociologist widely known for theorizing that the Protestant (Puritan) Ethic provided the spirit of capitalism in Western society.

Calvinists and Puritans differed from Luther, who believed that the importance of work lies not in producing wealth and prosperity, but rather in serving mankind and thereby bringing God glory.

Even though Weber's thesis has received some strong criticism, for instance, from Kurt Samuelsson, the Swedish economic historian,[18] social scientists continue to cite it as an acceptable theory regarding the effects that the Protestant Ethic has had on work and economic philosophy in Western society, especially in America.

Some have suggested that Weber's term "Protestant Ethic" should have been called the "Calvinist Ethic" or the "Puritan Ethic" because most of his illustrations are drawn from Calvinism or Puritanism rather than from Lutheranism, which comprised the bulk of Protestants at the time of Calvin. On the other hand, some, such as D. James Kennedy and Jerry Newcombe, believe that the Protestant Ethic ought to be called the "Christian Work Ethic."[19] They have a valid point. Christian Work Ethic is probably more accurate in that neither Luther nor Calvin were the first to introduce the work ethic within Christendom. Its roots really go back to what the Apostle Paul said to the Thessalonians, namely, that it was incumbent upon Christians to work. If they did not work, they had no right to eat. It should also be remembered that the Benedictine monks in the sixth century taught *laborare et orare* (to work is to pray). And of course, there was also the saying from the Middle Ages, "Idleness is the devil's workshop." These beliefs were already expressed by St. Jerome in the early part of the fifth century when he said, "Be always working at something so that the devil may always find you employed."

Thus, Weber would have been more accurate had he called the Protestant Ethic the Christian Work Ethic, because the value and necessity of hard work was not first introduced by Protestant Christianity; it was there from Christianity's beginning. Furthermore, the arrival of capitalism also preceded Calvin or Protestantism. For instance, the Medici of Florence, Italy, in the fourteenth century were productive businessmen. Some

MARTIN LUTHER was still a tonsured monk in the Roman Catholic Church in 1520, the year he wrote *An Open Letter to the Nobility,* hailed by many as a hallmark of Christian liberty and freedom. *(Lucas Cranach)*

medieval banks in southern Germany even charged interest and were not condemned by existing usury prohibitions.[20] And there were even some medieval monasteries that charged interest on loaned money.

The Christian Work Ethic has become a vital component in the economies of the Western world today. Business executives who regularly work long hours, often taking work home at night, and manual workers who work at second jobs ("moonlighting"), denying themselves leisure and pleasure, have internalized this work ethic. Although this ethic is quite descriptive of modern executives, businessmen, professionals, and even of manual laborers, there is one significant difference vis-à-vis the worker during the Middle Ages and the Reformation. In the past, work was to be done to the glory of God. Today that is all but forgotten. More and more workers, even many who are Christians, increasingly seem to work only for their family or for self-serving reasons. Yet even these modern workers, although they are not aware of it, are part of what Weber called "worldly ascetics" in that they often deny themselves benefits either for the family's welfare, or for their own future welfare that they hope to realize in their retirement years.

Some might wonder how the economic prosperity of modern Japan, whose people are also given to hard work, thrift, and self-denial in order to prosper, can be explained, since that country has never had a strong Christian influence. Does the Japanese example invalidate the Christian Work Ethic? The answer is no, because with the ascendancy of the Meiji philosophy, which began in the latter part of the nineteenth century, Japan intentionally adopted Western economic and industrial values and practices that were largely the product of the Christian Work Ethic. Japan did not have to adopt Christianity; it only needed to adopt the pertinent economic practices that are the product of its work ethic. As in many other areas of life, once the effects of a cause have become operative, they can be utilized apart from the original cause.

PROPERTY RIGHTS AND INDIVIDUAL FREEDOM

One's work and economic life have little or no dignity when one lacks the freedom and the right to own property. Both are rooted in two of the Ten Commandments, "You shall not steal" and "You shall not covet" (Exodus 20:15, 17). Both of these commandments assume that the individual has the right and freedom to acquire, retain, and sell his property at his discretion.

Private property rights are vital to people's freedom. The two cannot be separated. Yet this elemental truth is not very well recognized and is rarely taught in schools today, even in democratic countries. Promoters of socialism and especially communism often decry and berate private property rights, arguing that "human rights" are more important. Such talk is deceptive and lacks historical support, because where there are no private property rights there are also virtually no human or civil rights. What rights did the people under communism have in the former Soviet Union, where the state owned everything? Except for a few personal incidentals, private property rights were nonexistent. Not having the right to private property was closely linked to not having the right to freedom of religion, freedom of speech, or freedom of the press. Similarly, what human rights do the people have today in Cuba or China, where property rights are also nonexistent?

The American Founding Fathers, who were strongly influenced by biblical Christian values, in their wisdom knew that individual freedom—economically, politically, and socially—was intrinsically linked to private property rights. Even while Americans were still subjects of the British king, they made it clear that property rights and liberty were inseparable. Arthur Lee of Virginia proclaimed, "The right of property is the guardian of every other right, and to deprive a people of this, is in fact to deprive them of their liberty."[21] Thus, when the Constitution was written, its formulators included private property rights in the words of "writings and discoveries" (Article I, Section 8). The Third Amendment of the American Bill of Rights gives citizens the right to grant or deny housing on their property to soldiers. And the Fourth Amendment protects the property of citizens from unlawful searches and seizures.

But ever since the appearance of Karl Marx's economic and political philosophy known as communism, private property has been politically attacked, and it still is. *The Communist Manifesto* by Marx and Friedrich Engels in 1848 states, "The theory of the Communists may be summed up in the single sentence: Abolition of private property."[22] And immediately after the October 1917 Revolution, Lenin, the first communist leader of Russia, took the words of the *Manifesto* seriously when he secretly "ordered the destruction of all legal documents showing property ownership. . .in order to make it impossible for former owners to prove title."[23] Following the founding of the Communist party, numerous politicians and writers, even some theologians, have argued that socialism, a term often used interchangeably with communism in the *Manifesto*, is the most compatible economic and political philosophy with Christian values. For instance, during the Great Depression Jerome Davis said that Christianity, like socialism, holds human values to be higher than property values. While this statement is true, it is also misleading, for it implies that property values are the same as property rights. Moreover, he argued that human values are God-given, while property rights are merely human constructs.

It must be emphasized that nowhere in the Old or New Testament are property rights ever disparaged. To the contrary, the commandment "You shall not steal" underscores such rights. Moreover, in his parables and other teachings, Jesus often referred to property and material goods, but he never condemned anyone for possessing them. He only condemned people's overattachment to possessions because that interfered with loving God and one's neighbor. The parable of the Rich Young Man in Matthew 19 clearly illustrates this point. In another parable, Jesus has the owner of a vineyard say to one of this hired hands, "Don't I have the right to do what I want

JOHN CALVIN (1509–64), renowned theologian originally from France, became prominent in Geneva, Switzerland, and has been credited with giving rise to the Protestant (Puritan) Ethic and its affinity to capitalism. *(Lucas Cranach)*

with my own money?" (Matthew 20:15). Similarly, the book of Acts records Ananias, stricken dead by God, not for withholding some of his properties, but for having lied that he had given everything when he in fact had not. The possession of private property was assumed by Peter asking him, "Didn't it belong to you before it was sold?" (Acts 5:4).

It is unfortunate that political freedom, which Americans, especially, still enjoy to a great degree, is usually not recognized as an integral component of property rights. It is also unfortunate that their biblical and Christian roots are not recognized. Even the excellent book by James W. Ely, *The Guardian of Every Other Right* (1992), which documents the close relationship between freedom and property rights, makes no reference to any biblical or Christian contribution with respect to their existence.

ECONOMIC FREEDOM DIGNIFIED

Even though Christianity does not espouse a given economic ideology, it would be quite erroneous to conclude that therefore any economic ideology is compatible with Christian values and beliefs. Such a conclusion, however, is often made, especially by those who look favorably upon socialism. Many think, because some of the early Christians sold their possessions and "had all things in common," and gave to "each as anyone had need" (Acts 4:32, 35 NKJV), or because they were expected to be their brother's keeper, that current socialistic governments are therefore a modern reflection of Christianity. People who think this way make at least three mistakes. First, they fail to recall that not all of the early Christians in the New Testament era sold their possessions. For instance, Mary, the mother of Mark, retained her house (Acts 12:12); and Simon, a tanner in Caesarea, retained his house in which he hosted Peter (Acts 10:32). Second, they fail to note that the "socialism" that some of the early Christians practiced was totally voluntary. Whatever they shared in common was out of love for that individual whom Christ had redeemed, not because it was forced upon them by any governmental coercion. As noted in chapter 5, behavior that is forced, no matter how noble its objective, is no longer Christian. This point is all too often overlooked today, even by many Christians. And third, while Christ wanted all people to follow him, he also let them have the freedom to reject him, a precedent that God already established at the time of creation when he gave Adam and Eve the gift of a free will. Christ healed ten lepers, but only one returned to thank him. He had not denied the nine the freedom to reject him. Another time he said that he wanted to gather Jerusalem's people to himself spiritually, like a hen gathers her chicks, but they were unwilling. He even wept over Jerusalem's spiritual obstinacy, but spiritual compulsion was not his modus operandi.

Just as God does not want people to be coerced in spiritual matters, so too he does not want them to be coerced in earthly matters, for instance, in their economic activities. There is not a single reference in either the Old or New Testament in which God denies economic freedom to people, as do fascism, socialism, and communism. The parables of Jesus that touch on economic issues are always couched in the context of freedom. Consider his parable of the talents, which relates the case of one man having received five talents; another having two; and a third, one (Matthew 25:15–30). The implication is quite clear: each was free to invest or not to invest; there was no compulsion.

If we fail to understand that the involuntary, coercive nature of socialism and its state socialist programs is highly incompatible with the economic practices that some of the early Christians engaged in when they *voluntar-*

ily "had all things in common" (Acts 2:44 NKJV), we may think that social-ism is a good way to practice Christianity. This specious thinking led F. D. Maurice in 1848 to coin the term "Christian socialism."[24] As said earlier, something that is done involuntarily or as a result of compulsion is no longer Christian. "Christian socialism" is an oxymoron. Socialism, as the Austrian economist F. A. Hayek has argued, fails to tell people that its promises of freedom from economic care and wants can only happen "by relieving the individual at the same time of the necessity and of the power of choice."[25] Dostoyevsky expressed the incompatibility of socialism and Christianity by having Miüsov, in *The Brothers Karamazov,* say, "The socialist who is a Christian is more to be dreaded than a socialist who is an atheist."[26]

ECONOMIC FREEDOM: ITS RELATIONSHIP TO CAPITALISM

Ever since the atheist and communist Karl Marx wrote *Das Kapital* (Capital) in the mid-nineteenth century, the economic system of capitalism has been severely misunderstood and often castigated, partly because of Marx's definition of labor. He erroneously saw labor as an antithesis to cap-ital, when in reality capital is only labor transformed.[27] Another reason for the misunderstanding of capitalism stems from the lack of understanding what is meant by *capitalism.* Although Marx did not use the term, it soon became a scurrilous concept to his followers and sympathizers who used it in their anticapitalistic propaganda. Capitalism is often negatively portrayed in the mass media. Ironically, even many news anchors, who are paid mil-lions of dollars annually—a capitalist salary—cast aspersions on capitalism, in effect biting the hand that feeds them.

In reality, *capitalism* is only a synonym for *free enterprise* or *free mar-ket.* If the terms *free enterprise* or *free market* were consistently used instead of *capitalism,* socialists would have a more difficult time getting people to see capitalism as evil. This would be especially true in societies that have a strong tradition of freedom, such as the United States or even Canada and Great Britain. For people would ask: How can this economic system be evil if it is the product of political and economic freedom and has never been found to exist without such freedom?

A definition of capitalism by Pope John Paul II is relevant. In 1996, he asked rhetorically whether the eastern European countries, where commu-nism failed, should opt for capitalism. Said he, "If by 'capitalism' is meant an economic system which recognizes the fundamental and positive role of business, the market, private property and the resulting responsibility for the means of production, as well as free human creativity in the economic sector, then the answer is certainly in the affirmative."[28] This definition underscores, as noted above, that *capitalism* is only a synonym for *free enterprise*.

As John Chamberlain has pointed out, capitalism, or a free market, is not "Christian in and by itself; it is merely to say that capitalism is a material by-product of the Mosaic law."[29] In other words, capitalism is a by-product of Christianity's value of freedom applied to economic life and activities. To be sure, the economic freedom of capitalism can be abused and misused, and on occasion this has unfortunately happened. Also, unfortunately, that is often the only thing that the anticapitalists (communists and socialists) prefer to know about capitalism. Karl Marx believed that the abuses in capitalism would inevitably destroy it. As an atheist, he could not envision that the humanitarian spirit of Christianity internalized by countless leaders in the West would correct the economic abuses. Thus capitalism, or the free market, not only has survived, but it has given to a greater proportion of the people more prosperity and freedom than any other economic system in the history of mankind. As Milton Friedman has shown, in countries where the free market is not permitted to operate, the gap between the rich and poor is the widest.[30]

It can further be argued that a free market economy, or capitalism as it is practiced especially in America, is of all economic systems the most moral in that it does not coerce or compel individuals to make given economic transactions. It permits individuals or companies to act voluntarily. Individuals need not buy or sell their product(s) unless they so desire. Furthermore, individuals are not compelled to produce a product against their will as is the norm in socialist, or so-called planned economies.

Finally, given the positive relationship between economic freedom and a nation's prosperity, the following question needs to be asked: Is it merely accidental that the greatest amount of freedom and the accompanying economic prosperity happen to exist in countries where Christianity has had, and continues to have, a dominant presence and influence? The evidence shows rather decisively that "Christianity tends to create a capitalistic mode of life whenever siege conditions do not prevail."[31]

THE PROFIT MOTIVE IS HONORABLE

When the Bible, in both the Old and New Testaments, states that the laborer is worthy of his wages, as pointed out above, it simply assumes that the one who employs the worker must be able to make a profit, for without any profit he could not pay the worker. In Jesus' parable of the Talents, he in effect gave legitimacy to the profit motive, for the parable commends the one who invested and doubled his five talents, and it faulted and punished the one who out of timidity did not invest his one talent. Thus, the belief that the profit motive is evil and sinful does not come from the Bible or from Christian theology. It was Karl Marx, the communist, who said that profit, which he equated with what he called surplus value, was the product of labor not returned to the laborers.[32] Thus, profit is the exploitation of workers. The *Great Soviet Encyclopedia* reflects this Marxian belief when it states, "Under capitalism, the category of profit is a converted form of surplus value, the embodiment of unpaid labor of wage workers, which is appropriated without compensation by the capitalist."[33] Disdain for the profit motive is common among many intellectuals, who frequently harbor socialistic ideas. This accounts for books and articles that impugn profits. One such example is *In the Name of Profit* (1972) by Robert Heilbronner and associates. It mentions only the abuses in the business world, as it tries to cast a negative light on the entire profit motive. To be sure, profits can be and have been abused—and the Christian ethic does not condone abuse of any kind—but the potential for abuse makes profit no more evil than does eating food, which also can be and often is abused. The disdain for profit among intellectuals, says F. A. Hayek, may be admirable if one is an ascetic who is content with a minimal share of the world's riches. But it is another matter when this ascetic attitude is "actualized in the form of restrictions on profits of others, [for then it] is selfishness to the extent that it imposes asceticism, and indeed deprivations of all sorts, on others."[34]

ECONOMIC FREEDOM, THE GOSPEL, AND 1492

As is well known, Christopher Columbus set sail to find spices and other commodities in the Far East. Had there not been sufficient economic freedom in the Holy Roman Empire at this time, Columbus would probably never have thought about sailing to the Far East, let alone have been able to embark on his voyage, one that fortuitously resulted in his discovering the New World.

While Columbus certainly was economically motivated to undertake his venture, his being a Christian also played a major role. Believing in Christ's command to take the gospel to all nations, as is evident in his first report to King Ferdinand and Queen Isabella, he wanted to be true to Christ's

CHRISTOPHER COLUMBUS (1451–1506) appears before Queen Isabella and King Ferdinand of Spain in 1492 before they underwrote his pioneer voyage that serendipitously resulted in his discovering America.

command. In that letter he wrote, "Let Christ rejoice on earth, as he rejoices in heaven in the prospect of the salvation of the souls of so many nations [the natives] hitherto lost."[35] He also believed Christ's words that said the gospel had to be preached to all nations before the world would end (Matthew 24:14). Thus, by sailing to foreign lands where Christianity was unknown, he not only heeded Christ's command to extend the gospel, but he believed in God's plan for the world's consummation.[36]

Columbus was a man with strong Christian convictions, something that is not generally known. Samuel Morison, the well-known biographer of Columbus, says the explorer commonly undertook his tasks by saying, "In the name of the Holy Trinity I will do this."[37] His journal for his first voyage to America began, "In the Name of Our Lord Jesus Christ."[38] When he first set foot on the land of the New World, he "rendered thanks to Our Lord," according to his son Ferdinand.[39] One of his extant autographs states that his first trip to America was inspired by the Holy Trinity.[40] He regularly engaged in devotions and prayers.[41] Christian crosses were left standing as markers on all islands that he visited, and the first island he discovered he named San Salvador (Holy Savior). His letters were often signed as *XPO Ferens* (Christ Bearer), the meaning of his first name in Latin.

This Christian man's determination, which resulted in his discovering the New World, produced sea-change effects for the entire world. The discovery extended the geographic scope of Christianity as many American Indians were converted. And although European diseases and geographic dislocations, along with many immoral acts committed by some of Columbus's men and later by the Conquistadors, took heavy tolls on native inhabitants, the overall contributions that resulted from the discovery of America are still benefiting the world in a wide variety of ways.

The exportation of indigenous American food items to European countries gave Europeans a more balanced diet. Before Columbus, Europeans knew nothing of potatoes, tomatoes, sweet potatoes, corn, squash, peanuts, pecans, cashews, avocados, artichokes, cacao (chocolate), chili peppers, maple syrup, sunflower seeds, beans, pumpkin, vanilla, pineapple, and turkey meat. Bringing especially the potato to Europe brought an end to its many famines. Some of these new food items also benefited the continent of Africa, particularly sweet potatoes, corn, and green beans.[42]

Columbus's coming to America also brought other salutary changes to the American Indians. Less than a hundred years after 1492, the Indians adopted the horse ("sky dog") that was brought to the New World by the Spaniards. Horses improved buffalo hunting, particularly on the Great Plains, and they added a new dimension to Indian recreation. By the mid–1700s the white man's rifle made hunting more productive than the bow and arrow. The Navajos and Pueblos of the American Southwest incorporated the European sheep into their culture. Pigs and cattle from the Old World provided pork and beef to the Indians in Meso-America. And after Columbus (as noted in chapter 6), Cortes built hospitals for the Indians in Mexico.

Despite the numerous benefits that Columbus's discovering America yielded, together with his positive Christian demeanor, they have not insulated him in recent years from severe criticism, especially by promoters of multiculturalism. The governing board of the National Council of Churches in 1990, on the eve of the Columbus Quincentennial, accused him of having "invaded" America.[43] One writer, Kilpatrick Sale, in his book *The Conquest of Paradise* (1992), portrayed Columbus as a destroyer of the pristine paradise of the American Indians. Another critic has tried to link him to the origin of American racism.[44] And still another has accused him of practicing "Christian imperialism."[45]

In a number of instances, these harsh criticisms have spawned protest marches in the United States in recent years, most commonly around Columbus Day (October 12), a federal holiday. The protests are often initiated by the American Indian Movement (AIM) and its sympathizers; yet no members of AIM have ever stated that they would like to return to the primitive cultural practices that existed among the American Indians before Columbus arrived—an event that opened the doors to immigrants and their ensuing ideas that produced myriad cultural and technological conveniences that, for the most part, even the protesters seem to enjoy.

SOCIALISM OF JAMESTOWN AND PLYMOUTH FAILS

The first English settlers in America landed in 1607 and called their settlement in the New World Jamestown. Headed by Captain John Smith, the colonists were economically organized as a socialistic community, requiring all the settlers to give all products of their labor to "the common store." Individuals had no private property and no economic freedom. This system quickly turned disastrous, bringing famine and starvation. Said an early historian, "It was a premium for idleness, and just suited the drones, who promptly decided that it was unnecessary to work themselves, since others would work for them."[46] Even Smith's threats that if someone did not work, he would not eat did little to improve the economic malaise. Thus, beginning in 1611, Governor Thomas Dale began abolishing the common store system, and four years later he had the London Company grant fifty acres of land to each colonist if he would clear the trees and farm it. The injection of private property and economic freedom brought about a dramatic change in Jamestown. Now the colonists worked and prospered. The new economic system demonstrated that socialism does not work. It also showed, as one observer once noted, that "Christianity is not a socialistic chimera, intended to renew the customs of the world before changing the heart."[47]

A similar situation transpired in Massachusetts among the Pilgrims. When they landed on the shores of Cape Cod Bay in 1620 and set up the Plymouth Colony, they, like the Jamestown colonists, tried to equate Christianity with socialism. Their common store system also failed. The colony was experiencing economic disaster. Something had to be done. The colony's governor, William Bradford, like Governor Dale in Jamestown, assigned all able-bodied persons or families a portion of land as their own in 1623. Before long the

CAPTAIN JOHN SMITH (1580–1631) saw that the "common store" (socialistic system) fostered lethargy and poverty among the colonists of Virginia, leading him and Governor Thomas Dale to make private property available to colonists, which resulted in economic prosperity.

slothful and unproductive Pilgrims turned from laggards and idle-bodies to willing, productive workers. Men who previously "had feigned sickness were now eager to get into the fields. Even the women went out to work eagerly.... They now took their children with them and happily engaged in labor for their own family. The result was that the following harvest was a tremendous, bountiful harvest, and abundant thanksgiving was celebrated in America."[48] With the common stock system, "the Pilgrims had little incentive to produce commodities other than those needed for their immediate sustenance."[49]

The new system, based on economic freedom, revealed for the second time in America that when people own their own property, they become animated and energetic rather than lethargic and dependent on others. Socialism could only work if human beings were totally sinless individuals who would always seek the best for their neighbor. That kind of person, however, does not exist. For as both the Old and New Testaments teach, man is a fallen, sinful creature who does not first seek his neighbor's welfare. The psalmist says, "Surely I was sinful at birth, sinful from the time my mother conceived me" (Psalm 51:5). Similarly, the Apostle Paul declared, "For all have sinned and fall short of the glory of God" (Romans 3:23).

Thus, while Christianity does not advocate a given economic ideology, its support of human freedom and private property rights provides fertile ground for the existence of a free enterprise economic system as opposed to a planned or command economy such as socialism or communism, where human freedom is severely curtailed and private property proscribed. Nor is Christianity opposed to people being thrifty and productive, which can and often has resulted in many individuals' becoming wealthy. Abraham was one such person. Neither he nor his wealth were biblically condemned. It was not the possession of wealth that Christ condemned in the parable of the Rich Man, but the overattachment that the rich man had to his possessions.

While Christianity is not opposed to individuals becoming wealthy, it does not, however, countenance wealth as an end in itself. Christians have always been expected to use their acquired wealth to God's glory and to the welfare of their neighbor, as Luther and Calvin frequently emphasized.

CHRISTIANITY'S CONCEPT OF TIME

Closely related to the dignity of labor and economic freedom is Christianity's concept of time. The British historian Paul Johnson argues that one of Christianity's great strengths lies in its concept of time.[50] Unlike the Greeks, who saw time as cyclical, Christianity, given its Judaic background, has always seen time as linear, meaning that life and events proceed from one historical point to another. The Old Testament predicts the coming of the Messiah in that manner (see, for example, Daniel 9:25–26). St. Paul understood this when he said, "But when the time had fully come, God sent his Son" (Galatians 4:4).

Christianity's linear concept of time led to the invention of mechanical clocks in the Middle Ages. Daniel Boorstin, the venerable American historian, says that for centuries "man allowed his time to be parsed by the changing cycles of daylight, [remaining] a slave of the sun."[51] This state of affairs, says Boorstin, changed when Christian monks needed to know the times for their appointed prayers, giving rise to Europe's first mechanical clocks.[52] The appointed periods of prayer in the monasteries became known as "canonical hours."

PERSPECTIVES OF LABOR AND ECONOMICS

Pre-Christian Perspective	Christian Perspective
Greco-Roman	
—Labor is demeaning	—Labor is honorable (2 Thess. 2:10; Ex. 20:9)
—Labor is only for slaves	—Laborer deserves his wages (1 Cor. 9:9; Deut. 25:4)
—Free citizens do not labor	—Labor is a calling *(vocatio)* from God John Tauler (14th cent.) Martin Luther (16th cent.)
Hebrew	
—Labor is honorable (Ex. 20:9)	—Work ethic enjoined Martin Luther John Calvin (16th cent.)
—Laborer deserves his wages (Deut. 25:4)	—Dignity of labor produced a middle class
—Property rights enjoined (Ex. 20:15: "You shall not steal")	—Profit motive is honorable (Matt: 25:15–30: Jesus' parable of the Talents)

Referring to his second coming (the end of the world), Jesus said, "Therefore keep watch, because you do not know the day or the hour" (Matthew 25:13). This linear concept of time had the effect of Christians seeing time as limited and having an end point. Although Christ's warning referred to his sudden return and hence the need for Christians to be prepared, Paul Johnson argues that this awareness induced in Christians "a sense of anxiety about time, which made men dissatisfied by progress but for the same reason determined to pursue it."[53] Johnson refers to the British monk, the Venerable Bede of the eighth century, who said, "Write faster . . . there is so little time."[54] This time-related anxiousness motivated Christians to make the most of their time, economically and religiously. This motivation is clearly reflected by Annie Louisa Walker Coghill, who in 1854 wrote a hymn titled "Work for the Night Is Coming." And in a similar fashion, James Montgomery in 1853 penned his hymn "Work While It Is Today."

CONCLUSION

By giving dignity to labor and accenting the spirit of individual freedom, Christianity produced profound economic effects. Johnson says that "Christianity was one of the principal dynamic forces in the agricultural revolution on which the prosperity of Western Europe ultimately rested, and it was the haunting sense of time and its anxiety to accomplish, its eradicable urge to move and arrive, which gave men in the West the will to industrialize and create our modern material structure." Moreover, "Christianity provided the moral code, the drill and the discipline—as well as the destination—which enabled the unwieldy army of progress to lumber into the future."[55] In a related manner, Rabbi Daniel Lapin recently stated, "It's no accident that a capital market has never arisen indigenously in any non-Christian country."[56]

Finally, contrary to what is often erroneously assumed today, the dignity of labor and the economic freedom of the individual cannot exist in a socialist or nondemocratic society. As Milton Friedman has stated in his book *Capitalism and Freedom*, "A society which is socialist cannot also be democratic, in the sense of guaranteeing individual freedom."[57] And as shown above, individual freedom and economic freedom are inseparable. Both are products of the Christian ethic.

NOTES

1. Lynn D. White, "The Significance of Medieval Christianity," in *The Vitality of the Christian Tradition,* ed. George F. Thomas (New York: Harper and Brothers, 1945), 91.

2. Gerhard Uhlhorn, *Christian Charity in the Ancient Church* (New York: Charles Scribner's Sons, 1883), 107.

3. Ferdinand S. Schenck, *Christian Evidences and Ethics* (New York: YMCA Press, 1910), 94.

4. Uhlhorn, *Christian Charity,* 15.

5. White, "Significance of Medieval Christianity," 91.

6. Herbert B. Workman, *Persecution in the Early Church* (New York: Oxford University Press [1906], 1980), 72.

7. Kenneth Latourette, *A History of Christianity* (New York: Harper and Row, 1953), 246.

8. White, "Significance of Medieval Christianity," 91.

9. Edward Westermarck, *Christianity and Morals* (New York: Macmillan, 1939), 268.

10. Emil Brunner, *Christianity and Civilization* (New York: Charles Scribner's Sons, 1949), 61–62.

11. Latourette, *History of Christianity,* 246.

12. Workman, *Persecution in the Early Church,* 72.

13. Max Weber, *The Protestant Ethic and the Spirit of Capitalism,* trans. Talcott Parsons (New York: Charles Scribner's Sons, 1958), 35.

14. John Calvin, *Commentaries on the Four Last Books of Moses Arranged in the Form of a Harmony,* trans. Charles William Bingham (Grand Rapids: Wm. B. Eerdmans, 1950), 131.

15. Ibid., 132.

16. Ibid., 131.

17. Weber, *Protestant Ethic,* 121.

18. Kurt Samuelsson, *Religion and Economic Action: A Critique of Max Weber,* trans. E. Geoffrey French (New York: Harper Torchbooks, 1961).

19. D. James Kennedy and Jerry Newcombe, *What If Jesus Had Never Been Born?* (Nashville: Thomas Nelson, 1994), 115.

20. John Chamberlain, *The Roots of Capitalism* (Indianapolis: Liberty Press, 1976), 75.

21. Arthur Lee, *An Appeal to the Justice and Interests of the People of Great Britain, in the Present Dispute with America,* 4th ed. (New York: n.p., 1775), 14: cited in James W. Ely, *The Guardian of Every Other Right* (New York: Oxford University Press, 1992), 26.

22. Karl Marx and Friedrich Engels, *The Communist Manifesto,* ed. Samuel H. Beer (New York: Appleton-Century-Crofts, 1955), 24.

23. Harold Shukman, "Editor's Preface," in Dmitri Volkogonov, *Autopsy for an Empire: The Seven Leaders Who Built the Soviet Regime* (New York: Free Press, 1997), xi.

24. John E. Booty, "Christian Socialism," *Academic American Encyclopedia* (Danbury, Conn.: Grolier Publishing, 1996), 4:412.

25. F. A. Hayek, *The Road to Serfdom* (Chicago: University of Chicago Press, 1944), 100.

26. Fyodor Mikhaylovich Dostoyevsky, *The Brothers Karamazov,* trans. Constance Garnett (Chicago: Encyclopedia Britannica, Inc., 1952), 32.

27. Pope Leo XIII, *Rerum Novarum,* no. 4: cited in Adolpho Lindenberg, *The Free Market in a Christian Society,* trans. Donna H. Sandin (Montreal: St. Antoninus for Catholic Education in Business, 1999), 131.

28. Pope John Paul II, *Centesimus Annus,* no. 41, (Washington, D.C.: United States Catholic Conference, 1996), 81–82.

29. Chamberlain, *Roots of Capitalism,* 72–73.

30. Milton Friedman, *Free to Choose* (New York: Harcourt, Brace, and Jovanovich, 1979), 46.

31. Chamberlain, *Roots of Capitalism,* 72.

32. Karl Marx, *Capital: A Critique of Political Economy,* ed. Friedrich Engels (Chicago: Charles H. Kerr, 1909), 3:52–59.

33. R. D. Vinokur, *Great Soviet Encyclopedia* (New York: Collier Macmillan, 1979), 20:556.

34. F. A. Hayek, *The Fatal Conceit: The Errors of Socialism* (Chicago: University of Chicago Press, 1988), 105.

35. Christopher Columbus, "The First Voyage of Columbus," in *Christopher Columbus: Four Voyages to the New World,* ed. and trans. R. H. Major (New York: Corinth Books, 1961), 17.

36. Robert Royal, *1492 and All That* (Washington, D.C.: Ethics and Public Policy Center, 1992), 48.

37. Samuel Eliot Morison, *Admiral of the Ocean Sea: A Life of Christopher Columbus* (Boston: Little, Brown, 1942), 45.

38. Ibid., 47.

39. Ferdinand Columbus, *The Life of Admiral Christopher Columbus,* trans. Benjamin Keen (New Brunswick: Rutgers University Press, 1959), 59.

40. William Eleroy Curtis, "The Existing Autographs of Christopher Columbus," *Annual Report of the American Historical Association* (1894): 509.

41. Morison, *Admiral of the Ocean Sea,* 47.

42. John Schwartz, "The Great Food Migration," *Newsweek: Columbus Special Edition* (Fall/Winter 1991): 62.

43. James Muldoon, "The Columbus Centennial: Should Christians Celebrate It?" *America* (October 7, 1990), 300.

44. Jan Carew, "Columbus and the Origins of Racism in the Americas: Part One," *Race and Class* 33 (1988).

45. Stephen Greenblatt, *Marvelous Possession: The Wonders of the New World* (Chicago: Univesity of Chicago Press, 1991), 71.

46. John Esten Cooke, *Virginia: A History of the People* (Boston: Houghton Mifflin, 1897), 109.

47. C. Schmidt, *The Social Results of Early Christianity,* trans. R. W. Dale (London: Wm. Isbister, 1889), 161.

48. Kennedy and Newcombe, *What If Jesus Had Never Been Born?* 121.

49. Harry M. Ward, *Statism in Plymouth Colony* (Port Washington, N.Y.: National University Publications/Kennikat Press, 1973), 38.

50. Paul Johnson, *Enemies of Society* (New York: Atheneum, 1977), 32.
51. Daniel Boorstin, *The Discoverers* (New York: Vintage Books, 1985), 36.
52. Ibid.
53. Johnson, *Enemies of Society,* 33.
54. Ibid., 32.
55. Ibid., 118.
56. "Rabbi Lapin Calling America Back to Tradition," *Human Events* (October 20, 2000), 12.
57. Milton Friedman, *Capitalism and Freedom* (Chicago: University of Chicago Press, 1962), 8.

9

SCIENCE: ITS CHRISTIAN CONNECTIONS

"If I have been able to see farther than others,
it was because I stood on the shoulders of giants."

Sir Isaac Newton

Alfred North Whitehead, the renowned philosopher of science, once said that "faith in the possibility of science, generated antecedently to the development of modern scientific theory, is an unconscious derivative from medieval theology."[1] Similarly, Lynn White, the historian of medieval science, has stated that "the [medieval] monk was an intellectual ancestor of the scientist."[2] And the German physicist Ernst Mach once remarked, "Every unbiased mind must admit that the age in which the chief development of the science of mechanics took place was an age of predominantly theological cast."[3]

Crediting Christianity with the arrival of science may sound surprising to many, including many scientists. Why is that? The answer seems to go back to Andrew Dickson White, who in 1896 published *A History of the Warfare of Science with Theology in Christendom*. Ever since then, along with the growth of secularism, countless professors in colleges and universities

218

have uncritically accepted White's argument that Christianity is an enemy of science, so it seems unthinkable to many that it could possibly have fostered the arrival of science. Given this widespread bias, the old adage comes to mind: "A little knowledge is a dangerous thing."

CHRISTIAN PRESUPPOSITIONS UNDERLYING SCIENCE

There are numerous pronounced differences between Christianity and pagan religions. One is that Christianity, with its Judaic heritage, has always taught and insisted that there is only one God, a rational being. Without this Christian presupposition, there would be no science. The origin of science, said Alfred North Whitehead, required Christianity's "insistence on the rationality of God."[4]

If God is a rational being, then may not human beings, who are made in his image, also employ rational processes to study and investigate the world in which they live? That question, of course, was answered in the affirmative when some Christian philosophers linked rationality with the empirical, inductive method. One such person was Robert Grosseteste (ca. 1168–1253), a Franciscan bishop and the first chancellor of Oxford University, who first proposed the inductive, experimental method,[5] an approach to knowledge that was further advocated by his student Roger Bacon (1214–94), also a Franciscan monk, who asserted that "all things must be verified by experience."[6] Bacon was a devout believer in the truthfulness of Scripture, and being empirically minded, he saw the Bible in the light of sound reason and as verifiable by experience. Another natural philosopher, also a Franciscan monk, was William of Occam (or Ockham, 1285–1347). He too, like Bacon, argued that knowledge needed to be derived inductively.

Almost three hundred years later another Bacon, Francis Bacon (1561–1626), gave further momentum to the inductive method by actually recording his experimental results. He has been called "the practical creator of scientific induction."[7] In the context of rationality, he stressed careful observation of phenomena and collecting systematic information in order to understand nature's secrets.[8] His scientific interests did not deter him from also devoting time to theology, for he also wrote treatises on the Psalms and on prayer.

By introducing the inductive empirical method guided by rational procedures, Roger Bacon, William Occam, and Francis Bacon departed to a considerable degree from the ancient Greek perspective of Aristotle (384–322 B.C.). Aristotelianism, which had a stranglehold on the world for

FRANCIS BACON (1561–1626), a British Franciscan monk, was one of the pioneers of science who advocated the experimental method of acquiring knowledge that scientists now regard as a *sine qua non*.

fifteen hundred years, held that knowledge was only acquired through the deductive processes of the mind; the inductive method, which required manual activity, was taboo. As noted in chapter 7, physical activities were only for slaves, not for thinkers or freemen. Complete confidence in the deductive method as the only way of arriving at knowledge and understanding was also a view widely held by Christian monks, natural philosophers, and theologians until the arrival of Robert Grosseteste, Roger Bacon, William Occam, and Francis Bacon. Even after these empirically minded thinkers had introduced their ideas, the scholastic world, for the most part, continued to adhere to Aristotle's approach to knowledge.

Another prominent presupposition of Christianity is that God, who created the world, is separate and distinct from it. Aristotelian philosophy, on the other hand, saw God (or the gods in Aristotle's pagan thinking) and the universe of nature intertwined. This posits a pantheistic, panemanationist conception of the world.[9] Planets, for example, were seen as having an inner intelligence (*anima*) that induced them to move. This pantheistic view of planetary movement was first challenged by Jean Buridan (1300–1358), a Christian philosopher at the University of Paris.[10] Also contrary to Christian theology, which said that "in the beginning God created the heavens and the earth" (Genesis 1:1), was Aristotle's theory that the world neither had a beginning nor was created by God (see his *On the Heavens* 279–84).

Although Christianity very early in its existence condemned pantheism, its natural philosophers and scholastics for the longest time failed to see the pantheistic elements embedded in the Aristotelian philosophy that they used to explain the world of nature. Even after Roger Bacon and William Occam broke with Aristotle's perspective by advocating the inductive method, the natural philosophers and scholastics within Christendom clung to it contumaciously. Some—for example, the Franciscan order to which Bacon belonged—even saw Bacon's views as heretical, and in 1278 it imprisoned him for fourteen years.[11] Continued resistance to the inductive method together with the failure to see Aristotle's pantheistic view of the physical world delayed not only the arrival of science but also its progress, because pantheism, like the anti-inductive approach to knowledge, is antithetical to science. Pantheism implies that the scientific method, which manipulates various elements within the physical universe, is sacrilegious and an affront to the divine within nature. Thus, only in the Christian perspective, which sees God and nature as distinctively separate entities, is science possible. As has been rightly said, "Science could never have come into being among the animists of central or southern Africa or many other places in the world because they would never have begun to experiment on the natural world, since everything—whether stones or trees or animals or anything else—within it contained living spirits of various gods or ancestors."[12]

Had this major paradigm shift from Aristotle's pantheistic theory to a rational-inductive approach not occurred with men like Grosseteste, Buridan, the Bacons, William Occam, and Nicholas of Oresme, and later with men like Copernicus, Vesalius, Kepler, and Galileo, who from their knowledge of Scripture knew they were not investigating the divine in nature, there would be no science today. They saw themselves as merely trying to understand the world that God had created and over which he told mankind to have "dominion" (Genesis 1:28 NKJV). This paradigm shift is another example of Christianity's wholesome impact on the world.

Belief in the rationality of God not only led to the inductive method but also led to the conclusion that the universe is governed rationally by discoverable laws. This assumption is vitally important to scientific research, because in a pagan or polytheistic world, which saw its gods often engaged in jealous, irrational behavior in a world that was nonrational, any systematic investigation of such a world would seem futile. Only in Christian thought, which posits "the existence of a single God, the Creator and Governor of the universe, [one that] functions in an orderly and normally predictable manner,"[13] is it possible for science to exist and operate.

CHRISTIANS, THE PIONEERS OF SCIENCE

"From the thirteenth century onward into the eighteenth," says Lynn White, "every major scientist, in effect, explained his motivations in religious terms."[14] But if one looks at current textbooks in science, one would never know this was true. Today virtually all references to the Christian beliefs of the early scientists are omitted. This is especially unfortunate because these convictions often played a dominant role in their scientific work. Hence, the remaining part of the present chapter cites many Christian scientists who were pioneers and who made lasting contributions in major areas of science. To cite all of them would be beyond the scope and purpose of this book. However, those cited were, for the most part, on the "cutting edge" of science.

OCCAM'S RAZOR

One early cutting-edge concept was "Occam's razor" (no pun intended), named in honor of William Occam (1280–1349), which had a tremendous influence on the development of modern science. Simply stated, it is the scientific principle that says that what can be done or explained with the fewest assumptions should be used, meaning that a scientist needs to "shave off" all excess assumptions. It is a principle of parsimony. While this idea first arose with Peter of Spain (a Christian) in the thirteenth century, it was Occam who gave it plausibility. Modern scientists today use this principle in theorizing and explaining research findings.

As was common with virtually all of the medieval natural philosophers (harbinger scientists), Occam did not confine himself just to scientific matters. He also wrote two theological treatises, one dealing with the Lord's Supper and the other with the body of Christ. Both works had a positive influence on Martin Luther. Occam's theological writings and his Christian convictions affected Luther's theological thinking and were an integral part of his worldview.

HUMAN PHYSIOLOGY AND BIOLOGY

Most people think of **Leonardo da Vinci (1452–1519)** as a great artist and painter, but he was also a scientific genius. He analyzed and theorized in the areas of botany, optics, physics, hydraulics, and aeronautics, but his greatest benefit to science lies in the study of human physiology. By dissecting cadavers, which he often did at night because such activity was largely forbidden, he produced meticulous drawings of the human body. One historian says that "his drawings and comments, when collected in one massive volume, present a complete course of anatomical study."[15] This was a major breakthrough because before this time and for some time after, physicians really had very little valid knowledge of the human body. They were largely dependent on the writings of the Greek physician Galen (ca. 130–200), whose propositions on human physiology were in large measure extrapolated from lower animals such as dogs and monkeys. Leonardo's anatomical observations led him to question, for example, the belief that air passed from the lungs to the heart. He used a pump to test this hypothesis and found that it was impossible to force air into the heart from the lungs.[16]

Lest someone think Leonardo's scientific theories and drawings of the human anatomy were divorced from his religious convictions, it is well to recall his other activities. His paintings—for example, *The Baptism of Christ*, *The Last Supper*, and *The Resurrection of Christ*—are enduring reminders of his Christian beliefs.

The anatomical work of Leonardo was not forgotten. The man who followed in his footsteps was **Andreas Vesalius (1514–64),** a young, brash anatomist from Belgium. At age twenty-two, he began teaching at the University of Padua. In 1543 he published his famous work, *De humani corpis fabrica* (Fabric of the Human Body). The book mentions over two hundred errors in Galen's physiological writings. The errors were found largely as a result of his dissecting cadavers that he obtained illegally, even though some of the medical schools already studied cadavers legally in the 1300s. He often secretly took executed criminals off the gibbets at night.

When Vesalius exposed the numerous errors of Galen, he received no accolades. His contemporaries, like his former teacher Sylvius, still wedded to the Greek physician, called him a "madman." Others saw him as "a clever, dangerous free-thinker of medicine."[17] Indeed, he encountered more than his share of troubles. While in Spain as the physician of Charles V, he was not permitted to dissect any corpses. Yet after Charles's reign, according to one uncorroborated account, he did perform one dissection, an autopsy on a nobleman. Unknown to Vesalius, the nobleman was not quite dead. Opening his chest, according to reports, Vesalius and his assistants witnessed a beating heart. His enemies accused him of impiety and murder, for which the Inquisition sentenced him to death. However, King Philip II reportedly intervened and commuted his sentence on the condition that he would take a pilgrimage to the Holy Land. This he did, but on his way back he became seriously ill, and when his ship anchored at the island of Zante, he died. That he died on the island is true, but whether he went to the Holy Land to escape execution is not certain, because another uncorroborated story says that he went to Palestine to escape his wife's vicious tongue.[18]

It will probably never be known for certain why Vesalius went to the Holy Land. Could he simply have gone because he was a Christian? Although he questioned much of the existing physiological knowledge, he never questioned God's role in the construction of the human body. On one occasion he said, "We are driven to wonder at the handiwork of the Almighty."[19] He obviously was not condemned as a heretic, as some anti-church critics have implied, for at the time of his death he had an offer waiting for him to teach at the University of Padua, where he first began his career.[20] Whatever the reasons for his fateful trip, one thing is certain: he greatly advanced the knowledge of medicine and physiology, for which he is rightfully known as "the father of human anatomy."

Where would the study of genetics be today had the world not been blessed with the birth of **Gregor Johann Mendel (1822–1884)**? As often stated in science textbooks, it was his working on cross-pollinating garden peas that led to the concept of genes and the discovery of his three laws: the law of segregation, the law of independent assortment, and the law of dominance. The first law states that a sperm or an egg may contain either a shortness or a tallness factor (gene); the second law asserts that characteristics are inherited independently of one another; and the third says that one gene always dominates, for example, tallness over shortness of an organism.

Although Mendel was an Augustinian monk who spent most of his life in the monastery in Brno, Moravia, not much is known about his personal convictions as a Christian. It is known, however, that after he studied Darwin's theory of evolution, he rejected it.[21] Whether it was his Christian beliefs that prompted him to reach that conclusion is not clear.

ASTRONOMY

Four names loom large in the textbooks of astronomy: Copernicus, Brahe, Kepler, and Galileo. But the undeniable fact that these men were

NICOLAUS COPERNICUS (1473–1543), a canon of the Frauenburg Cathedral in East Prussia (right), proposed the heliostatic theory, resulting in what scientists call "the Copernican Revolution."

devout Christians, which influenced their scientific work, is conspicuously omitted in most science texts.

Nicolaus Copernicus (1473–1543) was born in Torun, Poland, although his childhood language was German, as was his mother and his name, Niklas Koppernigk. He belonged to a German fraternity at the university in Cracow, where he Latinized his name to Copernicus. Before World War I, historians saw him as Prussian, as did John Draper in his *The Intellectual Development of Europe* (1896). But after World War I, with Germany having fallen out of favor with British and American historians, he has been referred to as Polish.

While he was still a child, his father died, and he was sent to his mother's brother, a Catholic priest, who reared him. He earned a doctor's degree and was also trained as a physician; however, his uncle had him study theology, which resulted in his becoming a canon (not a priest) in the Frauenburg Cathedral in East Prussia. But the world, especially the scientific world, knows him best for having introduced the heliostatic theory (sometimes referred to as the "Copernican Revolution") that states that the sun, not the earth, is the center of the universe and that the earth revolves around the sun. His theory was not entirely new, for in the third century B.C. Aristarchus of Samos suggested that the earth might not be the center of the universe. And in the Middle Ages it was suggested that the earth might be in motion, "but nobody had troubled to work out the details of such a scheme."[22] Copernicus did, and therein lies much of his greatness.

Copernicus received a copy of his masterwork *De revolutionibus orbium coelestium* (Concerning the Revolutions of the Celestial Bodies) on his deathbed in 1543. He had hesitated to publish his work earlier, not because he feared the charge of heresy from the church, as has been often asserted without any documentation, but because he wanted to avoid the ridicule of other scientists, who were still strongly tied to Aristotle and Ptolemy. In fact, Arthur Koestler calls Copernicus "the timid canon."[23] It was his Christian friends, especially Georg Joachim Rheticus and Andreas Osiander, two Lutherans, who persuaded Copernicus to publish his work. Before its publication, Rheticus was so interested in Copernicus's research that he took a leave of absence from his mathematics professorship at Luther's Wittenberg University in order to visit him in Frauenburg. Rheticus arrived in 1539 and stayed for two years with Copernicus.

Thus, although Copernicus remained a moderately loyal son of the Roman Catholic Church, it was his Lutheran friends that made his publication possible. As one modern scholar has said, "No historian will cover up the facts that a Lutheran prince [Duke Albrecht of Prussia] subsidized the publication of his [Copernicus's] work, that a Lutheran theologian [Andreas Osiander] arranged for the printing, and that a Lutheran mathematician [Georg Joachim Rheticus] supervised the printing."[24]

This information is undoubtedly surprising to many people, including university students, because most only hear that Christian theologians condemned Copernicus's work. For instance, critics like to cite Luther, who reportedly called Copernicus a "fool." But as John W. Montgomery has shown, this frequently cited remark lacks reliable scholarly support. First, it comes from Luther's *Table Talks,* a late redacted copy, published twenty years after his death, of what some thought he said. Second, Copernicus is not named in the remark, so even if Luther did make that statement, it is not certain that he had him in mind. Third, if he did make the comment, it was conversational. Fourth, this is the only such remark in all of Luther's writings, which total nearly one hundred volumes. Fifth, "Luther elsewhere makes clear that he is quite willing to admit that the Biblical writers can and do describe physical phenomena from their own observational standpoint and not in absolute terms; thus the Joshua passage could not have been for him an insuperable barrier to the acceptance of the Copernican position."[25] And finally, Philipp Melanchthon, Luther's closest colleague, who initially was critical of Copernicus, stated publicly in 1549, "We have begun to admire and love Copernicus more."[26]

Another oft-cited scientist who furthered the cause of scientific astronomy is **Tycho Brahe (1546–1601)** of Denmark, a man who at age nineteen lost part of his nose in a university duel and artificially restored it with a nose of silver. In 1572 he published *De nova stella* (Concerning the New Star). It described an extremely bright star in the constellation of Cassiopeia. As a Lutheran, he wrote about "the divine works that shine forth everywhere in the structure of the world."[27] In 1577, one year after he built an observatory, he published a paper describing a newly sighted comet. In spite of his discoveries and calculations, however, he essentially remained an Aristotelian and never accepted the heliocentric theory.

When Brahe died in 1601, **Johannes Kepler (1571–1630)** succeeded him in Prague under an imperial appointment by Emperor Rudolph II. Kepler, who had studied for three years to become a Lutheran pastor, turned to astronomy after he was assigned to teach mathematics in Graz, Austria, in 1594.[28] Unlike his predecessor Brahe, who never did accept the heliocentric theory, Kepler did. In fact, Owen Gingerich, a Harvard University astronomer, says that Kepler, not Copernicus, deserves the real credit for the heliocentric theory. "Copernicus gave the world a helio*static* system, [but] it was Kepler who made it into a helio*centric* system." Gingerich further says, "We have grown so accustomed to calling this [heliocentric theory] the Copernican system that we usually forget that many of its attributes could better be called the Keplerian system."[29]

Kepler's mathematical calculations contradicted the old Aristotelian theory that said the planets orbited in perfect circles, an assumption that Copernicus continued to hold. This led Kepler to hypothesize and empirically substantiate that planets orbited elliptically, a finding known as his first law. He also found that planets do not move at a uniform speed, resulting in his second law. Later he discovered that the squares of the time it takes for any two planets to revolve around the sun are "as the cubes of their mean distances from the sun."[30] This discovery is his third law, also known as the harmonic law.

These three laws alone, often called the first "natural laws" in science, were enough to make Kepler famous. But he did much more. The list of his accomplishments is long. In 1597, at age twenty-six, he published

JOHANNES KEPLER (1571–1630), a devout Christian, studied for the Lutheran ministry, turned to astronomy, and became famous for discovering three laws of planetary motion.

Mysterium cosmographicum (Mystery of the Universe), and in 1604 his *Optics* was published. His most famous work, *Astronomia nova* (The New Astronomy), appeared in 1609. It spelled out his first two laws. Both laws contradicted the old Aristotelian doctrine, and Kepler made it clear that he had done so empirically.[31] In 1618 he published *Harmonice mundi* (Harmony of the Earth), in which he stated his third law.

He was the first to define weight as the mutual attraction between two bodies, an insight that Isaac Newton used later in formulating the law of gravity; and he was the first to explain that tides were caused by the moon. Three hundred years after he stated the inverse square law in optics, photometry confirmed his hypothesis.[32] He published an astronomy book, *Tabulae Rudolphinae*, in honor of Emperor Rudolph II, who conferred on Kepler the title of Imperial Mathematicus. This book contained tables and rules that were used for more than one hundred years to predict planetary positions.[33]

Many people today know that Dionysius Exiguus, the Scythian monk who gave the world the calendar's dating system that is based on the time

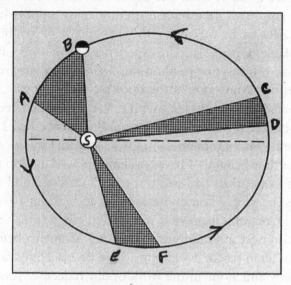

KEPLER'S SECOND SCIENTIFIC LAW, known as the law of equal areas, reveals that planets orbit faster when near the sun. In the diagram, for instance, the earth covers the shaded distance of A-B, C-D, and E-F in equal periods of time.

of Christ's birth, calculated Christ's birth several years too late. Kepler was the first to discover this error. His calculations placed Christ's birth between 4 and 5 B.C., a date commonly accepted today. Along with his many scientific discoveries, Arthur Koestler also credits him with being the first to pioneer differential calculus.[34]

Many of Kepler's achievements came amidst much personal suffering. Some of his hardships were a direct result of his Lutheran convictions, which cost him his position in Graz, where the Catholic Archduke of Hapsburg expelled him in 1598. Another time he was fined for burying his second child according to Lutheran funeral rites. His salary was often in arrears, even in Prague, where he had an imperial appointment. He lost his position in Prague in 1612 when Emperor Rudolph II was forced to abdicate. He was plagued with digestive problems, gall bladder ailments, skin rashes, piles, and sores on his feet that healed badly because of his hemophilia. Childhood smallpox left him with defective eyesight and crippled hands. Even death was no stranger to him. His first wife died, and several of his children from both his first and second wife also died. A number of times he was forced to move from one city to another, sometimes even from one country to another. Often he had no money to support his family or himself, largely because he was paid rather irregularly or lost his position.

Whether in fame or pain—and he experienced both—his Christian faith remained unshaken. In his first publication, *Mysterium cosmographicum,* he showed his Christian conviction at the book's conclusion wherein he gave all honor and praise to God.[35] Later, with reference to discovering his first law, he said, "I believe it was an act of Divine Providence that I arrived just at the time when Longomontanus [Brahe's assistant] was occupied with Mars."[36] Another time he said, "I have constantly prayed to God that I might succeed in what Copernicus had said was true."[37] Stressed and overworked as he often was, he would sometimes fall asleep without having said his evening prayers. When this happened, it bothered him so much that the first thing he would do next morning was to repent.[38] Moments before he died, an attending Lutheran pastor asked him where he placed his faith. Calmly, he replied, "Solely and alone in the work of our redeemer Jesus Christ."[39] Those were the final words of the man who earlier in his life had written that he only tried "thinking God's thoughts after him." He was still in that mindset when, four months before he died, he penned his own epitaph:

> *I used to measure the heavens,*
> *Now I must measure the earth.*
> *Though sky-bound was my spirit,*
> *My earthly body rests here.*[40]

Galileo (1564–1642), like Kepler, who was a contemporary of his, searched and described the heavenly bodies. He was the first to use the telescope to study the skies, although he did not invent it. That credit goes to Johann Lippershey, who first revealed his invention in 1608 at a fair in Frankfort. With the telescope Galileo discovered that the moon's surface had valleys and mountains, that the moon had no light of its own but merely reflected it from the sun, that the Milky Way was composed of millions of stars, that Jupiter had four bright satellites, and that the sun had spots. Apart from using the telescope, he determined, contrary to Aristotelian belief, that heavy objects did not fall faster than light ones.

Unfortunately, Galileo's observations were not well received by his Roman Catholic superiors, who saw Aristotle's view—not that of the Bible—as the final word of truth. Even letting Pope Paul V look through the telescope at his discoveries did not help his cause. His masterpiece, *A*

Dialogue on the Two Principal Systems of the World (1632), resulted in a summons before the Inquisition, where he was compelled to deny his belief in the Copernican theory and sentenced to an indefinite prison term. For some reason the sentence was never carried out. In fact, four years later he published *Dialogues on the Two New Sciences*. This work helped Isaac Newton formulate his three laws of motion.

Galileo was less pro-Copernican than Kepler, with whom he often disagreed. He largely ignored Kepler's discoveries, apparently because he was still interested in keeping the Ptolemaic theory alive.[41] He also criticized Kepler's idea of the moon affecting tides.[42] If he was less pro-Copernican than Kepler—and he was—then why did he get into trouble with the theologians who placed his books on the Index's forbidden books? The answer seems to be because he was Roman Catholic, while Kepler was Lutheran. As noted earlier, it was Lutherans, not Catholics, who encouraged and even financially underwrote the publication of Copernicus's work. Thus, when modern critics (including scientists) condemn the church or Christianity for its resistance to the Copernican theory, it must be noted and underscored that it was not the entire church that did so. The Calvinists also did not condemn the Copernican theory. It is therefore quite appropriate to credit Christianity with lending support to the Copernican theory, not only because of men like Copernicus, Osiander, Rheticus, Duke Albrecht, Brahe, Kepler, and others, but also because Christianity, at least three hundred years earlier, had spawned individuals like Grosseteste, Buridan, Oresme, Roger Bacon, and Francis Bacon, who introduced the inductive method that made it possible to discover and corroborate the heliocentric theory.

In the sixteenth and early seventeenth centuries Lutherans bolstered science, and after that the Calvinists (mostly Puritans) did much to advance science.[43] For example, the Calvinists founded the Royal Society of London in 1645, with seven of its ten scientists being Puritans. After royal recognition in 1661, it became the world's most prestigious scientific association. As Protestants in the sixteenth and seventeenth centuries helped keep the scientific movement alive, there were also some Catholic scientists (for example, Copernicus and Galileo), though they received little support from their church.

PHYSICS

In the area of physics and astronomy, the findings of Kepler reverberated after his death in 1630. One scientist who picked up some of these reverberations was **Isaac Newton (1642–1727),** who, like Kepler, was highly gifted in mathematics but especially in astronomical physics. It was

Kepler's planetary laws that helped Newton devise the inverse square law of gravitation. Without these laws, says Alfred Koestler, Newton "could not have arrived at his synthesis."[44] The discovery of the laws of gravity finally buried Aristotle's theory that each planet had an intelligence. Newton's *Mathematical Principles of Natural Philosophy* is considered "one of the greatest single contributions in the history of science."[45] One can argue that his discovery of gravity also confirmed the biblical statement that God "suspends the earth over nothing" (Job 26:7).

Some have charged that Newton was not an orthodox Christian, but Eric Bell states that he "had no intention of being anything else but a Christian."[46] In fact, some of his writings sound like an echo of the Apostles' Creed. For example, he says, "God governs the world invisibly, and he has commanded us to worship him, and no other God...he has revived Jesus Christ our Redeemer, who has gone into the heavens to receive and prepare a place for us, and...will at length return and reign over us...till he has raised up and judged all the dead."[47] On another occasion he cited Christ's post-resurrection appearance to Thomas as proof that Christ appeared, not as a spirit, but in a body after his resurrection. Specifically, he said Christ's resurrected body had "the consistency and solidity of flesh and bones."[48] Newton revered the Bible to such a degree that he searched it for a hidden code that would reveal the future.[49] Frank Manuel, an authority on Newton, says that he should not be seen as an eighteenth-century deist who saw Christ as just another prophet or inspired human being, "nor should Newton be transformed into a nineteenth-century New England Unitarian, though many have tried."[50]

E. A. Burtt corroborates Newton's Christian faith by quoting him: "The Father is omniscient, and hath all knowledge originally in his own breast, and communicates knowledge of future things to Jesus Christ, and none in heaven or earth, is worthy to receive knowledge of future things immediately from the Father but the Lamb."[51] In short, if Newton had some deistic inclinations, his scientific thinking continued to be strongly linked to the biblical postulates of Christianity.

We next encounter **Gottfried Leibniz (1646–1716).** Both he and Newton are credited with developing the theory of differential calculus, and because physics is so dependent on higher mathematics (the language of science) it can be argued that Leibniz's mathematical contribution was vital to science. As Herbert Butterfield has aptly stated, "Without the achievements of the mathematicians all scientific revolution, as we know it, would have been impossible."[52] Thus, some historians have credited Leibniz with being the founder of modern science.

Leibniz saw the Bible as God's authoritative word. As a Lutheran, he spoke of God's grace and maintained that there was no conflict between true faith and valid reason. He even remarked that, after having studied various theologians, he accepted the doctrines of the Augsburg Confession (the official Lutheran position presented to Charles V in Augsburg, Germany, in 1530), which strengthened his faith because of its irenic formulations.[53]

In physics the name of **Blaise Pascal (1623–62)** stands out, both for his scientific contributions and for his Christian convictions. Science knows him for Pascal's law, which says that liquid in a container exerts equal pressures in all directions; for his theory pertaining to measuring barometric pressures at different altitudes; for inventing the syringe and the hydraulic press; for constructing the first adding machine; and for Pascal's triangle. Computer science honors him today by having named a computer language after him, and Christian theology honors him for his strong defense of Christianity. He boldly said, "We know God only through Jesus Christ."[54]

Nearly a hundred years after Pascal, **Alessandro Volta (1745–1827)**, an Italian, discovered current electricity. He is honored every time the term *volt* or *voltmeter* is used by mechanics or electricians. Without pretense, Volta regularly reflected his Christian convictions as he participated in Catholic masses and various devotional activities. In one of this letters he wrote, "I am not ashamed of the Gospel, may it produce good fruit!"[55]

Another dedicated physicist, and a Christian who gave much to posterity, was **Georg Simon Ohm (1787–1854)** of Germany. Physicists know him as the formulator of the equation that measures electrical resistance, which today is called Ohm's law, and he is honored by the device known as the *Ohmmeter.* In writing his first volume of *Molecular Physics,* he indicated that he was planning to write additional volumes, "if God gives me the length of days."[56]

Another savant of science was **André Ampere (1775–1836),** whose name is enshrined in the language of electrical measurements. Electricians and motor mechanics regularly use the term *ampere* (or *amp*), a unit that measures the strength of an electric current. They also know that amperes equal volts divided by ohms.

After an earlier lapse in his Christian faith, Ampere returned to it with additional strength. He firmly believed that one can see the existence of God in nature; for example, he wrote, "One of the most striking evidences

GEORGE WASHINGTON CARVER (ca. 1860–1943) works in his laboratory at the Tuskegee Institute in Alabama, where he developed many by-products from peanuts and sweet potatoes.

of the existence of God is the wonderful harmony by which the universe is preserved and living beings are furnished in their organization with everything necessary to life."[57]

The discipline of physics reveals another scientific giant, **Michael Faraday (1791–1867).** He discovered electromagnetic induction, thus making electricity available for varied applications. This, however, was not his only contribution to science and technology. He was the first to make a liquid out of a gas, and he invented the generator. Although he was an Englishman, one year after his death the French Academy of Science characterized him as "the greatest scientist the Academy had ever counted among its members." In his religious life, he was a member of the Sandemanians or Glasists, a small fundamentalist Christian group that firmly believed in the Bible and in Jesus Christ as God's only Son. He not only read the Bible daily, but he also "donated a significant portion of his income to the church and frequently visited and tended the sick."[58]

William Thompson Kelvin (1824–1907) is still another great Christian physicist. Better known as Lord Kelvin, he made his mark in science by establishing the scale of absolute zero, by first conceptualizing energy, and by founding thermodynamics. The Kelvin scale, which measures absolute zero, bears his name. As a Christian, he saw the Christian religion and science as highly compatible. This stance was not well received by those who saw religion and science in conflict with one another. So he once said, "If you think strongly enough, you will be forced by science to the belief in God."[59]

CHEMISTRY

Most high school students encounter the name of **Robert Boyle (1627–1691)** in chemistry class when they learn about Boyle's law. They may also hear that he is recognized as "the father of chemistry." They may even learn that in 1645 he helped found the Royal Society of London for the Improvement of Natural Knowledge that became the most respected scientific association, commonly known as the Royal Society.[60] But few if any students hear or read that Boyle was as interested in Christian theology as he was in science. For instance, he wrote numerous theological essays and contributed money to support Bible translations. He served as governor of the Corporation for the Spread of the Gospel in New England, and in his will he left money for foreign mission work and for "Boyle Lectures" that would be directed to converting unbelievers.[61]

Half a century after Boyle, another prominent chemist, **Antoine Lavoisier (1743–1794)**, appeared. Like so many other scientists, Lavoisier was a Christian, though he had lapsed for a while during his career. This observant Frenchman showed the world that oxygen was a necessary condition for burning materials. He also demonstrated the law of the conservation of energy, that is, that matter cannot be created or destroyed. For these contributions and others, the French Academy of Sciences awarded him a gold medal. However, the French revolutionaries guillotined him five years after the revolution had begun. Many of his biographers note that he died confessing the Christian faith.

A devout Quaker, **John Dalton (1766–1844)**, was the first to publish the atomic weights of some elements. This earned him the title "father of atomic theory." He also formulated the law of partial pressure relative to gases. In 1831 he helped organize the British Association of Advancement of Science.[62] Medical science honors him with the term Daltonism, the alternate name for color-blindness, which he discovered and with which he himself was stricken. His Christian convictions, says Karl Kneller, were never in doubt.[63]

In a discussion pertaining to the discoveries in chemistry it is incumbent to cite **Joseph Priestley (1733–1804)**, the English chemist and clergyman who discovered oxygen. He also discovered hydrochloric acid, nitrous oxide ("laughing gas"), and sulfur dioxide. Even though he believed in Unitarianism as opposed to orthodox Christianity, especially in his sunset years, he continued to believe and argue for the superiority of the teachings and influence of Jesus Christ. In 1803, one year before he died, he published a monograph titled *Socrates and Jesus Compared* in which he contrasted Jesus to the Greek philosopher, saying that "Socrates was an idolater."[64] He also believed in Christ's physical resurrection. Writing to French philosophers and politicians, he said, "The certainty of his [Christ's] resurrection was also evident from the conduct and miracles of the apostles, acting in his name afterwards."[65] And he never saw God or Jesus Christ as irrelevant in his scientific pursuits, as is often the practice in science today.

Still another outstanding scientist and Christian was **George Washington Carver (1864?–1943),** a black American chemist. Born of slave parents, he worked his way through college and joined the faculty at Tuskegee Institute in Alabama. Here he not only became the country's top authority on peanuts and sweet potatoes, but he also developed over three hundred by-products from peanuts, ranging from instant coffee to soap and ink. From the sweet potato he made over one hundred by-products, including flour, shoe polish, and candy. He also used his knowledge to persuade farmers that they could grow peanuts, sweet potatoes, and pecans instead of only cotton. His heeded advice greatly diversified and enriched Southern agriculture.

Carver received numerous honors, one of which was the Roosevelt Medal in 1939. This award read, "To a scientist humbly seeking the guidance of God and a liberator to men of the white race as well as the black." These were fitting words, for Henry Morris writes that Carver was "a sincere and humble Christian" who never hesitated "to confess his faith in the God of the Bible and attribut[e] all his success and ability to God."[66]

MEDICINE

Among the ancient Greeks, the god Aesculapius was said to use serpents and dogs to heal sick people by having them lick the patients with their tongues. (Even today the serpent is a symbol of medicine.) Thus, a dog is often pictured standing beside Aesculapius.[67] But this kind of healing was far removed from any scientific methods.

The first real efforts to study the art and science of healing (medicine) occurred in the Abbey of Monte-Cassino, Italy, founded by the Benedictines in the year 528. Gabriel Compayre says that here the monks studied medicine "with marked devotion." From here "the taste of medical studies spread as far as Salerno, and by the eleventh century, the little town had become an intellectual center which attracted students from all parts of Western Europe."[68] Two hundred years later, Salerno's medical studies attached themselves to the University of Naples. By the mid-1300s the medical school at Montpellier (France) performed dissections on cadavers once every two years, and at the University of Paris at the rate of two per year.[69]

The early studies in medicine, however, like the studies in astronomy, did not always proceed smoothly. Some regional gatherings (synods) in the church—for example, the Synod of Clermont (1130) and the Synod of Lateran (1139)—ruled that monks were to refrain from studying medicine.[70] And (as noted above) in 1278 the Franciscan order condemned Roger Bacon and imprisoned him for fourteen years for advocating the inductive method. Before this unfortunate act, the Dominican order in 1243 had condemned his teachings and interdicted every monk of the order from the study of medicine.[71]

The actions of some synods, together with those by two monastic orders and isolated remarks made by some individual Christians, reflected an unscientific attitude on the part of some in the church. So did the church father Tertullian (d. ca. 220), who once criticized the Greek surgeon Herophilus for cutting up cadavers "in order to investigate the secrets of nature" (*De anima* 10). Similarly, St. Augustine (354–430) said anatomists who dissected dead bodies "inhumanely pried into the secrets of the human body to learn the nature of the disease and...how it might be cured" (*The City of God* 12.24). These examples have been exaggerated by secular critics to imply that the entire Christian church was anti-science. Not so! At no time did the entire church ever oppose, much less condemn, science.

With regard to these negative attitudes, at least two factors are regularly overlooked. One, as in the case of Copernicus and Galileo in the fifteenth and sixteenth centuries, the church's theologians and natural philosophers were so firmly wedded to Aristotle's deductive philosophy and Galen's writings that they saw the new methodology of science, such as dissecting human bodies, as wrong. Thus, it was not biblical or Christian doctrine that prompted opposition to dissecting cadavers, or to other aspects of science, but rather it was the pagan Greek theories that a few theologians within the church saw as the final word.

Second, cadavers were commonly obtained by robbing graves. Even Vesalius acquired many of his bodies in that way. Grave robbing is still a major taboo—and illegal too. Thus, the opposition to dissecting human bodies pertained in part to grave robbing and was not simply the result of theological obstinacy, as is often implied. In fact, there is evidence to the contrary. For instance, in 1556, as dissections became more common, some complaints came to Charles V. He referred the question to the theological faculty at the University of Salamanca. The response was positive: "The dissection of human cadavers serves a useful purpose, and is therefore permissible to Christians of the Catholic Church."[72] Moreover, as observed in chapter 7, there were at least three universities (Padua, Bologna, and Montpellier) that legally dissected cadavers in the 1300s. Hence, there never was a total ban on dissections. As unfortunate as the several acts of the opponents were, there is no evidence that they had any significant negative impact or that they really delayed the progress of medical science.

That the inductive study of medicine continued is evident, as we find the physician **Paracelsus (1493–1541)** engaged in espousing his theories and methods. His opponents called him the *Lutherus medicorum* (the Luther of medicine) because he introduced a number of new, unpopular ideas in medicine. He once wrote, "I am a Christian, I am no sorcerer, no pagan, no gypsy."[73] He was a meandering scientist, never living or teaching very long in one place, largely because of his arrogant, nonconforming, and bombastic demeanor. The latter characteristic even fit his German family name: Theophrastus Bombast von Hohenheim. He Latinized his name to Paracelsus by adding the prefix *para* to the name of Celsus, the famous first-century Roman physician and encyclopedist.

Given his nonconforming bent, although a Catholic, he enjoyed studying Luther's theological writings. Medically, he argued that external agents attacked the human body to produce illness, thus foreshadowing the germ theory. This idea was contrary to the old Galenic belief that disease resulted from internal imbalances of the body's humors. Fellow physicians and professors objected to his empirical methods and did not agree that chemicals should be used to treat diseases. He horrified them by burning the revered books of the Greek physician Galen and the medical writings of the Arab Avicenna.[74] By stating that illnesses were the result of external and natural causes, he spurned the belief that God or the saints (some diseases had saints' names) inflicted diseases. He once said, "We dislike such nonsensical gossip as it is not supported by symptoms."[75] As a Christian, he believed it was God's will that people should live long lives, and physicians were to work to achieve that end.[76] One historian stated that Paracelsus was a man "destined to awaken the scientific spirit among physicians and to spread the

LOUIS PASTEUR (1822–95), the discoverer of bacteria, treats a young person while surrounded by waiting patients.

contagion of the Renaissance to the field of medicine."[77] Indeed, a significant step forward!

Medicine, specifically surgery, received a gigantic boost from **Ambroise Pare (1509?–1590),** the French physician whom one medical historian called "the greatest of all time."[78] Until Pare's day, surgery was performed by barbers, executioners, bathhouse keepers, and vagabonds;[79] physicians saw it as beneath their dignity. Pare was particularly adept in treating gunshot wounds received by soldiers in battle. Rather than stop a wound's flow of blood by cauterizing it with a red-hot iron, he used ligatures to stop the bleeding as surgeons do today. He also introduced artificial eyes, improved existing artificial arms and legs, and implanted teeth.[80] On one occasion, an elderly woman told him that he should apply chopped onion to skin burns. Being open-minded, he did not reject the woman's suggestion. When a patient appeared with a badly burned face, he applied chopped onion to one side and left the other side untreated. The side with the onion did indeed heal more quickly. This experiment revealed his scientific bent; apparently

CHRISTIAN ADVOCATES
OF SCIENTIFIC KNOWLEDGE

Advocate	Contribution
Grosseteste, Robert (ca. 1175–1253)	First proposed the inductive, experimental method
Bacon, Roger (1214–94)	Argued all things must be verified by observation
William of Occam (1285–1347)	Introduced the principle of parsimony (Occam's Razor)
Buridan, Jean (1300–1358)	Introduced the theory of probability
Nicholas of Oresme (ca. 1320–82)	Introduced the mean-speed theorem
Copernicus, Nicholaus (1473–1543)	Wrote *De revolutionibus orbium coelestium* (Revolution of the Heavenly Bodies), 1543; proposed the heliostatic theory
Leonardo da Vinci (1452–1519)	Contributed to human anatomy, optics, physics, etc.
Paracelsus (1493–1541)	Argued that external agents caused diseases
Pare, Ambroise (ca. 1509–90)	Tied off arteries to prevent hemorrhaging; improved amputations
Vesalius, Andreas (1514–64)	Wrote *The Fabric of the Human Body*; called "father of modern anatomy"
Brahe, Tycho (1546–1601)	Wrote *Concerning the New Star*; discovered a new comet
Kepler, Johann (1571–1630)	Wrote a number of scientific treatises; discovered elliptical movement of planets; developed and confirmed three astronomical laws; first defined weight as the mutual attraction between two bodies; established the heliocentric theory
Galileo (1564–1642)	First to use the telescope to study the skies; saw lunar mountains; discovered phases of Venus
Harvey, William (1578–1657)	Discovered the circulation of blood
Pascal, Blaise (1623–62)	Discovered the law that liquid in a container exerts equal pressure in all directions; found barometric pressures varying with different altitudes; constructed first adding machine

Boyle, Robert (1627–91)	Discovered Boyle's law: the volume of gas varies inversely with its pressure
Newton, Isaac (1642–1727)	Discovered the law of gravity; also credited with inventing calculus independently of Leibniz
Leibniz, Gottfried (1646–1716)	Invented calculus independently of Newton; proposed theory of monads
Priestley, Joseph (1733–1804)	Discovered oxygen
Lavoisier, Antoine (1743–94)	Found that oxygen is needed for combustion
Volta, Alessandro (1745–1827)	Discovered current electricity; isolated methane gas
Dalton, John (1766–1844)	Developed the atomic theory; diagnosed color blindness
Ampere, Andre (1775–1836)	Discovered that electric currents produce magnetic fields
Ohm, Georg (1787–1854)	Formulated Ohm's law: the intensity of an electric current equals the magnetic force driving it, divided by the resistance of the conductor (wire)
Faraday, Michael (1791–1867)	Discovered electromagnetic induction
Simpson, James (1811–70)	First to use chloroform and ether medically
Pasteur, Louis (1822–95)	Founded microbiology; discovered bacteria and nullified spontaneous generation
Mendel, Gregor (1822–84)	Laid the foundation for modern genetics
Kelvin, William (1824–1907)	Discovered that molecular motion stops at minus 273 degrees centigrade (absolute zero)
Lister, Joseph (1827–1912)	Found that antiseptics reduce infection, a finding that revolutionized surgery
Carver, George Washington (ca. 1864–1943)	Developed numerous by-products from peanuts and sweet potatoes

he was the first physician to use science's experimental-control method. Reportedly, he was a man of tough fiber, but this quality did not overshadow his Christian humility. When complimented on his success in healing a soldier's wounds, he would say, "I dressed his wounds, but God healed them."[81]

Another giant in the advance of scientific medicine is **William Harvey (1578–1657)** of England, who was baptized in the Folkestone parish church. Like Vesalius, he studied medicine at the University of Padua.

Following the footsteps of Vesalius and Pare, he engaged in observations and experiments on deceased human bodies after returning to his home country. Daring to question the still-revered Galen, in 1628 he published *On the Motion of the Heart and the Blood*, a treatise demonstrating that blood circulated through the arteries of the body by the ventricles of the heart contracting simultaneously. His findings corroborated the biblical statement that "the life of the flesh is in the blood" (Leviticus 17:11 NKJV).

While space does not permit naming many other notable scientists in medicine who reflected their Christian faith, **Louis Pasteur (1822–1895)** cannot be overlooked. Although he was a chemist and microbiologist, his discovery of bacteria has been most helpful to medicine, enabling physicians to save millions of human lives. Working in the laboratory, this gifted Christian demonstrated how bacteria caused fermentation, spoiled food, and infected wounds. He also demonstrated the effective use of antiseptics, successfully treated hydrophobia, introduced inoculation, and gave the world the method of pasteurization, named after him. His research also led him to replace the old false hypothesis of spontaneous generation, which he replaced with the concept of biogenesis, that is, that life comes only from life. Like so many other Christians in science, scientific findings did not eclipse his faith. Said he, "The more I know, the more does my faith approach that of the Breton peasant."[82] When he died, "one of his hands rested in that of Mme. Pasteur [his wife], the other held a crucifix."[83]

Still another medical scientist whose Christian beliefs were an integral part of his scientific thinking was **James Simpson (1811–1870),** a Scottish obstetrician and gynecologist who discovered chloroform in 1847. His suggestion that chloroform be used to alleviate pain in childbirth brought him strong resistance from his medical colleagues. But after Queen Victoria received it at the birth of her seventh child (Prince Leopold), the medical establishment soon conformed.[84]

The discovery of chloroform laid the foundation for modern anesthesiology. Reportedly, it was the biblical account of God's having put Adam in a deep sleep when he created Eve from one of his ribs that inspired Simpson to discover chloroform.[85] If this account is reliable, it is not the only evidence of his biblical, Christian convictions. He also wrote a gospel tract in which he confessed his faith in Jesus Christ, and he told his friends that his greatest discovery was "that I was a sinner and Jesus Christ is the Saviour."[86]

Building upon Pasteur's discovery that fermentation was caused by bacteria, medical science was fortunate to have had **Joseph Lister (1827–1912),** a Quaker from England, who later became Queen Victoria's physician. He introduced and applied antiseptics to keep germs (bacteria) from multiplying in surgical or accidental wounds. Teaching physicians to wash their hands and to use only sterile instruments greatly reduced infections and the mortality rate of individuals. Before Lister's time, even minor surgeries resulted in high death tolls. Given his contributions, surgery is now divided into two periods: before Lister and after Lister.[87]

Numerous other scientists whose sincere Christian convictions motivated and influenced their scientific efforts as much as those already mentioned could be cited. In seeking information concerning the Christian beliefs of the early scientists, it soon becomes apparent that such information is quite sparse. This is especially true for scientists in the nineteenth and twentieth centuries, apparently because biographies have increasingly been written by secular historians who now assume that early scientists operated with twentieth-century "methodological atheism," to use Peter Berger's term.[88] Thus biographies, especially those written in the twentieth century, ignore the Christian values in the lives of scientists, let alone show how those values influenced their scientific theories. This is even true regarding scientists like Kepler, Copernicus, Boyle, Pasteur, Faraday, and Simpson, who were especially devout Christians, and who left plenty of evidence indicating that fact. Modern biographers of scientists seem oblivious to the fact that up to the end of the eighteenth century "most intelligent men, and thus most scientists, held that divine revelation could tell them what had happened in the beginning, how the Creator had, so to speak, set the stage of the world which their science was now newly investigating."[89] So for some time, college and university students, some of whom become scientists, have had no knowledge about the powerful and dynamic role that the teachings and the spirit of Jesus Christ played in the origin and development of science. This unfortunate state of affairs might be summed up in Shakespeare's words, "'Tis true 'tis pity; and pity 'tis 'tis true" (*Hamlet* II, 2).

CONCLUSION

This chapter began by asserting that modern science is an outgrowth of Christian theology of the Middle Ages. It proceeded to show that it was Christianity's values that provided the necessary *Weltanschauung* (worldview) and motivation to encourage many of its educated adherents (now called scientists) to study the world of nature. To conclude this chapter's thesis, the words of Stanley Jaki are relevant. He says the ancient Egyptians built great pyramids and had a highly developed form of phonetic writing, but they "failed to achieve a similar breakthrough, when it came to quantities, measurements, and calculations, which should have been more easily handled than the abstract symbolization of the spoken word. Egyptian mathematics and geometry remained a practical art."[90] Consider India, he says, with its pervasive animistic beliefs of Hinduism that reject competition and technological inventions and that also failed to open the gate to science. As Jaki notes, it was not because of Hinduism's absence of talent either, because the decimal, so vital to mathematics, was first discovered in India. Yet India, like Egypt, had "a standstill, a stillbirth, as far as science was concerned."[91] It was not much different in ancient China, where with its "quasi-pantheistic identification of man and society with Nature writ large, the Chinese of old...no longer felt confident that their limited mind could grasp and control the laws of the Nature because Nature itself was not the subject to a Mind and Lawgiver transcendent to it."[92]

Yet, in spite of Christianity's having provided the fertile stimulus for the development of science, students in the Western world—whether in elementary, secondary, or university classrooms—are regularly deprived by instructors and textbooks from learning and knowing about Christianity's connection to science. The tendency to omit this connection, whether in education or in the public square, began in the eighteenth century, when, as Jacques Barzun has noted, "the marriage of science with philosophical materialism" occurred.[93] In time this great omission became institutionalized, and thus today's students—and the public—are unaware that virtually all scientists from the Middle Ages to the mid-eighteenth century—many of whom were seminal thinkers—not only were sincere Christians but were often inspired by biblical postulates and premises in their theories that sought to explain and predict natural phenomena. These pioneering scientists, upon whose shoulders present-day scientists stand, knew and believed the words of the biblical writer: "The heavens declare the glory of God; the skies proclaim the work of his hands" (Psalm 19:1). To them, God could not be factored out. And concerning their Christian faith, they echoed the words of Kepler: "I am in earnest about Faith, and I do not play with it."[94] They were 180 degrees removed from the relativistic cliché of today's postmodernism that says, "What is true for you is not true for me." To them, truth was one, and God was its Author.

NOTES

1. Alfred North Whitehead, *Science and the Modern World* (New York: Macmillan, 1926), 19.

2. Lynn T. White, "The Significance of Medieval Christianity," in *The Vitality of the Christian Tradition*, ed. George F. Thomas (New York: Harper and Brothers, 1945), 96.

3. Ernst Mach, *Science of Mechanics,* trans. Thomas. J. McCormack (La Salle, Ill.: Open Court, 1960), 549.

4. Whitehead, *Science and the Modern World,* 18.

5. Thomas Goldstein, *Dawn of Modern Science: From the Arabs to Leonardo da Vinci* (Boston: Houghton Mifflin, 1980), 171.

6. Roger Bacon, *Opus majus,* trans. Robert Belle Burke (New York: Russell and Russell, 1962), 584.

7. Magnus Magnusson, ed., "Bacon, Francis, Baron Verulam of Verulam, Viscount St. Albans," *Cambridge Biographical Dictionary* (New York: Cambridge University Press, 1990), 88.

8. Herbert Butterfield, *The Origins of Modern Science, 1300–1800,* (London: G. Bell and Sons, 1951), 79.

9. Stanley L. Jaki, *The Savior of Science* (Edinburgh: Scottish Academic Press, 1990), 41.

10. Butterfield, *Origins of Modern Science,* 7–8.

11. Andrew Dickson White, *A History of the Warfare of Science with Theology* (Gloucester, Mass.: Peter Smith, [1896], 1978), 2:389.

12. D. James Kennedy and Jerry Newcombe, *What If Jesus Had Never Been Born?* (Nashville: Thomas Nelson, 1994), 95.

13. White, "Significance of Medieval Christianity," 96.

14. Lynn White Jr., *Dynamo and Virgin Reconsidered: Essays in the Dynamism of Western Culture* (Cambridge: MIT Press, 1968), 89.

15. Goldstein, *Dawn of Modern Science,* 206.

16. Butterfield, *Origins of Modern Science,* 39.

17. Agatha Young, *Scalpel: Men Who Made Surgery* (New York: Random House, 1956), 20.

18. Victor Robinson, *The Story of Medicine* (New York: Albert and Charles Boni, 1931), 259.

19. Cited in Howard W. Haggard, *The Doctor in History* (New Haven: Yale University Press, 1934), 244.

20. C. D. O'Malley, *Andreas Vesalius of Brussels, 1514–1564* (Berkeley: University of California Press, 1964), 309.

21. Henry Morris, *Men of Science—Men of God* (San Diego: Creation-Life Publishers, 1982), 80.

22. Ibid., 21.

23. Arthur Koestler, *The Sleep Walkers: A History of Man's Changing Vision of the Universe* (New York: Macmillan, 1959), 117.

24. Werner Elert, *The Structure of Lutheranism,* trans. Walter A. Hansen (St. Louis: Concordia Publishing House, 1962), 423.

25. John Warwick Montgomery, *In Defense of Martin Luther* (Milwaukee: Northwestern Publishing House, 1970), 91.

26. Cited in Montgomery, *In Defense of Martin Luther,* 92.

27. Cited in Montgomery, *In Defense of Martin Luther,* 99.

28. Rudolf Wolf, *Geschichte der Astronomie* (Munich: Verlag von R. Oldenboaz, 1877), 283.

29. Owen Gingerich, *The Eye of Heaven: Ptolemy, Copernicus, Kepler* (New York: American Institute of Physics, 1993), 333.

30. Koestler, *Sleep Walkers,* 394.

31. Ibid., 259.

32. Jaki, *Savior of Science,* 90.

33. Koestler, *Sleep Walkers,* 410.

34. Ibid., 397.

35. Max Caspar, *Johannes Kepler* (Stuttgart: W. Kohlhammer Verlag, 1948), 73.

36. Cited in Koestler, *Sleep Walkers,* 315.

37. Johannes Kepler, *Mysterium cosmographicum* (1596). Reprinted in the standard Kepler edition, *Johannes Kepler Gesammelte Werke* (Munich: JKGW, 1937), 1:11: cited by Gingerich, *Eye of Heaven,* 307.

38. Caspar, *Johannes Kepler,* 430.

39. Cited in Caspar, *Johannes Kepler.*

40. My translation of Caspar, *Johannes Kepler,* 430.

41. Butterfield, *Origins of Modern Science,* 50–51.

42. Hal Hellman, *Great Feuds in Science* (New York: John Wiley and Sons, 1998), 15.

43. Tim Dowley, *A History of Christianity* (Berkhamsted, England: Lion Publishing, 1977), 43.

44. Koestler, *Sleep Walkers,* 279.

45. Eric Temple Bell, "Newton, Isaac, Sir," *The World Book Encyclopedia* (Chicago: Field Enterprises Educational Corporation, 1958), 12:5619.

46. John Dillenberger, *Protestant Thought and Natural Science* (Garden City, N.Y.: Doubleday, 1960), 121.

47. Isaac Newton, "God and Natural Philosophy," in *Newton's Philosophy of Nature: Selections from His Writings,* ed. H. S. Thayer (New York: Hafner Publishing, 1953), 66–67.

48. Isaac Newton, *Yahuda MS* 15.7: cited by Frank E. Manuel, *The Religion of Isaac Newton* (Oxford: Clarendon Press, 1974), 60.

49. Michael Drosnin, *The Bible Code* (New York: Simon and Schuster, 1997).

50. Manuel, *Religion of Isaac Newton,* 60–61.

51. E. A. Burtt, *The Metaphysical Foundations of Modern Physical Science* (New York: Simon and Schuster, 1951), 283.

52. Butterfield, *Origins of Modern Science,* 77.

53. G. W. Leibniz, *Theodicy: Essays on the Goodness of God, the Freedom of Man, and the Origin of Evil,* trans. E. M. Haggard (La Salle, Ill.: Open Court, 1985), 67.

54. Blaise Pascal, *Pensées,* trans. A. J. Krailsheimer (London: Penguin Books, 1995), 56.

55. Cited in Karl A. Kneller, *Christianity and the Leaders of Modern Science,* trans. T. M. Kettle (Fraser, Mich.: Real-View Books, 1995), 118.

56. Ibid., 132.

57. Cited in Kneller, *Christianity and the Leaders of Modern Science,* 123.

58. Geoffrey Cantor et al., *Michael Faraday* (Atlantic Highlands, N.J.: Humanities Press, 1996), 18.

59. Cited in Kneller, *Christianity and the Leaders of Modern Science,* 38.

60. Morris, *Men of Science—Men of God,* 39.

61. Philip Schaff, "Robert Boyle," *The New Schaff-Herzog Encyclopedia of Religious Knowledge,* Samuel M. Jackson, ed. (Grand Rapids: Baker, 1977), 2:244.

62. Morris, *Men of Science—Men of God,* 71.

63. Kneller, *Christianity and the Leaders of Modern Science,* 180.

64. Joseph Priestley, *Socrates and Jesus Compared* (Philadelphia: Printed for P. Byrne, 1803), 3.

65. Joseph Priestly, *A Continuation of the Letters to the Philosophers and Politicians of France on the Subject of Religion* (New York: Kraus Reprint Company, 1977), 21.

66. Morris, *Men of Science—Men of God,* 104–5.

67. Walter Addison Jayne, *The Healing Gods of Ancient Civilizations* (New York: University Books, 1962), 285.

68. Gabriel Compayre, *Abelard and the Origin of Early Universities* (New York: Charles Scribner's Sons, 1899), 243.

69. Ibid., 245.

70. Carl Joseph von Hefele, *Conciliengeschichte* (Freiburg: Herder'sche Verlagshandlung, 1886), 5:441.

71. White, *A History of the Warfare,* 2:389.

72. Cited in Howard W. Haggard, *Devils, Drugs, and Doctors* (New York: Harper and Brothers, 1929), 147.

73. Preface to his *Philosophia sagax:* cited in Henry M. Pachter, *Magic into Science: The Story of Paracelsus* (New York: Henry Schuman, 1951), 93.

74. David Riesman, *The Story of Medicine in the Middle Ages* (New York: Harper and Row, 1936), 341.

75. Cited by J. F. C. Hecker, *The Epidemics of the Middle Ages* (London: Trubner and Company, 1859), 92.

76. Ibid.

77. Haggard, *Devils, Drugs, and Doctors,* 194.

78. Frances E. Cretcher, "Pare, Ambroise," *The World Book Encyclopedia,* 13:6104.

79. Samuel Evans Massengill, *A Sketch of Medicine and Pharmacy* (Bristol, Tenn.: S. E. Massengill, 1943), 257.

80. Haggard, *Devils, Drugs, and Doctors,* 225–26.

81. Ibid., 229.

82. Morris, *Men of Science—Men of God,* 84.

83. Rene Vallery-Radot, *The Life of Pasteur* (Garden City, N.Y.: Doubleday, Page, 1923), 464.

84. Haggard, *Devils, Drugs, and Doctors,* 117.

85. Morris, *Men of Science—Men of God,* 69.

86. Herbert Lockyer, *The Man Who Changed the World* (Grand Rapids: Zondervan, 1966), 1:177.

87. Massengill, *A Sketch of Medicine*, 220.

88. Peter L. Berger, *The Sacred Canopy: Elements of a Sociological Theory of Religion* (Garden City, N.Y.: Doubleday, 1969), 179–85.

89. Langdon Gilkey, *Religion and the Scientific Future: Reflections on Myth, Science, and Theology* (New York: Harper and Row, 1970), 8.

90. Jaki, *Savior of Science*, 23.

91. Ibid., 28.

92. Ibid., 33.

93. Jacques Barzun, *From Dawn to Decadence: 500 Years of Western Cultural Life, 1500 to the Present* (New York: Harper Collins, 2000), 365.

94. Cited in Koestler, *Sleep Walkers*, 280.

10

LIBERTY and JUSTICE
for ALL

"Where the Spirit of the Lord is, there is liberty."
St. Paul in 2 Corinthians 3:17 NKJV

The liberty and justice that are enjoyed by humans in Western societies and in some non-Western countries are increasingly seen as the products of a benevolent, secular government that is the provider of all things. There seems to be no awareness that the liberties and rights that are currently operative in free societies of the West are to a great degree the result of Christianity's influence. The architects of civic freedom and justice—men like St. Ambrose, Stephen Langton, John Locke, Baron de Montesquieu, Thomas Jefferson, and James Madison—all drew extensively from the Christian perspective regarding humanity's God-given freedoms, which had for most of human history never really been implemented.

NO ONE IS ABOVE THE LAW

One of the oldest means of depriving individuals of liberty and justice was for the top ruler (often a king or emperor) of a country to set himself above the law. Functioning above the law meant he was a law unto himself, often curtailing, even obliterating the natural rights and freedoms of the country's citizens. The pages of history are filled with examples of such rulers. One recalls some of the Hebrew kings in the Old Testament era, and most of the Roman emperors, who arbitrarily snuffed out the lives of individuals who were perceived as opposed to their policies. Whether such individuals were a threat to the welfare of the nation was irrelevant. What a ruler wanted was what he got. These rulers were not accountable to anyone (in Rome not even to the Senate) for their arbitrary and often bloody acts.

TWO OR MORE WITNESSES

More than a thousand years before the birth of Christ, Moses enjoined the Israelites not to execute anyone for an alleged capital crime without the testimony of at least two witnesses: "One witness is not enough to convict a man accused of any crime or offense he may have committed. A matter must be established by the testimony of two or three witnesses" (Deuteronomy 19:15). This biblical requirement became a vital component in the principle that "no man is above the law." Barring false witnesses, it checked arbitrary, capricious acts on the part of rulers or other officials. It told the accuser, "You must have at least two witnesses in order to convict the accused." This meant that the accuser, even a high-ranking official, could not arbitrarily incarcerate or execute the accused; he was subject to the law and could not act as though he were above it.

Requiring at least two witnesses is also mandated in the New Testament for use in ecclesiastical matters. Matthew cites Jesus' instructions regarding an erring Christian. If the wayward person, upon the urging of a fellow Christian, does not repent, then two or more witnesses are to confront the unrepentant individual, and if he still refuses to repent, then he is to appear before an assembly of Christians. If he continues to persist in his sin, he is then to be treated as a pagan and a tax collector (Matthew 18:15–17).

Today the criminal and civil justice systems of Great Britain, the United States, Canada, and many other free countries employ this Judeo-Christian requirement of having witnesses testify in a court of law. In British and American jurisprudence, witnesses are part of what is legally called "due process of law," a legal concept that first appeared in the fourteenth century under King Edward III.

ST. AMBROSE VERSUS THE EMPEROR

Bishop Ambrose, an early architect of liberty and justice, is usually ignored in secular discussions of the growth and development of civic freedom in the

BISHOP AMBROSE OF MILAN (ca. 340–97) rebukes Emperor Theodosius, indicating that no one, not even the Roman emperor, is above the law. *(Peter Paul Rubens)*

Western world. In A.D. 390 some people in Thessalonica rioted, arousing the anger of the Christian emperor, Theodosius the Great. He overreacted, slaughtering some seven thousand people, most of whom were innocent. Bishop Ambrose, who was located in Milan—which was also where the emperor lived—did not turn a blind eye to the emperor's vindictive and unjust behavior. He asked him to repent of his massacre. When the emperor refused, the bishop excommunicated him. After a month of stubborn hesitation, Theodosius prostrated himself and repented in Ambrose's cathedral, bringing tears of joy to fellow believers.[1]

It is unfortunate that Ambrose's action against Theodosius has often been portrayed as a power struggle between church and state rather than being the first instance of applying the principle that no one, not even an emperor or king, is above the law. The facts, indeed, support the latter interpretation. This is evident from Ambrose's letter to the emperor, which shows that he was solely concerned for the emperor's spiritual welfare. Like

King David, who deliberately had Uriah killed in battle, the emperor had placed himself above one of God's laws and committed murder, and for that Ambrose demanded genuine repentance.

Today modern democracies take pride in saying that no one is above the law, but they fail to note that this landmark of civilization, which is now commonly imitated in free societies, was first implemented by a courageous, uncompromising Christian bishop some 1,600 years ago. In a sense, Ambrose also set the stage for the Magna Carta that followed some eight hundred years later in England.

THE MAGNA CARTA

When the barons forced King John to consent to and sign the Magna Carta (the Large Charter) in 1215 at Runnymede, outside of London, they obtained a number of rights that they did not have before this historic occasion. Specifically, the charter granted that (1) justice could no longer be sold or denied to freemen who were under the authority of barons; (2) no taxes could be levied without representation; (3) no one would be imprisoned without a trial; and (4) property could not be taken from the owner without just compensation.[2] These achievements were monumental and history making. The era of the king being above the law had effectively come to an end. Commonly this document is hailed as ushering in English liberty and justice. Some five hundred years later it also served as a courageous precedent to the American patriots to establish liberty and justice in America. The early advocates of American independence often referred to the Magna Carta in support of their arguments.

The Magna Carta, like many other highly beneficial phenomena that lifted civilization to a higher plateau in the Western world, had important Christian ties. Its preamble began, "John, by the grace of God...," and stated that the charter was formulated out of "reverence for God and for the salvation of our soul and those of all our ancestors and heirs, for the honour of God and the exaltation of Holy Church and the reform of our realm, on the advice of our reverend [church] fathers."[3]

One of the "reverend fathers" involved in the birth of the Magna Carta was Stephen Langton, Archbishop of Canterbury (who is credited with dividing the Bible into chapters). Langton's involvement in the Magna Carta, together with the help of his Christian colleagues did not, however, have the approval of Pope Innocent III, who actually suspended him for two years. The pope's opposition, of course, does not nullify the argument

that the Magna Carta bears the marks of Christian influence. As church historians know all too well, this was not the first or the last time that a pope contradicted Christian values. Throughout the Middle Ages there were occasions, despite the popes, when Christians "let their light shine" as Jesus had commanded them. The formation of the Magna Carta is one of those occasions when the spirit of Christ moved his English followers to promote liberty and justice.

Finally, another Christian influence is worth noting. In 325 at the Council of Nicaea, Christian bishops wrote and adopted the Nicene Creed, a formal code of fundamental beliefs to which all Christians were expected to adhere. This was the first time in history that a formally written document of religious beliefs had ever been issued. The pagan Greco-Romans had no formal religious creeds or confessions.[4] Although the Magna Carta was a political document, it was also a type of creed in that it showed what the formulators as Christians (evident in the preamble) believed in regard to the king's and his subjects' expected adherence. Thus, in setting forth their beliefs regarding civic liberties, the architects of the Magna Carta followed a precedent set by the Christian bishops at the Council of Nicaea.

NATURAL LAW AND NATURAL RIGHTS

The concept of natural law has a long history going back to the Greco-Roman philosophers several hundred years before the birth of Christ. Although these philosophers' conceptions of the natural law varied somewhat, there was one essential point of agreement: natural law was understood as that process in nature by which human beings, through the use of sound reason, were able to perceive what was morally right and wrong. This natural law was seen as the eternal, unchangeable foundation of all human laws.

When Christianity came on the scene, it added an important element to the Greco-Roman view of the natural law. It said natural law was not an entity by itself but part of God's created order in nature through which he made all rational human beings aware of what is right and wrong. St. Paul expressed this position rather cogently when he said, "When Gentiles [pagans], who do not have the law [Ten Commandments], do by nature things required by the law, they are a law for themselves, even though they do not have the law, since they show that the requirements of the law are written on their hearts, their consciences also bearing witness, and their thoughts now accusing, now even defending them" (Romans 2:14–15). Simply put, Paul said that the natural law contains God's Ten Commandments, which, although not communicated in a visible or audible manner, tell the natural human being what is right and wrong behavior. Christian theologians who followed Paul, such as Justin Martyr, St. Augustine, St. Chrysostom, Thomas Aquinas, and Martin Luther, essentially all continued to hold to the Pauline understanding of natural law. Luther maintained that the Ten Commandments were the natural law stated more clearly. "Why does one then teach the Ten Commandments?" he asked. Answer: "Because the natural laws were never so orderly and well written as by Moses."[5]

In the seventeenth century the concept of natural law was applied to government in the context of people's natural rights. The physician and political philosopher John Locke (1632–1703) made this application, especially in his *Two Treatises of Government* (1690). He maintained that government existed merely to uphold the natural law and that governmental tyranny violated the natural rights of man. Natural rights were not given to people by kings or governments but belonged to the people by nature.

Locke's theory reflects St. Paul's Christian understanding of the natural law. Although he has often been referred to as a deist, it is clear from his writings that he considered himself a Christian. In his monograph *The Reasonableness of Christianity* (1695), he talks about sinners being "restored by Christ at the resurrection."[6] Frequently, he also cites Scripture references in support of his arguments.

THE AMERICAN DECLARATION OF INDEPENDENCE

In the eighteenth century, American patriots such as James Otis, Samuel Adams, John Adams, Christopher Gadsen, and others used the concept of natural law to argue for the natural rights of the American colonists. Similarly, in 1776 Thomas Jefferson, the author of the American Declaration of Independence, leaned heavily on Locke's natural rights philosophy. He even used some of Locke's phraseology, for instance, "but when a long train of abuses," and "consent of the governed."

Does the Declaration of Independence reflect a Christian influence? It does in several ways. First, the document clearly reflects its indebtedness to the Christian understanding of the natural law. The words "the Law of Nature and of Nature's God" in the Declaration show this to be true. These very words were used and interpreted by the renowned English legal scholar Sir William Blackstone in the context of Christian theology in his *Commentaries of the Laws of England* (1765), a work that was well known to the American colonists. Blackstone was required reading at almost all colonial colleges.[7]

Second, the Declaration of Independence specifically states that a government may be deposed when it violates people's "inalienable rights": "Whenever any form of government becomes destructive of these ends, it is the right of the people to alter or to abolish it, and to institute new government." This concept reflected "thoroughly medieval Christian notions" that by 1776 had become "equally American conceptions."[8]

Third, although Jefferson was essentially a deist, he was nevertheless greatly influenced by Christian values. Forty years after he penned the Declaration of Independence, he said of the teachings of Jesus, "A more beautiful or precious morsel of ethics I have never seen." Even his so-called Jefferson Bible, containing the teachings of Jesus that he cut out of the four Gospels, exclusive of Christ's miracles, was done to show, as he said, that "I am a real Christian."[9]

Fourth, the Declaration of Independence speaks about truths being "self-evident." This particular term has Christian roots going back to theological writings of the eighth century. To the medievalists, "self-evident" knowledge, says Gary Amos, "was truth known intuitively, as direct revelation from God, without the need for proofs. The term presumed that man was created in the image of God, and presumed certain beliefs about man's rationality which can be traced as far back as Augustine in the early fifth century."[10] Amos also shows that St. Paul in the Epistle to the Romans wrote that since the creation, even to the pagans, God's "invisible attributes are clearly seen" (Romans 1:20 NKJV), that is, self-evident. In the previous verse, Paul says that these truths are *phaneron estin en autois* (evident by themselves). Thus, it is quite plausible that Paul's biblical concept of "self-evident" knowingly or unknowingly influenced Jefferson when he declared, "We hold these Truths to be self-evident."

Fifth, the last paragraph of the Declaration of Independence uses the term "Supreme Judge," a term used in Locke's *The Second Treatise of Government,* where he refers to Jephthah calling God "the Judge" in Israel's fight against the Ammonites (Judges 11:27).[11] Amos says that if this term for God in the Declaration was taken from Locke's work, "then we have a direct link between the Bible and the Declaration of Independence."[12]

"READING THE DECLARATION BEFORE WASHINGTON'S ARMY, NEW YORK, JULY 9, 1776." *(Illustration by Howard Pyle originally published in* Harper's New Monthly Magazine, *July 1892)*

Sixth, some historians have persuasively argued that the rise of Americanism that is so clearly evident in the Declaration of Independence grew out of the Great Awakening of the 1730s. That movement, as is well known, was a Christian phenomenon.[13]

To argue that the Declaration of Independence is a secular document devoid of Christian influence, as is commonly done by American historians, reveals more about those making this argument than about the Christian ideas reflected in the document. Critics might say that even if Jefferson and others in the Continental Congress, who made some changes, were Christians, this does not necessarily mean that the Declaration contains Christian influences. While this is true, it can also be argued that if Jefferson and his editors (for example, Benjamin Franklin) were deists, that does not mean they were not influenced by Christian ideas. This is especially true because deists two hundred years ago were much more influenced by Christian teachings and values than are modern deists or Unitarians today. One need only read the writings in the 1790s of Joseph Priestley, a self-proclaimed Unitarian, to see how true this was. His writings have a strong Christian tone, as was noted in the chapter on science.

THE CONSTITUTION OF THE UNITED STATES

In documenting Christianity's influence on the American Constitution, which is heralded as the world's greatest charter of liberty and justice, it is not necessary to cite the church affiliation of its formulators, since it is well known by historians that the vast majority of the thirty-nine signers were Christians. But it is instructive to look at the political theorist whose thinking is commonly cited as having had the greatest influence on the writers of the Constitution: the French Christian and philosopher Baron de Montesquieu (1689–1755). His imprint on the Constitution is evidenced by the American government's three branches: legislative, executive, and judicial. One historian has said that Montesquieu's book, *The Spirit of Laws* (1748), "[gave] American Constitution writers their holy writ." In referring to Montesquieu, he called him "the godfather of the American Constitution."[14]

The incorporation of Montesquieu's political theory into the American Constitution was largely the result of the role taken by James Madison, the Constitution's principal architect, often referred to as "the father of the American Constitution." The Federalist Papers show that Madison borrowed extensively from Montesquieu's thinking. His indebtedness to the

French philosopher's political theory reveals at least an indirect Christian influence on him. But Madison also revealed a rather direct Christian influence on his political thinking. In defending his argument for the separation of powers, he reflected the Christian teaching of the fallen nature of man when he boldly asserted, "The truth [is] that all men, having power ought to be distrusted, to a certain degree."[15] And in his Federalist Papers (no. 51) he wrote, "If men were angels, no government would be necessary." These words clearly reflect the Christian doctrine of humankind's innate sinfulness. In Madison's thinking, the sinful nature of human beings required three branches of government so that each branch would keep a critical eye on the other and thereby maintain honesty and integrity.

Some believe that Madison in his "Memorial and Remonstrance" (1785) showed himself as being opposed to Christianity, for in that document he argued that "the establishment proposed by the Bill is not a requisite for the support of the Christian religion."[16] In response to those who see Madison as not having any concern for the well-being of Christianity, John Eidsmoe argues that the "Memorial and Remonstrance" actually demonstrates the very opposite because Madison believed that Christianity flourished best when it operated free of government support and control.[17] Eidsmoe is right. For in another portion of the document Madison states, "Whilst we assert for ourselves a freedom to embrace, to profess, and to observe the Religion which we believe to be of divine origin, we cannot deny an equal freedom to those whose minds have not yet yielded to the evidence which convinced us."[18] And at that time in America's history, the term *Religion,* as Madison and others used it, referred only to Christianity.

While many American history books have noted that the three branches of government in the United States are derived from Montesquieu's theory, none to my knowledge have ever noted how his argument for the three branches ("three powers," as he called them) was influenced by his admiration for Christianity. He saw Christian spiritual ideas as vital to a nation's liberty: "It is not enough for religion to establish a doctrine, it must also direct its influence. This the Christian religion performs in the most admirable manner, especially with respect to the doctrines of which we have been speaking. It makes us hope for a state which is the object of our belief; not for a state which we have already experienced or known."[19] Contrasting governments under Christianity to those under Islam, Confucianism, Hinduism, and Greek paganism, he found those under Christian influence far superior in fostering civic freedom. "The Christian religion," he maintained, "is a stranger to mere despotic power. The mildness so frequently recommended in the Gospel, is incompatible with the despotic rage with which a prince punishes his subjects, and exercises himself in cruelty."[20] Again, "[W]e shall see that we owe to Christianity, in government, a certain political law; and in war, a certain law of nations; benefits which human nature can never sufficiently acknowledge."[21] And he defended Christianity by chiding a critic who did not "distinguish between the orders for the establishment of Christianity, and Christianity itself."[22] It was these Christian convictions that led him to say, "There is no liberty if the judiciary power be not separated from the legislative and executive."[23]

To argue that Christian influences underlie the American quest for freedom, the War of Independence, the Declaration of Independence, and the construction of the Constitution of the United States may seem incredible to many Americans. If so, it is largely because secular historians, who have often been negatively predisposed to Christianity, have, as Sandoz has said, given the Christian influence "short shrift in recent political discussions," but, he continues, "it constitutes the deepest bases for ever asserting that there ought to be democracy or self-rule by the people."[24] The Christian values underlying the Constitution may not be well known to many Americans today, but they were taken for granted by the Founding Fathers and their contemporaries. For instance, John Adams, one of the signers of the Declaration of Independence and the second president of the United States, saw the American government as "grounded on reason, morality, and the Christian religion."[25]

Given that the Declaration of Independence and the American Constitution, which are extensions of the Magna Carta and other British documents of freedom, bear the marks of Christian influence is not to say they are Christian documents, like the Nicene Creed, for example. But it is to say that civic freedoms and liberties would not have occurred had it not been for the Christian values that prompted and shaped the formation of these documents.

FREEDOM AND RIGHTS OF THE INDIVIDUAL

Supporters of socialism, communism, fascism, and other highly centralized governmental systems have a strong distaste for the freedom of the individual because such freedom hampers and impedes authoritarian/totalitarian governments from controlling the expressions and movements of its citizens. Without freedom of the individual there is no real freedom, whether it is on the economic, political, or religious level.

When one examines the development of personal freedom, it soon becomes evident, as in many other areas of human life, that the influence of Christianity looms large. For instance, Jesus strongly emphasized the importance and the significance of the individual person. He proclaimed, "For God so loved the world that he gave his one and only Son, that *whoever* believes in him shall not perish but have eternal life" (John 3:16). These words make it very clear that no one gets to heaven unless he or she—as an individual—believes in the atoning merits of Jesus Christ. Jesus and the apostles on numerous occasions applied their message to individuals, meaning that every person is singly responsible and accountable to God. No one can obtain eternal life by virtue of belonging to a group.

The high value that Christianity, from its inception, placed on the individual person was in stark contrast to the Greco-Roman culture in which the individual was always subordinate to the state. "True liberty, individual right and respect for human personality, found no place in Greece or Rome."[26] Christianity's accent on the individual was a necessary condition for freedom and liberty to surface in the Magna Carta (1215), in England's Petition of Rights (1628) and Bill of Rights (1689), and, of course, in the American Bill of Rights (1791).

Political, economic, and religious freedom can only exist where there is liberty and freedom of the individual. Group rights that determine a person's rights on the basis of belonging to a given ethnic or racial group, as presently advocated by multiculturalists and by affirmative action laws, nullify the rights of the individual. Group rights greatly reduce the freedom of the individual in that his rights stem only from the group; if he does not belong to the group, his rights are greatly curtailed.

"Individual rights and group rights," says Balint Vazsonyi, "are mutually exclusive; we cannot have it both ways."[27] Ethnicity, race, sex, or party affiliation today increasingly determine the person's rights. This is reminiscent of Hitler, who once said, "The individual is nothing. The group [the Nazi Party] is everything." When group rights get the upper hand, gone are the "unalienable rights" given to the individual by his Creator so admirably expressed in the American Declaration of Independence. Indeed, the great documents of freedom cited in the previous paragraph know nothing of group rights, and neither does Christianity.

Individual freedom and rights are most prevalent where Christianity has had the greatest impact. This truth, which is often not known or recognized, needs to be told and retold. All freedom-loving people would do well to recall the words of Malcolm Muggeridge, once a non-Christian but later a strong defender of Christianity. Said he, "We must not forget that our human rights are derived from the Christian faith. In Christian terms every single human being, whoever he or she may be, sick or well, clever or foolish, beautiful or ugly, every human being is loved by his Creator, who as the Gospels tell us, counted the hairs of his head."[28]

Christianity's accent on the importance of the individual and his freedom demonstrates that God values each and every person. Spiritually speaking, God only saves individuals, never a group. No one can ride into heaven, so to speak, merely by being a member of some Christian group. Moreover, the Christian accent on the value of the individual was never intended to encourage or foster selfish individualism, an accusation that collectivists or socialists often make. When personal selfishness raises its ugly head, it is a serious abuse of basic Christian values.

Inherent in individual freedom and rights is the concept of individual responsibility. In recent years the latter has been virtually ignored, especially in the United States, where the concept of rights is so heavily accented that little or no emphasis is given to individual responsibility. Rarely does one hear people—for instance, teachers in schools—talk about the necessity of individual responsibility. Yet people's rights and freedom cannot be divorced from their responsibilities without eventually destroying both.

While Christian values have in large measure provided the infrastructure for individual freedom and rights in Western societies, they have never minimized individual responsibility. In fact, it can be argued that from the beginning Christians saw responsibility as more important than freedom or rights. Throughout the first three centuries of Roman persecution, there is no evidence that they ever insisted on their rights. St. Paul commanded the Christians in Rome to obey the governmental authorities even though they were persecuting them: "Everyone must submit himself to the governing authorities" (Romans 13:1). In short, he enjoined responsible behavior. In time, such behavior brought them freedom and rights. Moreover, it was the American Founding Fathers' strong sense of responsibility, imbued with Christian values, that resulted in their formulating specific rights for posterity in the Amendments to the Constitution of the United States. Irresponsible leaders do not care about the freedom and rights of others.

Bringing individual freedom into the human arena has had many positive effects in the history of Western society. For instance, the Austrian economic philosopher F. A. Hayek attributed the growth and advance of science to the freedom in Western society, for it led to "the unchaining of individual energies."[29]

FREEDOM OF RELIGION

As church historians know, there were times in the history of Christendom when some bishops and state rulers coerced individuals and even groups of people to accept Christianity. For instance, Emperor Theodosius I issued an edict in 380 compelling all government officials to embrace Christianity. In the sixth century, Emperor Justinian brought many into the church by involuntary means. And in the eighth century, Charlemagne the Great forced many to accept Christianity. As much as Christ wanted people to follow him, these leaders and others like them obviously forgot that he had never forced anyone to do so, even though it pained him to see people in their spiritual obstinacy spurn him and his message. He wept over Jerusalem's hardheaded rejection of him. His method for gaining converts was by teaching and preaching, not by coercion (Matthew 28:20). Thus, when people in the past were brought into the church by compulsion or through enticements of various sorts, the method and the spirit of Christ were grossly violated.

The freedom of religious beliefs was also transgressed when individuals were decapitated or burned at the stake for believing or teaching what some leaders in the church at various times called heresies. Only seventy-two years after Christianity had gained legal status in the Roman Empire in 313, Priscillianus, a Spanish bishop with gnostic leanings, was, in 385 under Emperor Gratian's direction, the first man to be tortured and decapitated for sorcery. But it must also be noted that St. Ambrose and Pope Siricius denounced the execution and refused fellowship with the accusers.[30] Charles the Bald in 844 began the Inquisition by enjoining bishops to interrogate teachers in the church to see whether they were teaching heresies. Space does not permit mentioning the Inquisitions that followed. In 1480 the frequently cited Spanish Inquisitions began, and they lasted until 1834. Equally horrible was burning the bones of John Wycliffe (thirty years after his death) for denying the Roman Catholic doctrine of transubstantiation, burning John Hus at the stake in 1416, and putting Jerome Savonarola to the flames in 1498. These are but a few examples of how the Roman Catholic Church before the Reformation violated the freedom of religious beliefs. Unfortunately, some major injustices also occurred among some of the Protestants. John Calvin, for instance, approved the execution of Michael Servetus for heresy in 1553, and the Dutch Calvinists hanged John of Oldenbarneveldt in 1619 for rejecting Calvin's doctrine of double predestination.

On the other hand, there were always prominent Christian leaders who proclaimed the right of individuals to believe according to their consciences. These leaders maintained this position even though they held firmly to Christ's teaching that there is no salvation outside of faith in him: "I am the way and the truth and the life. No one comes to the Father except through me" (John 14:6). Tertullian (d. ca. 220) said that "it is a fundamental right, a privilege of nature, that every man should worship according to his own convictions...to which free-will and not force should lead us" (*Ad Scapula* 2). Similarly, Lactantius (d. ca. 330) defended the freedom of religious belief. According to him, "It is religion alone in which freedom has placed its dwelling. For it is a matter which is voluntary above all others, nor can necessity be imposed upon any, so as to worship that which he does not wish to worship" (*The Epitome of the Divine Institutes* 49). In the fifth century St. Augustine (354–430), although an ardent defender of the Christian faith, never forced the pagans to accept Christianity.[31] And in the sixteenth century, Martin Luther (1483–1546) told the German princes in a letter that it was not the function of government to "forbid anyone to teach or believe or say what he wants—the Gospel or lies."[32]

Numerous other Christian theologians and leaders could be cited to document that the freedom of religious beliefs stems from biblical Christianity. To the skeptics who deny this fact, perhaps because many in the church often violated this principle, one need only ask: Where does one find the greatest amount of religious freedom? Is it in the Western countries where Christianity has had its greatest and longest presence, or is it in societies where Christianity has had little or no presence? The answer decidedly favors Christianity.

Despite some of the flagrant denials of religious freedom that occurred in the history of the church, the will of Christ eventually prevailed. God did not let evil conquer his church. He raised still another stalwart proponent of religious freedom in Martin Luther, who in 1521, before Emperor Charles V and the Diet of Worms, boldly declared, "Unless I am convicted by Scripture and plain reason—I do not accept the authority of popes and councils, for they have contradicted each other—my conscience is captive to the Word of God. I cannot and will not recant anything, for to go against conscience is neither right nor safe. God help me, Amen."[33] As historians know, a number of territorial princes of the Holy Roman Empire sided with Luther, and a new era of religious freedom dawned with the arrival of the Protestant Reformation.

When the framers of the American Constitution drafted the freedom of religion clause in the First Amendment, which states that "Congress shall make no law respecting an establishment of religion or prohibiting the free exercise thereof," they truly echoed the desire of prominent Christian forebears like Tertullian, Lactantius, Hus, Savonarola, and others, but especially Martin Luther. So powerful was Luther's breakthrough for religious liberty and freedom of conscience that Thomas Bailey, a secular historian, in his massive volume on American history credits him as one of the "indirect founding fathers of the United States."[34]

Alexis de Tocqueville, the observant French visitor to the United States in 1831, recognized the contributions that Christianity made to American individual liberty. Said he, "Americans combine the notions of Christianity and of liberty so intimately in their minds, that it is impossible to make them conceive the one without the other."[35]

EQUALITY OF INDIVIDUALS

In recent years there have been a plethora of political discussions regarding equality and inequality, virtually all of them in the secular vein. Once again, as with the many other influences that Christianity has contributed to Western civic freedoms, the concept of equality has definite Christian roots. But the Christian concept of equality must not be confused with the Marxian concept of economic equality or its understanding of egalitarianism.

The biblical and Christian understanding of equality focuses solely on the spiritual equality of human beings before God. Moses told the Israelites that spiritually God "shows no partiality" (Deuteronomy 10:17). Peter had these words in mind when he told Cornelius, "God does not show favoritism but accepts men from every nation who fear him and do what is right" (Acts 10:34–35). Similarly, the Apostle Paul told the Romans that "all have sinned and fall short of the glory of God" (Romans 3:23). Briefly put, all humans are equal as fallen, sinful creatures. And when sinful individuals place their faith in God's Son, they acquire a spiritual equality, as the Galatian Christians were assured: "There is neither Jew nor Greek, slave nor free, male nor female, for you are all one in Christ Jesus" (Galatians 3:28).

Early Christianity's concept of equality was largely confined to spiritual/fellowship interactions of its members. They treated each other as equals in terms of male-female relationships, mutual support, fellowship, and worship. And as indicated in the next chapter, even slaves had equal access to the church's rites such as baptism, the Lord's Supper, and other activities. But there never was any specific effort to extend equality beyond religiously oriented activities. In time, however, the notion of equality got extended. Some of those extensions were not always in conformity with Christ's precepts, especially with regard to economic equality. One such example was the twelfth-century Crusaders, who in pursuit of equality "decimated the nobles and divided their possessions."[36] They had forgotten Christ's words: "Man, who made Me a judge or arbitrator over you?" (Luke 12:14 NKJV).

Another incident in history that sought equality, this one in the context of politics, was the attempt by the Puritans, most notably the Independents, in the British Parliament during England's Civil War (1642–45). They believed that "all Christians were, as Christians, free and equal and therefore entitled to a voice in the affairs of a Christian State."[37] After the British monarchy was restored in 1660, however, the Puritan doctrine of political equality greatly diminished until it was revived by John Locke in 1689. From him it drifted across the Atlantic to America, where Puritans in New England kept the doctrine alive.[38]

The desire for a broader application of equality, especially in the realm of political life, continued to grow in the Western world. Thus, Alexis de Tocqueville argued that by the nineteenth century there was "greater equality of condition in Christian countries at the present day than there has been at any previous time, in any part of the world."[39] In his *Democracy in America* (first published in 1834) he also stated that the equality of condition was particularly pronounced in the United States.

As many Americans know, the American desire for equality is even enshrined in the Constitution of the United States. For instance, the formulators of the Constitution in 1787 stipulated in Section 9 that "No title of nobility shall be granted by the United States." The Constitution's writers also stated that the office of the President had to be "a natural born citizen" of the United States. Apparently the Constitution's designers wanted to avoid all semblance of European-like aristocracy, an old symbol of inequality. And given that most of the formulators had a Christian background, Christianity's concept of equality undoubtedly played a role in the wording of these two parts of the Constitution.

To cite Tocqueville, the analyst of American equality, one more time, it is noteworthy that he believed "equality pushed to the furthest extent, may be confounded with freedom."[40] Insightfully he added, "The taste which men have for liberty and that which they feel for equality are, in fact, two different things."⁴¹ These words indicate that nations that purportedly implement widespread equality—for instance, "economic equality," as was done by the communists in Russia, Cuba, China, and other like-minded countries—invariably sacrifice freedom. In all of these extreme socialist countries, in the name of equality people lost their personal freedoms such as the freedom of speech and the right to own private property. Such "equality" no longer has any relationship to Christianity's concept of equality. This is why many historians have called communism a Christian heresy.

SEPARATION OF CHURCH AND STATE

Does the concept of the separation of church and state reflect a Christian influence? If one listens to the media and to the American Civil Liberties Union, one gets the impression that this concept is a totally secular phenomenon designed to make certain that Christians do not establish a theocracy in the bosom of America's republic and that Christians stay out of civic affairs. How far this is from the truth! Contrary to the current faulty understanding of what separation of church and state means, one can argue that the church-and-state distinction has substantial Christian roots harking back to the response that Jesus gave to the Pharisees when they tried to entrap him by asking whether it was lawful to give tax money to the Roman Caesar, whom they despised. Jesus asked them to show him a Roman coin. "Whose image and inscription is on it?" he asked. "Caesar's," they replied. And Jesus answered, "Give to Caesar what is Caesar's, and to God what is God's" (Matthew 22:21).

Three hundred years after Jesus made this statement, Hosius, bishop of Cordoba, Spain, from 353 to 356, reprimanded Emperor Constantius II for meddling in ecclesiastical matters by trying to get the Western bishops to condemn Athanasius of Alexandria for opposing the Arian heresy. Said Hosius: "Intrude not yourself into ecclesiastical affairs. . . . God has put into your hands the [secular] kingdom; to us [bishops] He has entrusted the affairs of His church."⁴² In support of his reprimand, he cited Jesus' statement about rendering to Caesar the things that are Caesar's and to God the things that are God's.

The early Christians, during their first three hundred years of bloody persecutions, neither sought nor expected the government to support them in their religious activities. They only yearned for freedom to worship their Lord and Savior, Jesus Christ. They differed remarkably from the pagan Romans for whom religion meant being linked to a particular city or state.

The Latin word *religare* (from which we get the word *religion*) meant that there was a bond between the people and the state. The Christian idea of "an association of people bound together by a religious allegiance with its own traditions and beliefs, its own history, and its own way of life, independent of a particular city or nation," says Robert Wilkin, "was foreign to the ancients."[43] The fact that Christians were not linked to a city or state was one of the things that irritated Celsus, the second-century pagan critic of Christianity. He saw Christians as "sectarians." But when Constantine the Great legalized Christianity in 313 and soon involved himself in many of the church's affairs, the separation of church and state began to disappear, and for more than a thousand years after Constantine the church and state were largely intertwined.

When Hosius chided the emperor, it was the government that was attempting to make ecclesiastical decisions. But by the Middle Ages the situation had reversed itself. Now the church increasingly intruded in the affairs of government. This fusion of church and state activities angered Martin Luther in the sixteenth century. He especially criticized the papacy's role in secular government, seeing it as violating what he called the concept of the two kingdoms (realms). It was the church's task solely to preach and teach the gospel of Jesus Christ; this he called the spiritual kingdom or realm. The government's task was to keep peace and order in society by restraining and punishing the unlawful; this he called the worldly kingdom or realm. The secular government can only compel people to behave outwardly; it can never make a person's heart spiritually righteous. Only the preaching of the gospel (the spiritual realm) can do that. In the spiritual realm the Christian functions as a disciple of Christ; in the secular realm he functions as a citizen. Although the two realms are separate, the faithful Christian is active in both because God is active in both. In the spiritual realm he is active in proclaiming the gospel, whereas in the secular kingdom he is active by means of the law and the sword, or government. It is interesting that in Luther's lengthy discussion of the two realms (the spiritual and the worldly), he cites Jesus' statement about giving to Caesar what is his and to God what belongs to him; that is, the two realms (church and state) had separate functions.[44]

When America's Founding Fathers wrote the First Amendment to the Constitution, "Congress shall make no law respecting an establishment of religion, or prohibiting the free exercise thereof," they not only intended freedom of religion for the individual (as noted above), but in effect also said that the two kingdoms, to use Luther's terminology, were to be kept separate even though the words "separation of church and state" are not in the First Amendment.

The words "separation of church and state" (which in recent years have become a national preoccupation with many Americans) are the result of an inference made from a letter Jefferson sent to the Danbury Connecticut Baptist Association on January 1, 1802. In that letter he used the phrase "building a wall of separation between church and state." When he used these words, he had no intention of curtailing religious practices. Neither he nor the drafters of the First Amendment had even the remotest thought of outlawing governmental support for religion. He, like Luther, merely wanted to keep the government from making religious decisions. This is evident from some of his acts as president. For instance, he used federal money to build churches and establish missions for the purpose of bringing the gospel to the American Indians. "What the federal government was prohibited from doing, in Jefferson's view, was prescribing a particular set of religious rites or promoting a particular sect at the expense of others."[45] Jefferson also sent a treaty to the Congress that provided for a "Catholic church building" for the Kaskaskia Indians in 1803.[46] Note that this was after his "wall of separation" speech in Connecticut.

The Founding Fathers, including Jefferson, wanted the nation to have freedom *of* religion, not *from* religion. The latter is currently being promoted by the American Civil Liberties Union and its anti-Christian allies. In order to achieve freedom *from* religion, secularists have been using the state, with the help of the United States Supreme Court, to "free" the people from religion. Outlawing Christmas crèches and banning prayers in public schools are but two examples. When Jesus said "Give to Caesar what is Caesar's, and to God what is God's," he did not mean to have Caesar (the government) jettison God from public life.

So back to the question: Does the doctrine of separation of church and state reflect a Christian influence? Yes it does, but only as the First Amendment is actually worded, not as it has been interpreted (or misinterpreted) by the U.S. Supreme Court ever since the Everson v. Board of Education decision of 1947. Given that the Founding Fathers were well-read individuals and familiar with the teachings of Jesus Christ, they surely knew about Jesus' Caesar-and-God statement, about church-state conflicts in history, and about the monopoly that state churches had in Europe. Moreover, as is well known, they were also conversant with John Locke's

LIBERTY AND JUSTICE

Proclaimers	Principles
Moses, leader of Israelites and recipient of the Ten Commandments	Two or more witnesses (Deut. 19:16), ca. 1400 B.C.
Jesus Christ	"Give to Caesar what is Caesar's, and to God what is God's" (Matt. 22:21), ca. A.D. 28
St. Paul, 1st-cent. missionary to the Jews and Gentiles	"There is neither Jew nor Greek, slave nor free, male nor female, for you are all one in Christ Jesus" (Gal. 3:28), ca. 55
Tertullian, early 3rd-cent. African Christian apologist	Freedom of religion: Every man should be free to worship according to his own conviction (Ad Scapula), ca. 190
Lactantius, early 4th-cent. church father known as the "Christian Cicero"	Freedom of religion: No one should be compelled to worship against his will (Epitome of the Divine Institutes), ca. 320
Hosius, Christian bishop, Cordoba, Spain	Government is not to meddle in ecclesiastical affairs (spoken to Emperor Constantius II), ca. 355
St. Ambrose, 4th-cent. bishop of Milan	"No one, not even the emperor, is above the law": spoken to Emperor Theodosius I, 390
Stephen Langton, British archbishop and an architect of the Magna Carta	The king cannot be above the law (a reiteration of Ambrose's principle in the Magna Carta), 1215
Martin Luther, leader of the Protestant Reformation	Church and state must be separate realms (An Open Letter to the Christian Nobility, 1520)
John Locke, British political philosopher	People's rights are not given by governments but by the laws of nature (Two Treatises of Government), 1690
Baron de Montesquieu, French political philosopher	The powers (branches) of government must be separated (The Spirit of Laws, 1766)
Franz Pastorius, German immigrant	Anti-Slavery Proclamation, Germantown, Pennsylvania, 1688
Thomas Jefferson, author of Declaration of Independence	God has given people unalienable rights of life, liberty, and the pursuit of happiness (Declaration of Independence, 1776)
Adam Smith, Scottish political and economic philosopher	Liberty must also be present in people's economic affairs (The Wealth of Nations, 1776)
James Madison, father of the American Constitution	Freedom cannot be denied to those who do not believe ("Memorial and Remonstrance," 1788)
Abraham Lincoln, president of the United States	Emancipation Proclamation, giving freedom to American black slaves, 1863
Thirteenth Amendment to the Constitution of the United States	Outlawed slavery in the United States, 1865

writings, which reflected much Christian thinking. In light of Locke's scholarly bent, it is quite likely that he also was familiar with Luther's doctrine of the two realms. This is not idle conjecture, for in *A Letter Concerning Toleration*, Locke wrote, "All the power of civil government relates only to men's civil interests, is confined to the care of things of this world, and hath nothing to do with the world to come."[47] These words sound remarkably similar to Luther's two-realms doctrine. So it is quite plausible that the Founding Fathers, via Locke's Luther-like statement, together with Christ's Caesar-and-God teaching, imported this Christian understanding of the separation of church and state as they hammered out the First Amendment's freedom-of-religion clause.

The impression is sometimes given that keeping church and state separate occurred in the United States because most of the Founding Fathers were deists or secular-minded individuals who wanted to end all support for Christianity. This is not true. Most of the Founding Fathers professed to be Christians, and they had no intent of eliminating governmental assistance to religion, specifically Christianity. Their official acts clearly demonstrate this. For instance, presidents George Washington, John Adams, and James Madison, with approval of Congress, issued Thanksgiving Day proclamations. Madison took an active part in bringing chaplains to pray in Congress. And presidents James Monroe, John Quincy Adams, Andrew Jackson, and Martin Van Buren, with Senate approval, proposed and signed Indian treaties that provided for the government to support various Christian religious needs of the American Indians. Robert Cord, in his *Separation of Church and State* (1982), an extensively researched work, cites numerous Indian treaties that gave federal financial assistance to Catholic churches on reservations as well as other religious support.[48]

These examples and others show that for more than a hundred years neither the American presidents nor the country's Supreme Court saw any conflict in giving aid to religion or religious activities. Clearly, America's presidents and judges understood what Jesus meant when he introduced the distinction between Caesar and God as well as understood the arguments made by Martin Luther regarding the separation of church and state — namely, that the state and church were two very different entities and that such a separation did not necessarily give support for taking religion or God out of publicly, tax-supported activities. Nor did Christ's and Luther's position say that governmental assistance to some religious activities eliminated the distinction between state and church, reminiscent of the Middle Ages, but rather that both served complementary roles in a civilized society.

CONCLUSION

In whatever nations Christianity has had a prominent presence, there has been marked improvement in liberty and justice as opposed to societies that have been, or continue to be, dominated by non-Christian religions. Nowhere has there been a better example of liberty and justice than in the United States of America. Why? American liberty and justice has been profoundly influence by Christian principles. Alexis de Tocqueville recognized the connection when he said, "There is no country in the world where the Christian religion retains a greater influence over the souls of men than in America."[49] Or as Kevin Abrams, a Jewish author, has recently noted, "The American civilization rests on the basic principles of Christian morality which have their origin in the Hebrew Scriptures."[50]

In short, the great emphasis on liberty and justice in the United States is not mere happenstance. It exists because the American architects of liberty and justice were influenced to a large degree by Christianity's biblical values and beliefs. Thus, as Abrams asserts, "Remove the Bible as the constellation that guides the American Ship of State and the whole edifice of American civilization collapses."[51] And regarding Western countries outside of the United States, the historian Carlton Hayes has remarked, "Wherever Christian ideals have been generally accepted and their practice sincerely attempted, there is a dynamic liberty; and wherever Christianity had been ignored or rejected, persecuted or chained to the state, there is tyranny."[52]

NOTES

1. Augustine, *The City of God Against the Pagans* (Cambridge: Harvard University Press, 1963), 5:273.

2. See the Magna Carta in J. C. Holt, *Magna Carta* (Cambridge: Cambridge University Press, 1965), 317–37. Quotations below are from this work.

3. Ibid., 317.

4. Leon McKenzie, *Pagan Resurrection Myths and the Resurrection of Jesus* (Charlottesville: Bookwrights Press, 1997), 49.

5. Martin Luther, "Against the Heavenly Prophets in the Matter of Images and Sacraments," *Luther's Works*, trans. Bernard Erling, ed. Conrad Bergendoff (Philadelphia: Muhlenberg Press, 1958), 40:98.

6. John Locke, *The Reasonableness of Christianity* (Stanford: Stanford University Press, 1958), 29.

7. Gary T. Amos, *Defending the Declaration: How the Bible and Christianity Influenced the Writing of the Declaration of Independence* (Brentwood, Tenn.: Wolgemuth and Hyatt, 1989), 42.

8. Ellis Sandoz, *A Government of Laws: Political Theory, Religion, and the American Founding* (Baton Rouge: Louisiana State University Press, 1990), 94.

9. Thomas Jefferson, in *Jefferson Himself: The Personal Narrative of a Many-Sided American*, ed. Bernard Mayo (Charlottesville: University of Virginia Press, 1970), 322.

10. Amos, *Defending the Declaration*, 78.

11. John Locke, *The Second Treatise of Government* (Indianapolis: Bobbs-Merrill, 1952), 14.

12. Amos, *Defending the Declaration*, 56.

13. Sandoz, *Government of Laws*, 99.

14. Robert Wernick, "The Godfather of the American Constitution," *Smithsonian* (September 1989): 183.

15. James Madison, *The Papers of James Madison,* ed. Robert A. Rutland (Chicago: University of Chicago Press, 1977), 10:98.

16. James Madison, "Memorial and Remonstrance," in *The Papers of James Madison,* ed. Robert A. Rutland and William M. E. Rachal (Chicago: University of Chicago Press, 1973), 8:301.

17. John Eidsmoe, *Christianity and the Constitution: The Faith of Our Founding Fathers* (Grand Rapids: Baker, 1987), 107.

18. Madison, "Memorial and Remonstrance," 300.

19. Baron de Montesquieu, *The Spirit of Laws,* trans. Thomas Nugent (Cincinnati: Robert Clarke, 1886), 2:134.

20. Ibid., 2:121.

21. Ibid., 2:122.

22. Ibid., 2:124.

23. Ibid., 1:174

24. Sandoz, *Government of Laws,* 13.

25. C. F. Adams, ed., *The Works of John Adams* (Boston: Charles C. Little and James Brown, 1851), 4:293.

26. C. Schmidt, *The Social Results of Early Christianity,* trans. R. W. Dale (London: Sir Isaac Putman and Sons, 1889), 76.

27. Balint Vazsonyi, *America's 30 Years War* (Washington, D.C.: Regnery Gateway, 1998), 79.

28. Malcolm Muggeridge, *The End of Christendom* (Grand Rapids: Wm. B. Eerdmans, 1980), 19.

29. F. A. Hayek, *The Road to Serfdom* (Chicago: University of Chicago Press, [1944] 1994), 19.

30. Michael M. Smith, *The History of Christianity* (Herts, England: Lion Publishing, 1977), 142.

31. Jacques Chabanes, *St. Augustine,* trans. Julie Kernan (New York: Doubleday, 1962), 164.

32. "Letter to the Princes of Saxony Concerning the Rebellious Spirit," *Luther's Works,* trans. Bernard Erling, ed. Conrad Bergendoff (Philadelphia: Muhlenberg Press, 1958), 40:58.

33. Cited by Roland H. Bainton, *Here I Stand: A Life of Martin Luther* (Nashville: Abingdon Press, 1978), 144.

34. Thomas Bailey, *The American Pageant* (Lexington, Mass.: D. C. Heath, 1975), 3.

35. Alexis de Tocqueville, *The Republic of the United States of America and Its Political Institutions, Reviewed and Examined,* trans. Henry Reeves (New York: A. S. Barnes, 1851), 335.

36. Alexis de Tocqueville, *Democracy in America,* ed. Philips Bradley (New York: Vintage Books, 1945), 1:5.

37. James Bryce, *Modern Democracies* (New York: Macmillan, 1921), 1:28.

38. Tocqueville, *Democracy in America,* 1:6–7.

39. Ibid., 1:6.

40. Ibid., 2:100.

41. Ibid.

42. "Hosius to Constantius the Emperor," *Athanasius,* in *The Nicene and Post-Nicene Fathers of the Christian Church* (Grand Rapids: Wm. B. Eerdmans, 1980), 4:286.

43. Robert Wilken, *The Christians as the Romans Saw Them* (New Haven: Yale University Press, 1984), 124–25.

44. Martin Luther, "Temporal Authority: To What Extent It Should Be Obeyed," in *Luther's Works,* ed. Walther I. Brandt and Helmut T. Lehmann (Philadelphia: Muhlenberg Press, 1962), 45:111.

45. Benjamin Hart, *Faith and Freedom: The Christian Roots of American Liberty* (Dallas: Lewis and Stanley, 1988), 349.

46. Robert L. Cord, *Separation of Church and State* (New York: Lambeth Press, 1982), 41.

47. John Locke, *Treatise of Civil Government and A Letter Concerning Toleration,* ed. Charles L Sherman (New York: Appleton-Century-Crofts, 1937), 175.

48. Cord, *Separation of Church and State,* 66–73.

49. De Tocqueville, *Democracy in America,* 314.

50. Kevin Abrams, "Preface," in Scott Lively and Kevin E. Abrams, *The Pink Swastika: Homosexuality in the Nazi Party* (Keizer, Ore.: Founders Publishing Corporation, 1966), viii.

51. Ibid.

52. Carlton J. H. Hayes, *Christianity and Western Civilization* (Stanford: Stanford University Press, 1954), 21.

11

SLAVERY ABOLISHED: a CHRISTIAN ACHIEVEMENT

"No longer as a slave, but better than a slave, as a dear brother."
St. Paul in Philemon 16

Slavery was indigenous to African and Arab countries before it made its way to Europe.[1] But by the time of Christ, slaves made up an estimated 75 percent of the population in ancient Athens and well over half of the Roman population. Slavery was also widely practiced by many tribes of the American Indians long before Columbus set foot on the shores of the New World. With few exceptions kings, priests, and philosophers approved of it. Aristotle, the influential Greek philosopher, saw it as natural, expedient, and just (*Politics* 1.1255).

Unlike in more recent history when slaves performed only unskilled labor, in ancient Greece slaves not only did all of the menial work but also the work that required skilled labor. The freeborn and property owners (the citizens) in Greece, as noted in chapter 8, did not engage in manual labor. This state of affairs was similar in Roman culture: slaves performed virtually all of the physical or manual work. Thus, the Appian Way, the Seven Wonders of the World, and even the beautiful sculptures from that period were the work of slaves. Every time present-day tourists are impressed by the magnificent ancient buildings and statues—now mostly in ruins or badly damaged—in the countries of the Middle East or in Europe, they are looking at products of slave labor.

Many do not know that the tragedy of slavery continued in a number of countries for more than a hundred years after it was outlawed in the United States in 1865. Ethiopia had slavery until 1942, Saudi Arabia until 1962, Peru until 1964, and India until 1976. Moreover, it still exists to this day in Sudan, Africa's largest country.[2] When people do not know—and many do not—that slavery is still present today in Sudan, their ignorance is largely the fault of the mass media's reluctance to report it. Politically correct media and school textbooks give the impression that slavery has primarily been a sin committed by white people who enslaved blacks. The fact that only about 25 percent of the Americans in the South had slaves before the Civil War is commonly not mentioned, nor is the fact that (according to the United States census of 1830), for example, 407 black Americans in Charleston, South Carolina, alone owned black slaves.[3]

Nor have the mass media made any effort to report that a Christian organization in Sudan known as Christian Solidarity International currently buys slaves, most of whom are black Christians, in order to set them free. In some instances this organization pays 50,000 Sudanese pounds per slave.[4] Nor have the mass media reported that in the past several years more than three million Sudanese Christians and animists, mostly slaves, have been executed in recent years.

EARLY CHRISTIAN OPPOSITION TO SLAVERY

As the biblical citation accompanying this chapter's title indicates, St. Paul told Philemon that he was no longer to treat Onesimus, his onetime slave, as a slave but rather as a brother. Onesimus had run away and was being returned to Philemon, his owner. Paul in effect told Philemon that as a Christian he was no longer to practice slavery. Similarly, he told the Galatian Christians that from the Christian perspective there was "neither Jew nor Greek, slave nor free...for you are all one in Christ Jesus" (Galatians 3:28). And given the culturally ingrained practice of slavery that had existed for centuries in the ancient world, Paul's words were revolutionary. The Philemon and Galatians passages laid the foundation for the abolition of slavery, then and for the future.

In addition to Paul's antislavery statements made to Philemon and the Galatians, numerous other actions and statements that were incompatible with slavery soon surfaced in the early church, even though many Christians did not fully heed Paul's antislavery statements. Here are a few examples of the changes that were happening. Christians interacted with slaves as they did with freemen. Slaves communed with Christians at the same altar. This behavior contrasted sharply with that of the Romans who held slaves in contempt.[5] Slaves fared no better among the Greeks, whose philosopher Aristotle argued that "a slave is a living tool, just as a tool is an inanimate slave. Therefore there can be no friendship with a slave as slave" (*Nichomachean Ethics* 8.11).

In many instances, Christians freed slaves. During the second and third centuries, according to Robin Lane Fox, the early Christians "were most numerous in the setting of urban households where freeing [of slaves] was most frequent." He further states that "the freeing of slaves was performed in church in the presence of the bishop."[6] How many slaves were freed during the early years of Christianity can never be known, but that there were many is illustrated by W. E. H. Lecky, who says, "St. Melania was said to have emancipated 8,000 slaves; St. Ovidius, a rich martyr of Gaul, 5,000; Chromatius, a Roman prefect under Diocletian, 1,400; Hermes, a prefect under Trajan, 1,200. [And] many of the Christian clergy at Hippo under the rule of St. Augustine, as well as great numbers of private individuals, freed their slaves as an act of piety."[7] It is also known that Constantine in A.D. 315, only two years after he issued the Edict of Milan, imposed the death penalty on those who stole children to bring them up as slaves.[8]

Freeing slaves not only took Christian conviction, but it took courage as well. Edicts issued by Roman emperors did not favor liberating slaves. In time, however, an emperor (Justinian, 527–65) arose who was sympathetic to what his fellow Christians were doing. He abolished all laws that prevented freeing slaves. This change, together with the numerous slaves who had already been freed and who still were being liberated, was consistent with what some of the leading theologians had been saying. Early in the fourth century Lactantius (the "Christian Cicero") in his *Divine Institutes* said that in God's eyes there were no slaves. St. Augustine (354–430) saw slavery as the product of sin and as contrary to God's divine plan (*The City of God* 19.15). St. Chrysostom, in the fourth century, preached that when Christ came he annulled slavery. He proclaimed that "in Christ Jesus there is no slave....Therefore it is not necessary to have a slave....Buy them, and after you have taught them some skill by which they can maintain

SAN VITALE CHURCH in Ravenna, Italy, is named after a Christian slave who was martyred in the early fourth century.

themselves, set them free" *(Homily 40 on 1 Corinthians 10)*. These words and actions as well as others had continuing salutary effects. Slavery was also condemned in the fifth century by St. Patrick in Ireland. For several centuries bishops and councils recommended the redemption of captive slaves, and for five centuries the Christian monks redeemed Christian slaves from Moorish servitude.[9] By the twelfth century slaves in Europe were rare, and by the fourteenth century slavery was almost unknown on the Continent.[10] The honor, acceptance, and freedom that Christianity extended to slaves resulted in "multitudes" of them embracing the new faith, according to Lecky. Some even became priests of the church. In the early third century Callistus, a onetime slave, became not only a priest but also a bishop. In fact, the Roman Catholic Church lists him as one of its early popes. Some slaves were even honored as martyrs. For instance, in the first half of the sixth century Emperor Justinian built and dedicated the grandest example of Byzantine architecture in Ravenna, Italy, the Church of San Vitale, in memory of a martyred slave of the fourth century.[11]

Some Erring Christians Condoned Slavery

Although slavery in Europe had virtually come to end by the fourteenth century, it is important to remember that in spite of St. Paul's words to Philemon and to the Galatians, for more than a thousand years many Christians had owned slaves. This included even prominent church leaders such as Polycarp, a second-century bishop of Smyrna, and Athenagoras, a second-century Christian philosopher. Others, such as Clement of Alexandria and Origen, both third-century church fathers, spoke approvingly of slavery. Similarly, in the thirteenth century St. Bonaventure saw slavery as a divine institution, and in 1548 Pope Paul III granted to all men, and to the clergy, the right to keep slaves.

The erring Christians who supported and owned slaves indicate at least three important truths: (1) as sinful beings, they were either ignorant of Paul's words or knowingly ignored them; (2) they let the prevailing culture of pagan societies influence their behavior; and (3) they ignored Christ's words that said his followers were to be in the world but not of it.

The British Revival of Slavery and Its Abolition

It is important to note that although by the fourteenth century slavery had essentially come to an end in Europe, including England, it was revived by the British in the seventeenth century, especially in England's colonies. A London church council decision of 1102, which had outlawed slavery and slave trade, was ignored.[12] Slaves were transported from Africa to the colonies in the British West Indies as well as to the American colonies and to Canada. The Portuguese and the Spanish also went to Africa to get slaves and then shipped them to their colonies in Brazil, Central America, and parts of South America.

This revival of slavery was lamentable because this time it was implemented by countries whose proponents of slavery commonly identified themselves as Christians, whereas during the African and Greco-Roman eras, slavery was the product of pagans. However, some serious-minded Christians saw slavery as a gross violation of basic Christian beliefs and values, and before too long some courageous individuals came to the forefront of the battle against slavery.

One such courageous abolitionist was William Wilberforce (1759–1833), a member of England's House of Commons. As a devout Christian, he declared, "The Christian's motto should be, 'Watch always, for you know not in what hour the Son of man will come.' Also 'Help me, O Jesus, and by Thy Spirit cleanse me from my pollutions; give me a deeper abhorrence of sin; let me press forward.'"[13] His biographer, John Stoughton, says, "He believed in Jesus Christ as the image of the invisible God; he believed that we are saved by grace; he believed in justification by faith; he believed in the work of the Holy Spirit; he believed in the world to come. These beliefs with their practical consequences and applications were as dear to him as life."[14] Sir Walter Scott credited Wilberforce with being the leader of the religious members in Parliament. A gifted orator, he delivered many powerful speeches during his twenty-some years in Parliament against Britain sending slaves to the West Indies. According to his biographer, his speeches were most effective when he "appealed to the Christian consciences of Englishmen."[15] In 1823, two years before he had to relinquish his seat in the House of Commons because of ill health, he presented a petition to the House of Commons to abolish slavery, a petition that a close associate of his, Thomas Fowell Buxton, moved "as a resolution declaring slavery repugnant to Christianity and the Constitution."[16] A few days before he died on July 26, 1833, he received word that Parliament had passed the Abolition Act. This act resulted in freeing 700,000 slaves by England in its

"UNE VENTE D'ESCLAVES AUX ÉTATS-UNIS" shows an auction of slaves, once practiced in the United States as well as other countries. *(Gustave Doré)*

West Indies colonies.[17] Upon hearing this good news, he exclaimed, "Thank God that I should have lived to witness a day in which England is willing to give twenty millions sterling for the Abolition of Slavery."[18] It is difficult to find a better example than Wilberforce to show the powerful effect the teachings and spirit of Christ have had in fighting the social sin of slavery. No proponent for the abolition of slavery ever accomplished more. Largely as a result of his indefatigable efforts, slavery came to a complete end in all of the British Empire's possessions by 1840, making it the first modern country to outlaw slavery.

SLAVERY AND ITS ABOLITION IN AMERICA

Even after slavery came to an end in the British Empire in the 1830s, it continued unabated to the north and south of the adjacent British West Indies, most notably in the United States, Brazil, and Mexico. In the United States it had become a deeply entrenched institution, especially in the Southern states, despite the fact that only about 25 percent of the Southerners owned slaves.[19]

Given that this "peculiar institution," as it was often called, was so firmly entrenched in the South, it had many ardent defenders. Unfortunately, many of them called themselves Christians. Virtually every American church denomination had pro-slavery advocates. In support of their position, they cited man's innate sinfulness, historical precedent, black people's perceived inferiority, and economic necessity. A common argument in favor of slavery was its presence in the Old Testament. Here they engaged in faulty reasoning, giving descriptive passages in the Bible prescriptive meaning.

Slavery became an intensely heated issue politically and even theologically in both the American North and the South. This occurred despite the fact that the United States had received a relatively low percentage of the ten million African slaves that had been imported to the New World between 1502 and the 1860s. It had received about 7 percent; Brazil, 41 percent; the British and French colonies in the Caribbean, along with the Spanish settlements, 47 percent; and the Dutch, Danish, and Swedish colonies, 5 percent.[20]

Pro-slavery advocates and defenders were not backward or illiterate. For the most part they were well educated; some were presidents of colleges in the North. And among the pro-slavery clergy, for example, Yale and Princeton had the highest representation.[21] But although slavery in America was condoned and defended by many who were members of Christian denominations, there were also strong countervailing voices of prominent

Christian leaders who came to be known as abolitionists. The Christian abolitionists not only had the mind of Christ and powerful references of the New Testament on their side, but they also had noteworthy antislavery precedents in Christian history, as cited earlier.

Many American defenders of slavery, as has already been mentioned, called themselves Christians, and every state also had its clergy who argued that slavery was compatible with biblical Christianity. But the abolitionist movement had a considerably higher percentage of Christian clergy than did the pro-slavery defenders. Two-thirds of the abolitionists in the mid–1830s were Christian clergymen.[22] This made for a phalanx of vociferously active clergy abolitionists.

CHRISTIAN CLERGY'S IMPACT ON ABOLITION

Elijah Lovejoy, who was accosted and killed by rioting pro-slavery radicals in his printing office in Alton, Illinois, in November 1837, is often cited as the abolitionists' first martyr. He was a Presbyterian clergyman who had attended Princeton Theological Seminary. His strong stand against slavery, prompted by his Christian convictions, cost him his life. Two years before he was murdered, he wrote in the newspaper that he published, "I shall come out, openly, fearlessly, and as I hope, in such a manner as becomes a servant of Jesus Christ, when defending His cause."[23]

A close friend and supporter of Lovejoy was Edward Beecher, who resided sixty miles north of Alton in Jacksonville, Illinois, where he served as president of Illinois College. Beecher, who visited Lovejoy shortly before his brutal death, was also a strong promoter of the abolitionist cause, largely through the auspices of the college. Black students, for instance, were welcomed as students, a rare phenomenon in those days. The college, a Christian institution, was labeled by the *Illinois State Register* of Springfield, Illinois, as a "freedom-shrieking tool of abolitionism."[24] Like his friend Lovejoy, Beecher was a Presbyterian clergyman. And he was the brother of Harriet Beecher Stowe, the author of *Uncle Tom's Cabin.*

Another strong clergy connection that provided considerable stimulus to the abolitionist movement was Lane Theological Seminary in Cincinnati, Ohio. The seminary was founded in the early 1830s by New York evangelicals as an outpost of revivalism in the Midwest to train clergy who would urge Christians to live holier and more sanctified lives.[25] Lyman Beecher, a Congregationalist and one of New England's well-known evangelistic (but not a revivalist) preachers, became the school's first president. He was also the

WILLIAM WILBERFORCE (1759–1833) was a prime mover in getting the British Parliament to outlaw slavery throughout the British Empire in 1833.

father of Henry Ward Beecher, Edward Beecher, and Harriet Beecher Stowe.

Along with its evangelistic emphasis, Lane Seminary also had ties to Ohio and New York antislavery societies. Arthur and Lewis Tappan, two strong abolitionists and wealthy businessmen from Boston, provided financial funding for the school.[26] Lewis Tappan, a former Unitarian, had turned Presbyterian because "the Unitarian denomination did not give equal evidence with the Orthodox of their spirituality and liberal giving" and because they were "deficient in a devotional frame of mind."[27] The Tappan brothers funded the seminary, and they also sought to make it an abolitionist school by bringing Theodore Weld from the Oneida Institute in New York to the seminary. Weld was a zealous abolitionist, an evangelistic preacher, and a convert of revivalist Charles Finney, once an eastern attorney. Together with others, Weld soon made the seminary "a citadel of Yankee abolitionism."

Weld had little patience. Soon he, along with some faculty members and most of the students, adopted immediatism, meaning that slavery had to end immediately. The seminary's trustees became alarmed and asked the faculty and students to "disband their anti-slavery society."[28] Lyman Beecher was unable to effect a compromise. So Weld and forty students (some of whom were already ministers) severed their seminary ties, and before long they relocated at the new and fledgling Oberlin College. The rebellion entered even Beecher's family, as daughter Catherine sided with her father, and daughter Harriet agreed with the seceders. According to one historian, "The Lane debate reverberated throughout the nation."[29] Almost simultaneously with the founding of Lane Seminary, another zealous abolitionist, the Reverend John Jay Shipperd, began the Oberlin Institute in Elyria, Ohio, in 1833. In less than a year's time, however, this venture encountered severe financial problems. Shipperd contacted the Reverend Asa Mahan, a trustee of Lane Seminary and a firm abolitionist. Seeking to revitalize the Oberlin Institute, Mahan contacted the Tappan brothers for funding. They complied, providing that the new school would have an anti-slavery orientation. It became Oberlin College.[30]

At Oberlin College, Charles Finney, a former Freemason and a charismatic preacher of revivalism, joined the faculty in 1836 to teach theology and later became the college's president. In the 1820s he used his charisma to convert large audiences to evangelicalism in his revival meetings in the eastern part of the country.[31] Now in the Midwest he also used his charisma to convert people to abolitionism. One of Finney's eastern converts, both with regard to Christianity and to antislavery, was Theodore Weld, who soon joined the Oberlin faculty. Later, in 1839, he wrote a best-selling book on antislavery, *Slavery As It Is*. This book was one of the resources that Harriet Beecher Stowe used in writing *Uncle Tom's Cabin*. Oberlin College assumed a number of roles in promoting abolitionism. It opened its classrooms to blacks, hired abolitionist instructors, and sheltered black fugitives.

Still another clergyman who had a powerful effect on the antislavery movement was Charles T. Torrey, "the father of the Underground Railroad." His leadership in the fugitive slave movement is credited with having helped 100,000 fugitive slaves escape northward to freedom. Torrey, whose involvement in abolitionist causes went back to Lovejoy's chronicles,[32] died a martyr's death in a Maryland jail while serving time for having abetted escaped slaves.

Christ's teachings definitely have to be credited with having moved Christian clergy like Lovejoy, the Beechers (Harriet, Henry, and Edward), Mahan, Shipperd, Finney, Weld, Torrey, and others too numerous to mention. That is also how Lyman Beecher saw it. One researcher cites him as saying that abolitionism was the offspring of the Great Revival that preceded it in the eastern states.[33]

Abolitionist clergy in the South encountered more difficulties than their Northern soul mates. Antislavery-minded ministers commonly were muzzled verbally, many lost their positions, and some were even imprisoned. David Chesebrough in his *Clergy Dissent in the Old South, 1830–1865* described the difficulties that antislavery clergy experienced in the South. One, J. D. Paxton, was forced to leave his parish in Cumberland, Virginia, for having authored a small book, *Letters on Slavery*, in which "he called slavery a moral evil and declared that Christians were morally obligated to work for its destruction."[34] John Hersey, a Methodist pastor in Virginia, wrote a book titled *Appeal to Christians on the Subject of Slavery*. After the book's third edition (1843) appeared, matters became very intense for him. Soon copies of his book were burned in Richmond, and he was finally com-

THIS STATUE IN ALTON, ILLINOIS, commemorates Elijah Lovejoy, an ardent opponent of slavery, who in 1837 became the first martyr of the American abolitionist movement.

pelled to migrate to the North.[35] Another clergyman, John Fee, founded Berea College in Berea, Kentucky. Modeled after Oberlin College in Ohio, it was the only racially integrated school in the South, a phenomenon that did not sit well with the pro-slavery proponents. Over the course of several months (1854–55) Fee was attacked by a mob, thrown into the Ohio River, and eventually forced to flee to Cincinnati.[36]

The impact of Christ's teachings that so moved hundreds of abolitionist clergy did not, of course, remain with them alone. Through their teaching and preaching they converted many lay people to the abolitionist cause. The fact that there were also clergy, both in the North and especially in the South, who defended slavery does not nullify the argument that the Christian antislavery spirit achieved its eventual goal: freedom for the enslaved. Numerous faithful clergy, motivated by the spirit of Jesus Christ, helped attain that goal.

NONCLERGY ROLE IN ABOLITIONISM

While clergy, most of them of the evangelical stripe, made up two-thirds of the abolitionist movement, it is important to remember that many

Christian lay people also played vitally important roles in abolishing American slavery. The Tappan brothers and Harriet Beecher Stowe are excellent examples of lay people who worked tirelessly to bring an end to it. But there were many other lay people who took active roles, some as supporters of the abolitionist clergy and some independent of them.

One of the prominent and influential laymen in the abolitionist movement was William Garrison, a Baptist from Massachusetts. His associate, Benjamin Lundy, a Quaker, called him "ultra-orthodox" in his religious beliefs. He founded his own periodical, *The Liberator,* which for years published strong and frequently strident articles promoting abolition. As a Christian, he "often quoted the passage from Christ's parable: 'a house divided against itself cannot stand.'"[37] So strong were his antislavery beliefs that he sometimes chastised Christian denominations for doing too little to end slavery. Often clergy were the object of his ire. Thus he once wrote, "The cause [abolition] must be kept in the hands of laymen, or it will not be maintained."[38] He said this even though at a typical meeting of the New England Anti-Slavery Society, which he had founded in 1833, two-thirds of its delegates were clergy.[39]

Garrison once burned a copy of the Fugitive Slave Act of 1850 as well as a copy of the U.S. Constitution. Hence, many saw him as radical and impatient even though he always advocated Christian nonresistance. Whatever the accusations, his contributions to abolitionism were immense. They were summarized well in President Lincoln's words: "The logic and moral power of Garrison and the antislavery people of the country and the army have done it all."[40] It should be remembered that Garrison's Christian beliefs and convictions played a major role in all of his contributions to the abolitionist cause.

Space does not permit discussing many other outstanding laymen in the abolitionist cause. But James G. Birney, a Southerner from Kentucky and Alabama and a onetime slave holder, needs to be mentioned. Birney became an active abolitionist and, like virtually all of the antislavery promoters, he was motivated by Christian principles. Another was Joshua Giddings, a convert of Theodore Weld who later served as a United States Congressman. Referring to the Fugitive Slave Act of 1850, Giddings said, "We cannot be Christians and obey it."[41] Still another abolitionist worthy of note was Julia Ward Howe. Although she was Unitarian, her early Christian influence is apparent in some of the lyrics in her "Battle Hymn of the Republic" (1862), an antislavery song that stirred the minds and emotions of countless

135,000 SETS, 270,000 VOLUMES SOLD.

UNCLE TOM'S CABIN

FOR SALE HERE.

AN EDITION FOR THE MILLION, COMPLETE IN 1 Vol, PRICE 37 1/2 CENTS.
" " IN GERMAN, IN 1 Vol, PRICE 50 CENTS.
" " IN 2 Vols, CLOTH, 6 PLATES, PRICE $1.50.
SUPERB ILLUSTRATED EDITION, IN 1 Vol, WITH 153 ENGRAVINGS,
PRICES FROM $2.50 TO $5.00.

The Greatest Book of the Age.

HARRIET BEECHER STOWE (shown later in life) is best known for her famous novel, *Uncle Tom's Cabin,* published in 1852 when she was age forty-one. The advertisement not only boosted sales for the book but also publicized Stowe's intense antislavery stand.

Americans. And finally, we must remember the prominent nonclergy role of Abraham Lincoln as the president of the United States, especially his Proclamation of 1863, which officially granted black slaves freedom.

HARRIET BEECHER STOWE'S CHRISTIAN IMPACT

Most Americans have heard about *Uncle Tom's Cabin* (1852) and how it depicts the misery of America's enslavement of the Negro. Many even know that this book brought the tragedy of American slavery to the attention of the entire world. Unfortunately, one rarely hears about the Christian motivation that moved Harriet Beecher Stowe to write her revealing, antislavery novel.

Harriet casts Uncle Tom in the role of the suffering servant as he suffers physically under the hands of his last slave master. Christlike, he refuses to take revenge despite powerful urgings from his fellow slaves; he clings to the promises of Christ up to his death, which was caused by the beatings his slave owner inflicted on him. As one analyst has well observed, "Uncle Tom [the book] takes a Christian approach that suffering is redemptive and that evil will be atoned for."[42]

The book abounds with biblical passages, and throughout its emotionally stirring pages the author reveals the deep spiritual tensions, induced by

Christian values, that existed among the slave owners. In noting these tensions, Stowe seeks, of course, to show how slavery violated the teachings of Christ, teachings that she personally had internalized from her Christian upbringing. On one occasion, a sea captain who met her said that he was pleased to shake the hand that wrote *Uncle Tom's Cabin*. She responded that she did not write the book. "God wrote it," she said, "I merely did his dictation."[43] In writing *Uncle Tom's Cabin*, Harriet Beecher Stowe, a Christian, contributed greatly to the shattering of American slavery. Her book "took the sting of fanaticism out of abolitionism, and its popularity gave incalculable weight to the idea of emancipation as a moral and historical inevitability."[44]

CHRISTIANITY SUSTAINED THE SLAVES

In all of the pain and suffering that the American blacks endured during slavery, they were greatly aided by Christianity's presence in their lives through the vehicle of black churches. The Negro church was virtually the only place where slaves were allowed to congregate, to experience a spiritual union with other slaves, and to feel equal to the white man, especially in the eyes of God. In addition, black preachers could go to the white slave master and beg for trivial favors.[45] Even Eugene Genovese, once a Marxist, credits Christianity as the institution that enabled the black slaves in America to survive the prolonged dehumanization process.[46]

In the North during the antebellum era, numerous black churches functioned as "stations" of the Underground Railroad as well as centers of abolitionist activities. While the churches helped slaves overcome dehumanization during the slavery decades, they also served other important functions, as is noted by various studies: (1) opportunities for emotional release where individuals could express their oppression; (2) social interaction with one's own kind; (3) educational opportunities so that many individuals learned to read and write; (4) socioeconomic assistance to the sick and bereaved; (5) social cohesion that gave a sense of belonging; (6) solace and comfort; (7) leadership opportunities. With regard to the latter, Franklin Frazier, a black sociologist, remarked that black congregations provided "full opportunity for the development of leadership and character."[47] This was especially true after the Civil War.

The Christian religion continues to be highly important to American blacks even today, more than a century after slavery was constitutionally outlawed in 1865. Sociological research consistently shows that blacks attend weekly church services in higher percentages than do whites. In

1993 a Gallup poll showed that 49 percent of American blacks attended church in a typical week, compared to 40 percent for American whites. This poll also revealed that only 7 percent of the blacks never attend church, compared to 14 percent of the whites.[48]

THE FIRST ANTISLAVERY PROCLAMATION

In most of the antislavery discussions in American history books and articles, a rather significant event is commonly and unfortunately overlooked. This event happened more than a century before the American abolitionist movement arose when an unknown German immigrant issued America's first formal proclamation against slavery in 1688. He was Franz Daniel Pastorius, a Mennonite, who spoke several languages and had studied law in Germany. William Penn met him in Germany, where he and a number of other Germans were persuaded to migrate to the colony of Pennsylvania. Upon arriving in America, Pastorius purchased 5,000 acres of land and founded Germantown, Pennsylvania, now in the suburbs of Philadelphia.

When Pastorius came to Pennsylvania in 1683, he soon encountered slavery, which in those days was not unusual even in the North. Negro slavery was repulsive to him and his fellow German settlers, most of whom were Mennonites from the Rhine River area. In 1688 Pastorius approached his Quaker friends in the Germantown area with a protest against slavery. The formally written protest, which was signed by Pastorius and several other German immigrants, invoked the Golden Rule, among other arguments. In part it read, "There is a saying that we shall doe [sic] to all men, like as we will be done ourselves, making no difference of what generation, Descent or Colour they are, and those who steal or rob men, and those who buy or purchase them, are they not all alike?"[49] This was part of the protest's rationale to condemn slavery. The Quakers were indifferent to his proposal. This shocked him and his fellow Germans. How could these pious people harmonize slavery with their religious beliefs?[50] In spite of trying several more times to get the Quakers to approve the proclamation, Pastorius and his several co-signers did not succeed. But his efforts were not entirely lost, for in 1705 the Quakers did at least take a stand against slave trade.

There is no doubt that Pastorius's antislavery proclamation was motivated by his Christian convictions. Just before he came to America he had formed close ties with some of the German members of the Pietist movement that tended to emphasize the Christian's sanctification more than justification. One of the Pietists whom Pastorius met was Philipp Spener, the father of the Pietistic movement.[51] There is good reason to believe that Pietism, an offshoot of Lutheranism, stimulated Pastorius to issue the proclamation against slavery.

AMERICAN CIVIL RIGHTS AND THE CHRISTIAN CONNECTION

While slavery in the United States officially came to an end in December of 1865, one of its accompanying practices was still alive and very active: racial segregation, which was formally legitimated by the United States Supreme Court in 1896 in its Plessy v. Ferguson decision. This decision established the "separate but equal" principle, a racially discriminatory practice that existed legally throughout the nation until the Supreme Court overturned the 1896 ruling in its Brown v. Board of Education decision in 1954. With this high court decision, a new era of civil rights began.

Three years later, in 1957, Martin Luther King Jr. helped found the Southern Christian Leadership Conference (SCLC), an organization that dedicated itself to ending racial segregation by getting the nation to accept and adopt racial integration in all of its public facilities. The organization's name reveals its indebtedness to Christian teachings, beliefs, and values. As such, it assumed a posture of Christian nonviolence to promote its objectives. King, its first president, frequently made the organization's nonviolence clear in his speeches. He wanted the organization's members and eventually all Americans to imitate the early Christians, who, he said, "were small in number but big in commitment. They were too God-intoxicated to be 'astronomically intimidated.' They brought an end to such ancient evils as infanticide and gladiatorial contests."[52] He wanted American Christians, in a similar manner, to end the evils of segregation and racism.

As civil rights laws were passed by Congress in the early 1960s and public demonstrations were occurring in the North and South, a new phenomenon occurred. Clergy from many Christian denominations joined the peaceful, nonviolent marches that were led by King. These marches called on Americans to end racial prejudice and discrimination. The march that occurred in March of 1965 in Selma, Alabama, where numerous marchers were brutally beaten, is of particular note. Clergy had come from across the nation to participate and to lend support to the efforts of the SCLC. One reporter summed up the Selma event by saying, "In the age of Martin Luther, churches discovered the individual conscience. In the age of Martin Luther King, the churches may be discovering how to put the individual conscience to work."[53] Critics sometimes accuse Christians and the churches

SOME PROMINENT AMERICAN ABOLITIONISTS

Abolitionists	Status	Contribution
Pastorius, Franz	German immigrant	Issued first formal antislavery proclamation in America, Germantown, Pennsylvania, 1688
Lovejoy, Elijah	Clergyman and publisher; shot in 1837, Alton, Illinois	Published articles opposing slavery
Beecher, Edward	Clergyman, president of Illinois College	Enrolled black students at the college
Tappan, Arthur	Wealthy businessman	Funded Lane Seminary, a strong antislavery school, Cincinnati, Ohio
Tappan, Lewis	Wealthy businessman	Helped his brother fund Lane Seminary
Finney, Charles	Revivalist preacher, president of Oberlin College	Promoted abolitionist causes at Lane Seminary and Oberlin College
Weld, Theodore	Evangelistic preacher	Promoted abolitionism at Lane Seminary; published Slavery As It Is, best-seller
Stowe, Harriet Beecher	Author	Published Uncle Tom's Cabin, a stirring antislavery novel
Shipperd, John Jay	Clergyman	Founded Oberlin Institute, Elyria, Ohio
Mahan, Asa	Clergyman	Helped found Oberlin College
Torrey, Charles T.	Clergyman	"Father of the Underground Railroad"
Paxton, J. D.	Clergyman, author	Published Letters on Slavery
Hersey, John	Clergyman, author	Published Appeal to Christians on the Subject of Slavery
Fee, John	Clergyman	Founded Berea College, a racially integrated school, in Berea, Kentucky
Garrison, William	Publisher	Published The Liberator, an abolitionist periodical; burned a copy of the Fugitive Slave Act of 1850
Birney, James G.	Former slave owner	Promoted abolitionist causes
Giddings, Joshua	Convert of Theodore Weld	Condemned the Fugitive Slave Act of 1850
Howe, Julia Ward	Social activist	Wrote "Battle Hymn of the Republic," 1862
Lincoln, Abraham	President of the United States	Issued his Emancipation Proclamation of 1863 that freed all black slaves

for not having been involved in promoting racial integration until it was forced upon them by secular authorities and the new antisegregation laws that followed the Supreme Court's decision of 1954. Not quite true! This accusation overlooks the fact that a number of Christian denominations had already issued statements and passed resolutions that urged their members to accept and implement racial integration several years earlier. In 1949 the Presbyterian Church in the United States (PCUS) issued a lengthy document in support of civil rights for American blacks, and the Southern Baptist Convention denounced the Ku Klux Klan and its use of the Christian cross, calling the Klan's practice "a presumptuous sacrilege."[54] Also in 1949, the Federal Council of the Churches of Christ, composed of twenty-seven denominations, moved toward supporting racial integration.

Skeptics who ignore or deny that slavery was first abolished in the Western world as a result of Christianity's influence need to ponder the following questions: Was slavery first abolished in countries where Christianity had a major or minor presence? Did Christianity have a major or minor presence in the countries that retained slavery into the twentieth century? In Sudan, Africa's largest country, where slavery is still present today, has Christianity been the dominant religion there or has it been virtually non-existent? The answers to these questions make it clear that slavery and Christianity are poor companions; historical evidence shows a high correlation between Christianity and the abolition of slavery.

CONCLUSION

Both the abolition of slavery and rejection of racial segregation have their roots in the earliest teachings of Christianity. As the great historian Will Durant has shown, Christianity was not a segregated religion: "It offered itself without restriction to all individuals, classes, and nations; it was not limited to one people, like Judaism, nor to the freemen of one state, like the official cults of Greece and Rome"[55] And as noted above, the early Christians received slaves into the church's membership and often freed them where they were able to do so. Slaves regularly communed at the same altar with Christians who were not slaves. Receiving and accepting slaves as equals, and having some of them in leadership roles, as in the case of Callistus, says Herbert Workman, was in some instances another reason for persecuting Christians: "Roman governors, conscious of the vast slave populations, were ever anxious lest there should be a servile outbreak."[56]

Thus, the effort to remove slavery, whether it was Wilberforce in Britain or the abolitionists in America, was not a new phenomenon in Christianity. Nor were the efforts by Martin Luther King Jr. and the American civil rights laws of the 1960s to remove racial segregation new to the Christian ethic. They were merely efforts to restore Christian practices that were already in existence in Christianity's primal days.

NOTES

1. David R. James, "Slavery and Involuntary Servitude," in *Encyclopedia of Sociology*, ed. Edgar F. Borgatta and Marie L. Borgatta (New York: Macmillan, 1992), 4:1792.
2. Brian Eads, "Slavery's Shameful Return to Africa," *Reader's Digest* (March 1996): 77–81.
3. United States census data for 1830, cited in Larry Koger, *Black Slaveowners: Free Black Slave Masters in South Carolina, 1790–1860* (Columbia: University of South Carolina Press, 1995), 20.
4. Lisa Anderson, "Paying for Slavery," *Chicago Tribune*, 17 May 1999, 1.
5. W. E. H. Lecky, *History of European Morals* (New York: Vanguard Press, 1926), 77.
6. Robin Lane Fox, *Pagans and Christians* (San Francisco: Perennial Library, 1986), 298.
7. W. E. H. Lecky, *History of European Morals: From Augustus to Charlemagne* (New York: D. Appleton, 1927), 2:69.
8. C. Schmidt, *The Social Results of Early Christianity*, trans. R. W. Dale (London: Wm. Isbister Limited, 1889), 430.
9. Edward Ryan, *The History of the Effects of Religion on Mankind: In Countries Ancient and Modern, Barbarous and Civilized* (Dublin: T. M. Bates, 1802), 151.
10. Lecky, *History of European Morals*, 2:71.
11. Ibid., 69.
12. Kenneth Scott Latourette, *A History of Christianity* (New York: Harper and Brothers, 1953), 558.
13. John Stoughton, *William Wilberforce* (New York: A. C. Armstrong and Son, 1880), 134, 138.
14. Ibid., 112.
15. Ibid., 79.
16. Ibid., 78.
17. D. James Kennedy and Jerry Newcombe, *What If Jesus Had Never Been Born?* (Nashville: Thomas Nelson, 1994), 21.
18. Stoughton, *William Wilberforce*, 210.
19. Kenneth Stamp, *The Peculiar Institution: Slavery in the Ante-Bellum South* (New York: Alfred Knopf, 1956), 85.
20. Robert William Fogel, *Without Consent and Without Contract: The Rise and Fall of American Slavery* (New York: W. W. Norton, 1991), 18.
21. Larry E. Tise, *Proslavery: A History of the Defense of Slavery in America, 1701–1840* (Athens: University of Georgia Press, 1987), 124–79.
22. Sherwood E. Wirt, *The Social Consequences of the Evangelical* (New York: Harper and Row, 1968), 39.
23. Joseph C. Lovejoy and Owen Lovejoy, eds., *Memoir of the Rev. Elijah P. Lovejoy* (Freeport, N.Y.: Books for Libraries Press [1838], 1970), 156.
24. Donald Mundinger, "Statement by President Mundinger," in *Sesquicentennial Papers: Illinois College*, ed. Iver F. Yaeger (Carbondale: Southern Illinois University Press, 1982), 156.
25. James Brewer Stewart, *Holy Warriors: The Abolitionists and American Slavery* (New York: Hill and Wang, 1976), 35, 57.
26. Louis Filler, *The Crusade Against Slavery: 1830–1860* (New York: Harper and Brothers, 1960), 67.
27. Cited in Filler, *Crusade Against Slavery*, 31.
28. Stewart, *Holy Warriors*, 58.
29. Gilbert Hobbs Barnes, *The Anti-slavery Impulse: 1830–1844* (Gloucester, Mass.: Peter Smith, 1973), 69.
30. Ibid.

31. Ibid., 8–9.

32. Filler, *Crusade Against Slavery,* 163.

33. Ibid., 72.

34. David B. Chesebrough, *Clergy Dissent in the Old South, 1830–1865* (Carbondale: Southern Illinois University Press, 1996), 42.

35. Ibid.

36. Ibid., 46.

37. Ibid., 125.

38. Cited in Barnes, *Anti-slavery Impulse,* 98.

39. Ibid.

40. Cited in Henry Mayer, *All On Fire: William Lloyd Garrison and the Abolition of Slavery* (New York: St. Martin's Press, 1998), 568.

41. Cited in Stewart, *Holy Warriors,* 153.

42. Josephine Donovan, *Uncle Tom's Cabin: Evil, Affliction and Redemptive Love* (Boston: Twayne Publishers, 1991), 12.

43. Annie Fields, *Life and Letters of Harriet Beecher Stowe* (Boston: Houghton Mifflin, 1898), 377.

44. Mayer, *All On Fire,* 423.

45. Gunnar Myrdal, *An American Dilemma: The Negro Problem and Modern Democracy* (New York: Harper and Brothers, 1944), 860.

46. Eugene Genovese, *Roll, Jordan, Roll* (New York: Pantheon Books, 1974), 161–68.

47. Franklin E. Frazier, *The Negro Family in the United States* (Chicago: University of Chicago Press, 1939), 31.

48. Gallup Poll, "Emerging Trends," *Princeton Religion Research Center* (March 1993): 4.

49. Albert Bernhardt Faust, *The German Element in the United States* (Boston: Houghton Mifflin, 1909), 1:46. The original copy of this protest is housed in the library of the Historical Society of Pennsylvania in Philadelphia.

50. Ibid.

51. Ibid., 33.

52. Martin Luther King Jr., "Letter from Birmingham Jail," in *A Testament of Hope: The Essential Writings and Speeches of Martin Luther King Jr.,* ed. James Melvin Washington (San Francisco: Harper Collins, 1991), 300.

53. "Selma, Civil Rights, and the Church Militant," *Newsweek,* 29 March 1965, 78.

54. "Southern Baptists Denounce Klan," *Christian Century,* 14 September 1949, 1059.

55. Will Durant, *Caesar and Christ: A History of Roman Civilization and of Christianity from Their Beginnings to A.D. 325* (New York: MJF Books, 1971), 602.

56. Herbert B. Workman, *Persecution in the Early Church* (New York: Oxford University Press, [1907], 1980), 62.

CHRISTIANITY'S STAMP on ART and ARCHITECTURE

"Nothing can come out of artist that is not in man."

H. L. Mencken

In this brief survey of Christianity's contribution to art and architecture, this chapter portrays only a small number of the vast array of the magnificent works that were created, primarily in the Western world, during the last two millennia. That the great works of art and architecture during this time were crafted by artists who were moved and influenced by the life, death, and resurrection of Jesus Christ is apparent in virtually all of their works. For instance, Christian art differed radically from that of the Greeks. As Peter Forsyth has said, the Greeks loved nature, especially human nature; whereas Christians loved not the natural but the supernatural, "the God Man, the human God, whose grace offered Himself to love."[1] This Christian accent was to a large degree also reflected in Renaissance art until the so-called Age of Enlightenment, the eighteenth century.

EARLY CHRISTIAN ART

During their first three centuries the early Christians contributed very little to the world of art. Given that art flourishes best in the context of freedom, which the early Christians did not have, this is not surprising. When people are harassed, imprisoned, and even killed for their beliefs, as were many of the early followers of Christ, there is neither opportunity nor energy left for art. Yet in spite of the persecutions, some drawings and frescoes were produced. Most of these were done in the catacombs near Rome, where the Christians often went for divine services and where many of their loved ones were buried. Their pictures commonly depicted biblical accounts. For example, the Catacomb of Domitilla (third century) has a scene of the Good Shepherd, showing Christ with a sheep draped around the back of his neck while some sheep stand on both sides of him. The Catacomb of Priscilla, also from the third century, depicts the Virgin Mary and the Christ child, illustrating the fulfillment of the Old Testament prophet's prediction in Isaiah 7:14. And the Catacomb of Callistus has a number of biblical scenes, including the Woman of Samaria and the Lord's Supper.[2] Some catacombs also have carved portraits on sarcophagi, generally depicting biblical events or Christian symbols.

By the early second century the fish had become a common symbol of Christian art. It was chosen because the Greek word for fish (ΙΧΘΥΣ or *ichthus*) formed the acrostic: Jesus Christ God's Son Savior. The fish symbol is found on cemetery art, amulets, carved stones, and other objects. In some instances it also symbolized baptism or Jesus' feeding the five thousand, who were miraculously fed with five barley loaves and two fish. (It is interesting to note that the Christian fish symbol today is experiencing a revival of sorts. For instance, one often sees it portrayed on the back of automobiles.)

After Constantine the Great legalized Christianity in A.D. 313, art among Christians increased significantly. It appeared most often in churches, and here too virtually all of the art depicted biblical stories or events. By the early fifth century the Santa Maria Maggiore church in Rome was decorated with glass mosaic panels, one of which was *The Parting of Lot and Abraham*. Glass mosaics were a Christian innovation. Previous mosaics, such as those crafted by the Greeks, were made of marble pieces.

With the arrival of the sixth century, Christian art became rather common, though it was still largely confined to churches. The most noteworthy of the early churches decorated with mosaic art was Hagia Sophia in

Constantinople (now Istanbul). This large cathedral was built by the Christian emperor Justinian the Great in a mere five years (A.D. 532–37). Its massive dome, nearly two hundred feet high, resting on four arches, had its interior beautified with gold-covered glass mosaic cubes, about one hundred fifty million of them, made of one thousand tons of glass.[3] "It created an image of the concept of the world governed 'from above.'"[4] The building thus functioned as a symbol of theocracy. Tradition says that when Justinian had completed this awe-inspiring structure, the largest church ever built (81,375 square feet), he declared, "Glory to God, who has deemed me worthy of fulfilling such a work. O Solomon, I have surpassed thee."

After a thousand years of Christian habitation, Hagia Sophia fell into the hands of the Muslim Ottoman Turks when they conquered Constantinople in 1453. Hagia Sophia became a mosque. In the early 1930s the building, still under Islamic control, largely became a secular museum meant to attract tourists. It functions in that capacity today. In the 1700s the Muslims covered the beautiful gold mosaic of this majestic domed ceiling with white plaster; the marbled floor was covered with hundreds of rugs; lights were suspended from the ceiling; and Arabic inscriptions defaced the pendentives. Even today the dome's beauty has been only partially restored. Some of the paneled figures on the walls, however, are still visible. These were added after Justinian's time; some of them show the *Virgin and the Christ Child, Archangel Michael, St. John the Baptist,* and the *Head of Christ.* Some of the original art panels, thought to have contained pictures of Christian saints and of Christ, were destroyed during the Iconoclastic Controversy in the eighth and ninth centuries. Now, as one architect has sadly noted, "Gone are the believers, the priests, the incense, the colors, the music, the choirs, the murmurs, and the rituals."[5]

THIS MARBLE SCULPTURE from about A.D. 350, depicting Christ as the Good Shepherd, is typical of much early Christian art found in numerous locations.
(Lateran Museum, Rome)

CHRISTIAN ART IN THE MIDDLE AGES

Numerous other churches and cathedrals were built after Hagia Sophia (meaning Holy Wisdom, referring to Christ), and nearly all were enhanced with painted or mosaic portraits and with sculptures of biblical figures. Whether the panels were made of mosaic or painted on frescoes, they were all crafted to glorify God and to edify the believers who viewed them as they came to hear the gospel of Jesus Christ, spoken and sung in the churches where they assembled. This biblically based art was most widely portrayed in the Western churches and cathedrals of the Middle Ages.

Churches and cathedrals, with their biblically based art, became "the Bible of the poor and illiterate Christians." For it was through the mosaics, frescoes, stained-glass windows, and sculptures that most Christian laymen learned about the content of the Bible. Most could not read Latin, but those who could also were not permitted to read the Bible for themselves, even if one were available. In 1229 the Synod of Toulouse (France), in response to two reform-minded groups (the Cathari and Waldensians), outlawed Bible reading for the laity. Martin Luther, for instance, reportedly had not seen a Bible until he was a student at the University of Erfurt. Later he broke this three-hundred-year-old ban on Bible reading when he translated the New Testament into German in 1522. A few years later he also translated the Old Testament.

Many of the works of art in the churches and cathedrals that depicted biblical characters and events were so well crafted and of such high artistic caliber that they are still discussed and featured in art history textbooks to this very day. These books not only show the works of well-known artists like Michelangelo, but also of lesser-known artists. Works such as the following are commonly listed and discussed: *Christ Enthroned with the Apostles,* a fourth-century mosaic in the apse of Santa Pudenziana in Rome; *The Multiplication of Loaves and Fishes* in Santa Apollinare Nuova in Ravenna; *The Crucifixion,* an eighth-century fresco in the church of Santa Maria Antiqua; *Adam and Eve Expelled,* a fresco panel in Brancacci Chapel in Florence; *The Last Judgment* in the Autun Cathedral; *The Last Supper,* a gold relief in Aachen Cathedral in Germany; and *Melchizedek and Abraham,* a sculpture in Reims Cathedral in France. These are but a few found in churches from the Middle Ages that artists continue to see as lasting works of great accomplishment. Even secularists who view these and other Christian masterpieces in a textbook or in person as tourists visiting churches and cathedrals in Europe are impressed by their beauty and aesthetic quality. The fact that these and other Christian works are still viewed and admired demonstrates that this art has had wholesome effects on the art of the world. Had Jesus Christ not entered this world, these contributions would not exist and civilization would be the poorer for it.

GOTHIC CHURCH ARCHITECTURE

From the time that Christianity became a legal religion in 313 to the end of the first millennium, churches were mostly built in the style of the Roman basilica. The basilica church buildings to a degree still retained some of the pagan architecture, such as Greek pillars supporting the flat ceiling and round Roman arches over the doorways. It was not a style that lifted or exalted the human spirit. It was a time in which the "Christian spirit was still acquiring an individuality of its own, which in due course would express itself in an art of its own."[6]

Following the basilicas, from approximately 1000 to 1150, Christian churches were constructed in the Romanesque style. Built in the shape of the Latin cross, these churches still used the Roman arched vault of the pagan era, but they dispensed with the beams, and the roof became semicircular. Although an improvement over the basilica, the Romanesque architecture did not really express Christian aspirations and the spiritual beauty of the Gothic churches that appeared in the twelfth century.

Gothic architecture, which began with the construction of St. Denis Cathedral in 1144, flourished well into the Renaissance era. It has often been described as the architecture that best exemplifies Christianity. Its pointed arches soared to the heavens. Its cathedrals had a number of other outstanding characteristics: (1) they were (and still are) physically aesthetic; (2) no two were alike; (3) they took decades (some more than a century) to construct; (4) they were adorned with biblically based art, statues, frescoes, and sometimes engravings; (5) they towered above everything else in a city or town; (6) they were visible from miles away; (7) their bells regulated the town's activities; and (8) their stained-glass windows added to the overall grandeur.

Gothic cathedrals were—and still are—spiritually uplifting; they made man "aware of the invisible and infinite, and that the divine became immanent."[7] As one art historian notes, they "symbolized man's awareness of the divine as well as his own self consciousness."[8] Another art historian says, "The very stone and structure becomes spiritualized—the piers high, slender, and supple, the vaulting losing itself in dizzy altitudes, the towers and

TWO VERSIONS OF A COMMON SUBJECT—"Pietà": (left) this example of Gothic sculpture, fashioned from wood and painted, is from the early fourteenth century and stands 34½ inches high *(Provinzialmuseum, Bonn)*; (right) the painted limestone statue, 29½ inches in height, comes from the Seeon Monastery near Salzburg, Austria *(Bayerisches Nationalmuseum, Munich)*.

pinnacles dissolving in a spray of upward movement."[9] Indeed, when standing inside one of these majestic edifices, one has to be spiritually and esthetically obtuse not to be positively affected by the features of these magnificent structures. For example, ever since it was built, on long summer evenings, the west end of the grandiose Chartres Cathedral has shown Christians its biblical statues that "glow in the setting of the sun, calling to mind not just the end of that particular day, but the end of time itself in the Last Judgment."[10] Indeed, this cathedral and others were the "Bible in stone and glass."

"No architecture like the Gothic so spiritualizes, refines, and casts heavenward the substance which it handles,"[11] wrote Peter Forsyth. Unlike any other medium, the cathedrals provided "an actual picture of Heaven which the human senses can perceive."[12] Given the inspiring grandeur of the Gothic cathedrals, one cannot help but wonder what the pagan Celsus of the second century would have said had he lived a thousand years later, for it was he who ridiculed the Christians for not having any temples.

Michael Camille says that today's viewers of the Gothic cathedrals often fail to see and understand these buildings' real message, "not because the visual forms are so different, but because they were meant to be seen within a totally different temporality, an eschatological framework in which the past, present, and future were often combined."[13] Modern viewers often fail to see that the tall, ornately carved pillars, the lofty pointed arches, and the streaming shafts of light were crafted to reveal the message of God's infinite glory and man's finiteness. Medieval Christians standing inside or near these majestic houses of God could hardly fail to apprehend this spiritual message, a message that no building in the twentieth century is capable of conveying. By comparison, the Empire State Building in New York City and the Sears Tower in Chicago, although they reach higher into the sky than the Gothic cathedrals, convey no majesty, no glory to God. They are modern towers of Babel, whose builders, like those of Babel, sought to show the greatness of man rather than the majesty and grace of God. The devout medieval Christians, knowing that in Jesus Christ God came down from heaven in human flesh, were conscious of the latter and that changed everything, including the design of churches and cathedrals. Today, in an age of secularism and neo-paganism, they would grieve deeply to see that their spirituality uplifting cathedrals have become mere museum objects or Christian relics.

The Gothic architects did not just shape pillars and arches of stone, but they also adorned these materials with the beauty of frescoes, statues, and engravings depicting biblical messages. The following are some artistic examples: the Chartres cathedral has a tympanum above one of the doors that pictures a sculpture of Christ seated above the apostles and surrounded by angels; the cathedral in Cologne has its solemnity enhanced by a fresco of *The Adoration of the Magi* and the six-foot wood carving of *The Gero Crucifix;* the Gothic St. Lawrence church in Nuremberg enriches the spiritual environment with its sculpture of *The Angelic Salutation;* and the Reims cathedral has, among other items, the sublime statues of *The Angel of the Annunciation* and *The Virgin of the Annunciation.* Many more could be cited to show that biblically derived art was an integral part of the Gothic cathedral.

A discussion of Gothic cathedrals would not be complete without considering their beautiful stained-glass windows. There is some evidence, although not overly convincing, that some type of stained-glass windows were already used by Christians in their churches before A.D. 500; however, the earliest known stained-glass window pieces, decorated with human fig-

THE MAINZ CATHEDRAL in Germany typifies the Romanesque architecture with its heavy (thick) and relatively unadorned walls.

ures, date from the early 1000s. The oldest stained-glass windows still to be seen in their original setting are *The Prophets,* five larger-than-life-sized figures in the windows of the Cathedral of Augsburg, Germany. These windows were made from about 1100 to 1130.[14] Thus, it is important to note that stained-glass windows, which were such an important part of the medieval cathedrals, are another product that Christianity bequeathed to the world of art and architecture.

Historians for the most part do not know the names of the architects or the builders of the Gothic churches, but they do know that they were laymen, not clergy. Nor is it known who first developed the pointed arch.

Even if its concept first came out of the Middle East, as some think, it matters little, because nothing came of it until Christian craftsmen made it the heart and soul of the Gothic churches and cathedrals. This shows that Christ's spirit made its impress on the general populace of Christendom to such a degree that the Christian laity fashioned, as Peter Forsyth has said, "a beautiful garment of Christian piety and praise."[15]

Finally, what moved the designers of the Gothic cathedrals to fashion them so that Christians would have to cast their eyes and spirit heavenward? The answer is simple. It was the influence of Jesus Christ. The Gothic architecture contrasts notably with the architecture of the Egyptian pyramids, which are colossal but devoid of any spiritually awe-inspiring beauty. A similar contrast exists with regard to the Greek and Roman temples, which convey much architectural skill with their tall Ionian, Doric, or Corinthian capped pillars, but they, similar to the pyramids, also did not shower light from above as did the shafts of light that came through the peaked roofs of the Gothic cathedrals.

BYZANTINE CHURCH ART AND ARCHITECTURE

Enthralled as many Western Christians are with Gothic church architecture, they may note the Hagia Sophia cathedral (mentioned above) as an example of Christian architecture outside of the West but then fail to consider the many other examples of ecclesiastical art and architecture of eastern Europe or western Asia. Sometimes it is assumed that the Byzantine's domed churches began with Hagia Sophia in the sixth century, but in reality the Church of San Vitale in Ravenna, Italy (see picture in chapter 11), originated six years before Hagia Sophia received its dome, also built by Emperor Justinian, who resided in Constantinople. This church is sometimes cited as an example of Italo-Byzantine art and architecture. San Vitale's dome is much smaller and less prominent in height and grandeur than the massive dome of Hagia Sophia in Constantinople (the town of Bzyantium before Constantine the Great). Built as an octagonal structure, San Vitale departed from the long-drawn rectangular design of previous basilica churches.

Although Hagia Sophia is essentially a domed basilica, most Byzantine domed churches, located east of the Adriatic Sea, departed from the basilica design, as did the Church of San Vitale in the West. But these churches also engaged in another departure by adopting the model of the cruciform. The cruciform plan took the form of the Greek cross, whose four arms are of equal length. This resulted in church buildings with a square floor plan. Each cruciform church was capped with at least one dome. These churches were a notable contrast to the Gothic cathedrals and churches of Europe that kept the rectangular basilica floor plan. The basilica plan lent itself to structuring the building in the form of the Latin cross whose left and right arms intersect the vertical shaft near its upper end. The church's center aisle resembled the vertical shaft of the cross, and the transcept in front of the main altar formed the left and right arms of the cross. Many Gothic churches also reflect the Latin cross from the outside, especially when viewed from above the roofline.

Later in the Byzantine era, especially in Russia and the Balkans, churches retained the dome concept from Hagia Sophia but redesigned the domes resembling the shape of onions. Many of these churches were built with multiple domes, one being a main (larger) dome. The main dome symbolized the heavenly abode of God, the smaller usually some of the apostles or some more recent Christian saints. Usually the exterior roofs of the onion domes were crowned with a cross, and thus each dome conveyed a dual Christian symbolism (God and Christ's crucifixion). Not infrequently, a dome has a cross with three arms, two being parallel to the earth's surface and one having its arms slanted at about forty-five degrees in honor of St. Andrew, the patron saint of the Russian Orthodox Church. Tradition says that St. Andrew was martyred on a cross in the form of an X.

The interior of the Byzantine churches, especially their interior domes, were typically decorated with brightly colored mosaics, a practice started by Justinian when he built the Church of San Vitale in Ravenna. The mosaics, both on the dome's interior and on the walls, frequently depicted Christ the Pantocrator (Ruler of the Universe), the Crucifixion, the Virgin Mary, revered Christian saints, and sometimes portraits of emperors. Byzantine emperors viewed their office as one of divine kingship (noted earlier), so some mosaics (for instance, Justinian and his attendants in the Church of San Vitale) depict the emperor and members of his court as being more celestial than human.[16]

Few would deny that the art and architecture of Byzantine Christianity made salutary contributions to civilization. It did so by synthesizing certain Roman and Greek elements with Christ and Christian theology at the center. And art historians have noted that Byzantine Christianity also contributed to Islamic art and architecture, for instance, in the design of mosques. The Islamic (Muslim) religion appeared a hundred years after the

THE APSE OF SANT' APOLLINARE in Classe, Ravenna, Italy, was built in about A.D. 525 by Emperor Justinian I and reveals that some Byzantine art appeared in the Western empire.

construction of Hagia Sophia, and when Muslims began constructing mosques, the concept of Hagia Sophia's dome was essentially replicated. Thus numerous mosques are domed, with their interiors resembling Byzantine domes, portraying, however, only geometric designs.

RENAISSANCE ARTISTS AND THEIR ART

The term *renaissance*, derived from the Latin *rinascere*, means "reborn." It did not become a popular word until the nineteenth century. The assumption is that from about the tenth to the fourteenth centuries learning and the arts had essentially died, but they were reborn in the fourteenth century. Thus, some books refer to the Middle Ages as the "Dark Ages." That designation, however, is very questionable, for it is known today that the Middle Ages were by no means wholly dark or void of learning. Many advances in learning and the arts germinated during the so-called Dark Ages, advancements that ensuing centuries built upon. It is also assumed by many that Renaissance art largely focused on the humanistic spirit of man rather than on the religious themes of biblical Christianity. Although the humanistic nature of Renaissance art did indeed become very prominent in the latter stages of the Renaissance era, especially among Italian artists, in the early years of this era numerous works of art depicted a strong emphasis on the biblical themes and events surrounding the work of Christ and his followers.

One of the earliest Renaissance artists was Masaccio (1402–29). Although his life was extremely brief, he nevertheless left his mark. One of his noteworthy frescoes is *The Holy Trinity.* His Renaissance orientation is best seen in *The Expulsion from the Garden,* which shows Adam and Eve being expelled from the Garden of Eden. This was the first portrayal of the human body in the nude for an ecclesiastical painting.[17] Yet when one looks at this panel, the nudity of Adam and Eve has not the slightest suggestion of sensuousness, but rather it accents the couple's rejection and loss of everything, spiritually and materially, as a result of their fall into sin.

Masaccio influenced the works of Leonardo da Vinci (1452–1519) and Michelangelo (1475–1564), who both produced magnificent works of Christian art. Leonardo's *Last Supper* is hailed as the one of the greatest paintings in the world. He also painted other great pieces that conveyed biblical messages, such as *St. John the Baptist, The Madonna and Child and St. Anne,* and *The Annunciation.* Michelangelo, like Leonardo, also gave to the world marvelously crafted Christian art. Although he was primarily a sculptor (along with being an architect and poet), his paintings in the Sistine Chapel of St. Peter's in Rome are universally acclaimed for their greatness. These include *The Creation of Adam, The Creation of Eve, The Expulsion from Paradise,* and others. His last work, *The Last Judgment,* shows God as a stern judge, surrounded by the apostles, who look questionably at his acts of condemnation as demons carry away the condemned. Great as this work is, it overlooks the Christian gospel, namely, that there is also forgiveness for those who by faith in Christ "repent, and believe in the good news" (Mark 1:15 NRSV). This shortcoming of *The Last Judgment* is also true of some other Christian art produced during the late Middle Ages as well as during the earlier years of the Renaissance, whose many biblical teachings are often portrayed in the context of God's condemning law.

Some other great Renaissance artists who produced significant Christian art were men like Raphael (1483–1520), Tintoretto (ca. 1512–1594), Albrecht Dürer (1471–1528), and Rembrandt (1606–69), to cite only a few. Some noteworthy paintings of Raphael are *Christ Bearing the Cross, The Sistine Madonna, The Conversion of Saul,* and *The Transfiguration.* The latter work, unfinished at the time of his death, was used in his funeral procession as a sign of respect and honor. His religiously based paintings have earned him the title of "Divine Raphael." Tintoretto, often credited with originating baroque art, painted such panels as *Christ with Mary and Martha, The Miracle of St. Mark, The Last Supper,* and *Paradise.* The latter is reputed to be the largest painted canvas in existence and is housed in Doges Palace in Venice.

On the popular level, Albrecht Dürer is perhaps best known for *The Praying Hands* (a wood engraving). However, he also created other masterpieces such as *The Adoration of the Magi* and *The Knight, Death, and the Devil,* which portrays a knight as a soldier of Christ "on the road of faith toward the Heavenly Jerusalem and undeterred by the hideous horseman threatening to cut him off, or by the grotesque devil behind."[18]

One writer reports a moving story behind the carving of *The Praying Hands.* Being economically poor, Dürer and a friend, also an artist, agreed to share the same living quarters; and one of them would work while the other would apply his artistic talents. Dürer volunteered to work, but his friend, seeing that Dürer had the greater talents, wanted him to be the first to paint and carve. When the time came to trade places, the hands of Dürer's friend were too gnarled and stiff to hold a brush to paint. One day Dürer found his friend, not bitter or angry, in his room praying with folded hands. This sight so moved the German artist that it inspired him to carve the well-known *Praying Hands.*[19]

Biographical writings of many artists who created great Christian works of art are often silent about the artists' Christian faith and commitment, but not so with Dürer. His Christian faith so permeated his life and work that biographers cannot ignore it. He once remarked, "There is nothing good in us except it becomes good in Christ. . . . If we will what is good, Christ wills it in us."[20] He was an avid follower of Martin Luther's teachings, although he reportedly remained a member of the Roman Catholic Church.

The Dutch artist Rembrandt gave to the world of art such notable works as *Christ at Emmaus, The Prodigal Son, Simeon in the Temple,* and *Descent from the Cross.* But the panel that best reveals his Christian faith is

CHARTRES CATHEDRAL, begun in the mid-twelfth century by an unknown architect, is one of the first Gothic cathedrals; its rose window appeared in the thirteenth century.

The Elevation of the Cross. This work shows a man, wearing a blue beret, raising Christ's cross at his crucifixion; that man is Rembrandt himself. Francis Schaeffer says that Rembrandt wanted "all the world to see that his sins sent Christ to the cross." Schaeffer continues, "Rembrandt understood that Christ is Lord of all life. As a Christian, he lived in the midst of God's world and did not need to make himself God. Rather, he could use God's world and its form in his painting."[21]

The above sample of artists and their art reveals that many of the greatest masterpieces in the world have had Christian themes or bases. It also shows that significant art since the decay of the Roman Empire was largely

GATE CHURCH OF THE RESURRECTION in the Kremlin in Moscow typifies the onionlike domes of the Russian Orthodox Church.

dominated by artists who were inspired by the teachings and love of Jesus Christ. They produced paintings, statues, carvings, and architectural works with Christian themes and messages that dominated the world of Western art for more than a thousand years.[22]

FROM THE SUBLIME TO THE IRRATIONAL

In order to appreciate further the contributions of the Christ-inspired art, from which much of the world has benefited for centuries, it seems appropriate to note by way of contrast some of the modern art, particularly that which art critics refer to as "irrational." While it may not be edifying to mention some of the modern productions, sometimes it is instructive to see the "other side" in order to cherish more fully the beauty of classic productions.

Forty years ago Hans Sedlmayr, an art historian, informed the artistic world that much modern art in Western societies was giving "visible form to the irrational."[23] Similar is the observation of D. James Kennedy and Jerry Newcombe, who say, "Much art started to become irrational as the West began to move away from God and His divine revelation."[24] During the past two or three decades some of the irrational art has moved into the realm of the sacrilegious.

For much of the twentieth century the philosophy of relativism, which says that there is no absolute truth because everything is relative, has been promoted in schools, universities, and textbooks and by the mass media in Western societies. Irrational art is a logical product of relativism. Belief in relativism is a chasm-wide leap away from the Christian beliefs and convictions that motivated the great works of art discussed in this chapter. The great artists of the Middle Ages, the Gothic era, the Reformation age, and the early Renaissance period were no relativists. They knew and believed that there was a God whose Word was absolutely true, not relative, and their work reflected it. Like Luther, they saw art as an activity that should serve God.[25] To these talented artists, life had meaning in spite of their living at a time when disease and famine were frequently out of control, when poverty was widespread, when human comforts were limited and rare, and when life expectancy was only about thirty-five years.

Today, when these vicissitudes have been greatly reduced in Western societies, man has ironically become increasingly alienated from God as he sees values and morals as relative, even absurd. This attitude is reflected in modern art, which began with cubism, then continued with surrealism, and still later with dadaism. The latter uses ridicule and nonsense in art to show that life is absurd. Thus, for example, Marcel Duchamp painted his *Mona Lisa* with a goatee and moustache. From these philosophies of art, it was a small step to irrational art.

In recent years sacrilegious art has often desecrated Christian symbols. For instance, in 1987 Andres Serrano, a fallen Catholic and a homosexual who died two years later of AIDS, presented a portrait that he called *Piss Christ*. It showed a crucifix submerged in a glass container of human urine. Some might dismiss Serrano's portrayal as merely the work of an eccentric artist. But numerous art galleries in a number of American cities gave it prominent display, thereby giving it respectability. One wonders whether these art galleries or the mass media would have condoned similar irrational and sacrilegious art if it had depicted Jewish or Muslim symbols in a similar manner.

Two years after Serrano's irrational or sacrilegious portrait appeared, another blasphemy in the name of art was shown to the public by John Fleck, who in a play on stage "publicly urinate[d] on a picture of Christ."[26] In another of his presentations, *Blessed Are All the Little Fishes* (1989), Fleck displayed on stage a toilet bowl turned into an altar that he urinated on and mimed vomiting into.[27] And in the fall of 1999 yet another sacrilegious portrait appeared. It was Chris Ofili's *Sensation*, shown in New York's Brooklyn Museum of Art. It is a painting of the Virgin Mary splattered with elephant dung and floating bits of female pornography. Also displayed at the same time in the Brooklyn Museum were 3-D acrylic women with erect penises for noses,[28] another example of dadaism.

Recently feminists have appropriately spoken out against "art" that degrades women, arguing that art which demeans women is not art. If this is true with art regarding women, it must also be true for other types of art, such as that which degrades Christianity or any of its sacred symbols. If the feminist definition of art is accepted, then Serrano's portrait and Chris Ofili's portrait are clearly not art. Although the mass media and art galleries appear to concur with the feminist definition regarding the demeaning portrayal of women in art, they have ignored it when Christianity has been demeaned by some so-called recent art.

Kurt Vonnegut, the renowned novelist, defined art as that which makes the soul grow.[29] And George Santayana, the American philosopher, said art is not art unless it has a sense of beauty. Either one of these definitions, as well as the one offered by feminists, nullifies Serrano's and Ofili's work as art, for no one can argue that their productions are capable of making human souls grow.

These modern presentations are illustrations of what the Spanish critic Ortega y Gasset has called the "dehumanization of art," namely, that it is art in which the artist "has deliberately resolved to shatter and dehumanize the human image."[30] The painters or sculptors, he said, no longer turn to reality, but against it. They are in a rebellion against tradition, producing art that "ridicules art itself."[31] And it is a sea-change departure from the art that the Christ-minded artists produced in Western and Byzantine works of art.

THE DECLINE OF MODERN CHURCH ARCHITECTURE

Similar to noting how some modern art departs from the classic works of art long influenced by Christianity, it would also appear helpful to take a brief look at how much current architecture of North American churches has departed from the Christian symbolism and influence of the past.

When one drives through American or Canadian countryside and villages, it is still common to see relatively small churches. These congregations did not have the financial resources to build large cathedral-like churches, but their members nevertheless erected churches that in a meager and limited way reflect some aspects of the European Gothic architecture. These churches, whether of brick or stone or wood, have pointed roofs with crosses on steeples that tower well above the roof lines of other buildings in the vicinity. The steeples or spires point heavenward, seeking to imitate the European churches from which they borrowed their design. Evidently their members, similar to the patrons of the Gothic churches in Europe, wanted these peaked and tall structures to help them look upward rather than horizon-

"PRAYING HANDS" is one of the most famous works of Albrecht Dürer (1471–1528), who was a painter but is best known for his woodcuts and engravings. *(Albertina Museum, Vienna)*

tally like the Greco-Romans, whose pagan temples were relatively low, flat, and earthbound. These rural churches, like their more grandiose predecessors in Europe, were the product of Christianity's contribution to church architecture.

Today many modern churches, low in height and often without steeples as well as without crosses on the exterior (and sometimes none in the interior), have lost much of the formerly inspiring Gothic resemblances. A. Welby Pugin, a historian of architecture, laments this trend: "Churches are now built without the least regard to tradition, to mystical reason, or even common propriety. A room full of seats at the least possible cost is the present idea of a church, and if any ornament is indulged in, it is a mere screen to catch the eye of the passerby, which is a most contemptible deception to hide the meanness of the real building."[32]

CHRISTIAN ART AND ARCHITECTURE

Era	Art Work	Architecture	Selected Edifices
Pre–Edict of Milan (ca. A.D. 29–313)	3rd-cent. frescoes of biblical scenes and characters found in catacombs, relief art of biblical scenes on sides of sarcophagi	Christian churches before the Edict of Milan resembled the Roman basilica, destroyed during Emperor Diocletian's persecution (303–5); no intact, extant church of the first three centuries remains	Christians worshiped in family houses and synagogues; excavated church at Dura-Europa (Syria), a converted house church, ca. 232
Basilica (ca. 320–1000)	Mural frescoes of saints, gold and marble mosaic decorations, mosaic paved naves	Longitudinal plans with flat roofs, two rows of large columns, central nave, two side aisles, apse above altar, small windows, west entrance with narthex	Church of the Nativity (Bethlehem); Santa Maria Maggiore (Rome)
Byzantine (324–1453)	Highly idealized figures of saints, biblical characters, and rulers; brightly illuminated glass and gold mosaics, frescoes, and icons	Some longitudinal and some cruciform plans, domed arches accenting the celestial and theocratic, mosaics in the apse above altar and other domes	Hagia Sophia (Istanbul); St. Sophia (Thessalonica); St. Irene (Istanbul)
Romanesque basilica (1000–1150)	Illuminated manuscripts, mural frescoes on ceilings and walls, mosaic-colored marble, stained-glass windows, embellished altars	Longitudinal plan, large interiors spanned by barrel vaults, thick walls, small windows, Latin cross transepts, biblical sculptural scenes on the tympana	Cathedral in Mainz (Germany); Cathedral of Pisa (Italy); Church of the Apostles (Cologne, Germany)
Gothic (1150–1600)	Sculptured figures, decorated walls, tympana, large stained-glass windows	Tall pointed arches, ribbed vaults, flying buttresses, thin walls, tall spires, Latin cross transepts, slender columns, lancet windows, west entrances	St. Denis Cathedral (France); Cologne Cathedral (Germany); Houses of Parliament (London)
Renaissance (1400–1550)	Richly decorated ceilings in churches, cartouches (ornamental panels in form of scrolls), graffito paintings	Semielliptical domes with eye on top, domes over the church's transepts, columns with Corinthian capitals	St. Peter's Dome (Rome); St. Pietro in Montoris (Rome)
Baroque (1600–1800)	Sculpture and art accent movement, complexity, and highly ornate interior and exterior decorations; frescoes spiritually tense	Oval ground plan, light and shadow effects; illusionary ceilings, interior has theater appearance, giant columns, ornamental windows, side chapels lining the walls	Frauen Kirche (Dresden, Germany); St. Peter's Piazza (Rome)
Neoclassical (1750–1900)	Seeks to instruct the mind, not only please the eye; shows accents on freedom	Imitates ancient Greco-Roman architecture; use of the dome; lack of spatial depth	Cathedral of the Trinity (St. Petersburg); U.S. Capitol building, D.C.
Contemporary (1900–2000)	Much iron and glass, abstract art scenes, some forms of expressionism	Eclectic styles; much steel, glass, and concrete; very tall buildings with numerous windows, functional design	U.S. Air Force Academy Chapel (Colorado Springs)

This modern trend is unintentionally giving aid to the wishes of Le Corbusier, the French architect, who in our modern era wanted no conspicuous church edifices such as cathedrals. "The heart of our ancient cities," he said, "with their spires and cathedrals must be shattered to pieces."[33] The desires of Le Corbusier also receive support from many American suburbs that no longer permit Christians to build churches with spires that tower above suburban housetops. The Christian spirit that once prompted the building of Gothiclike churches is slowly fading into history.

Having said the above, I am aware that there is no biblical command that binds Christians to only one type of architecture and that some Christians can be spiritually edified hearing and responding to the gospel of Jesus Christ in the context of plain, nonsymbolic structures. To be sure, Christ said that "where two or three come together in my name, there am I with them" (Matthew 18:20). He also told the Samaritan woman that the time had come for God's people to worship him "in spirit and truth" (John 4:23). Moreover, the earliest Christians, while under persecution in the Roman Empire, were spiritually nurtured in house churches and in the catacombs. They had little in terms of Christian architecture. Yet it is evident that already before the Edict of Milan in 313, Christians were motivated to build church edifices that would enhance the service of God's Word. Most of these churches were destroyed as a result of Emperor Diocletian's edict in 303 that sought to eradicate the Christians and their churches; however, after 313 the building of architecturally edifying churches resumed.

After the Edict of Milan, for about three decades many churches were built by Helena, the mother of Constantine the Great. She built them in various parts of the empire. While most of her churches were later destroyed by warring parties, one still stands. It is the Church of the Nativity in Bethlehem, in the Holy Land, reportedly situated on the very site of Jesus' birth. Built in 326 and restored by Emperor Justinian in 529, it is a basilica that has five naves separated by columns, and the original floor consists of fourth-century mosaics. When visiting this church, one is impressed by its large size and its imposing columns of colored marble. This ancient, impressive edifice does not equal the Gothic cathedrals that came a thousand years later. Yet this church shows that the early Christians, through Helena's efforts, understood that they needed to be reminded architecturally that a church building, in the words of architect Steven J. Schoelder, should "nourish [the] soul with meaning, symbolic content, and beauty."[34]

Architecturally the Church of the Nativity is still admired by multitudes of visitors from all parts of the world as they come to see where Jesus Christ, the man who changed the course of history, was born some two thousand years ago. The church also helps keep alive the memory of Constantine's mother, who in the annals of church history is know as St. Helena.

CONCLUSION

Francis Schaeffer once said that Christian art in the Reformation era was not "an aesthetic value divorced from considerations of truth and religious significance."[35] This understanding of art was true from Christianity's beginning, as is evident even in the limited artwork of the third-century catacombs. The truth and religious significance of Christian art was not a mere end in itself, but rather an intimate part of human life, and as such, as Emil Brunner has noted, it was seen as having the potential to renew man's life.[36] Hence, whether in Christianity's early years, in the Middle Ages, in the Renaissance, or in the Reformation era, Christian art regularly shows human life scenes, which in the light and context of biblical history convey a cosmic awareness that God, either by his divine Spirit or through his Son Jesus Christ was always present. Viewers of Christian art—whether that of Da Vinci's *Last Supper,* Tintoretto's *Christ with Mary and Martha,* Rembrandt's *Christ Healing the Sick,* or Dürer's *Knight, Death, and the Devil*—could easily identify with the subjects in these and other human life portraits and perceive that such identification offers the renewal of life. It was this quality of Christian art that resulted in its becoming such a great and long-standing contributor to the world of art.

With regard to Christianity's influence on architecture, it is especially the Gothic style of the European cathedrals that remains an unequaled accomplishment, and it has left a magnanimous, abiding impression on much of the world. It was the Gothic architecture that became the "language" of Christian architecture, as one art historian has phrased it.[37]

It is axiomatic that the architecture of the Gothic cathedrals has spiritually uplifted millions of Christians over the centuries, because, as has been said, its "unfathomable height expressed the aspiration of humanity toward a God to be loved and sought in the nave by the light of day, as well as in the penumbra of the candlelit chapels."[38] Moreover, it is noteworthy that this magnificent architecture continues to impress not only countless Christians but also many non-Christians. It is well known that even secular Europeans are proud of their cathedrals, and each year thousands of tourists come from various sectors of the world to view these renowned edifices. These responses provide ample evidence that the Gothic contribution, shaped by Christianity's influence, lives on, not just in art history books, but also in the lives of countless people in the twenty-first century.

NOTES

1. Peter Taylor Forsyth, *Christ on the Parnassus: Lectures on Art, Ethic and Theology* (London: Independent Press, 1911), 78.

2. D. Talbot Rice, *The Beginnings of Christian Art* (Nashville: Abingdon Press, 1957), 26–27.

3. Fatih Cimock, ed., *Hagia Sophia* (Istanbul: A Turizm Yayinlari, 1995), 46.

4. Hubert Faesen and Vladimir Ivanov, *Early Russian Architecture* (New York: G. P. Putnam's Sons, 1972), 15.

5. Mario Salvadori, *Why Buildings Stand Up: The Strength of Architecture* (New York: W. W. Norton, 1980), 258.

6. Forsyth, *Christ on the Parnassus*, 170.

7. Albert E. Elsen, *Purposes of Art* (New York: Holt, Rinehart and Winston, 1967), 74.

8. Ibid., 70.

9. Emerson H. Swift, *Roman Sources of Christian Art* (New York: Columbia University Press, 1951), 215.

10. Michael Camille, *Gothic Art: Glorious Visions* (New York: Harry N. Abrams, 1996), 71.

11. Forsyth, *Christ on the Parnassus*, 184.

12. Hans Sedlmayr, *Art in Crisis: The Lost Center* (Chicago: Henry Regnery, 1958), 228.

13. Camille, *Gothic Art*, 71.

14. Hans Huth, "History of Stained Glass," *The World Book Encyclopedia* (Chicago: Field Enterprises Educational Corporation, 1958), 15:7678.

15. Forsyth, *Christ on the Parnassus*, 180.

16. H. W. Janson and Anthony F. Janson, *A Basic History of Art* (New York: Prentice-Hall, 1987), 99.

17. William Felming, *Arts and Ideas* (New York: Holt, Rinehart and Winston, 1963), 346.

18. H. W. Janson and Joseph Kerman, *A History of Art and Music* (New York: Harry N. Abrams, n.d.), 124.

19. Laura Armstrong Athearn, *Christian Worship for American Youth* (New York: Century Publishing, 1931), 192–93.

20. Cited in G. G. Coulton, *Art and the Reformation* (New York: Alfred A. Knopf, 1938), 119.

21. Francis Schaeffer, *How Should We Then Live? The Rise and Decline of Western Thought and Culture* (Old Tappan, N.J.: Fleming H. Revell, 1976), 98.

22. Emil Brunner, *Christianity and Civilization* (New York: Charles Scribner's Sons, 1948), 77.

23. Sedlmayr, *Art in Crisis*, 117.

24. D. James Kennedy and Jerry Newcombe, *What If Jesus Had Never Been Born?* (Nashville: Thomas Nelson), 177.

25. Coulton, *Art and the Reformation*, 408.

26. Michel Medved, *Hollywood vs. America: Popular Culture and the War on the Arts* (New York: New Press, 1992), 343.

27. Steven C. Dubin, *Arresting Images: Impolitic Art and Uncivil Actions* (New York: Routledge, Chapman and Hall, 1992), 155.

28. Charles Krauthammer, "The Mayor, the Museum, and the Madonna," *Weekly Standard*, 11 October 1999, 14.

29. "Art Is What Makes the Souls Grow, Vonnegut Says," *Journal-Courier* (Jacksonville, Ill.), 13 September 1999.

30. Jose Ortega y Gasset: cited in Sedlmayr, *Art in Crisis*, 157.

31. Jose Ortega y Gasset, *The Dehumanization of Art and Notes on the Novel* (Princeton: Princeton University Press, 1948), 48.

32. A. Welby Pugin, *The True Principles of Pointed Architecture* (New York: St. Martin's Press, 1973), 52.

33. Cited in Gasset, *The Dehumanization of Art*, 111.

34. Steven J. Schoelder, "A Return to Human Architecture," *Intercollegiate Review* (Fall 1998): 25.

35. Schaeffer, *How Should We Then Live?* 89.

36. Brunner, *Christianity and Civilization*, 85.

37. Otto von Simson, *The Gothic Cathedral* (New York: Pantheon Books, 1956), xxiii.

38. Mario Salvadori, *Why Buildings Stand Up* (New York: W. W. Norton, 1980), 207–8.

13

The SOUND of MUSIC: ITS CHRISTIAN RESONANCE

"Music is well said to be the speech of angels."

Thomas Carlyle

Pagan Rome," says one observer, "made no contribution to musical progress." Its music was "a degenerate form of music that was used in temple, theatre, and circus in the time of the empire."[1] It was into this cultural environment that the Christians brought a very different kind of music. Following the Old Testament tradition, they initially sang biblical psalms, and in time they progressed from monophonic to polyphonic singing, always influenced by the life, death, and resurrection of Jesus Christ. Whether in formal or informal contexts, Christians praised and honored God through music and song. As one observer expressed it, "The Christian Church was born in song."[2]

MUSIC IN THE EARLY CHURCH

Two of the Gospels, Matthew and Mark, note that before Jesus and his disciples left the upper room to go to the Garden of Gethsemane, they sang a hymn. The New Testament also states that St. Paul encouraged the

Christians in Ephesus to "speak to one another with psalms, hymns and spiritual songs. Sing and make music in your heart to the Lord" (Ephesians 5:19). To the believers in Colossae he wrote similar words.

At first the early Christians, like their Jewish ancestors, sang psalms, but as they moved into Asia Minor and Europe, and with Gentiles joining the church, they increasingly began singing hymns as lyrics set to music. References to hymns and spiritual songs are also found in the New Testament (written from about A.D. 50 to 95)—for instance, in 1 Corinthians 14:26, Ephesians 5:19, and Colossians 3:16. In St. Paul's first epistle to Timothy he quotes a fragment of a hymn that Christians sang before Paul composed this letter in about A.D. 64. The fragment reads:

> He [God] appeared in a body,
>   was vindicated by the Spirit,
> was seen by angels,
>   was preached among the nations,
> was believed on in the world,
>   was taken up in glory. (1 Timothy 3:16)

Thus, it is not surprising that Pliny the Younger reported to Emperor Trajan in about A.D. 111 that the Christians sang hymns. Specifically, he told Trajan that they assembled on a "fixed day before it was light, when they sang in alternate stanzas songs to Christ as to a god" (*Epistolae,* or *The Letters of Pliny* 10.96).

We know that during the first three centuries the Christians worshiped and sang in the privacy of their homes as well as in house churches and in catacombs. Clement of Alexandria (late second century) says Christians also sang at mealtimes and before retiring at night (*Stromata* 7.7). Tertullian (ca. A.D. 198) states that Christians sang as lamps were brought in at suppertime. And from Pliny's description quoted above, we know that they also sang hymns outside of their homes.

From Socrates, the fifth-century church historian, we know that St. Ignatius (martyred in A.D. 107) wrote a hymn to Christ (*Ecclesiastical History* 6.8). We also have an extant hymn, "A Hymn to Christ, the Savior," that is appended to Clement of Alexandria's work *Pedagogus,* written about A.D. 170. It reveals the content and the style of the hymns that apparently were sung by the early Christians. Penned in Greek, this hymn has a lyric meter. It is "a hymn of praise and thanksgiving on the part of those newly received into the Church."[3] In the early third century, Hippolytus reportedly composed a number of hymns accenting Christ's redemption. And toward the end of the third century, the "Hymn of Thekla" appeared with each of its twenty-four stanzas followed by a chorus refrain.[4]

MUSICAL INNOVATIONS IN THE MIDDLE AGES

After Constantine legalized Christianity in 313, Ambrose (340–97), the bishop of Milan, made some noteworthy contributions to Christian music. Although psalms were first chanted in Latin in Carthage of northern Africa,[5] it was Ambrose who first had members of his congregation sing psalms antiphonally, which led to the formal singing of hymns in his cathedral. He created the Latin hymn as we know it today, and he established the tradition of congregational song in the West. It was he who made it possible for all people to participate in the morning and evening church services by setting the words of his hymns to "an easy metrical form, the iambic dimeter."[6] "O Splendor of God's Glory Bright" is one of his hymns still being sung. He also introduced what became known as the Ambrosian chant.

Another early Christian hymn writer was the Spanish lawyer and poet Prudentius (348–413). One of his hymns, "Of the Father's Love Begotten," is well known and is sung by many Christians today. He also wrote "O Chief of Cities, Bethlehem," a hymn that apparently inspired "O Little Town of Bethlehem" so familiar to us today.

PLAINSONG

Although the Ambrosian chant arose during the latter part of the fourth century, by the ninth century the Christian church made much use of the Gregorian chant, or plainsong, sung monophonically; that is, all voices sang a simple melody without accompaniment and without harmonization. Named in honor of Gregory the Great (pope from 590 to 604), it was commonly sung by choirs composed mostly of monks. In varying degrees, the Gregorian chant can still be heard in some of the liturgies—for instance, the *Gradual*—in many Catholic, Episcopalian, and Lutheran churches.

CHURCH OPERAS

As early as the ninth century, biblical stories were dramatized and performed in song in the altar area of French churches. One well-known church drama in the early tenth century was *Visitatio sepulchri* (The Visit to [Christ's] Sepulcher). There is good reason to believe that operas, which became popular in concert halls during the Renaissance era, evolved out of the church dramas, whose origin go back five hundred years before the

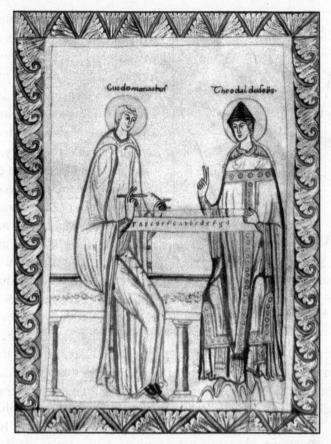

THE MONK GUIDO OF AREZZO (ca. 990–1050), who reformed musical notation, demonstrates his method of sight singing to Bishop Theobald, in an illustration from a German codex of the twelfth century.

Renaissance.[7] This musical fact has been forgotten by many modern opera lovers.

POLYPHONIC MUSIC

Up to the tenth century the church's singing was largely monophonic. A major change occurred when Ubaldus Hucbald (840–930), a French Benedictine monk, in his famous *De institutionae harmonica* ushered in a form of music known as *polyphony,* which is the parallel movement of melodic lines, combining two or more melodies in harmony.[8] A little more than a century after Hucbald, an additional advance occurred in the development of polyphony when Guido of Arezzo (ca. 995–1050), a Benedictine monk,

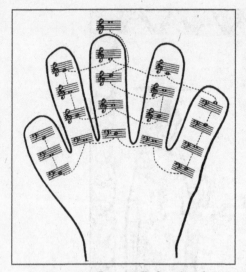

THE "GUIDO HAND" reportedly functioned as a mnemonic device to teach singers the hexachord, a six-tone scale.

introduced the staff of four lines on which the pitch of notes could be written. His invention now enabled musicians to notate music. It brought to an end the lament of Isidore of Seville, who, in the seventh century, said if music is not retained in one's memory, it is lost, since it cannot be written down.

Guido of Arezzo also devised a system known as solmization that consisted of six syllables: *ut (do), re, mi, fa, sol,* and *la.* They are still in use today.[9] His six syllables comprised a *hexachord,* providing a span of six successive notes. Now musicians have added two to Guido's first six; they are: *ti (si)* and *do.* These eight syllables are known to most people today, even to those who have only an elementary knowledge of music. Guido's contribution was "as crucial to the development of music as written language is to literature."[10]

Although historians consider 1600 as the end of the polyphonic era, "polyphony was by no means finished," according to Marion Bauer. "A century later Bach wrote some of the finest polyphonic music the history of music has known."[11] The creation and development of polyphonic, "multi-voiced music," says Henry Pleasants, "sets Western music off from the music of other civilizations."[12] Today the beauty of polyphonic music is taken for granted, and many may think that music has always been that way. Indeed not, for without Hucbald and Guido of Arezzo laying the foundation of polyphonic music, the world today would not have the beauty of *St. Matthew's Passion* by Bach, *Messiah* by Handel, and countless other outstanding polyphonic compositions in both sacred and secular music.

THE MOTET

Derived from the French word *mot,* meaning "word," motets appeared in the Western world in the thirteenth century from Notre Dame's music theorists in Paris. From their beginning, motets were vocal or vocal combined with instrumental compositions based on sacred texts and sung in church services. The most important polyphonic music during the Middle Ages and the Renaissance, motets were sung by choruses and comprised most of the divine services in churches.[13] Beginning with the Renaissance, motets were increasingly performed in nonchurch settings and conveyed secular themes. Both Bach and Mozart, for example, wrote a number of motets that continue to be enjoyed by lovers of secular music.

THE MADRIGAL

When madrigals appeared in the fourteenth century, they were polyphonic songs with religious texts and prayers. Apparently that is why they "did not at first differ in musical construction from the church chorus."[14] By the sixteenth century madrigals took on a completely different complexion both poetically and musically. Since then, they have been quite unrelated to the fourteenth-century madrigals. Nevertheless, it is worth remembering that these delightful musical renditions owe their existence to the influence of musically creative Christians. Orlando di Lasso (1532–94), a prominent writer of sacred music within the confines of the church, wrote numerous madrigals. His contemporary, Giovanni Palestrina (1525–94), another composer of sacred music, crafted more than one hundred madrigals.

THE ANTHEM

It is common in the United States to refer to "The Star Spangled Banner" as the country's "national anthem," the same expression that is used in Canada when "O Canada" is sung. The anthem, as vocal music, has Christian roots. It evolved out of the church's motets in England during the sixteenth century. When the anthem first appeared, it was sung alternately or responsively in the vernacular in the low-church Anglican churches of England that did not follow the prescribed liturgy.[15] So when the word *anthem* is used, whether in the context of sacred or secular music, it is noteworthy that it is another of the many contributions that Christianity has made to the world of music.

THE ORATORIO

In the sixteenth century, sometime after the motets appeared, the oratorio (from the Latin *oratorius:* prayer) made its debut. It began in Rome in the 1560s as an outgrowth of a devotional movement among laymen led by Fillip Neri, an Italian priest.[16] Neri gave devotional lectures, accompanied by hymns, in the oratory (prayer hall) of Rome's San Girolamo church. These presentations were known as *oratorani*. They included Bible readings, sermons, and spiritual lauds, which involved fine musicians such as Giovanni Palestrina and were done more and more by professionals as time progressed. "From these lauds, or perhaps from the whole context, the oratorio was born," according to Paul Westermeyer, who says that oratorios "can be viewed not only as a gift of the church to the world, but as a tradition of proclamation in the world."[17] Handel's *Messiah*, Mendelssohn's *Elijah,* and Haydn's *Seven Last Words of Christ* are but a few of the well-known oratorios.

THE SYMPHONY

Another significant component in the world of music is the symphony. Few people realize that the symphony grew out of the context of the church in the late 1500s. Giovanni Gabrieli, who introduced the sonata, composed his *Sacrae symphoniae* in 1597. This work included motets, a mass, *Hodie Christus natus est* (Christ Is Born Today), and other compositions. Thus, while most symphonies today are performed in secular concert halls, it should not be forgotten that this popular form of music, like so many others, first evolved out of Gabrieli's sacred music.

THE SONATA

Although the sonata did not originate as church music, it was created by a gifted church musician in the sixteenth century, Giovanni Gabrieli, who spent much of his career at St. Mark's in Venice. Late in the 1500s he introduced the sonata, a musical performance played by one or two instrumentalists. When he first initiated the sonata, he had to make it clear that it was a form of music meant to be played rather than sung, as was commonly done. A four-movement sonata, for example, begins with *allegro;* the second is *andante, adagio, or largo;* the third is *scherzo;* and the fourth or last consists of the *finale.* The world is perhaps most familiar with Beethoven's many piano sonatas. Of course, other Christian musicians, for example, Mozart and Haydn, also composed numerous sonatas.

THE CANTATA

The name *cantata* is derived from the Latin *cantare* (to sing). When the cantata first appeared in the early seventeenth century, it was a vocal music as opposed to a sonata, which was performed instrumentally. As music fans know, today a cantata is a poem or story for one or more voices accompanied by musical instruments. It is sung by choruses and typically includes solos, duets, trios, and quartets. Unlike the oratorio, which is generally based on a biblical story, a cantata is usually shorter, has no scenery and no acting, and may or may not have a religious theme. Some of Bach's inspiring church cantatas have also been called oratorios. Many well-known cantatas are religious, for example, Bach's *Christ Lay in the Bonds of Death* and his *Awake My Soul,* and Dubois's *Seven Last Words of Christ. Hodie* and *The Sons of Light* are two well-known cantatas composed by Ralph Vaughan Williams.

THE CONCERTO

The concerto, a composition for instruments, appeared during the last two decades of the seventeenth century during the Baroque era (ca. 1550–1750). Its predecessors were the sonata and the sinfonia. Like these two, concertos originally were played "in the church as 'overtures' before Mass or at certain moments in the ceremony."[18] Thus, this style of music, which today is commonly heard in concert halls rather than in churches, is still another form of music that had its origin in the Christian church. Bach, Beethoven, Handel, and Mozart made concertos popular as well as musically beautiful.

REFORMATION AND POST-REFORMATION MUSIC

The Reformation brought vast improvements to music, some of which later spread to nonchurch music. The many great musicians that arose during and after the Reformation era were highly influenced by the Reformation's gospel-centered theology. Space permits citing only a few.

MARTIN LUTHER

The Reformation began on October 31, 1517, with Martin Luther's posting of his Ninety-five Theses to the door of All Saints Church, the university church in Wittenberg. Luther not only reformed and restored the church's theology, but he also reformed its music. Congregational singing by lay members, as it was practiced by the early Christians during the reign of Emperor Trajan (early second century) and in Bishop Ambrose's cathedral in the fourth century, had disappeared from the church. Only choir groups (commonly monks) sang in Latin, a language not understood by the common church member. In 1526 Luther translated and reformed the Latin Mass into *Die Deutsche Messe* (*The German Mass*) so that parishioners could participate in their native tongue.

Luther loved music, and he never tired of saying that music was the handmaiden of Christian theology. Christian music was a servant of God's word, the *"viva voce evangelii"* (living voice of the gospel). Being musically talented, he wrote thirty-six hymns, of which "A Mighty Fortress Is Our God," often called "the battle hymn of the Reformation," is his best known.

Two of Luther's contemporaries also affected the Reformation and its music. One was Ulrich Zwingli (1484–1531), an ex-monk from Switzerland who did nothing good for music. Because of his theology, Zwingli banned music from church use in Zurich, where he wielded his authority. Interestingly, of the three reformers, Zwingli was the most musically gifted.[19] The other was John Calvin (1509–1564), who disliked polyphonic chorales. He had members only sing psalms monophonically and did not permit instruments or choirs in church.[20] Later, in Strasbourg, upon hearing "the Germans sing Luther's hymns, he turned French Psalms. . . into modern meters set to congregational tunes."[21] The Puritans brought Calvin's original musical thinking to America. In time, however, polyphonic music, in spite of Calvin and the Puritans, became more and more common in the American Reformed and Calvinistic churches.

In England, the music of the Methodists, through Charles Wesley's contact with the Moravians, reflected the Moravian love of church music. The Moravians inherited much of their musical tastes from their Hussite predecessors and some from their contact with Lutherans. Thus, Luther's love for polyphonic chorales gained the upper hand, and by the late sixteenth century the term *chorale* had become synonymous with the vernacular hymns in Europe and America. The many hymns that now are sung in various denominations are all polyphonic arrangements. The monophonic or noninstrumental music favored by Calvin and the Puritans have all but disappeared from church services.

JOHANN SEBASTIAN BACH

One hundred fifty years after Luther, Johann Sebastian Bach (1685–1750) entered the world of music as one of the most gifted musicians the world has ever known. He has been called the "composer's composer whose analytical mind, belief in God, and melodic genius led him to create some

THESE ARE THE KEYBOARD and pedals of the organ that Bach played while at Arnstadt, Germany. The organ is now in the town hall.

of the greatest religious music we have."[22] Some have called him "the fifth evangelist." He set Christian theology and its gospel to music.

Bach's music reflected his strong Lutheran theological convictions. He faithfully read and studied the Bible, along with other Christian writings. At his death, his private library was found to contain "some eighty books, including Luther and Lutheran pillars of the seventeenth and eighteenth centuries."[23] His Christian convictions were evident in his well-known oratorios, such as the *St. Matthew Passion* and the *Magnificat,* and in all of his church music. The titles of his chorales give further evidence of his strong Christian faith. For brevity's sake I shall only note three: "O Man, Bewail Thy Great Sins," "I Call on Thee, Lord Jesus Christ," and "Before Thy

Throne I Now Appear." The latter number was his last composition. Given that he was almost blind and his hands paralyzed, he dictated it one week before he died.[24] As a Christian he looked forward to meeting Jesus Christ upon his heavenly throne.

Before he began writing his musical compositions he commonly wrote the initials "J. J." (*Jesu Juva:* Help Me, Jesus) or "I. N. J." (*In Nomine Jesu:* In the Name of Jesus). At the end of the manuscript he would write "S.D.G" (*Soli Deo Gloria:* To God Alone All Glory), a concept that goes back at least to Johannes Tinctoris (1435–1511).[25] "To Bach these were not trite religious slogans but sincere expressions of personal devotion," says Patrick Kavanaugh.[26] Reportedly, Bach would tell his students that unless they committed their talents to Jesus Christ, they would never become great musicians.[27] For him "thinking in music was a necessary consequence of a belief in its divine origins."[28]

Like so many other past and present Christians, Bach was not insulated from tragedies in his life. By the grace of God, he knew how to bear the cross of sorrow and suffering. His first wife, who bore seven children, died suddenly leaving him with four small ones. With his second wife he had thirteen more children. In all, only ten lived to maturity. To stand at the graveside of one family member is more than enough grief, but he did it eleven times. In addition to family deaths, he also had a wayward son, Johann Gottfried Bernhard Bach, who left town without paying his several financial debts. Regarding this delinquency, the great musician wrote, "What can I do or say more, my warnings having failed, and my loving care and help having proved unavailing? I can only bear my cross in patience and commend my undutiful boy to God's mercy, never doubting that He will hear my sorrow-stricken prayer and in His good time bring my son to understand that the path of conversion leads to him."[29]

This musical giant composed a multitude of chorales, preludes to chorales, chamber sonatas, concertos, toccatas, cantatas, music for orchestras, and fugues. He wrote every kind of music except operas. He is credited with introducing a new fingering technique to play keyboard instruments with five fingers instead of four as was the practice previously when the thumb was not used. And he "created the 'well-tempered' scale, so that from any note on the piano or organ one could begin a scale which was impossible before that time."[30] But he did even more. Professional musicians also know him for his contrapuntal, fugal complexities, "the foundation of what we today call 'classical music.'"[31]

Bach spent most of his professional life as cantor at St. Thomas Lutheran Church in Leipzig, where he composed most of his music: over two hundred cantatas; more than two hundred fifty chorales; numerous concertos for organ, violin, and fugue; plus numerous organ preludes, sonatas, and suites. Many of these compositions also include beautiful secular music, for example, his six *Brandenburg Concertos, The Well-Tempered Clavier, Fantasia and Fugue in D Minor,* and many other secular pieces. In his mind, however, there was no sacred-secular distinction in music. All of his compositions, even his "secular" music, was dedicated to God's glory.[32]

This brief sketch of Bach's magnificent achievements shows that when God made him, he threw away the mold. As Alfred Einstein said, "Bach is of the company of those masters with whom every age and every individual must arrive at a new understanding; and still his greatness has not been appraised, nor can be ever."[33] The many and varied musical contributions that he left behind, however, have not been thrown away. They remain for the world, both inside and outside the church, to enjoy, even though many may not know that much of their musical enjoyment owes a debt of gratitude to a man whose work was spurred by the grace and love of Jesus Christ. One can confidently say that had there never been a Jesus Christ, the world today would not be in possession of the majestic music that the Christian genius of Johann Sebastian Bach produced. But in today's age of secularism it is not uncommon to read articles about Bach's great achievements and never see a single reference to his Christian convictions and how they shaped his music.[34]

GEORGE FRIDERIC HANDEL

What is the statistical probability for two geniuses to excel in the same area of expertise (music), to be born in the same year (1685), to hail from the same country (Germany), and to confess the same religious faith (Lutheran)? It must be extremely low. Yet that is precisely what happened in the case of Johann Sebastian Bach and George Frideric Handel (1685–1759). While these two gifted men had these characteristics in common, their careers were remarkably different. Bach devoted most of his entire musical career to writing and playing music primarily in the context of the church to enrich the liturgy and hymns for the common person in the pew. Handel, on the other hand, spent his life writing and performing before audiences seated in theaters, often for audiences of high social status, including royalty. Bach stayed in Germany his whole life; Handel migrated to England and stayed there. Bach sired twenty children; Handel never married.

When Handel went to England at the youthful age of twenty-five, he was already an accomplished master of Italian opera. In addition to writing operas, he also wrote music for instrumental suites and sonatas. He wrote biblically based oratorios such as *Esther, Joseph and His Brethren, Saul,* and *Israel in Egypt.* His Christian faith also moved him to compose a number of explicitly Christian pieces, for example, "In the Lord, I Put My Trust"; "As Pants the Hart"; and "Have Mercy Upon Me." According to Herbert Weinstock, Handel never forgot the sermon that his sister's pastor preached at her funeral. Its topic was "I Know that My Redeemer Liveth," the title of which was later used in one of his most famous arias.[35] Handel's most famous oratorio is *Messiah,* which portrays the life, death, and resurrection of Jesus Christ. This majestic composition masterfully pulls together passages from the Old and New Testaments, thereby showing that Christ was the Messiah predicted by the Hebrew prophets hundreds of years before his birth. In this masterpiece, Handel not only unfolded the messianic prophecies but also revealed his own Christian convictions. Newman Flower reports that while Handel was working on *Messiah,* which took him only twenty-four days to write, his servant found that he often left his food untouched. "He was unconscious of the world during that time, unconscious of its press and call; his whole mind was in a trance. He did not leave the house." One day tears began rolling down his face, and he was heard saying, "I did think I did see all Heaven before me, and the great God Himself."[36] This was not just a onetime remark reflecting his Christian faith, for a few days before his death he said he wanted to die on Good Friday so that could meet his "Lord and Savior, on the day of his Resurrection."[37]

The moving effect of *Messiah*'s spiritual quality was not confined to its composer. Patrick Kavanaugh notes that when the renowned musician Haydn first heard the Hallelujah Chorus, "he wept like a child."[38] Another observer, one hundred years ago, said that *Messiah* "has probably done more to convince thousands of mankind that there is a God about us than all the theological works ever written."[39] Yet it took a number of years for this marvelous piece of music to attain its present fame and acclaim. Strange as it may seem, initially, it received serious criticism from British clerics.

As most people know, when *Messiah* is performed, the audience rises during the Hallelujah Chorus, a tradition that began with King George II, who in London in 1743 rose to his feet as the chorus sounded forth its jubilant voices. This honorary custom, 250 years old, testifies to the fact that *Messiah* is, as one observer has remarked, "the greatest feat in the whole his-

"MOZART SINGING HIS REQUIEM" shows the musician presenting his last composition moments before he died. *(Thomas W. Shields)*

tory of musical composition."[40] It has rightly been called a "Christian epic in tones."

Much more could be said about Handel, the talented Christian musician. When one surveys his life and work, it is evident that, as in the lives of so many other Christians, what he produced was inspired and motivated by the gospel of Jesus Christ. His outstanding contributions to music, especially *Messiah,* which have lifted the spirits of countless listeners, give added understanding to Christ's saying that man does not live by bread alone.

CHRISTIAN INFLUENCE REFLECTED BY SOME OTHER GREAT MUSICIANS

There is a long train of noteworthy musicians who followed Bach and Handel, all of whom made varying contributions to the world of music.

One of them is **Wolfgang Amadeus Mozart (1756–91)**, a brilliant musician who, at age five, wrote a piano concerto that was "too difficult for anyone to play."[41] Mozart enriched the music world with his orchestral symphonies, string quartets, piano sonatas, and piano concertos. And what would music be without his *Eine kleine Nachtmusik*, his *Requiem*, or his operas such as *The Magic Flute* or *The Marriage of Figaro*?

In comparing Mozart's religious life with that of Bach or Mendelssohn, one might conclude that his Christian beliefs were not especially important to him, perhaps because he wrote far more secular than religious music. It is also known that his father once complained about his being lax in going to confession.[42] Yet it would be unwise to see him as religiously indifferent, for there are a number of instances in his life that reveal that he was a serious Christian. For instance, after his mother's death, he recalled the good contacts that he had with her and how those incidents affected his faith, saying, "I found that I never prayed so fervently, confessed and communicated so devoutly, as when I was at her side."[43] But his Christian faith is probably best reflected in the *Requiem*, written while he was literally dying. While composing this famous work, he said to his wife Constanze that he felt it was written for himself. The day before he died, friends rehearsed the unfinished *Requiem* with him lying on his death bed. "During the 'Lacrimosa' movement, Mozart burst into tears, and his final rehearsal ended. He died early next morning, December 5, 1791. His last action was to initiate the kettledrums in his…*Requiem*."[44] Otto Jahn, a biographer of Mozart, believes that the *Requiem* reveals Mozart's "innermost spirit."[45] It can be argued that his Christian beliefs are also reflected in his *Missa Brevis, Mass in C Minor, Epistle Sonatas*, and *Ave Verum Corpus*.

Ludwig van Beethoven (1770–1827) is another musical genius to which the world is indebted. This talented man's life, from childhood on, was filled with misfortunes, so much so that it is difficult to read about them and not be emotionally stirred. His father was an alcoholic and often mean-spirited, the family lived in dire poverty, and his mother died of consumption.[46] As a child, he had smallpox, which left him with bad eyesight and even worse hearing, later resulting in total deafness. These unusual childhood experiences apparently gave him a highly erratic personality, one that often stood in the way of his making friends and getting married. Several women whom he wanted to marry saw him as too temperamental and rejected his proposals. He once said, "I have no friend. I must live by myself. I know, however, that God is nearer to me than others; I go without fear to Him."[47]

Beethoven wrote music that at times reflected, and at other times transcended, his personal problems. Although there was a certain ambiguity during much of his life regarding his Christian faith, there is this documented account. While he was on his deathbed, his sister-in-law asked him to take communion. After doing so, he said to the priest, "Father, I thank you. You brought me comfort."[48] Many of his musical works reveal definite Christian imprints. These are plainly evident in *Missa Solemnis* and in *Christ on the Mount of Olives* as well as in other religious compositions.

Beethoven wrote string quartets, piano sonatas, choral music, and symphonies. Some of these, such as the famous *Ninth Symphony* and the *Concerto for Violin,* have been enjoyed by secular concert audiences for generations, and today countless individuals delight in hearing these selections on compact discs in the solitude of their homes. We need to remember that it was Beethoven "who gave to the symphony orchestra the final basic shape we know today."[49] The world of music, ecclesiastical or secular, would be much poorer had God not so richly blessed the talents of this musical giant.

A contemporary of Beethoven was **Felix Mendelssohn (1809–47),** another noteworthy Christian musician. Although he was born of Jewish parents, his father had him baptized as an infant in the Lutheran church so that he would be better accepted in German society. But Felix was no nominal Christian. He not only remained a devout Lutheran throughout his life, but he also composed a number of sacred hymns reflecting his firm belief in Jesus Christ and the Holy Scriptures. He believed unwaveringly in the Bible and was shocked when others did not. When setting music to a biblical text, he would take the utmost care not to deviate one iota from the text.[50]

Mendelssohn loved Johann Sebastian Bach's music and is often credited with having brought Bach to the attention of the music world. For nearly a century after Bach's death his music was unrecognized by musicians. It seemed that during Bach's life musicians saw his contrapuntal music, as did his own children, as "old-fashioned."[51] But Mendelssohn thought otherwise. Upon discovering the manuscript of Bach's *St. Matthew's Passion,* which had been lost for a hundred years, he said that he was giving "to the people the greatest Christian music in the world."[52] He performed it for the first time with the chorus of the Berlin *Singakademie* on March 11, 1829, exactly one hundred years after Bach had written it.[53]

Mendelssohn himself wrote *Elijah* and also *St. Paul,* two highly acclaimed oratorios. The well-known Christmas carol "Hark the Herald

Angels Sing," written by Charles Wesley, was set to music by Mendelssohn. Secular listeners are probably most familiar with Mendelssohn's overture to *A Midsummer Night's Dream,* which he composed at the early age of seventeen, and his *Wedding March.* Among other works, he also wrote piano and chamber music that modern concertgoers continue to delight in hearing, for example, his *Violin Concerto in E Minor.*

When one considers the many other Christian musicians who have enriched the world of music, the name of **Franz Joseph Haydn (1732– 1809)** cannot be overlooked. Born and reared as a Roman Catholic in Austria in very ordinary circumstances, he later performed some of his compositions before the upper classes of society. He composed over one hundred symphonies as well as a number of chamber music pieces. In the context of sacred music, he produced many moving pieces that conveyed his joyful understanding of the gospel of Jesus Christ.[54] *The Seven Last Words of Christ, The Seasons,* and *The Creation* are three of his most revered oratorios. Regarding one of them, he said, "Never before was I so devout as when I composed *The Creation.* I knelt down each day to pray to God to give me strength for my work."[55] Thus, when listeners enjoy Haydn's musical selections, it is fitting to remember that like Bach, Handel, Mozart, and Mendelssohn, he was highly motivated by his Christian beliefs and values.

In the history of the musically gifted one also finds **Franz Peter Schubert (1797–1828)**, a Catholic, often called "the most poetic musician that ever lived." This man's short life was filled with disappointments and misfortunes, one of which was poverty. He received neither adequate financial rewards nor much recognition for his musical efforts. It is said that he saw himself as not belonging to this world.[56] Unhappy experiences, however, did not daunt his Christian faith that is so apparent in the titles of some of his musical renditions. To Catholics he is known for his "Ave Maria." "Great Jehovah" is another of his noteworthy Christian numbers. In the secular concert world, his *Unfinished Symphony* is well known. Schubert wrote more than six hundred songs and nine symphonies as well as piano and chamber music. Kavanaugh says, "Through the tribulations of his tragic life, it was the combination of two elements in his nature—his faith in God and his God-given talent—that enabled him to create without applause or acclaim the many masterpieces we treasure today."[57]

Another noteworthy musician, often cited as one of the three great Bs of music, is **Johannes Brahms (1833–97)**. Born and raised a Lutheran, he assiduously studied Johann Sebastian Bach's music.[58] He was also "a diligent student of Martin Luther's German translation of the Bible, as well as

Luther's book *Table-Talks*."[59] Thus, Bach and Luther, two outstanding Christians, influenced Brahms's music. His *German Requiem*, though a concert composition, has been called "the only great Lutheran Requiem Mass."[60]

Brahms also wrote numerous musical pieces that continue to be played in concert halls. These include symphonies, piano and violin concertos, and chamber music such as quintets, sextets, motets, sonatas, waltzes, ballads, and rhapsodies. Some of his music furnished joyful songs, such as his well-known *Wiegenlied*, sometimes called "Brahms' Lullaby." In short, his music has esthetically enriched the lives of countless people, Christians as well as non-Christians.

Ralph Vaughan Williams (1872–1958), a British musician commonly referred to as Vaughan Williams, made many contributions to the world of music, including church music. He was a great admirer of Johann Sebastian Bach and arranged and performed Bach's *Mass in B Minor, St. John's Passion,* and *St. Matthew Passion*. With regard to the latter, he insisted that its performance was an act of worship, so he placed large notices on the walls of the concert hall requesting "NO APPLAUSE PLEASE"; and during the Institution of the Eucharist portion, he insisted that the audience stand.[61]

Vaughan Williams wrote and arranged a number of Christian hymns. His church music includes "O Praise the Lord of Heaven," "O Taste and See," "Te Deum and Benedictus," "Magnificat and Nunc Dimittis," and more. Other Christian pieces are *The Sons of Light*, a cantata; *Pilgrim's Progress*, an opera; and *Te Deum in G*, a choral number sung by men and boys only, which has been cited as his greatest composition, although many musicians see his hymn "For All the Saints" as his greatest. For concert audiences he wrote symphonies, of which *A Sea Symphony* is best known. He also wrote folk songs for schools, concertos for violins, cantatas, chamber music, and music for films.

In spite of his writing and performing majestic Christian music, his wife's biography of Vaughn Williams says that he was not a Christian.[62] This is surprising, for when he performed Bach's *St. Matthew Passion*, he would become very involved emotionally. For instance, its words "Truly this was the Son of God" would so move him that "his face contorted with intensity of feeling." And this *Passion's* words, "Be near me, Lord, when dying," prompted him to tell his choir members, "Sing this to yourself."[63]

Given his wife's account, some have wondered whether his atheism during the earlier years of his life and his later agnosticism might have come from reading *The Origin of Species*, written by his great-uncle, Charles

Darwin.[64] His wife, however, says there is no evidence that he ever read the book. According to her, his agnosticism came from his student days at Charterhouse and Cambridge.[65] If her account is true, Vaughan Williams serves as a good example of how Christianity's beliefs and values can shape a person's artistic work without his actually being a Christian.

Igor Stravinsky (1882–1971), an exiled Russian native who spent the last thirty years of his life in the United States, became an acclaimed musician known worldwide. After becoming a Christian at age twenty-six, he never hid his religious beliefs, in spite of his fame. He once remarked, "The more one separates himself from the canons of the Christian church, the further one distances himself from the truth."[66] He believed that in order to compose religious music one had to be "not merely a believer in 'symbolic figures,' but in the Person of the Lord, the Person of the Devil, and the Miracle of the Church."[67] So sacred was his concept and belief in God that when he was preparing his opera *The Tower of Babel* and someone suggested that he use a narrator who would speak as God, he unequivocally rejected this suggestion. He felt it would be sacrilegious for a human to assume such a role.[68] Such were the Christian convictions that moved him to write his musical selections, whether they were religious or not.

Some of his noteworthy religious numbers include *The Flood*, an opera based on the Genesis account; *Pater Noster*, an a cappella liturgical rendition; *Abraham and Isaac*, a sacred ballad; and "A Dove Descending Breaks the Air," an a cappella anthem for a British hymnal. He also produced many nonreligious compositions for orchestras as well as concertos, piano music, chamber music, and, of course, operas such as *The Nightingale, Mavra,* and *The Rake's Progress.*

SOME GREAT HYMNS AND SONGS

The world of music has been blessed with many great hymns and songs from the talents of numerous Christian musicians, especially during the last five hundred years. They are songs that virtually everyone has heard, but space permits noting only some of the most outstanding and most widely known.

"A MIGHTY FORTRESS IS OUR GOD"

One of the all-time great hymns is "A Mighty Fortress Is Our God," written by Martin Luther in 1529 at the height of Reformation. This hymn has been called the "*Marseillaise* of the Reformation." It continues to be sung by millions of Christians in many denominations throughout the world. Although long seen as an undesirable hymn by Roman Catholics, mainly because Luther wrote it in defense of the opposition that he encountered in his call for the church's reformation, it is today found in some Catholic hymnals. It has been translated into more languages than any other hymn in Christendom.[69] One musician has remarked, "The good that this hymn has done, the faith it has inspired, the hearts it has comforted, the influence it has exerted, cannot be measured and will first be revealed to us in eternity, where the saints of God will praise their Lord and redeemer for many blessings, not the least of which will be the privilege of having known and sung this hymn on earth."[70]

"NOW THANK WE ALL OUR GOD"

The hymn "Now Thank We All Our God" has been called the "Lutheran *Te Deum*." Like "A Mighty Fortress," it has crossed denominational lines. It was sung at the opening of the Cathedral of Cologne in 1880, at the cornerstone laying of the Reichstag in Berlin in 1884, at the end of the Boer War in South Africa in 1902, and at other victorious and national events.[71] "Now Thank We All Our God" is the creative work of Martin Rinckart (1586–1640), a Lutheran pastor who served in the little Saxon town of Eilenburg during the Thirty Years War (1618–48). The town had been ravaged three times by invading armies. In addition to the dead from the war, pestilence and famine struck the town, resulting in the death of some eight thousand residents. For a while (especially in 1636 and 1637), Rinckart was the only pastor in town to bury the dead. Some days he buried forty to fifty people; within two years he buried over four thousand people, one of which was his wife, who died in 1637.[72] Despite the dire, long-lasting pestilence, God spared his health.

When the Swedish general whose army occupied Eilenburg imposed an excessive tax on the town's remaining people, Rinckart pleaded with the general, saying the people could not pay what he demanded. The general ignored the plea. So Rinckart said, "Come, my children, we can find no mercy with men, let us take refuge with God," and they sang the hymn "When in the Hour of Utmost Need." This act so softened the general's heart that he reduced the tax to one-fifteenth of his original demand. In the midst of all the horrific tragedies, Rinckart did what most people would find unthinkable. He wrote "Now Thank We All Our God," a spiritually uplifting hymn that has been sung by countless Christians ever since, in recent years especially at Thanksgiving time.[73]

THE COMMON DOXOLOGY

There are probably very few Christians who have not sung the joyful words of the doxology:

> *Praise God, from whom all blessings flow;*
> *Praise Him all creatures here below;*
> *Praise Him above, ye heavenly host;*
> *Praise Father, Son, and Holy Ghost!*

Its writer was Thomas Ken (1637–1711), a bishop in the Church of England. The tune for its poetic words is from the *Old Hundredth,* which stems from the sixteenth century.[74] Some see Ken's doxology, derived from "All Praise to Thee, My God, This Night," as a modern *Te Deum.*

"OUR GOD, OUR HELP IN AGES PAST"

One of the most familiar hymns written by the talented hymn writer Isaac Watts is "Our God, Our Help in Ages Past." Called "the father of English hymnody," Watts wrote some seven hundred hymns, including "When I Survey the Wondrous Cross," "Joy to the World!" and "Jesus Shall Reign." "Our God" was penned about 1714 during an anxious time in England, the death of Queen Anne. "Her death halted the enactment of the Schism Act that would have suppressed Dissenters (of whom Watts was one) and would undoubtedly have brought persecution upon them."[75] This hymn, based on Psalm 90, accents the fleeting nature of time and the brevity of human life in contrast to the everlasting nature of God. Christians have often sung this song, and still do, at the end of the calendar year or sometimes at funerals, to remind themselves of the ephemeral nature of time and life, while remembering that God is the one thing that is constant and their only "hope for years to come" (sixth stanza).

"SILENT NIGHT"

Of all the Christmas carols, "Silent Night" is the best known and the most loved. It is the creation of Joseph Mohr, who was a young Catholic priest in St. Nikolaus Church in Oberndorf, Austria. Shortly before Christmas of 1818, the church's organ broke down, creating the need for some music that could be played on Christmas Eve without an organ. So Mohr wrote a six-stanza carol that he gave to Franz Gruber, the parish organist, to set to music. On Christmas Eve Gruber, using his guitar, sang the carol with Mohr for the first time as a small choir of village girls repeated in harmony the last two lines of each stanza.[76] In 1827 this beautiful carol, now commonly sung in only three stanzas, was brought to the United States by the Renner family, a folk-singing group that toured the nation.[77] Today this spiritually edifying carol is frequently heard in Christmas concerts, Christmas church services, and often in stores and shopping malls during the Christmas season.

Other Christmas carols could be mentioned, such as "Hark the Herald Angels Sing," "It Came Upon a Midnight Clear," "O Come All Ye Faithful," "Away in a Manger," and "O Holy Night." They all reveal the powerful influence that the life and work of Jesus Christ has had on their authors, an influence that also moves countless people today to sing and listen to these Christ-centered songs.

THE CHURCH AS PATRON AND PROMOTER OF THE MUSIC ARTS

The Christian church that transmitted the teachings of Christ not only inspired and motivated most musicians to compose and play music, but it also patronized many of the musicians and their compositions. It was the churches of Santa Maria Maggiore and Capella Julia that patronized Giovani Palestrina (1525?–94) as he composed his spiritual madrigals and motets and his many masses for the Catholic Church. And it was St. Thomas Church in Leipzig that employed Bach when he wrote most of his chorales, cantatas, preludes, and oratorios for the Lutheran Church.

But even more important was the friendly alliance that the church had established with the royal courts that patronized much of the music, especially during the Baroque era. Without this alliance many, perhaps most, of the great musical compositions, particularly the sacred numbers, would never have come into being. As Friedrich Blume states, "Court and church blended so intimately that the Baroque became without ado the age of the court art and aristocratic cultivation of music, and the aristocratic spirit set its stamp upon music."[78] It was the courts that patronized, at least in part, Haydn, Mozart, Handel, Brahms, Liszt, and other musicians. Even Johann Sebastian Bach was employed for a while by Prince Leopold in Köthen before he assumed his position as cantor at St. Thomas Church. It was in the prince's court that he wrote his Brandenburg concertos and some of his chamber music.

Through its churches, Christianity also patronized and promoted music by using and distributing the sacred motets, madrigals, sonatas, preludes, chorales, and oratorios. The church further promoted music as its members installed high-quality pipe organs in churches and cathedrals throughout Europe. The organ has been primarily associated with the church for nearly two millennia. And in eighteenth-century America, the Moravian Christians cultivated and promoted many varieties of music for churches, orchestras, and chamber groups, using the music of Mozart, Haydn, Stamitz, and Johann Christian Bach.[79]

MODERN MUSIC'S REVOLUTIONARY NOTES

As noted earlier, Luther saw music as ancillary to Christian theology, and Bach told his music students that unless they committed their talents to Jesus Christ they could not become great musicians. Igor Stravinsky believed that religious music was meant to praise God. He saw it offering more praise to God than the most beautiful cathedral architecture. Said he, "It is the Church's greatest ornament."[80] On the other hand, neither Luther, Bach, nor Stravinsky saw anything amiss in having and enjoying music that was not specifically religious. To them even nonreligious music was to be used to the glory of God in the sense of St. Paul's words spoken to the Corinthians: "So whether you eat or drink or whatever you do, do it all for the glory of God" (1 Corinthians 10:31).

But then came the twentieth century with its modern music, music that flaunted the words of Samuel Johnson, who said that "music is the only sensual pleasure without vice." The idea that music was to be used to God's glory had become greatly undermined. Thus, much of today's modern music, as it caters to sensual pleasure, is often a revolt against God, biblical values, and even against society. Richard Weaver, in his *Ideas Have Consequences,* saw this revolt even in the music of jazz, which, he said, gave the fullest freedom to the individual to "express himself as an egotist. Playing now becomes personal; the musician seizes a theme and improvises as he goes; he develops perhaps a personal idiom, for which he is admired. Instead of that strictness of form which had made the musician like the celebrant of a ceremony, we now have individualization." Jazz, he argued, "has helped to destroy the concept of obscenity. By dissolving forms, it has left man free to move without reference, expressing dithyrambically whatever surges up from below. It is music not of dreams—certainly not of our metaphysical dream—but of drunkenness." He further stated that the chief devotees of jazz are "the young, and those persons, fairly numerous, it would seem, who take pleasure in the thought of bringing down our civilization."[81]

ROCK 'N' ROLL MUSIC

A half dozen years after Weaver's analysis of jazz, rock 'n' roll music appeared in 1954. Far more than jazz, it accented the sensual pleasures and was often accompanied by vice, for instance, as in heavy metal music. Rock 'n' roll began with Alan Freed, a Cleveland, Ohio, disk jockey, who "began playing 'race music'—rhythm and blues records made and bought by blacks—for the white teenagers of middle America."[82] That same year, Elvis Presley made his debut with his rock 'n' roll song called "That's All Right, Mama." Some of us remember that this number and other selections, such as "You Ain't Nothin' But a Hound Dog," caused a national stir in the mid–1950s. So uncomfortable were people, including the television media, with Presley's music and his physical gyrations that when he appeared on the *Ed Sullivan Show* in September of 1956, he was only shown from the waist up. Even so, the *New York Times* criticized this appearance because of Elvis's "gyrating figure and suggestive gestures." The writer of this piece also accused TV of being merely interested in making a "fast buck" while ignoring that Elvis's music sexually "overstimulated" teenagers.[83] When the author of this article spoke of Elvis sexually overstimulating teenagers, did he have in mind the original meaning of rock 'n' roll? That meaning, according to the *Rolling Stone Encyclopedia of Rock and Roll*, is a blues euphemism for sexual intercourse. In another article, the *New York Times* said that Presley had "no discernable singing ability" but that this did not seem to be a requirement for his audience of "squealing teenagers."[84] As one observer noted, "Rock and roll triggered a crisis in cultural authority."[85] If jazz had no need for intelligence, as one of its defenders once said, but only feeling, then rock 'n' roll music met this definition even more, because that is what aroused the teenagers when they heard Elvis's music.

Now, more than forty years after the arrival of rock music, it is heard on numerous radio stations, television channels, and compact disks; and millions of young people flock to hear rock concerts. A couple of observations are needed: The beauty and majesty once so artfully conveyed in sacred and secular music by Bach, Handel, Beethoven, Mozart, Stravinsky, and other great composers are totally absent in rock music. It is not music that lifts and inspires the human emotions, but rather music with a rebellious tone and beat. Four years after rock 'n' roll first was played by Alan Freed, a riot erupted in Boston at a rock concert that Freed had organized.[86] In the 1960s the consummate consumers of rock music—the youth of America—

rioted on many university campuses. Many observers say that rock 'n' roll music showed its propensity for the rebellious at Woodstock, New York, in 1969, where numerous rock music bands gathered before some quarter of a million rebellious youth who engaged in sex, drugs, and alcohol. Although Weaver's words about jazz being the music of young people and those who take pleasure in "bringing down our civilization" seem to be an overstatement in regard to jazz, they appear more accurate with reference to rock 'n' roll music, especially hard rock.

In the early 1980s the concerns of many accelerated as rock music performers introduced "heavy metal" rock, whose disseminators openly admitted that there were few moral restraints in either their music or their behavior. This admission corresponds with Martha Bayles's observation that heavy metal rock music is derived from "William S. Burrough's fictional celebration of pedophilia, sadomasochism, heroin addiction, and ritual murder."[87] Furthermore, it "regards itself as an abject failure if all hell *doesn't* break loose."[88] Thus, soon after the appearance of heavy metal rock music, the public heard "rock videos depicting female victims chained, caged, beaten, and bound with barbed wire, all to whet the appetites of twelve- and thirteen-year-olds for onstage performances."[89] Many may recall some of the sadistic songs of the rapper Ice-T—for instance, his outrageous "Cop Killer." The titles and lyrics of many other hit songs are too bizarre or barbaric to be cited here.

Indeed, heavy metal rock music and much of the music on MTV has become increasingly rebellious—rebelling against all Christian values, including sexual morality, human decency, the sanctity of life, human dignity, civilized language, and, of course, against the beauty and serenity of music itself. Behind the rebellion lies the rejection of God and his only begotten Son, Jesus Christ, who for centuries inspired great musicians to write music that raised the human spirit. It is its rebellious nature that has produced music that has a hole in its soul, as Martha Bayles says in her book, *Hole in Our Soul: The Loss of Beauty and Meaning in American Music* (1994). The real tragedy of rock music, especially its heavy metal type, is not that it has a hole in its soul, but that it has no soul at all.

SOFT ROCK MUSIC

It is tempting for those of us who love music by classical artists such as Bach, Beethoven, Mozart, Haydn, and others, or even traditional popular music, to see all rock music as of one genre, as Allan Bloom does in his

THE PROGRESS OF MUSIC DURING THE CHRISTIAN ERA

Monophonic music (pre-10th cent.)
—Ambrosian chant (late 4th cent.)
   —Antiphonal singing (late 4th cent.)
   —Congregational singing (late 4th cent.)
—Plainsong (4th cent.)
—Gregorian chant (late 6th cent.)

Polyphonic music (late 9th cent.)

Church operas (9th cent.)

Solmization (10th cent.)

Staff of four lines (10th cent.)

Motet (13th cent.)

Madrigal (14th cent.)

Anthem (16th cent.)

Oratorio (16th cent.)

Symphony (16th cent.)

Sonata (16th cent.)

Cantata (17th cent.)

Concerto (17th cent.)

Well-tempered scale (18th cent.)

Five-finger technique for keyboard instruments (18th cent.)

book, *Closing of the American Mind* (1987). He argues that "rock music has one appeal only, a barbaric appeal, to sexual desire—not love, not *eros,* but sexual desire undeveloped and untutored."[90] This definition certainly fits heavy metal and MTV music, but it does not quite do justice to what is called "soft rock." Although the lyrics are set to a rock beat, its music is gentle, not deafening, not sexual, not rebellious, not political, and not performed by males only.

To a large degree, soft rock has become today's popular music. Performers such as Sarah McLachlan, Celine Dion, Bruce Hornsby, Marty Robbins, Mariah Carey, and others perform music that still has a relatively wholesome quality, even though it has a rock beat. Also many country-western singers, such as Faith Hill, Mark Wells, and Shania Twain, set their lyrics to soft rock and thus are essentially following the tradition of popular music selections whose lyrics still speak about age-old problems of love and romance. In short, soft rock, unlike hard rock or heavy metal, is music without a rebellious attitude and can be used to God's glory.

"CHRISTIAN" ROCK

In light of the wide exposure that the mass media have given, and continues to give, to rock 'n' roll, together with the ever-present phenomenon of secularization, it seemed inevitable that rock music would someday invade Christian circles—and it did. Its users call it "Christian rock." Often it is also called "contemporary Christian music." Some of the popular bands or groups in 2000 were the Newsboys, Audio Adrenaline, Petra, MXPX, P.O.D (Payable on Death), and Jars of Clay. Many songs are also performed by individual singers such Michelle Tumes, Clay Crosse, Twila Paris, Michael Card, Amy Grant, and others. Some Christian rock songs have religious titles or themes while others focus only on love and romance. In regard to the latter, there often is little or no difference in the lyrics of these songs from those of non-Christian rock music. Even selections that have religious titles or themes often reflect a theology that indirectly praises humans rather than God. For example, one song ("Cartoons" by Chris Rice) says it is great to sing "praise in a whole new way."

Some of the Christian rock music, like secular rock, also plays notes of rebellion. A few years ago Undercover, a Christian punk rock group, took the well-known Christian hymn "Holy, Holy, Holy" and recorded it in speed rock form, greatly diminishing its sacred qualities.[91] By altering this widely sung hymn, the Undercover group displayed a form of rebellion. Still other Christian rock music sometimes faults (at times rightly) the institutional church of today for having forgotten the poor and the downtrodden. Such music is probably more accurately seen as a social critique than an example of rebellion, especially if we remember the early church's deep commitment to charity and compassion, as discussed in chapter 5.

Even Christian rock that is not rebellious—and much of it is not—still leaves much to be desired in terms of good Christian theology. Often little or nothing is said about the nature of God other than the fact that he loves people. But that God is Father, Son, and Holy Spirit is rarely heard, if at all, in Christian rock music. Many recordings speak about God's grace, but they do not say how man receives that grace. That God's grace in Christ comes through faith as heard from his Word is typically missing. Also, far too many selections accent people's subjective spiritual feelings, as singers note how they feel about God rather than how he felt about them as sinful beings whom he chose to redeem through the death and resurrection of his Son, Jesus Christ.

Finally, in considering Christian rock, one must ask whether its performers and those who listen to it are not conforming to the world, contrary to Romans 12:2, where St. Paul reminds Christians, "Do not conform any longer to the pattern of this world, but be transformed by the renewing of your mind. Then you will be able to test and approve what God's will is—his good, pleasing and perfect will." The following indicate that conforming to the world is definitely a part of many so-called Christian rock selections, for they sometimes present a worldly or even a blasphemous picture of God. Here are some examples. Robert Sweet of the now defunct Stryker band used to display the words "JESUS CHRIST ROCKS" on the back of his drummer chair. The Messiah Prophet Band has called Jesus Christ "the Master of Metal"; Petra has said that God is "the God of Rock and Roll," and Daniel Band plays a song called "Party in Heaven" that says, "There's a party in heaven/The bread is unleaven/The tree of life is growin' fine/It's past eleven/My number is seven/The Lamb and I are drinkin' new wine."[92]

CONCLUSION

For centuries both sacred and secular music in Western society, much of it written by Christians or by musicians influenced by Christianity, had a highly edifying effect on people. But with the continued growth of secularization and relativism, there has been a steep and rapid decline in the wholesomeness and beauty of music. Hence, one wonders what the future holds, especially since much current rock music, including heavy metal and rap music, not only has assumed a major role but is preempting and displacing wholesome music of the past. It is not an exaggeration to say that as far as the East is from the West, so far have hard rock musicians and their music moved from the goal that music should be performed "to the glory of God and the recreation of the mind."[93] Christian rock, although different than hard rock in some respects, also appears to be contributing to this displacement.

Western music attained its greatness because its composers, such as Ambrose, Bach, Handel, Mozart, Mendelssohn, Stravinsky, and Vaughan Williams, were inspired by Christ's life, death, and resurrection. Unlike the God-denying and morally defiant writers of hard rock music, who see human life as meaningless and absurd, musicians in the past knew that God existed and guided their lives. They believed that God willed their existence and that they were not biological flukes. Their lives had meaning, and their music resonated those convictions. That is why Bach, for instance, felt that all music, even his secular music, was "an expression of divinity."[94] In a great deal of rock music, especially hard rock, this noble conviction is not only totally absent but is often rebelled against as well.

From Christianity's earliest years and for centuries thereafter, Christian musicians gave beauty and majesty to Western music, even to secular pieces. They reflected the influence of Jesus Christ. As Donald Grout has said, "The history of Western art music properly begins with the music of the Christian Church."[95] Once the Christian influence no longer plays a significant role in the music of Western society, which is increasingly becoming the case, it will continue to deteriorate and sink to even baser levels. One is reminded of the Greek philosopher Plato who said, "Give me the songs of the nation and it matters not who writes its laws."

NOTES

1. Edward Dickinson, *The Study of the History of Music* (New York: Charles Scribner's Sons, 1937), 13.

2. Ralph Martin, *Worship in the Early Church* (Westwood, N.J.: Fleming H. Revell, 1964), 39.

3. Ruth Ellis Messenger, *Christian Hymns of the First Three Centuries* (Fort Worth: Hymn Society of America, 1942), 23.

4. Ibid., 24.

5. Louis F. Benson, *The Hymnody of the Christian Church* (New York: George H. Doran, 1927), 67.

6. Ruth Ellis Messenger, *Latin Hymns of the Middle Ages* (Fort Worth: Hymn Society of America, 1948), 2–3.

7. Paul Griffiths, "Opera," in *The Oxford Companion to Music,* ed. Denis Arnold (New York: Oxford University Press, 1983), 3:1291.

8. Basil Smallman, "Church Music," in *The Oxford Companion to Music,* 1:389.

9. Beekman C. Cannon, Alvin H. Johnson, and William G. White, *The Art of Music* (New York: Thomas Y. Crowell, 1960), 79.

10. James D. Kennedy and Jerry Newcombe, *What If Jesus Had Never Been Born?* (Nashville: Thomas Nelson, 1994), 182.

11. Marion Bauer, "Polyphony, Polyphonia," in *The International Cyclopedia of Music and Musicians,* ed. Oscar Thomas (New York: Dodd, Mead, 1964), 1656.

12. Henry Pleasants, *The Agony of Modern Music* (New York: Simon and Schuster, 1955), 97.

13. Jerome Roche, "Motet," in *The Oxford Companion to Music,* 2:1205.

14. Dickinson, *Study of the History of Music,* 65.

15. Edmund H. Fellowes, "Anthem," in *Grove's Dictionary of Music and Musicians,* ed. Eric Blom (New York: St. Martin's Press, 1966), 1:166.

16. Homer Ulrich and Paul A. Pisk, *A History of Music and Musical Style* (New York: Harcourt Brace Jovanovich, 1963), 264.

17. Paul Westermeyer, *Te Deum: The Church and Music* (Minneapolis: Fortress Press, 1998), 237.

18. Donald Grout, *A History of Western Music* (New York: W. W. Norton, 1973), 400.

19. I am indebted to Dr. John Behnke, a noteworthy musician at Concordia University, Mequon, Wisconsin, for the information regarding Zwingli's musical talent.

20. Westermeyer, *Te Deum,* 157.

21. Benson, *Hymnody of the Christian Church,* 80.

22. Doris Flexner, *The Optimist's Guide to History* (New York: Avon Books, 1995), 100.

23. Charles Sanford Terry, *Bach: A Biography* (London: Oxford University Press, 1928), 275.

24. Henry A. Simon, "Bach at Journey's End," *The Lutheran Witness* (July 2000): 15.

25. Gerhard Herz, "Bach's Religion," *Journal of Renaissance and Baroque Music* (June 1946): 128.

26. Patrick Kavanaugh, *Spiritual Lives of the Great Composers* (Grand Rapids: Zondervan, 1996), 20.

27. Kennedy and Newcombe, *What If Jesus Had Never Been Born?* 187.

28. Lawrence Dreyfus, *Bach and the Patterns of Invention* (Cambridge: Harvard University Press, 1996), 95.

29. Letter to Johann Klemm, in Karl Geiringer, *Johann Sebastian Bach: The Culmination of An Era* (New York: Oxford University Press, 1966), 87.

30. Kennedy and Newcombe, *What If Jesus Had Never Been Born?* 186.

31. Ibid., 185.

32. Kavanaugh, *Spiritual Lives,* 20.

33. Alfred Einstein, *A Short History of Music,* trans. Eric Blom (New York: Alfred A. Knopf, 1965), 137.

34. One such example is the recent article on Bach in the magazine *German Life* (April/May 2000).

35. Herbert Weinstock, *Handel* (New York: Alfred A. Knopf, 1959), 90.

36. Newman Flower, *George Frideric Handel: His Personality and His Times* (New York: Charles Scribner's Sons, 1948), 289.

37. Robert Turnbull, *Musical Genius and Religion* (London: S. Wellwood Publishers, 1907), 27: cited in Kavanaugh, *Spiritual Lives,* 32.

38. Kavanaugh, *Spiritual Lives,* 30.

39. Robert Manson Myers, *Handel's Messiah: A Touchstone of Taste* (New York: Macmillan, 1948), 238.

40. Ibid.

41. Henry Thomas and Dana Lee Thomas, *Living Biographies of Great Composers* (Garden City, N.Y.: Halcyon House, 1940), 54.

42. Maynard Solomon, *Mozart* (New York: Harper Collins, 1998), 31–33.

43. Friedrich Kerst, ed., *Mozart, the Man and the Artist Revealed in His Own Words,* trans. Henry Kriehbiel (New York: Dover, 1965), 98.

44. Kavanaugh, *Spiritual Lives,* 51.

45. Otto Jahn, *Life of Mozart,* trans. Pauline D. Townsend (New York: Cooper Square, 1970), 3:391.

46. Edouard Herriot, *The Life and Times of Beethoven,* trans. Adelheid Mitchell and William Mitchell (New York: Macmillan, 1935), 31.

47. Philip Kruseman, *Beethoven's Own Words* (London: Hinricksen Edition, 1947), 53.

48. "Beethoven's Last Hours," in Paul Nettl, *The Book of Musical Documents* (New York: Philosophical Library, 1948), 197.

49. Yehudi Menuhin and Curtis W. Davis, *The Music of Man* (New York: Methuen, 1979), 148.

50. Kavanaugh, *Spiritual Lives,* 77–78.

51. Paul Henry Lang, *Music in Western History* (New York: W. W. Norton, 1941), 513.

52. Herbert Kupferberg, *The Mendelssohns: Three Generations of Genius* (New York: Charles Scribner's Sons, 1972), 130.

53. Curt Sachs, *Our Musical Heritage: A Short History of Music* (Englewood Cliffs, N.J.: Prentice-Hall, 1955), 277.

54. Kavanaugh, *Spiritual Lives,* 40.

55. Neil Butterworth, *Haydn: His Life and Times* (Tunbridge Wells, England: Midas Books, 1977), 122.

56. Alfred Einstein, *Schubert: A Musical Biography* (New York: Oxford University Press, 1951), 312.

57. Kavanaugh, *Spiritual Lives,* 71.

58. Erwin L. Lueker, *Lutheran Cyclopedia* (St. Louis: Concordia Publishing House, 1954), 153.

59. Kavanaugh, *Spiritual Lives,* 144.

60. Lueker, *Lutheran Cyclopedia,* 152.

61. Celia Newbery, ed., *Vaughan Williams in Dorking* (Dorking, England: Local History Group, 1979), 20.

62. Ursula Vaughan Williams, *R.V.W: A Biography of Ralph Vaughan Williams* (New York: Oxford University Press, 1964), 29.

63. Newbery, *Vaughan Williams in Dorking,* 20.

64. Byron Adams, "Scripture, Church, and Culture: Biblical Texts in the Works of Ralph Vaughan Williams," in *Vaughan Williams Studies,* ed. Alain Frogley (New York: Cambridge University Press, 1996), 101.

65. Williams, *R.V.W.,* 29.

66. Kavanaugh, *Spiritual Lives,* 186.

67. Igor Stravinsky and Robert Craft, *Conversation with Igor Stravinsky* (Berkeley: University of California Press, 1960), 125.

68. Eric Walter White, *Stravinsky: The Composer and His Works* (Berkeley: University of California Press, 1966), 378.

69. Fred L. Precht, *Lutheran Worship: Hymnal Companion* (St. Louis: Concordia Publishing House, 1992), 317.

70. W. G. Polack, *The Handbook to the Lutheran Hymnal* (St. Louis: Concordia Publishing House, 1942), 194.

71. Ernest Edwin Ryden, *The Story of Our Hymns* (Rock Island, Ill.: Augustana Book Concern, 1930), 82, 83.

72. James Mearns, "Rinckart, Martin," in *A Dictionary of Hymnology* (London: John Murray, 1905), 962.

73. Ryden, *Story of Our Hymns,* 83.

74. Colonel Nicholas Smith, *Hymns: History of Famous Hymns* (Chicago: Advance Publishing, 1901), 46.

75. Precht, *Lutheran Worship,* 198.

76. Ibid., 77.

77. Ibid.

78. Friedrich Blume, *Renaissance and Baroque Music: A Comprehensive Survey,* trans. M. D. Herter Norton (New York: W. W. Norton, 1967), 157.

79. Ulrich Homer and Paul A. Risk, *A History of Music and Musical Style* (New York: Harcourt Brace Jovanovich, 1963), 635.

80. Stravinsky and Craft, *Conversation,* 124.

81. Richard M. Weaver, *Ideas Have Consequences* (Chicago: University of Chicago Press, 1948), 86.

82. Janet Podell, "The Birth of Rock and Roll," *Rock Music in America* (New York: H. W. Wilson, 1987), 7.

83. Jack Gould, "Elvis Presley: Lack of Responsibility Is Shown by TV in Exploiting Teen-Agers," *New York Times,* 16 September 1956, X13.

84. Jack Gould, "Elvis Presley Rises to Fame as Vocalist Who Is Virtuoso of Hootchy-Kootchy," *New York Times,* 6 June 1956, 66.

85. Robert Walser, "The Rock and Roll Era," in *The Cambridge History of American Music,* ed. David Nichols (Cambridge, England: Cambridge University Press, 1998), 357.

86. Martha Bayles, *Hole in Our Soul: The Loss of Beauty and Meaning in American Music* (New York: Free Press, 1994), 43.

87. Ibid., 247.

88. Ibid., 259.

89. Ibid., 254.

90. Allan Bloom, *The Closing of the American Mind* (Chicago: University of Chicago Press, 1987), 73.

91. Jay R. Howard, "Contemporary Christian Music: Where Rock Meets Religion," *Journal of Popular Culture* (Summer 1992): 128.

92. David Cloud, "Does Jesus Groove to Rock Music?" *The Christian News,* 24 July 24 2000, 18.

93. Cited by Harold C. Schonberg, *The Lives of Great Composers* (New York: W. W. Norton, 1997), 37.

94. Ibid., 6.

95. Grout, *History of Western Music,* 2.

14

HALLMARKS of LITERATURE: THEIR CHRISTIAN IMPRINT

"Literature is the thought of thinking souls."

Thomas Carlyle

T he selected hallmarks of literature that are briefly described in this chapter have for decades been required or recommended reading in higher education. Although not all of the selections are Christian literature per se, and while some were written by non-Christian authors, they all reveal definite Christian imprints. While these influences can be ignored, it would be difficult to argue that these works were not shaped by Christian teachings, either directly or indirectly. In fact, they would not have been authored had Christ not come down from heaven and walked the dusty roads of Palestine. Thus, out of a large number of books penned in Western society over a period of fifteen hundred years, the works described below were chosen because they address a variety of ever-present human concerns from which the authors could not withhold the Christian perspective, whether it was theirs or their society's.

Christians have always believed, taught, and confessed that in Jesus Christ "the Word became flesh" (John 1:14), and that through the spoken or written word, the gospel of his redemptive work is imparted to people. It was this Christian conviction that produced the New Testament. And after the New Testament books were written, numerous other Christian writings appeared to spread the good news of Jesus Christ.

LITERATURE IN THE EARLY CHURCH

Post-New Testament literature, written between A.D. 100 and the mid-fourth century, can be classified as exhortational, polemical, and apologetic. By the early Middle Ages Christian authors addressed other topics as well.

EXHORTATIONAL WRITINGS

Since the early Christians were widely and frequently persecuted during the church's first three centuries, some of the first writings, which appeared after the New Testament books were authored, exhorted them to cling to Jesus Christ. *The Epistle of Barnabas* (written about A.D. 130) was largely directed toward this end; it urged Christians not to lapse into law-oriented Judaistic teachings. Some writings also exhorted the believers to live God-pleasing lives. Clement of Rome (d. A.D. 97), in his *Epistle to the Corinthians,* implored Christians to heal the schisms that existed among them. *The Shepherd of Hermas* (ca. A.D. 120–150) exhorted Christians to live a life of constant repentance and not to forget who they were in their daily activities. The *Didache* (The Teaching of the Twelve), written between about A.D. 85 and 110, exhorted and instructed the early believers in the basic elements of the Christian faith. The writings of Polycarp (martyred in A.D. 156) reminded Christians that their faith must always adhere to the death and resurrection of Jesus Christ and that Christ is to be adored as God. *Pedagogus* (The Teacher), written around A.D. 200 by Clement of Alexandria, exhorted the believers to adhere to the teachings of Jesus Christ. The prolific writer Tertullian (d. ca. A.D. 220), whose writings focused on several subjects, also admonished Christians with regard to moral living. For example, he taught that marriage was indissoluble. Cyril of Jerusalem (fourth century) in his *Catechetical Lectures* spelled out what individuals needed to learn and believe doctrinally in order to become members of the church, and he exhorted them to live morally upright lives.

POLEMICAL WRITINGS

The Apostle Paul predicted to Timothy, his co-worker, that "the time will come when men [within the church] will not put up with sound doctrine. Instead, to suit their own desires, they will gather around them a great number of teachers to say what their itching ears want to hear. They will turn their ears away from the truth and turn aside to myths" (2 Timothy 4:3–4). Christians, he said, would need to "fight the good fight of the faith" (1 Timothy 6:12). Paul was right. False teachers soon entered the church, espousing heretical doctrines that were disseminated in a variety of writings. Thus, a tradition of polemical writing was born—disputations and refutations of religious and often controversial principle and practice.

One of the first false doctrines promoted was Gnosticism. Although parading as Christians, gnostics taught that salvation was attainable through special, esoteric knowledge, apart from the inspired Scriptures of the Old Testament prophets and New Testament apostles. The written or spoken word of the Old Testament and the apostolic writings of the New Testament were largely rejected. Gnostics also denied the incarnation and the physical resurrection of Jesus Christ because to them matter was evil, and thus Jesus, if divine, could not have assumed a material human body.

The first and most eloquent opponent of Gnosticism was Irenaeus (ca. 120–203), who became bishop of Lyons, France, after Bishop Pothinus was martyred in that city's intense persecution of numerous Christians in 177. Irenaeus attacked the gnostic teachings in his *Adversus haereses* (Against Heresies) in which he argued that Gnosticism uprooted the fundamental Christian teachings and that this heresy essentially sought to revive pagan religion and philosophy in Christian mask. His book urged all Christians to reject gnostic teachings.

Another powerful writer and rhetorician in the early church was Lactantius (d. ca. 330). He bravely defended the Christian faith, for when Emperor Diocletian unleashed the "Great Persecution," he had the courage to write *The Divine Institutes,* a polemical and apologetic work. This persecution essentially lasted from 293 to 311, during which time all Christians were purged from the military; some were imprisoned, tortured, and executed; churches and the sacred Scriptures were systematically burned. Lactantius spoke out against the worship of false gods and against false teachings and the false wisdom of the pagan philosophers. Known as the "Christian Cicero," he so impressed Constantine the Great that he was retained to teach Constantine's son Crispus.

In 325 the Christian church took a polemical position when it convened its first ecumenical council at Nicaea, where it formulated the Nicene Creed, rejecting the teachings of Arius, who taught that Jesus Christ was not God but merely the son of God. The Arian heresy lingered for many years.

Athanasius (ca. 295–373), whose persuasive influence at the Council of Nicaea helped the orthodox Christians overrule the Arian party, wrote a polemical work known as *Discourses Against the Arians.*

APOLOGETIC WRITINGS

Some of the early Christian writers took an apologetic tack, defending the Christian faith and its teachings. These writings urged the believers not to fall prey to the various attacks voiced by the skeptics and mockers. As early as about A.D. 120, *The Apology of Aristides on Behalf of Christians* appeared. Addressing the Emperor Hadrian, Aristides argued that the Christian concepts of God and of morality were superior to the religion of the pagans. He further stated that religious truth was not attainable in the teachings of the barbarians, the Greeks, or the Jews, but only in Jesus Christ. Justin Martyr (ca. 110–165) composed two apologetic works in addition to his *Dialog with the Jew Trypho.* He maintained that Christ was the only true Logos (Word) and that Christians were unjustly persecuted.

The lay philosopher Athenagorus (second half of the second century), in *A Plea for the Christians,* defended Christians, saying that they were loyal citizens, not atheists, to counter the accusation often levied against them. Minucius Felix, a Christian lawyer, authored *Octavius* (ca. A.D. 200). He countered the arguments of Caecilius, a pagan, by showing that Christianity was not foolish, unpatriotic, or incestuous. And in the first decade of the third century, the Latin church father Tertullian penned his eloquent *Apology,* in which he defended his fellow Christians for opposing the pagan practices of Rome.

Moving from northern Africa, where Tertullian defended the Christian faith, we find Origen (d. ca. 254) in the East, who in his many writings also defended Christianity. His *Contra Celsum,* a detailed defense of Christianity against the vocal critic and pagan skeptic Celsus, is the most notable. In his learned manner, Origen argued that Christianity was not barbaric, childish, low class, or treasonable, nor was it a religion mostly for women (a common Roman sneer).

Another strong apologist who exerted considerable influence on the Christian church was St. Jerome (ca. 342–420). In his book *Concerning Illustrious Men,* he marshaled a wide array of prominent Christian orators, writers, philosophers, and scholars to show that Christians had reached a cultural level superior to that of the Greco-Romans. The book also helped establish an early confidence among Christians as they increasingly assumed leadership roles

EUSEBIUS, the fourth-century church historian, wrote the classical work *Ecclesiastical History*.

in society not long after three hundred years of persecution had come to an end. Jerome's work underwent numerous editions, especially from the fifteenth and to the nineteenth centuries.[1]

While Jerome was in the East (Palestine), a contemporary of his, St. Augustine (354–430), served the church in northern Africa. After living a pagan, sensual life during his youth and early adult years, he was converted to Christianity at age thirty-two. The prayers of Augustine's mother, Monica, were finally answered. After he became a Christian, his brilliant mind assimilated all aspects of Christian theology, which he then made known to the church at large through his many published writings. His many works expounded on a variety of Christian doctrines. Some were exegetical expositions of Scripture; some were designed to educate; others were apologetic. His most famous work is *De civitate Dei (The City of God)*, completed in 426. Although this book is primarily an apologetic treatise and thus could appropriately be discussed here, it is discussed in the next section.

Whether the Christian writings were exhortational, polemical, or apologetic, they had the effect of not only reinforcing the faith of the readers but also inspiring Christians to serve God and their fellow human beings in the life of society. These writings, as well as many others too numerous to mention, buoyed and bolstered the spirit behind Christian charity and compassion that aided and astounded even the pagans, as described in chapter 5.

SOME LITERARY HALLMARKS: EARLY MIDDLE AGES TO 2000

The early Middle Ages are commonly thought to have begun at about the time of St. Augustine and St. Jerome, late fourth century. Following the earthly departure of these two scholars, Christianity had an ever-growing number of theologians, philosophers, poets, and others who wrote treatises and monographs that reflected the influence of their Christian faith and values. What follows is a selection of literary masterpieces that reveal not only their Christian influences but also the contributions they made to the world of literature.

ECCLESIASTICAL HISTORY

Although Eusebius (ca. 280–339) technically antedates the early Middle Ages by several decades, his *Ecclesiastical History* is nonetheless relevant to the Middle Ages. Without this work we not only would know very little about the many significant events that transpired in the church's first three hundred years, but we would also understand considerably less regarding the later life of the church in the Middle Ages.

To be sure, Eusebius's *Ecclesiastical History* is not equal to the scholarly historical writings of today's trained historians. Nevertheless, it is an outstanding work for which the author is rightly called "the Christian Herodotus." The vast number of historical details and characters chronicled and discussed in this work are truly astounding, given the extremely limited means of collecting data and information available to Eusebius in the early fourth century. The work is a major contribution to the discipline of history.

THE CITY OF GOD

The first half of this highly significant work, authored in the early fifth century by St. Augustine, boldly critiques the pagan gods as false and useless. It also asserts that Christians are not to be blamed for weakening the Roman Empire, making it possible for the Goths to sack Rome in 410. The second half of the work introduces the concept of two "cities": the City of

God and the City of Man. The former is characterized by self-sacrifice, obe-dience, and humility; the latter by pride, selfishness, and personal ambition. The two cities are in constant conflict, and the Christian lives in both. The struggle between the two cities provides the content of history. Contrary to the Roman view, history has meaning, says Augustine, because God is the Lord and pedagogue of history; and as a consequence, Christians can, in part, discern God's will in the events of history. To Augustine history is not, as Henry Ford once said, "more or less bunk."[2]

"*The City of God,*" says one scholar, "is one of the most important books ever written. It is the classic statement of the Christian philosophy of life and understanding of history."[3] It has been called "the Charter of Christendom." Over the years, more copies of it have been published than any other book except the Bible.[4] And the fact that the work has for years been one of the titles in Encyclopedia Britannica's *Great Books of the Western World* is proof of its value to Western literature.

AN ECCLESIASTICAL HISTORY OF THE ENGLISH NATION

This work, written by St. Bede (673–735), "the Venerable Bede," an erudite English monk, was completed in 731. It is a masterpiece for at least three reasons. First, it provided the first useful history of the Christian church in England of the Middle Ages. One analyst says this work "will probably continue to stand in the first rank of literary works because of its simple, unaffected style, and its sure handling of the picturesque and the dramatic."[5] Second, the work introduced the science of historiography. And third, it was the first to use the expression *anno ab incarnatione Domini* (after the Lord's incarnation) with reference to the occurrence of some event. With this precedent, historians abbreviated the Latin phrase as A.D. The abbreviation of B.C., counting back from the birth of Christ, however, did not come into use until the seventeenth century.[6]

By dating an event as having occurred *anno Domini,* St. Bede was indebted to Dionysius Exiguus (d. 544), an abbot, a mathematician, and a canon lawyer from Scythia (modern Moldavia), who in 532 proposed to the pope that the chronology of the calendar be revised by using Christ's birth as the new reckoning of time.[7] When Exiguus introduced his new chronology, he calculated that Christ was born December 25 in the Roman year of 753 A.U.C. (*ab urbe condita:* from the founding of the city [Rome]). Thus one week later, January 1, which would have been 754 A.U.C., became year 1. Although Exiguus miscalculated Christ's birth by four to six years too late, his system of reckoning time, together with Bede's innovation, both of which were incorporated into the Gregorian calendar in the sixteenth century, are now used for commercial and travel purposes throughout the world. The Chinese, Israelis, and others may celebrate their new year on dates other than January 1, but in their daily standards of recording time they use the dating system of Bede and Exiguus.

RHETORIC AND VIRTUE

In the eighth century England produced another highly educated man, similar to the Venerable Bede, in the person of Alcuin (735–804). He toiled fervently to convert pagans with the gospel of Christ rather than by force. Recognizing his intellectual talents, Charlemagne recruited him from the city of York to the Continent to reform and expand education in the Holy Roman Empire, Europe. In the early 790s Alcuin wrote *Rhetoric and Virtue*, a work that provided Western society's Latin language with standards for rhetoric and writing. "For centuries," says one scholar, "rhetoric, as taught by Alcuin and developed and modified by later educators, influenced not only the art of speaking, but the writing of letters, petitions, legal documents, and other forms in which Western Europeans have expressed and transmitted their ideas."[8]

OPUS MAJUS (MAJOR WORK)

Behind this lackluster title lies an immense amount of profound learning and knowledge, some of it radically new. Its author was the gifted Franciscan monk Roger Bacon (1214–94) from Oxford, England. Many historians believe Bacon was the most learned Christian man of the Middle Ages. In *Opus majus* he discusses the causes of error and the importance of studying foreign languages, philosophy, optical science, experimental science, and moral philosophy. Although Bacon was partly indebted to his teacher, Bishop Robert Grosseteste, the major significance of *Opus majus* lies in its being the first serious, formal publication to argue that knowledge of the natural world needs to be acquired by the use of empirical methodology, that is, by using inductive procedures rather than by the deductive thinking that was common to the Greek philosophers and also to the scholastics within the church.

Being a sincere Christian, he never subordinated the Scriptures to his thinking, even though he believed that the empirical method (discussed in chapter 9) was the best way to learn about God's created world. Today modern science takes for granted the empirical method advocated in Bacon's *Opus magus*. Thus, the world received a major contribution from a highly gifted Christian thinker.

THE DIVINE COMEDY

A generation ago, nearly every graduate from a reputable liberal arts college was required to read Dante Alighieri's *Divine Comedy* (written in about 1321). Today, however, professors who seek to be politically correct often omit this work from what they derisively call the "Canon" of Western literature. Political correctness not withstanding, the *Divine Comedy* is one of the classic works of art and communication in Western culture. It "has survived in a large number of MSS [manuscripts], been the subject of commentaries from an early date, been widely translated, and has exercised a deep influence, especially on nineteenth century English literature and art."[9]

One may be critical of some of Dante's (1265–1321) medieval Catholic beliefs, for example, his portrayal of purgatory, which has no biblical basis. But as a whole this allegorical drama provides a vivid portrait of how medieval Christians viewed hell, purgatory, and heaven. It also reveals how man's spiritual journey takes him through the dark woods of life, bringing to mind the biblical words that all Christians "must go through many hardships to enter the kingdom of God" (Acts 14:22). And since the West has for centuries identified itself with Christianity, and also in some way with Dante's experience portrayed in the *Divine Comedy*, this work has appropriately been included in the *Great Books of the Western World*.

THE CANTERBURY TALES

Many of us can recall having to read in college or university the intriguing *Canterbury Tales* as told by a variety of individuals whom Geoffrey Chaucer (ca. 1343–1400) calls "pilgrims." He chose twenty-nine individuals from various walks of life, including a priest, two nuns, a miller, a knight, the wife of Bath, and a seller of indulgences, to travel from London to the shrine of St. Thomas Becket in Canterbury. To occupy the time while traveling, each pilgrim was to tell four stories, two on the way there and two on the way back.

Although Chaucer, a Christian, reveals in this poem that not all was well in the organized church of the Middle Ages, he never rejects its basic doctrines. He portrays the character of the Monk as one who loved hunting game more than his religious duties, but he does not reject or castigate monasteries. The Wife of Bath, who has her fifth husband, relates the joys and sorrows of married life, but Chaucer does not have her reject the church's teaching on the importance of marriage. In charity, he even seems to tolerate the selling of indulgences, for he has the Pardoner tell his tale about how he cajoles people into buying fake relics. In spite of these and other problems that sinful people and an imperfect church frequently display, Chaucer in essence tells his readers that one does not throw out the proverbial baby with the bath water. Indeed, he ends his poem by having the Parson give a sermon on the Seven Deadly Sins. Finally, if the "retraction" at the poem's end is authentically Chaucer's, he repents for having written his tales. But even if this last part is not by Chaucer—and it likely is not—the poem as a whole underscores rather than rejects the importance of Christian theology.

Chaucer's work has been praised for having introduced the pentameter couplet that later became "the favorite metrical form for English narrative poetry."[10] Once again we see that the spirit and influence of Christ not only produced a gifted writer with keen Christian insights in a period of time that some have called the "Dark Ages," but also one who made a lasting contribution to the field of English literature. So great is his contribution that G. K. Chesterton argued that Chaucer's Prologue to *The Canterbury Tales* is "the Prologue of Modern Fiction."[11]

THE PRAISE OF FOLLY

Written by the learned humanist Desiderius Erasmus (1466–1536) in 1511, *The Praise of Folly* is both a satire and an irony, revealed by Folly herself, not wisdom, who reveals human follies. The book argues that all people, regardless of their position in society, are given to folly, that is, foolishness, in everything they do. Erasmus, a priest who never functioned as one but spent his life in scholarly pursuits, exposes the foolish pretensions of the common populace as well as of learned and high-ranking people. He faults the priests, the monks, the bishops, the cardinals, and the popes for their pomp, selfishness, and worldliness; and he exposes the pretensions of titles with which its various holders are so greatly enamored.

Erasmus's exposure of the serious corruption of the church's leadership brought him close to being condemned as a heretic, a verdict that he managed to avoid, largely because he was a weak-kneed and timid soul. He took no action to correct the ecclesiastical corruption that went far beyond the ordinary follies of mankind. He lacked the spiritual fortitude of his contemporary, Martin Luther, who, it has been said, hatched the egg that Erasmus laid.

The Praise of Folly has gone through hundreds of editions. For nearly five hundred years it has conveyed a powerful message. It subtly restates the

ERASMUS, the Dutch scholar and philosopher, published *The Praise of Folly* in 1509. *(Holbein)*

biblical doctrine of the fallen nature of man, which humans so easily forget. The book reminds us of man's persistent, endemic follies that are by-products of a fallen world, a universal truth that makes it a masterpiece of Christian literature.

AN OPEN LETTER TO THE CHRISTIAN NOBILITY

Martin Luther (1483–1546) wrote this treatise when his struggle with his opponents in the Roman Catholic Church was most intense. Of the numerous tomes that he penned, this is by many considered his greatest work. Published in June 1520, the book appeared six months before Luther in December burned the pope's bull, *Exsurge Domine*, which formally excommunicated him in January 1521.

Luther argued that every baptized Christian was part of God's "royal priesthood," as spelled out in 1 Peter 2:9. Every baptized Christian, not just a priest, was "as truly a priest as though all bishops and popes had consecrated him." And he further added that "whoever comes out of the water of baptism can boast that he is already consecrated priest, bishop, pope, though it is not seemly that everyone should exercise the office."[12] Moreover, the sacred Scriptures, said Luther, know nothing of a pope as head of the church or as having authority over the temporal realm. Thus, the *Open Letter* asked the princes and other civic leaders to rule and govern as lay Christians, apart from the pope or the church, and further asserted that church authorities were to confine themselves entirely to the spiritual realm by not assuming roles of secular government. Christian values, to be sure, were to be operative in government; but they were to be exercised only through the efforts of individual Christians.

Historians credit the *Open Letter* with introducing the modern concept of the separation of church and state. Although Luther can in part be credited for this idea, it needs to be remembered that he merely repeated (as noted in chapter 10) what Jesus had said to the Pharisees fifteen hundred years earlier, namely, that there were two realms, Caesar's and God's. The *Open Letter*, which abounds with biblical references in support of Luther's arguments, provides powerful evidence that the words and spirit of Jesus Christ not only shaped Luther's thinking but also influenced modern governments of the Western world to become responsive to the voice of the people. This influence makes this work a noteworthy addition to the canon of Western literature.

THE AUGSBURG CONFESSION

Ten years after Luther's *Open Letter*, another hallmark of Western literature came to the fore. Although Luther had already been excommunicated and declared a heretic and an outlaw at the Diet of Worms in 1521, one more attempt was made by Emperor Charles V to conciliate the differences between the Protestants (primarily the Lutherans) and the Church of Rome. The emperor wanted to keep the empire united for political reasons, to ward off the Turks who had already gained a foothold in what is now Bosnia and Kosovo. So he summoned an imperial diet to convene in Augsburg, Germany. It included princes (electors) of territories and representatives from free cities within the empire. The elector of Saxony asked the theologians from the University of Wittenberg to prepare a statement of the beliefs and practices of the churches that sided with Luther.

The formal presentation of the Lutheran position at the diet became known as the *Augsburg Confession*. It was signed by a number of princes on June 25, 1530. While this conciliatory document sought to emphasize the agreements that existed between the Church of Rome and the Lutherans, it was nevertheless rejected by the Catholic constituency. The breach or schism was not mended, and the *Augsburg Confession* became a landmark in annals of historical Christian literature. It gave formal birth to the Lutheran church; it lent organizational support to the arguments of Luther's *Open Letter* and other Lutheran documents; and its adherents were now formally called "Protestants," a term first applied primarily to Lutherans in 1529.

UTOPIA

Many books and articles have cited *Utopia* by Thomas More (1478–1535), first published in 1551, comparing it to *The Republic* by the Greek philosopher Plato, who actually advocated the implementation of a utopian society. This is a false comparison, for More knew that the Greek word *utopia* meant "no such place." Hence, his book does not propose a heaven-on-earth social world, but it is really a fable mocking utopian thinking rather than providing a blueprint for actual implementation. However, this has not stopped many socialists and communists from pointing to this book as an inspiration or model for a new society.

If More did not intend for *Utopia* to be understood as advocating a society that would have all things in common, then what did he intend? This question has produced much debate, and that is in part what has made his work so intellectually desirable to many in the field of literature. While the real answer may never be known conclusively, one can with good reason argue that More, a Christian with a strong social conscience, wanted to draw attention to the corruption that his society practiced economically and socially, rather than to propose a perfect society. As one commentator has observed, "He knew. . .that the roots of evil run far too deep in men to be destroyed by a mere rearrangement of the economic organization of society."[13] Thus, this book, like *The Praise of Folly*, is another attempt to remind readers, who at the time of its publication were all members of the Christian church, that they must never underestimate the sinful nature of human beings and its many harmful effects. This reminder is as relevant today as it was in the sixteenth century, and that is undoubtedly why it is still one of the *Great Books of the Western World*.

THE INSTITUTES OF THE CHRISTIAN RELIGION

John Calvin (1509–64), a French lay theologian aroused by the persecution of the Reformed Protestants (Huguenots) in France, published a small treatise of six chapters in 1536 on behalf of the Protestants that he titled *The Institutes of the Christian Religion*. By 1559 this work had grown to seventy-nine chapters. Written in a readable style, it covers the basic Christian doctrines.

The Institutes has had a prominent influence on a large segment of the non-Lutheran Protestants, especially in America. Calvin's theology not only permeated much of the thinking of many Protestant denominations in the Western world, but it also influenced a great deal of the thinking of the Founding Fathers of the United States. Hippolyte Taine, a non-Christian French historian, said that the followers of Calvin "founded the United States."[14] George Bancroft, the American historian, remarked, "He who will not honor the memory and respect the influence of Calvin knows but little of the origin of American liberty."[15] Others have made similar observations.

The Calvinistic imprints on America are not only evident in the political philosophy that led to the War of Independence, the formation of the Constitution, and the Federalist Papers, but they also underlie America's concept of a republic, a government of duly elected representatives with no regal authority above them. This type of government was already well established in the American Protestant churches long before 1776, especially among Congregationalists and Presbyterians. Loraine Boettner is correct in saying that "Calvinism has been the chief source of [the American] republican government."[16] James Kennedy and Jerry Newcombe maintain that "Calvinism and republicanism are related to each other as cause and effect."[17] Indeed, much of the Calvinistic influence in America comes from Calvin's *Institutes*.

ASTRONOMIA NOVA (THE NEW ASTRONOMY)

Briefly noted in chapter 9 in regard to the development of science, *Astronomia nova* was published in 1609. It is the magnum opus of Johannes Kepler (1571–1630), a devout Christian and prominent scientist. The book states and discusses two laws without which present-day astronomy would not exist. The first law states that planets orbit elliptically rather than in a circular motion. This discovery jettisoned the revered theory that planets move in perfect circles, a theory that even Galileo, a contemporary of Kepler's, continued to believe. The second law says that planets do not

358

"I SAW A MAN CLOTHED WITH RAGS" portrays a view of the Christian Pilgrim in *The Pilgrim's Progress*, written by John Bunyan while he was in prison in 1675. *(Engraving by Frederick Barnard)*

move at a uniform speed in their orbits, that they move faster when they are closer to the sun.

Kepler's laws are "a landmark in history. They were the first 'natural laws' in the modern sense: precise, verifiable statements about the universal relations governing particular phenomena, expressed in mathematical terms."[18] Being the serious-minded Christian that he was, Kepler, who had nearly completed his theological studies for the Lutheran ministry before he began his astronomy research, believed that nothing in nature existed without God's having a plan for it. Hence, he concluded that there must be a geometrical structure in the universe that accounted for the stars and planets and their relative distance from the sun.[19] This hypothesis led him, in 1618, to discover his third law, sometimes called the harmonic law. It states that the squares of the periods of the revolution of any two planets around the sun are proportional to the cubes of their mean distances from the sun.

Scientists rank *The New Astronomy* as one of the major publications in the literature of science. The Harvard astronomer Owen Gingerich has said that "Kepler's *Astronomia Nova* of 1609 revolutionized celestial physics."[20] Whether it was the findings in this seminal work, or his other discoveries, he believed they were all the result of God's providence and guidance.[21] If ever there was a scientific work that uninhibitedly admitted the powerful influence that Christian beliefs had in motivating and directing one's scientific research, *The New Astronomy* is most definitely it.

THE PILGRIM'S PROGRESS

This classic work by John Bunyan (1628–88), a self-taught Puritan preacher and writer of religious prose, has stirred the spiritual emotions of readers for generations. Written while Bunyan was imprisoned for his religious beliefs, *Pilgrim's Progress* portrays a lonely pilgrim named Christian, who travels from the City of Destruction to the Celestial City. As he travels, he encounters numerous difficulties. He falls into the Slough of Despond; he comes to the Hill of Difficulty; he enters the grounds of the Doubting Castle, where he wonders whether Christianity is true or not. Here every follower of Christ can identify with the pilgrim. This is but one example of why *Pilgrim's Progress* is a classic of Christian literature. As one observer has said, "*The Pilgrim's Progress* is a book which, when once read, can never be forgotten. We too, every one of us, are pilgrims on the same road, and images and illustrations come back upon us from so faithful an itinerary, as we encounter similar trials, and learn for ourselves the accuracy with which Bunyan has described them."[22] Obviously, Bunyan's allegorical story of Christianity's plan of salvation was primarily written for Christian readers. The names of the book's many characters—Sloth, Presumption, Hypocrisy, Faith, Hope, Envy, Mr. Hate-light, Mr. Cruelty, Mr. Love-lust, Mr. Liar, Hopeful, Little-faith, and others—convey powerful messages to Christians. For three hundred years this work has enlightened countless Christians, great numbers of whom have been college and university students. It has been translated into virtually every language, another evidence of its great appeal. Unfortunately, *The Pilgrim's Progress* is today excluded from many college and university curricula because it is seen as part of the "Western Canon."

PARADISE LOST

Composed by John Milton (1608–74) in 1667, this poem has been called the greatest poem in the English language. *Paradise Lost* presents the biblical account of the devil and his evil angels having been cast out of heaven along with the fall into sin by Adam and Eve in the Garden of Eden, hence its title. It also seriously portrays death as the result of man's fall into sin, the reality of heaven and hell, the Archangel Michael's message of the coming of the Messiah (Christ) to redeem man, the incarnation of God in Jesus Christ, the resurrection of Christ, and Christ's ascension to heaven.

While Milton underscores the basic doctrines of Christianity, he also reveals his concern for the continuing consequences of man's fall in everyday life. Some argue that it is the latter that is Milton's ultimate point in *Paradise Lost.*[23] If this is Milton's main point, as it appears to be, then he has made a major contribution in reminding us that man's expulsion from Paradise and its dire consequences are ever with us.

PENSÉES (THOUGHTS ON RELIGION)

Pensées (mentioned briefly in chapter 9) first appeared in 1670, eight years after its author, Blaise Pascal (1623–62) died. It is the product of a brilliant French philosopher who, in today's secular society, is more frequently known for his mathematical and scientific achievements than for his work in Christian theology. *Pensées* is a collection of notes that Pascal made in preparation for a book on the merits of Christian theology. It consists of fragmented comments, some of them several paragraphs long and others merely short sentences. Throughout this edited work, Pascal consistently defends the Christian faith, using rigorous logic and biblical citations as his main weapons.

"It is not only impossible but useless to know God without Jesus Christ,"[24] he boldly states. And, he asserts, "Without Jesus Christ the world would not exist; for it should needs be either that it would be destroyed or be a hell."[25] Pascal also argued that he would rather believe the writings of the apostles, who died for their testimony, than the words of those who did not: "I believe only the histories of witnesses who got themselves killed."[26] And he once said, "I would have far more fear of being mistaken, and of finding that the Christian religion was true, than of not being mistaken in believing it true."[27] This has come to be known as Pascal's Wager. Expressed another way, the wager says, "If I believe Christianity is true and it turns out to be false, I have lost nothing, but if I believe it to be false and it turns out to be true, I have lost everything."

THE WEALTH OF NATIONS

In 1776, one year after the American War of Independence broke out, a Scottish professor who taught Christian moral philosophy at the

University of Glasgow, wrote a book that had profound effects on the political economy of the Western world. The author was Adam Smith (1723–90), and the book was *The Wealth of Nations*. As is widely known, Smith was the first to advocate a free market economy, one in which the government would not control the supply or the demand. This monograph was also the first social science work that used empirical data in its arguments. It has been credited with laying the philosophical ground work for modern capitalism, or the free enterprise system.

Smith's renowned work clearly reflects Christian values. In one part of the book he says that people should love their neighbors as they love themselves. In another portion he cites the words of Moses: "Love the LORD your God with all your heart and with all your soul and with all your strength" (Deuteronomy 6:5).[28] This passage is also cited by Jesus in Matthew 22:37. Thus, Smith shows his indebtedness to Moses and to Christ.

Scholars have sometimes noted that Smith was leaning toward deism and hence was no longer an orthodox Christian. That he had deistic inclinations appears to be true. However, that does not negate his being influenced by Christian teachings and values, for the Christian perspective imbued nearly all scholarly, academic, and scientific thinking of that era. For example, he refers to a teaching of Jesus as "our Saviour's precept."[29] Although this expression was common in the eighteenth century even among deists, it indicates that the deists of that era were not like the deists of the twentieth century, because today no deist, or Unitarian, would refer to Jesus Christ as "our Savior." In all, had the spirit and freedom of Jesus Christ never appeared, it is highly unlikely that the world today would have *The Wealth of Nations* on its libraries' shelves, together with the immense influence this work has wielded in the realm of economics and business.

THE DECLINE AND FALL OF THE ROMAN EMPIRE

This classic work of six volumes by Edward Gibbon (1737–94) took twenty years to complete. Once a Roman Catholic, Gibbon later developed a negative attitude toward Christianity. Despite some of his critical comments regarding the role of the Christian church, he nonetheless notes many events and incidents that show Christianity's beneficial influence. For instance, he credits Christianity with changing the life of Clovis (a sixth-century king of the Franks) after he became a Christian. Says Gibbon, "When Clovis ascended from the baptismal font, he alone in the Christian world deserved the name and prerogatives of a catholic king."[30] Also, Ian Wood points out, "For Gibbon the impact of Christianity on the barbarians...was largely positive."[31]

Gibbon's work has been translated into many languages. It has made a major contribution to the world's understanding of early Christianity vis-à-vis the Greco-Roman world. Its many citations and accounts of the events that transpired over a period of several centuries often supplement and corroborate some of the incidents and occurrences that were written by some of the church fathers and by the fourth-century church historian Eusebius. *The Decline and Fall of the Roman Empire* has added much to the knowledge and understanding of Christianity's impact on the world.

GOETHE'S *FAUST*

The late medieval legend of Dr. Faust, with its various versions, first fascinated its readers in Germany and then later in England. During the Middle Ages it had become one of the most enduring legends in Western literature. As a magician and astrologer, Faust sold his soul to the devil, Mephistopheles, for a limited time in exchange for knowledge and power, and in the end the devil took Faust's soul to hell.

But in the *Faust* of Johann Wolfgang Goethe (1749–1832) the story takes a different turn in that his Faust does not sell his soul for knowledge and power but to find supreme happiness. He finds it by giving himself unselfishly in the service of mankind. He also does not end up in hell, as in the older legends, but rather Goethe has him obtaining redemption. These departures from the old Faust legends, it can be argued, indicate that Goethe was to some degree influenced by the redemptive component in Christian theology, even though he was essentially a pantheistic rationalist who "had no true conception of the real character of sin, [and] he had no appreciation for the Christian doctrine of redemption."[32] This is evident as Goethe's Faust is redeemed, not by grace through faith in Jesus Christ (Ephesians 2:8–9), but by his own good works. Thus, while Christian theology apparently exerted some influence on Goethe as he wrote *Faust*, it did not erase his pantheistic rationalism. Nevertheless, he would probably not have written his version of *Faust* had he not in part been influenced by Christianity's doctrine of a devil, a hell, and redemption.

A CHRISTMAS CAROL

Written in 1843 in London by the British novelist Charles Dickens (1812–70), this small book was an instant success. It has been said that this book, more than any other writing, has engraved in many people's minds that Christmas is a time for goodwill and giving. Whether that was the intent of Dickens is not known, but if it was, he likely extrapolated it from Luke's account of Jesus' birth that has the angels saying to the shepherds, "Glory to God in the highest, and on earth peace, good will toward men!" (Luke 2:14 NKJV). Some ancient biblical manuscripts say "to men *of* good will."

Children know *A Christmas Carol* best for its main character, Mr. Scrooge. They know him for saying "bah" and "humbug" to those who found joy in Christmas as they greeted one another by saying "Merry Christmas." Scrooge sees nothing good about celebrating Christmas. He has no goodwill, and he does not care to receive any. But after he goes to bed on Christmas Eve, three ghosts appear to him in his dreams. The ghost of Christmas Past tells Scrooge about his years as a young boy; the ghost of Christmas Present reminds him about the economically poor Bob Cratchit

"A CHRISTMAS CAROL" is an illustration for Charles Dickens's popular story published in 1843. *(Illustration by John Leech)*

family (Bob works in Scrooge's business). The third ghost tells him of Christmas Yet to Come, alluding to the possibility that no one may mourn him when he dies. The three ghost stories deeply affect Scrooge, and as he awakes on Christmas Day, he is a changed man. He is kind to the Cratchits, he raises Bob's salary, and he even says "Merry Christmas" to his associates.

Although Dickens's Christmas story fails to note the real purpose of Christmas, namely, that it is a holiday celebrating God becoming man in Jesus Christ in order to redeem a sinful mankind, he at least accents the goodwill that is a by-product of Christmas, as shown by the change in Mr. Scrooge. In this context, *A Christmas Carol* has had a number of wholesome effects. A friend of Dickens said that this book "had done more good than all of the pulpits in Christendom."[33] Another stated that it was "the greatest little book in the world."[34] It has also been credited with reversing the New England Puritans' rejection of celebrating Christmas.[35] And not to be overlooked, this little book introduced the Christmas turkey, for it was Mr. Scrooge who gave the Cratchits a turkey for Christmas as part of his newly gained goodwill. One recent author, who is highly negative about Christmas celebrations, says that as a result of Dickens's little story, "Christmas had been born anew. . .[and it] left the holiday more sentimental in character and more universally observed than ever before."[36]

UNCLE TOM'S CABIN

This famous book by Harriet Beecher Stowe (1811–96), discussed in another context in chapter 11, would never have been written had Stowe not witnessed the evils of American slavery through a Christian lens. The book's Christian accents are plainly evident—first, in the way Uncle Tom, a Christian and a slave, is depicted as taking on the role of the suffering servant, a Christlike figure who does not rebel; and second, in the way the book shows slavery to be incompatible with Christianity.

President Lincoln recognized the impact this book had on the consciences of the American people when he said, upon meeting Stowe, "So this is the little lady that caused this great war." *Uncle Tom's Cabin* is not great literature because it is filled with suspense and intriguing plots, but because it is filled with the spirit of Jesus Christ that prompted St. Paul to tell the early Christians, "There is neither Jew nor Greek, slave nor free, male nor female, for you are all one in Christ Jesus" (Galatians 3:28). One cannot imagine how such a book could have been written without the spirit and teachings of Jesus Christ.

THE BROTHERS KARAMAZOV

Published in 1880, this Russian novel is frequently hailed as Fyodor Dostoyevsky's (1821–81) greatest work. It has been said that during much of Dostoyevsky's life he struggled with his own poverty and ill health, but especially with his conflict between doubt and faith, as is shown in the godless brother Ivan and the believing brother Alyosha. In the portraits of these two very different brothers and in other parts of the novel, the author to a large degree reflected his own struggles and experiences (and apparently those of many other Russians as well) by projecting them onto the characters in his novel.

As is well known, Dostoyevsky has Ivan, the blasphemous brother of the Karamazov boys, declare that since there is no God, everything is lawful. Believing his brother's blasphemy, Smeerdyakov ends up murdering his father, Fyodor Karamazov. Thus Dostoyevsky, who shows great familiarity with Christ's teachings and the duties of a Christian, demonstrates what happens when doubt preempts a person's faith in God and Jesus Christ. It is not an overstatement to say that this novel, which portrays abiding universal human traits in its characters, reveals a distinct Christian influence.

BEN-HUR

Lewis Wallace (1827–1905), a Hoosier, a high school dropout, and a onetime officer in the United States Army during the Civil War, wrote this award-winning novel in 1880. Its subtitle is "A Tale of the Christ." Before he wrote this novel, Wallace had a conversation with the infidel Robert Ingersoll. This exchange did not go well, he said, for he was unable to counter Ingersoll's arguments. This prompted him to learn more about the life and circumstances of Jesus; and as one reads the novel, it is evident that he did his homework well. Even his details of Jerusalem's geography are impressive.

The story focuses on Judah Ben-Hur, a young Jewish male whose enemy, Messala, falsely accuses him of plotting to kill the Roman governor of Judea. He is sentenced to the galleys, and his mother and sister are thrown into a dungeon, where they become infected with leprosy. After he attains his freedom, upon saving the life of the shipwrecked Roman officer Arrius he is adopted by Arrius and taken to Rome. Later, he is confronted by Messala in a dramatic chariot race in which he defeats his old enemy. Still later, in Jerusalem, he sees Christ perform miracles, including the healing of his mother's and sister's leprosy. He witnesses Jesus' crucifixion and recalls his saying "I am the resurrection and the life."[37] Ben-Hur and his wife become Christians, and in time he returns to Rome and gives all of his wealth to promoting the Christian gospel.

This novel, which sold over two million copies during Wallace's lifetime, shows what can happen when one is not awed by the doubts of an unbeliever but proceeds to examine for himself whether the historical facts of Jesus' life, death, and resurrection are true or false. Those facts convinced the author, who said he once left the teaching of religion in his family to his wife. He wrote this novel not only to counter Ingersoll's atheistic comments but also to reveal the powerful effects of the life and work of Jesus Christ. *Ben-Hur* is still in print. The movie version continues to be shown on television, usually during the Easter season, thus revealing its long-standing appeal to millions of viewers.

THE PROTESTANT ETHIC AND THE SPIRIT OF CAPITALISM

The German sociologist Max Weber (1864–1920), whose father was religiously indifferent and his mother a pious Lutheran, saw himself being "out of tune," as he phrased it, with regard to being a Christian.[38] His religious agnosticism, however, did not deter him from writing the classic work, *The Protestant Ethic and the Spirit of Capitalism*, in 1905.

It has been said that Weber, an adherent to the philosophy of idealism, wrote this book to counter the materialism of Karl Marx. Idealism holds that the human mind—the idea—is the most important element in the nature of reality and history. This is contrary to the philosophy of materialism, which says that what people need materially to live is the only thing that determines the course of their lives and history. Weber chose the Protestant ethic (as noted in chapter 8) to show that it was the Protestant belief in the importance of hard work, thrift, personal responsibility, and worldly asceticism that gave rise to the spirit of capitalism. In short, this Protestant idea shaped an economic (material) system. The fact that Weber selected the Protestant ethic to support his philosophy of idealism indicates that even he, as a non-Christian, was influenced by Christianity to such an extent that, consciously or unconsciously, he could not ignore it, hence his classic treatise.

THE SOCIAL TEACHINGS OF THE CHRISTIAN CHURCHES

This work, published in 1912 by Ernst Troeltsch (1865–1923), has, like Max Weber's classic, been of great interest to historians and sociologists both for its interpretive analysis and for the hypotheses it suggests. The work's main contribution has often been seen, especially by sociologists, in its positing the church-sect typology that has resulted in a plethora of sociological research showing how Christian sects arise and how in time they often become institutionalized churches. Troeltsch defined the church type as an organization that tolerates the secular order of society, cooperates with the state, possesses a formal system of doctrine, has a professional ministry, grants membership at birth through infant baptism, has most of its members from the upper and middle classes, and is governed less democratically. In the sect these characteristics are reversed in that it rejects the secular order of society, resists the state, possesses no formal system of doctrine, has no professional ministry, receives most of its members by adult conversion, draws most of its members from the lower classes, and operates more democratically.

In addition to the typology, Troeltsch's study also discusses the interrelatedness of Christian theology and the social dimensions of culture by showing that it is not always that theology affects society and culture, but that often society and culture affect theology. Since this work appeared, the latter effect has become much more pronounced, a phenomenon that does not bode well for the church. As Troeltsch says at the end of his study, "The churches are losing their hold on the spiritual life of the nations."[39] In short, the beneficial influences that Christianity exerted for almost two millennia are losing their force and effectiveness in modern society.

THE SCREWTAPE LETTERS

C. S. Lewis (1898–1963), a onetime lapsed Anglican who later became a powerful apologist for Christianity, used words and imagery in his writings that caught the attention of the twentieth-century man. *The Screwtape Letters* (1942) is one such work. The book is an account of a conversation between Screwtape (the devil in hell) and Wormwood (his delegate on earth), telling him how to get human souls to end up in hell. Screwtape calls God "the Enemy."

Screwtape knows the weaknesses of modern Christians. So he tells Wormwood to encourage them to look for a church that suits their personal tastes, a church where the traditional liturgy is watered down, where a lot of new psychology is used, and where novelty is in vogue. He is also told that he should introduce Christians to illicit sex, intemperate drinking, and other sensual pleasures, because these are excellent means of getting them

SOME LITERARY HALLMARKS

Name of Work	Type of Literature	Author's Name and Status
Ecclesiastical History	Historical	Eusebius (ca. 280–339), theologian, historian
The City of God	Apologetic	Augustine (354–430), bishop, theologian
An Ecclesiastical History of the English Nation	Historical	The Venerable Bede (673–735), monk, historian
Rhetoric and Virtue	Educational	Alcuin (735–804), monk, scholar
Opus Majus	Scientific	Roger Bacon (1214–94), monk, philosopher
The Divine Comedy	Allegorical	Dante Alighieri (1265–1321), poet
The Canterbury Tales	Moral	Geoffrey Chaucer (ca. 1343–1400), poet
The Praise of Folly	Satire	Desiderius Erasmus (1466–1536), priest, scholar
An Open Letter to the Christian Nobility	Doctrinal	Martin Luther (1483–1546), theologian, reformer
Augsburg Confession	Doctrinal	Philipp Melanchthon (1497–1560), theologian
Utopia	Satire	Thomas More (1478–1535), monk
The Institutes of the Christian Religion	Doctrinal	John Calvin (1509–64), theologian, reformer
The New Astronomy	Scientific	Johann Kepler (1571–1630), scientist
The Pilgrim's Progress	Allegorical	John Bunyan (1628–88), Puritan preacher
Paradise Lost	Allegorical	John Milton(1608–74), poet
Pensées (Thoughts on Religion)	Apologetic	Blaise Pascal (1623–62), philosopher
The Wealth of Nations	Philosophical	Adam Smith (1723–90), moral philosopher
Decline and Fall of the Roman Empire	Historical	Edward Gibbon (1737–94), historian
Faust	Allegorical	Johann Wolfgang Goethe (1749–1832), poet
A Christmas Carol	Moral	Charles Dickens (1812–70), writer
Uncle Tom's Cabin	Moral	Harriet Beecher Stowe (1811–96), novelist
The Brothers Karamazov	Moral	Fyodor Dostoyevsky (1821–81), writer
Ben-Hur	Historical fiction	Lewis Wallace (1827–1905), statesman, writer
The Protestant Ethic and the Spirit of Capitalism	Historical	Max Weber (1864–1920), professor, sociologist
The Social Teachings of the Christian Churches	Historical	Ernst Troeltsch (1865–1923), professor, sociologist
The Screwtape Letters	Apologetic	C.S. Lewis (1898–1963), professor, writer
Mere Christianity	Apologetic	C.S. Lewis (1898–1963), professor, writer

to desert the Enemy's camp. But do not use reason and logic, warns Screwtape, because both favor Christianity.

In typical C. S. Lewis fashion, this work pulls no punches regarding the basic teachings of the Christian church. It does not soft-pedal the biblical teachings concerning the existence of the devil and hell. Both are presented as real and authentic. The book does not pander to those in today's world who no longer find the existence of the devil and hell as palatable to their intellectual taste. Upon reading *The Screwtape Letters*, the modern Christian is not only reminded that there is a devil and a hell, but that every Christian stands in danger of being captured by the devil's delegate and taken there. Lewis also assures the Christian that God through his Son, Jesus Christ, has provided the way to escape from the clutches of the devil and his evil angels. It is amazing to see how Jesus Christ's two-thousand-year presence has inspired so many of his followers. C. S. Lewis is one of them.

MERE CHRISTIANITY

One year after C. S. Lewis wrote *The Screwtape Letters*, he published another book, *Mere Christianity* (1943). In this hallmark of Christian literature, he shows that Christianity makes sense, that it is not some pie-in-the-sky religion. The book explains what Christians believe and how those beliefs translate into the practices of daily living, such as social morality, sexual morality, Christian marriage, forgiveness, charity, faith, and so forth. In Lewis's usual manner, he confronts a number of modern misconceptions regarding Christianity, one of them being that Jesus was indeed a great teacher but not God. With simple and forceful logic, he annihilates this trite but commonly heard refrain. A man who is merely a man does not say the things that Jesus said, for if he did, he would not be a great teacher but a lunatic. "You must make your choice," Lewis continues. "Either this man was, and is, the Son of God, or else a madman or something worse. You can shut Him up for a fool, you can spit at Him, and kill Him as a demon; or you can fall at His feet and call Him Lord and God. But let us not come with any patronizing nonsense about His being a great human teacher."[40] This is a convincing rejection of an old and hackneyed argument.

CONCLUSION

As indicated at the outset of this chapter, many of the literary works described above have for decades been recommended or required reading in higher education. Their bearing the marks of Christian influence was not, however, the reason these works and others were read. That is not even why they were chosen in church-related colleges. They were chosen because they were good literature, written in unexcelled literary form and style that meaningfully engaged the reader. But perhaps more important, they were read because they engaged readers in what Robert Hutchins once called "the Great Conversation." Said he, "No civilization is like that of the West. . . . No dialogue in any other civilization can compare with that of the West in the number of great works of the mind that have contributed to this dialogue. The goal toward which Western society moves is the Civilization of Dialogue. The spirit of Western civilization is the spirit of inquiry. Its dominant element is the Logos."[41]

Hutchins's words, however, are currently not well received by those who see the literary works discussed in this chapter as well as Hutchins's *Great Books of the Western World* as culturally biased works of the "Western Canon." Thus, many of these great works of literature are unfortunately no longer used as texts in many high schools or colleges or universities.

In spite of this trend of slighting many of the hallmarks of literature, it is significant to note that Christianity not only has made immense contributions to the world of literature, but also has a legacy of being highly supportive of literature. Christians did so first by revering the biblical texts as the Word of God, then honoring the extrabiblical works of the church fathers, and also by using many writings of secular authors whose insights were compatible with Christian principles.

Christianity's affinity for literature plus its numerous scholars and scientists (noted in previous chapters) show that its alleged anti-intellectualism does not stand the historical test. Even secular and pagan literature such as the writings of Greco-Roman poets and philosophers received support from many noteworthy Christian leaders. For example, Ulfilas (ca. 311–81), a bishop and missionary to the Goths (ancient Germans), translated some of Aristotle's works. Similarly, Cassiodorus (ca. 477–570), a Christian monk, copied numerous classics, some of them pagan writings, for Christians to read. Neither Cassiodorus nor Ulfilas was indifferent to Christianity's teachings, nor were they interested in promoting paganism; rather, they felt that these works had value for their insights regarding the drama of human life. That is why Martin Luther advocated studying these ancient writings even though he called them "heathen books."[42]

Lynn D. White, an expert on medieval science, has said that had it not been for the Christian monks' enthusiasm for the classic Greco-Roman literature, and the Christian teachers using them, "we should know as little about the writings of Rome as we do about the Mayan literature which once flourished in the jungles of Yucatan."[43] The Christian interest in literature obviously continued, prompting many others to write also, as is attested by this chapter's selections. Behind this interest lay the motive so clearly spelled out by St. Paul when he said, "Whatever you do, whether in word or deed, do it all in the name of the Lord Jesus, giving thanks to God the Father through him" (Colossians 3:17).

NOTES

1. E. G. Weltin, *"De Viris Illustribus,"* in *Masterpieces of Catholic Literature,* ed. Frank N. Magill (New York: Harper and Row, 1965), 150.

2. Interview with Charles N. Wheeler in the *Chicago Tribune,* May 25, 1916.

3. Thomas P. Neill, "The City of God," in *Masterpieces of Catholic Literature,* 189.

4. Ibid.

5. Frank N. Magill, *Masterpieces of Christian Literature* (New York: Harper and Row, 1963), 186.

6. Daniel J. Boorstin, *The Discoverers* (New York: Vintage Books, 1985), 598.

7. E. G. Richards, *Mapping Time: The Calendar and Its History* (New York: Oxford University Press, 1998), 106.

8. Mary Evelyn, "Concerning Rhetoric and Virtue," in *Masterpieces of Christian Literature,* 265.

9. "Alighieri, Dante, *Divine Comedy"* in *Oxford Dictionary of the Christian Church,* ed. F. L. Cross and E. A. Livingstone (New York: Oxford University Press, 1997), 491.

10. John H. Fisher, *The Importance of Chaucer* (Carbondale: Southern Illinois University Press, 1992), 34.

11. G. K. Chesterton, *Chaucer* (New York: Farrar and Rinehart, 1932), 5.

12. Martin Luther, *An Open Letter to the Christian Nobility,* in *Three Treatises* (Philadelphia: Muhlenberg Press, 1960), 15.

13. J. H. Hexter, *More's Utopia: The Biography of an Idea* (Princeton: Princeton University Press, 1952), 72.

14. Hippolyte Alphonse Taine, *The History of English Literature,* trans. H. Van Laun (New York: Henry Holt, 1874), 2:472.

15. George Bancroft: cited in Taine, *The History of English Literature,* 390.

16. Loraine Boettner, *The Reformed Doctrine of Predestination* (Grand Rapids: Wm. B. Eerdmans, 1932), 392.

17. D. James Kennedy and Jerry Newcombe, *What If Jesus Had Never Been Born?* (Nashville: Thomas Nelson, 1994), 61.

18. Ibid., 314.

19. C. D. Hellman, "Johannes Kepler," in *New Catholic Encyclopedia* (San Francisco: McGraw-Hill, 1967), 8:163.

20. "The New Astronomy: Introduction" in *Readings from Scientific American: Frontiers in Science,* ed. Owen Gingerich (San Francisco: W. H. Freeman, 1970), 247.

21. Arthur Koestler, *The Sleep Walkers: A History of Man's Changing Vision of the Universe* (New York: Macmillan, 1959), 315.

22. James Anthony Froude, *Bunyan* (New York: Harper and Brothers, 1988), 153.

23. E. L. Marilla, *Milton and Modern Man* (Tuscaloosa: University of Alabama Press, 1968), 31.

24. Blaise Pascal, *Pensées,* in *Great Books of the Western World,* ed. Mortimer Adler (Chicago: Encyclopedia Britannica, Inc., 1996), 267.

25. Ibid., 272.

26. Ibid., 278.

27. Ibid., 217.

28. D. D. Raphael and A. L. Macfie, eds., *Adam Smith: The Theory of Moral Sentiments* (Oxford: Clarendon Press, 1976), 171.

29. Ibid., 178.

30. Edward Gibbon, *The Decline and Fall of the Roman Empire* (Chicago: William Benton, 1952), 1:611.

31. Ian Wood, "Gibbon and the Merovingians," in *Edward Gibbon and the Empire,* ed. Rosalind McKitternick and Roland Quinault (New York: Cambridge University Press, 1997), 124.

32. "Goethe, Johann Wolfgang von," in *Lutheran Encyclopedia,* ed. Erwin L. Lueker (St. Louis: Concordia Publishing House, 1954), 420.

33. Genevieve Taggard, "Dickens, Charles," *The World Book Encyclopedia* (Chicago: Field Enterprises Educational Corporation, 1958), 4:1984.

34. Monica Dickens, "Introduction," in Charles Dickens, *A Christmas Carol: The Original Manuscript* (New York: Dover, 1967), ix.

35. Tom Flynn, *The Trouble with Christmas* (Buffalo: Prometheus Books, 1993), 102.

36. Ibid.

37. Lewis Wallace, *Ben-Hur: A Tale of the Christ* (New York: Harper and Brothers, 1904), 535.

38. H. H. Gerth and C. Wright Mills, *From Max Weber: Essays in Sociology* (New York: Oxford University Press, 1946), 25.

39. Ernst Troeltsch, *The Social Teachings of the Christian Churches,* trans. Olive Wyon (Chicago: University of Chicago Press, 1976), 2:1008.

40. C. S. Lewis, *Mere Christianity* (New York: Macmillan, 1960), 41.

41. Cited in Robert McHenry, ed., *The Great Conversation: A Reader's Guide to Great Books of the Western World* (Chicago: Encyclopedia Britannica, Inc., 1994), 31.

42. Martin Luther, "Selected Psalms," *Luther's Works,* ed. Jaroslav Pelikan (St. Louis: Concordia Publishing House, 1956), 13:199.

43. Lynn D. White, "The Significance of Medieval Christianity," in *The Vitality of the Christian Tradition,* ed. George F. Thomas (New York: Harper and Brothers, 1941), 93.

15

ADDITIONAL INFLUENCE: HOLIDAYS, WORDS, SYMBOLS, and EXPRESSIONS

"Isn't life a series of images that change as they repeat themselves?"

Victor Bokris

As I have noted previously, during their first three hundred years Christians, often suffering severe persecution, had no voice in the public affairs of the pagan Roman society. Nevertheless, they soon commemorated and celebrated the key events that highlighted the life and acts of Jesus Christ as well as some of their early experiences. After Constantine legalized Christianity in 313, these commemorative events in time became widely institutionalized in the Western world and even elsewhere.

HOLIDAYS (HOLY DAYS)

Holidays is a religious word. It once meant "holy days," a term of Christian origin dating from the Middle Ages. Christmas Day, Easter, Good Friday, and Pentecost were considered to be holy days by Christians in the past because of what God had done for them on these days through his

Son, Jesus Christ. Ironically, in the English-speaking world today, the word *holidays* is increasingly used to avoid conveying any religious meaning. So when people say "Happy Holidays" during the Christmas and New Year season, they usually intend a greeting that is religiously neutral, one that avoids any reference to the birth of Jesus Christ. Until recently, the observance of these days was not divorced from Jesus Christ. In Canada this divorce is even further evident in that Canadians call their summer vacation "holidays."

SUNDAY

Since Christ physically rose from the dead on the first day of the week, the apostles and their fellow believers honored and celebrated Christ's resurrection by choosing that day as their formal day of worship. The Younger Pliny, a Roman consul, wrote to the Emperor Trajan (as noted above in chapter 13) in about A.D. 111 that the Christians assembled "on a certain fixed day" (*Epistolae,* or *The Letters of Pliny* 10.96). He had Sunday in mind.

The apostolic Christians also chose Sunday because it was on this day (Easter Sunday) that the risen Christ first met with his disciples. Later, it was on a Sunday that he breathed the Holy Spirit on his disciples (John 20:19–22), and it was fifty days after Easter, on the day of Pentecost, another Sunday, that Christians received the outpouring of the Holy Spirit (Acts 2). Thus, Sunday replaced Saturday, the Hebrew Sabbath, as a day of worship in the early church. It soon came to be known as the "Lord's Day," as noted in the *Didache,* a Christian handbook written sometime between about A.D. 85 and 110.

Given that the early Christian church for the first 150 years was composed largely of Jewish converts, the change from Saturday to Sunday was a major departure from the Judaic religious custom. By this change the apostolic Christians not only underscored the importance of Christ's physical resurrection, but they also showed they were no longer bound to the ceremonial laws of Moses. As followers of Christ, St. Paul told the Christians in Colossae, "Therefore do not let anyone judge you by what you eat or drink, or with regard to a religious festival" (Colossians 2:16). It was important that they worship Christ, their risen Lord. On what day this was done was of no importance, according to Paul. So they chose the first day of the week, Sunday.

Some have argued that the pagan Mithras cult of the sun, from which the name *dies solis* (sun day) is derived, influenced the selection of Sunday by the early Christians. This argument really lacks credibility, because it overlooks the significance of Christ's resurrection and other significant events that occurred on Sunday. It also ignores the fact that, although the early Christians assembled on the first day of the week, to them the day was nameless. This is evident from St. Paul's words in 1 Corinthians 16:2, where he asked the congregation to take up a collection for needy Christians. He writes, "On the *first day of every week,* each one of you should set aside a sum of money."

In extrabiblical literature the first reference to Christians worshiping on "the day of the sun" is from Justin Martyr, a Christian apologist (defender) of the mid-second century (*Apologia* 1.67). A half-century later (between 190–200) Tertullian, another Christian apologist, argued that the Christian practice of worshiping on Sunday had nothing to do with the sun god and denied that their praying toward the east conveyed any pagan influence (*Ad nationes* 13). Thus, it appears that the early Christians chose to call the first day of the week "Sunday" quite apart from any influence of the cult of Mithras. For instance, biblical precedent for the word *Sunday* (day of light) also relates to John's Gospel, which calls Jesus "the *light* of the world" (John 8:12), and Luke's reference to him as the "*light* to bring revelation to the Gentiles" (Luke 2:32 NKJV).

While there is no evidence that the early Christians during the first three centuries abstained from work on Sunday, for some reason the Emperor Constantine in A.D. 321 decreed that "the venerable day of the sun" was to be a day of rest for urban residents. However, the decree did not apply to rural people. Constantine's act of making Sunday a legal holy day also gave official status to the seven-day planetary week among the Romans.[1] In 538 the Council of Orleans (France) threatened to punish Christians if they worked in the fields on Sundays. The church leaders wanted Christians to be able to attend divine services. And in 789 Charlemagne the Great, who was highly supportive of the church, outlawed all labor on Sunday. This decree set off a type of Old Testament sabbatarian legalism that functioned in many Christian denominations in Europe, the United States, Canada, and other countries of the West. In the United States and Canada, for instance, where the Calvinist/Puritan influence has been strong, numerous "blue laws" were enacted that prohibited certain work and outlawed public entertainment on Sundays. These laws sometimes also restricted the movement of trains on Sundays. Canada even had a federal law called "The Lord's Day Act" that was one of the country's federal statues until 1985.

Many of these laws, however, were not enforced, and by the mid-twentieth century virtually no violators were prosecuted.

Given that the laws banning work and many other activities on Sunday went far beyond what the early Christians did or envisioned, it can be argued that these laws often did not reflect the true spirit of Jesus Christ, but rather a type of pharisaical legalism. Jesus, it will be recalled, was once upbraided by the Pharisees for allowing his disciples to pick grain on the Sabbath. To this criticism he responded, "The Sabbath was made for man, not man for the Sabbath" (Mark 2:27). About the only merit the blue laws had was to serve as a reminder that it was good for people to rest on one day of the week and to attend church.

Even in today's secular environment, where Sunday has become much like any other day of the week, the day still retains somewhat of a special status in the Western world; for it is on Sundays that millions of Christians attend church, not only in Western countries but also in many non-Western nations. Of all the days of the week, Sunday is still the day that has the least amount of people working. It is also seen by many as a day of leisure and relaxation, more so than any other day of the week. All who appreciate these aspects of Sunday are benefiting from one of the many by-products of Christianity.

CHRISTMAS DAY

The word *Christmas* once literally meant "Christ's Mass," which was performed in churches on the day that Christians honored the birth of Jesus Christ. The name is derived from *Cristes Maesse,* two Old English words from the twelfth century. In German it is *Weihnachten;* in French, *Nöel;* in Spanish, *Navidad;* and in Russian, *Rozhdestovo*. None of these words use the name of Christ to commemorate the day of his birth as does the English language.

Frequently one hears that Christmas Day, like Sunday, is a holiday that evolved out of the religious cult of Mithraism—namely, that the date of December 25 comes from the Roman emperor Aurelian's edict in A.D. 274 that established the festival of *Natale Solis Invicti* (Birth of the Unconquerable Sun)[2] as he dedicated a new temple to the sun as god near the Mausoleum of Augustus.[3] The widely held belief that Christmas Day came about as a result of Christians having Christianized sun-god worship fails to consider the argument that Christians in some geographic areas—in northern Africa (primarily in Egypt), for example—were already observing Christmas Day as early as December 25, in A.D. 243, thirty years before

"The Departure of St. Augustine of Hippo from Milan" is a fresco by Benozzo Gossoli of the fifteenth century. *(Church of St. Augustine, San Gimignano, Tuscany)*

Aurelian's edict. They associated Christ's birth with the Old Testament prophecy in Malachi 4:2, which calls the predicted Messiah "the sun of righteousness" (*Natalis Solis Iustitiae* in Latin).[4] If this argument is true, then the Christians did not choose December 25 to Christianize Aurelian's decision, but rather the emperor, by establishing the Birth of the Unconquerable Sun, may have tried to paganize the Christian observance of the birth of Christ, the "sun of righteousness."[5] The latter gains added plausibility when one recalls that Emperor Diocletian in the Great Persecution of 293–305 reinforced Aurelian's edict in order to "expunge Christianity."[6] Moreover, also in the mid-fourth century, Christians considered March 25 "to be the actual date of both Christ's Passion and Resurrection *and his conception* [*sic*] so that December 25—exactly nine months later—was originally chosen from a computation based on the assumed date of Jesus' death, resurrection, and conception."[7] Hence the attempt to link Christmas Day with Mithraism's sun god festival does not have unequivocable historical support.

In spite of the many secular, accretions that accompany the Christmas season today—for example, songs such as "Rudolph the Red-nosed Reindeer," "Jingle Bells," and "I'm Dreaming of a White Christmas"—it continues to have a salutary effect on countless people, especially in Western countries. Who would argue that the beauty and solemnity of the carols, even when heard in a modern department store, do not lift the spirits of millions each Christmas season? The emphasis on goodwill to all men and the gift giving that occurs at Christmastime may sometimes seem ritualistic and routine, but few would argue that these activities have no wholesome effects on people's lives.

New Year's Day

Of all the days that are the product of Christianity's presence, New Year's Day has become the most secularized. During the Christmas season one still hears some carols that proclaim the birth of Jesus. On Easter Day, camouflaged as it is with colored eggs and bunnies, one can still hear about the resurrection of Jesus Christ, even though that message is very much couched in what Christians believe, rather than what happened historically. However, New Year's Day is totally devoid of any reference to Christianity. Gone is the awareness that New Year's Day, eight days after Jesus' birth, commemorates the circumcision of Jesus (an act that was done in accordance with Leviticus 12:3), a day that the church since the middle of the sixth century liturgically called "the Feast of Circumcision." And gone also is any awareness that it was the eighth day after Jesus' birth that he publicly received his name.

For centuries Christians saw New Year's Eve as a symbol of what awaits all human beings at the end of their life cycle and therefore a reminder that they should always be prepared to meet their Lord. It was a time for Christians to attend church services to pause and reflect, asking God to guide and protect them from all harm and danger in the new year, and most of all, to keep them in the Christian faith.

Easter

It is odd that the greatest event in all history, the physical resurrection of Jesus Christ, has been named, according to the Venerable Bede (673–735), after the goddess Eastre, or Ostra, who represented light or spring to pagan Anglo-Saxons. This new name replaced what the early Christians called the week of *hebdomada alba* because newly catechized Christians wore white garments at their baptism during Easter week.[8] It is equally odd that Easter activities today have camouflaged much of the meaning and significance of Christ's resurrection with the use of Easter eggs and bunnies. These pagan accretions are even accepted by many well-meaning but apparently indifferent or uninformed Christians.

For centuries in Europe and in North America, Easter was celebrated on both Sunday and Monday, making Monday a holiday for urban and rural workers. Christians attended church services on both days. With increasing secularization, however, the second day of Easter has all but faded into oblivion as a time for religious activities. Nevertheless, Easter Sunday still receives some attention as a major holiday, especially in the West. And in many European countries, following an old Christian observance, Easter Monday continues to be a business holiday.

HALLOWEEN NIGHT

For centuries the Christian church honored its deceased members on All Hallows' Day (All Saints Day), November 1. The night before was known as "Hallowed Eve." The liturgical churches—Catholic, Episcopalian (Anglican), and Lutheran—still celebrate All Saints Day, but as most everyone knows, the evening of October 31 is no longer a hallowed evening. It has become quite unholy, even though the etymology of the word *Halloween* would indicate otherwise.

Some historians believe that the church in Europe, which celebrated All Hallows' Day as early as the seventh century, moved All Saints' Day to November 1 in the eighth century in order to Christianize the pagan custom that honored the dead on the night of October 31. Pagans (for example, the Celts) believed this evening was filled with ghosts, elves, and evil spirits that came out to harm people, and witches that were believed to be capable of flying. So bonfires were made to scare off these evil entities.[9] How well the church Christianized the pagan rite at one time is difficult to determine. Today, however, All Saints Day and Halloween Night are completely unrelated events. Moreover, present-day Halloween activities have in part reverted, at least symbolically, to some of the ancient pagan customs by displaying spooky jack-o'-lanterns, ghosts, skeletons, and witches riding on brooms. Perhaps it is a dubious honor to note that the name Halloween would be unknown had it not been for Christianity's efforts in the Middle Ages to hallow what once was an unhallowed, pagan festival.

THANKSGIVING DAY

Giving formal thanks to God did not begin with the Pilgrims in Massachusetts in 1621 as many Americans believe, for numerous thanksgiving accounts are portrayed in the Old Testament, where one finds Noah, King David, King Hezekiah, Nehemiah, and Daniel thanking God for material and spiritual blessings. Likewise, we read about the apostolic Christians in the New Testament giving thanks for their blessings. Thus, when the Pilgrims of the Plymouth Colony formally thanked God for three days, they did what God's thankful people had done for centuries. Nevertheless, several things were new and different in the Pilgrims' thanksgiving. Their leader, Governor William Bradford, issued a formal proclamation commanding the people to give thanks to God for having received divine protection during a terrible winter and for having received their first harvest. It was also new that the Pilgrims celebrated their thanksgiving by eating wild turkey (an indigenous bird) and venison.

When President George Washington, in response to both houses of Congress, proclaimed the nation's first Thanksgiving Day on October 3, 1789, he reflected his and Congress's spirit of thankfulness. Washington said that the country's National Thanksgiving Day was to be "a day of public thanksgiving and prayer."[10] After Washington's first proclamation, Americans celebrated Thanksgiving Day irregularly. But in 1863 President Lincoln made Thanksgiving Day an annual holiday, and when he did so, he noted that Americans were to give "praise to our beneficent Father who dwelleth in the Heavens."[11] Americans have observed this day every year since Lincoln's proclamation.

The American Christian influence that prompted the observance of Thanksgiving Day in the United States spread to Canada in 1879. Canadian Thanksgiving Day, like the American day, was first celebrated in November, but it now takes place on the second Monday in October. Although Canadians make less ado about Thanksgiving Day than Americans, like the Americans they also celebrate the day with a turkey dinner.

While Thanksgiving Day definitely reveals its biblical and Christian origins, it has become a rather secular holiday. Much talk is heard about thanksgiving, but one rarely hears to whom thanks is to be given. God is essentially factored out of this great American holiday ritual. The verbal utterances concerning Thanksgiving Day are mostly focused on visiting friends and loved ones, and of course, eating a bountiful turkey dinner. Yet without the biblical precedent of God's people giving thanks, along with the example of the Pilgrims, we would not have this noteworthy holiday.

COMMON WORDS AND SYMBOLS

Although Christianity has contributed many words to a number of languages, this chapter focuses only on some of the words that have become a part of the English language. Many of those words and symbols have become so common that their Christian origins are often no longer known or recognized.

B.C. AND A.D.

When St. Bede in 731 in his *Ecclesiastical History of England* first used the term *anno Domini* (A.D.) to date an event, he honored Jesus Christ. And when the abbreviation B.C. was added in the seventeenth century to refer to events before Christ's birth, he was honored once more. Even non-Christians were (and are) reminded that the symbols B.C. and A.D. put Christ at the center of time and history. Today, however, with the inclination toward political correctness, historians and many other writers are abandoning the use of B.C. in favor of B.C.E. (Before the Common Era), and A.D. is changed to C.E. (Common Era). This is a radical change. In effect, intentionally or unintentionally, it removes Christ from history and the people's historical consciousness. It is a grave matter to remove any significant person from history, but exceedingly more so with Jesus Christ, given the countless, unequaled contributions that his life and teachings have bequeathed to the world for two thousand years.

By increasingly using B.C.E. and C.E., the two-hundred-year-old goal of removing Jesus Christ as history's time marker may be succeeding where other attempts have failed in the past. For instance, the French Revolutionaries in 1793 replaced the so-called Christian calendar, the Gregorian calendar, introduced by Pope Gregory XIII in 1582. The new "republican calendar" eliminated the designations of the A.D. and B.C., and its ten-day week sought "to abolish Sunday, the saints, the churches, religion, the clergy, and God."[12] The efforts of the revolutionaries failed, however. By 1805 the Gregorian calendar, along with Sunday, was restored in France.[13]

In 1929 the atheistic Soviets in Russia took their turn in trying to abolish all the Christian vestiges in the calendar, along with replacing the seven-day week with a five-day week, the fifth day being a day off from work. Like the French attempt, it also erased Sunday; and like the French experience a century earlier, the people in the rural areas failed to conform to the new calendar. Thus, in 1934 the Soviets restored the old calendar but not the seven-day week.[14] By June 1940, however, the Russian Communists also restored the seven-day week. Again, the Christian influence in the reckoning of time prevailed.

BAPTISM

The word *baptism* is a rather common word today in the English language. It is derived from the Greek word *baptizo,* meaning "to wash," or "to cleanse" and has largely had for two thousand years a distinctive Christian meaning. From the very beginning, baptism signified a person's entry into the church's membership. In nonreligious contexts the word is sometimes used as a metaphor—for example, "baptism of fire"—when someone for the first time has undergone or experienced an unusual ordeal. *Baptism* would likely not be in the English vocabulary had Jesus Christ not commanded his disciples to make more disciples by "*baptizing* them in the name of the Father and of the Son and of the Holy Spirit" (Matthew 28:19), and had the church not heeded his command for two millennia by baptizing all new members.

CATHEDRAL

To most people in the English-speaking world, the word *cathedral* brings to mind a beautiful, large stone structure—a church building of Gothic design. But it is more than a large church. The word is derived from the Latin *cathedra,* meaning "a seat or bench." From the early Middle Ages on, it was where the bishop had his official seat and from which he discharged his duties to all Christians within a geographic jurisdiction, or diocese. Commonly, the cathedral was the largest church building in the bishop's diocese. In a sense, it was the bishop's church. Although many no longer associate the cathedral with the office of the bishop, virtually everyone thinks of the Christian church when the word *cathedral* is mentioned. Thus, for centuries the word has had an exclusive Christian meaning.

CEMETERY

As was briefly indicated in chapter 1, the early Christians, given their strong faith in the resurrection of the dead, taught that the deceased were "asleep" in their graves until Christ returns to resurrect them. Those

Christians took Jesus at his word: "I will raise [them] up at the last day" (John 6:40). Their belief that the dead were asleep was derived from the teaching of both the Old and New Testament. In the Old Testament the prophet Daniel said, "Multitudes who *sleep* in the dust of the earth will awake" (Daniel 12:2). In the New Testament St. Paul declared, "We believe that Jesus died and rose again and so we believe that God will bring with Jesus those who have fallen *asleep* in him" (1 Thessalonians 4:14). So convinced were they of their future resurrection that they called every burial site a *koimeterion,* a Greek word that referred to a dormitory or temporary sleeping place. It was a word that already by the middle of the first century was "used exclusively of Christian burial grounds."[15] And from this Greek term the word *cemetery* entered the English language. Thus, when English speakers use the word *cemetery,* they are echoing (intentionally or not) the Christian doctrine that says all the dead are asleep until Christ's second coming, when he will resurrect the dead and, as the Apostles' Creed says, "judge the living and the dead."

CHAPEL

For a long period of time, the word *chapel* has been used in Christian circles as a secondary or smaller place of worship. In the Middle Ages a chapel was often a smaller unit within a larger church or cathedral, used for small gatherings of Christians. Today its structure and function has broadened somewhat. It is often seen as a separate church building or place used for special Christian services, such as on college campuses and more recently in funeral homes. The latter commonly have a "chapel" as part of their premises. As with the word *cathedral,* the term *chapel* has a distinctive Christian connotation.

CHRISTENING

It has been a long-standing practice that when a new ship is about to be launched on its maiden voyage, it is formally given a name by splashing bottles of champagne on it and thereby "christening" it, that is, giving it a name similar to an infant receiving his or her name when christened (baptized). In February 2000, a new airline company in the United States known as Jet Blue went into operation. All of its planes were brand new, so they were "christened" by showering bottles of champagne on each one. Obviously, the term *christening* and its symbolic significance is borrowed from Christianity. The name that an infant received at baptism was the recipient's first, or "Christian" name. In fact, before the current concern for political correctness, American and Canadian application forms commonly asked the applicant to give his "Christian" name, preceding the surname.

CHRISTIAN

Not too long after Christ's followers were dispersed to Asia Minor, they were called "Christians" in Antioch (Acts 11:26). The historian Tacitus (55–120) said the name *Christianos* was a "vulgar appellation" (*Annals* 15.44), apparently because Christians did not conform to Rome's pagan lifestyles. They rejected the Greco-Roman gods and the many immoral acts that were in vogue. It is ironic that the name Christian, derived from the most righteous person who ever lived, was from the beginning seen as pejorative. But to the informed Christian this is no surprise, for Jesus told his disciples, "You will be hated by all for My name's sake" (Matthew 10:22 NKJV). Hated or not, today the name Christian is borne by one-third of the world's population. And although the name has often been degraded (and it still is) by many who bore it, the world still expects more virtuous behavior (and rightly so), from those who identify with the name Christian than from those who do not.

CHRISTMAS TREE

Many interesting stories abound regarding the origin of the Christmas tree; however, most of them cannot be verified or documented for historical accuracy. One legend holds that in the eighth century St. Boniface persuaded the pagan Teutons "to give up their cruel practice of sacrificing a child before a great oak tree during their winter festival. Instead, he said, 'Cut down a fir tree, take it home, and celebrate around it with your innocent children.'"[16] Another legend credits Martin Luther with having originated the Christmas tree. Neither of these legends, however, can be corroborated.

The custom of decorating the Christmas tree with lights is also sometimes linked to Luther. Reportedly, he was impressed with God's grandeur as he stood one night in the midst of the forest, viewing the beauty of the twinkling stars in the sky. As the story goes, this experience prompted him to place lighted candles on a little evergreen tree to simulate for his children the scene that he had witnessed in the forest.[17] Whether or not this is the reason, the Christmas tree became so common in German culture that a Christmas carol, "O Tannenbaum" (O Christmas Tree), was written and is still sung today.

From Germany the custom of decorating Christmas trees spread. In 1841 Prince Albert, the German husband of Queen Victoria, introduced the custom in England.[18] In America August Imgard, an immigrant from Bavaria, is credited with having introduced the first Christmas tree in 1847 in Wooster, Ohio. And in 1851 Pastor Henry Schwann is credited with having been the first to bring a Christmas tree into the chancel of a church, specifically, the Zion Lutheran Church in Cleveland, Ohio.[19]

Today Christmas trees are found in millions of homes in many countries. In the United States, for example, aside from the many artificial trees, thirty-two million American families bought a real tree in 1998. There are currently fifteen thousand Christmas tree growers, who employ more than one hundred thousand people in the United States.[20] Each year a Christmas tree is erected on the lawn of the White House in Washington, D.C., an event that receives national television coverage. But although it is called a Christmas tree, it is usually devoid of Christian symbols. The absence of these symbols is evidently the effect of recent United States Supreme Court decisions that have banned the display of Christian symbols—for instance, Christmas creches—on tax-supported public properties.

CHURCH

The word *church* is derived from the Greek term *kyriakos,* which literally means "a house that belongs to the Lord." As is well known, the word commonly refers to a physical structure where Christians assemble for divine services, as opposed to a synagogue for Jews or a mosque for Muslims. The word *church,* of course, is also used with reference to the collective body of Christians. In both instances, it is a term of exclusive Christian origin.

CREED

The word *creed* is very common today, even in a society that increasingly seeks to become creedless. Antidiscrimination documents commonly state that discrimination is not practiced relative to national origin, race, sex, or *creed.* But the concept of a creed, in terms of what one believed religiously, did not exist until the early Christians required their Christian associates to state what they believed. Although the word comes from the Latin *credo* (I believe), it had no religious connotations to the Romans. To them *credo* merely meant "I believe," that is, believing a person, a statement, or event to be true.

Although the pagans in the Greco-Roman era sacrificed to gods and goddesses, they had no creeds that formally stated their religious beliefs. The pagans, as Robin Lane Fox says, had no concept of heresy, heterodoxy, or orthodoxy, and hence no creeds.[21] The Christians, on the other hand, were totally different. Irenaeus (ca. 115–202), in his treatise *Against Heresies,* said that Christians had a "rule of faith," apparently a creed that stated what each Christian was required to believe. The Christian idea of having a creed has its source in the question that Jesus asked Peter: "Who do you say I am?" And Peter's answer, "You are the Christ, the Son of the living God" (Matthew 16:15, 16), is a creedlike response.

Only twelve years after Constantine legalized Christianity, the Council of Nicaea met in 325 to counter the Arian heresy that questioned the divinity of Christ. The council formulated a creed, now known as the Nicene Creed, which spelled out the orthodox Christians beliefs regarding the human and divine nature of Jesus Christ. By formulating creeds such as The Apostles' Creed, The Nicene Creed, and the Athanasian Creed, Christians not only started something new religiously, but they also coined the word *creed.* Hence, every time this word is spoken or written, even in a non-Christian context, it reflects Christianity's pervasive influence.

CROSS (CHRISTIAN)

The Romans executed non-Roman citizens or slaves by nailing them to crosses. And as the world knows, that is how Jesus was executed. Little did the enemies who crucified Jesus Christ realize that the cross would someday become a symbol used by his followers to commemorate his death, or that it would be used to mark the religious identity of buildings and people. What was once an ignominious object to the Romans soon became a symbol of God's love and redemption to Christ's followers.

The cross as a meaningful religious symbol appeared early in the life of the early Christians. Already in about the year 200 Tertullian said, "At every forward step and movement, at every going in and out, when we put on our clothes and shoes, when we bathe, when we sit at the table, when we light the lamps, on couch, on seat, in all ordinary actions of daily life, we trace upon the forehead the sign [cross]" (*De Corona* 3).

THE CHI-RHO CROSS, a common early Christian cross designed from two Greek letters, functioned as an abbreviation for Christ, and the letter rho symbolized the shepherd's staff for Christ, the Good Shepherd.

Even today, making the sign of the cross is practiced by the majority of the world's Christians. It is not a mere Roman Catholic custom, as many American and Canadian Protestants often falsely conclude. Christians in the Greek Orthodox, Russian (Eastern) Orthodox, Anglican (Episcopalian), and the Lutheran church also make the sign of the cross. Martin Luther, for instance, in his *Small Catechism* (still widely used in confirmation instruction) wrote a morning and evening prayer for family devotions, and before either prayer is prayed, he tells Christians, "In the morning when you get up, make the sign of the holy cross. . . .In the evening when you go to bed, make the sign of the holy cross."[22]

The cross has also been used as a metaphor to symbolize the suffering of those who follow Jesus Christ. Jesus first spoke of the cross in this manner when he said, "Anyone who does not take his cross and follow me is not worthy of me" (Matthew 10:38). It was in this sense that St. Paul wrote, "May I never boast except in the cross of our Lord Jesus Christ, through which the world has been crucified to me, and I to the world" (Galatians 6:14). Bearing one's cross is a very difficult theological concept for the average Christian to accept. It runs counter to the innate nature of every human being who wants to experience the glory of God reflected in good health, prosperity, and other blessings. A Christian accepting his cross is what Luther called "the theology of the cross." It means that the Christian, when experiencing trials, painful suffering, and tribulations does not fault God. Instead, he tries to accept his "cross," remembering that his afflictions are minuscule in comparison with what Christ endured on the cross as he took upon himself the sins of the entire world.

Thus, aside from the simple portrayal of two intersecting lines at right angles, a plus sign, or a picture of a road intersection, the cross has for two thousand years been a distinctive Christian symbol, both visually and metaphorically. It has had, and continues to have, a major impact on the world.

HEAVEN AND HELL

The Bible speaks of heaven as the place where God and his angels are, whereas hell is where the devil and his evil angels exist. Both heaven and hell were places that Jesus mentioned in his teaching. He stated that his Father was in heaven, as he taught the disciples in the Lord's Prayer. Regarding hell, he warned people, "Do not be afraid of those who kill the body but cannot kill the soul. Rather, be afraid of the One who can destroy both soul and body in *hell*" (Matthew 10:28).

To orthodox Christians, heaven and hell are real places, just as they were to Jesus. The early Christians confessed in the Apostles' Creed that Jesus Christ "suffered, was crucified, dead, and buried; he descended into hell; on the third day he rose again from the dead; and he ascended to heaven." The words *heaven* and *hell* in the Apostles' Creed, as well as in the Bible, have left an indelible mark on the minds of countless people for centuries.

Both words have become part of many people's exclamatory vocabulary. Many Christians and non-Christians alike at times exclaim "Good heavens!" or "For heaven's sake!" Or some will describe a good experience as "heavenly." The word *hell* is also frequently invoked, usually in a profane sense. It is common to hear individuals say, "To hell with that," "Go to hell," "There was hell to pay," and so forth. Although the words *heaven* and *hell* are often used as expletives, their usage reveals that even individuals who deny the reality of both have been influenced by these Christian concepts more than they realize.

HERESY

The word *heresy* is derived from the Greek *hairesis*, or Latin *heresia*. At the time of early Christianity it meant choosing, choice, or a faction that came about as a result of choice. Given their concern for orthodox teachings and creeds, Christians saw a faction (*hairesis*) as a serious threat to accepted Christian doctrines, and hence the concept of heresy arose. Among the Greco-Romans, who had no creeds, a group that chose to hold to different views was primarily seen as just another school of thought. But to Christians a person or group that believed and taught different doctrines was a very serious matter because it violated Christ's words: "I am the way and the truth and the life. No one comes to the Father except through me" (John 14:6).

THE CHRISTIAN CONNECTION TO COMMON WORDS AND SYMBOLS

Word/Symbol	Origin/Source	Meaning
A.D.	Venerable Bede in England, A.D. 731	*Anno Domini:* in the year of our Lord (Christ) after his birth
B.C.	England, 17th cent.	Before the birth of Christ
Cathedral	*Cathedra* (a seat in Latin)	Church of a bishop's seat
Cemetery	*Koimeterion* (in Greek literature, a sleeping place, a dormitory)	For Christians a temporary sleeping place for the dead
Chapel	*Capella* (Latin, 12th cent., France)	Secondary sanctuary for Christian worship
Christen	Medieval English; the act of giving persons their given (Christian) names at baptism	A synonym for Christian baptism; more recently also used for naming of ships and planes
Christian	Coined in Antioch (Acts 11:26), ca. A.D. 40–60	Someone who believes in Jesus Christ as Lord and Savior
Christmas (evergreen) tree	Reportedly introduced by Martin Luther, 1530s	Signifies Christ's birth as the Tree of Life
Church	*Kyriakos* (in Greek a house belonging to a lord)	A building for divine services and synonym for Christianity
Creed	*Credo* (Latin for "I believe")	A formal statement of beliefs, especially Christian doctrine
Cross	Instrument of Roman execution for noncitizens and slaves	Symbol of Christ's death and identity symbol of Christians
Heaven	*Shemayin* (biblical Hebrew); *Ouranos* (New Testament Greek)	The abode of God and the angels, also of those who die believing in Christ
Hell	*Sheol* (biblical Hebrew); *Gehenna/Hades* (New Testament Greek)	Place of eternal torment for those who die without Christ (Matthew 10:28)
Heresy	*Hairesis* (a faction in Greek)	A teaching that denies basic Christian doctrine(s); more recently also a teaching contrary to accepted beliefs in secular areas of knowledge
Martyr	*Martyr* (in Greek a witness)	A Christian persecuted or executed for witnessing to his faith, more recently also someone who dies for a cause
Pagan	*Paganus* (in Latin a rustic, rural person)	A non-Christian or unbeliever
Parish	*Paroika* (in Greek a side-house dwelling)	A geographic area of church members, also a Christian congregation
Pastor	*Poimaen* ("shepherd" in Greek; spiritual shepherd in the New Testament)	The spiritual head (shepherd) of a group of Christians
Santa Claus	St. Nicholas (a Christian saint of the 6th cent.)	White-bearded man in a red suit who brings gifts at Christmastime
Trinity	*Trias* (Greek word for numeral three)	God as Father, Son, and Holy Spirit, more recently also any threefold phenomenon

THIS ALTAR TO "THE UNCONQUERABLE SUN GOD" displays the nimbus, or arc of the sun, around the head. Worship of the sun god was established by Emperor Aurelian in 274.

Today the word *heresy* is widely used, even in nonreligious contexts. We hear about "heresies" in politics, medicine, education, science, and other areas. Moreover, these are usually seen as serious, similar to the seriousness that Christianity over the centuries attached to heresies within its fellowship.

MARTYR

Originally, the word *martyr* in the Greek language (as noted in chapter 1) simply meant being a witness. But when the early Christians were severely persecuted, beginning with the latter part of the first century, the word *martyr* took on the meaning of someone who was put to death or imprisoned for witnessing to the Christian faith. Ever since those hateful, cruel days that the early Christians endured for three centuries, the word *martyr* has been applied to someone who suffered and died for his or her beliefs. For instance, people who were (and still are) put to death by communist governments are called martyrs. The Christian connection to this word may often not be known today;

yet had there been no persecution of the early Christians, this word would still likely be confined to the Greek language and would refer only to someone who is a witness.

PAGAN

With the advent of Christianity, the Latin word *paganii* (a rustic or nonurban persons) received a new meaning. The early Christians were mostly urbanites. So common was the urban phenomenon of Christianity that by the fourth century, Christians referred to unbelievers as *paganii*. Later, as the monk Cassiodorus (ca. 477–570) said, unbelievers and non-Christians were not "from the City of God" (*Canticles* 7.11). Although Cassiodorus used the expression "the City of God" metaphorically to refer to Christians, it was another way to point out that non-Christians were *paganii*. The word *pagan*, even as some pagan beliefs are being revived today, still has a strong, uncomplimentary connotation, reflecting Christianity's influence.

PARISH

The word *parish,* derived from the Greek *paroika* (a side-house dwelling), made its way into the English language in the Middle Ages when it came to mean a British church district that had its own clergyman. Although somewhat altered today, the word still has an ecclesiastical meaning. Episcopalians (Anglicans) and Roman Catholics speak of their parish priest(s), and Lutherans are accustomed to saying that their pastor is in the "parish ministry," as opposed to being a clergyman in a bureaucratic or administrative context. In some geographic regions the word *parish* refers to a civil governmental unit, for instance, in Louisiana where a parish is the counterpart of a county in other parts of the United States. Thus, whether the term *parish* is used in the ecclesiastical or in the civil government sense, it is one of Christianity's contributions to the English language.

THE GREEK CROSS, with horizontal and vertical arms of equal length, is a prominent symbol of the Greek Orthodox Church.

PASTOR

Jesus called himself the "good shepherd" of his people (John 10:11). To Peter he said, "Feed my sheep" (John 21:17), meaning that he was to assume the role of a shepherd vis-à-vis the people of his spiritual flock. The words spoken to Peter set the precedent for the leader of a Christian group to be called *pastor*, a term meaning "shepherd" in Latin.

The word *pastor* is not uniformly used in all Christian denominations. Catholics are more prone to using "priest" instead of "pastor," and most Protestant denominations tend to call the spiritual head of a congregation their "minister," whereas Lutherans usually address their congregation's spiritual leader as "Pastor Anderson," for example. When Jesus told Peter to feed his sheep, he likened him to a shepherd, a pastor—and the word has been with us ever since then.

SANTA CLAUS

Even though the current trend in Western societies is to desacralize all events and items that have some Christian symbolism, the name Santa Claus has thus far been left untouched. The jolly, white-bearded man, dressed in a red suit trimmed in fur, who is seen as a religiously neutral symbol, continues to be affectionately called Santa Claus, which really means "Saint Claus," as derived from the Dutch *Sante Klaas*.

Santa Claus's very existence is, of course, a Christian symbol. Some historians link his name with Saint Nicholas, the bishop of Myra, who reportedly attended the Council of Nicaea in 325, and who died December 6, 326. But this linkage is apparently incorrect because there is no historical record of Nicholas having attended the Nicaean council. Others believe that the idea of Santa Claus comes from Nicholas of Sion, who lived at the time of Emperor Justinian in mid-sixth century. It is this Nicholas who was known to have brought children gifts on December 6, a onetime church festival honoring Nicholas, the bishop of Myra, as a saint. Thus, when we hear children sing "Jolly Old Saint Nicholas," a popular song at Christmas time, a prominent Christian saint is honored, whether it is Nicholas of Sion or Nicholas the bishop.

In spite of today's pervasive secularization and so many people not knowing that Santa Claus symbolizes a Christian saint, his presence during every Christmas season is testimony to Christianity's continuing influence. This is not to say that Santa Claus communicates a clear-cut Christian message; but it does say that despite the many non-Christian accretions of this symbol, he still symbolizes the Christian spirit of giving that began with the Wise Men from the East, who brought gold, frankincense, and myrrh to the Christ child in Bethlehem two thousand years ago.

TRINITY

The word *trinity* is derived from *trias,* the Greek word for three. Theophilus of Antioch apparently was the first to use the word *trias* to refer to the Triune God. He used it late in the second century in his *Ad autolycus,* an early Christian apology. Tertullian, the African church father, used the Latin word *trinitas* to say that there is "one God: Father, Son, and Holy Spirit" (*On Modesty* 21). The trinitarian concept of God, as noted by Theophilus and Tertullian, was derived from Jesus' telling his disciples to baptize people "in the name of the Father and of the Son and of the Holy Spirit" (Matthew 28:19). In 325 the Council of Nicaea formulated the Nicene Creed that stated that God was one divine essence in three persons: Father, Son, and Holy Spirit. For centuries the acceptance or denial of the doctrine of the Trinity has been used to determine whether or not an individual is a Christian or not.

During most of the Christian church's history, numerous congregations have been named Trinity—for example, Trinity Episcopal Church. Before the Reformation, churches having this name were simply called Trinity Church. Some colleges have also chosen this name—for instance, Trinity College of Cambridge University in England, Trinity University of San Antonio, Texas, and others.

VERBAL EXPRESSIONS AND SAYINGS

Christianity has contributed a number of verbal expressions that have enriched the language of various countries. I will note only those that have become a conventional part of the English language, although other languages, especially in Europe, have also absorbed various Christian sayings and expressions.

"A GOOD SAMARITAN"

The Good Samaritan, whom Jesus mentioned in one of his parables, has become a prototype and example of someone who gives of him- or herself to help others beyond what most people are inclined to do. Had Jesus never uttered the parable of the Good Samaritan, the world would lack one of the most altruistic models of human behavior known to mankind. Although many Christian expressions and symbols today are increasingly being banned from public usage, one may still call someone a "Good Samaritan" without its being seen as a biased Christian term.

"AVOID IT LIKE THE PLAGUE"

This expression comes from St. Jerome (early fifth century), who used these words in a rather narrow context. He said, "Avoid, as you would the plague, a clergyman who is also a man of business."[23] Today people use this expression much more broadly, indicating that they will avoid anything that might seriously harm them.

"BROTHER"

Before the advent of Christianity, the word *brother* (Greek *adelphos*) was primarily a biological concept, referring to male siblings having the same father. But when Jesus said, "Whoever does God's will is my *brother*" (Mark 3:35), he gave the word a spiritual kinship meaning that was soon being used by the apostles and the early Christians to address one another. St. Paul told the Christians in Rome, "I urge you, brothers"; and to the believers in Thessalonica he wrote, "*Brothers*, pray for us." St. John says, "Do not be surprised, my *brothers*, if the world hates you."[24]

Addressing each other as "brother" was a common and regular form of greeting among early Christians. Tertullian informs us that using this form of greeting was an additional reason why the pagan Romans hated Christians. Says he, "And they are wroth with us too, because we call each other brethren" (*Apology* 39). Tertullian also explains that Christians called one another brother because they had a common father in God (*Apology* 39).

During the late Middle Ages the fellowship meaning of the term *brother* spread beyond the circle of Christian usage as guilds and secret orders called its members "brothers." This practice spread to secret fraternal orders such as Freemasonry, Odd Fellows, and others. University fraternities also adopted this form of address for its members. Even many labor unions used the word in their organizations' official names, for instance, the Brotherhood of Railroad Workers. Thus, we have another example of Christianity's influence that went beyond the church itself.

"DOUBTING THOMAS"

Another common expression that has become a part of the English language is the label "doubting Thomas" applied to someone who is given to

"THE DOUBTING THOMAS" portrays Christ giving the evidence his disciple Thomas demanded in order to believe that Christ had truly risen from the dead. (*Julius Schnorr*)

persistent doubt, whether in religious matters or otherwise. The label usually has an uncomplimentary connotation.

Thomas, one of Jesus' twelve apostles, at first refused to believe the report of his fellow apostles that they had seen their resurrected Lord on the evening of the day he rose from the dead. Thomas insisted that he would not believe them, saying, "Unless I see the nail marks in his hands and put my finger where the nails were, and put my hand into his side, I will not believe it" (John 20:25). One week after Jesus had first appeared to the apostles, he again entered their midst behind closed doors. This time Thomas was present. Jesus, knowing of Thomas's doubts, asked him to see and touch his wounds. Upon doing so, Thomas declared, "My Lord and my God!" (John 20:28). His words were an astounding confession, perhaps greater than Peter's confession before Christ's death and resurrection. Yet Thomas is remembered negatively as the great doubter.

The expression, "doubting Thomas," is derived from a misunderstanding of the text that gives the impression that the veracity of Christ's resurrection rests on mere faith. But Thomas, unlike many modern Christians, would not accept the resurrection of Christ on the basis of mere faith. To him faith did not establish the veracity of Christ's resurrection; rather, the veracity of Christ's resurrection was necessary to establish the validity of his faith. What he wanted was consistent with what St. Peter later wrote: "We did not follow cleverly invented stories. . .but we were eyewitnesses of his majesty" (2 Peter 1:16). One might say that Thomas wanted to be certain that, if he was to preach the resurrection of Christ, he had to have the evidence that it had really happened. To have faith in something that might not have happened was not good enough for him.

Today many well-meaning Christians, including clergy, cite the Thomas incident, especially the last words of Jesus, "Because you have seen me, you have believed; blessed are those who have not seen and yet have believed" (John 20:29), to argue that Christ's resurrection rests entirely on faith. This is an unfortunate misreading of the text, because Jesus did not say that the veracity of his resurrection is a matter of faith. Not at all. If that were what he intended, he would not have given Thomas the empirical evidence of his resurrection. Moreover, Jesus' words indicate that other individuals, such as you and I, who would someday only be able to hear or read the apostles' report of Christ's resurrection, would be blessed for believing their account. In short, Jesus' words to Thomas do not say that Christ's resurrection is a faith event. It is only the *benefits* of his resurrection that are received through faith, but the physical resurrection of Christ itself was—and remains—a historical event, similar to all other historical occurrences, quite independent of any Christian's faith.

Would history (and the church) not have done Thomas more justice if it had portrayed him as a hero, a wise man not given to gullibility? To him the resurrection of Christ was too important to be left to human credulity. One can argue that receiving empirical verification of Christ's resurrection not only gave Thomas the courage to declare this unique historical event to others but also that the knowledge of his experience was an added factor in transforming the early Christians, who were unequivocally convinced that they were worshiping not a dead carpenter, but one who had indeed risen from the dead. It was the historical certainty of Christ's physical resurrection (as noted in chapter 1) that transformed them, motivating them to stand firmly against the many pagan values and practices, and that in time transformed the Greco-Roman world.

"FILTHY LUCRE"

Today this expression is often applied to money in general. It comes from the widespread influence of the King James Version of the Bible's original usage, where in St. Paul's letter to Titus he warns his co-worker that false teachers were in his midst, teaching false doctrines for "filthy lucre's sake" (Titus 1:11 KJV). Paul's use of the words "filthy lucre" in Greek meant ill-gotten money or some other illegitimate economic gain.

"THE GOSPEL TRUTH"

Before the nineteenth century, no one seriously doubted the four Gospel accounts of Jesus' life and work. They were seen as God's inspired recordings of what actually happened regarding his teachings, his miracles, how he was falsely accused, crucified, and raised from the dead—hence the saying, "It's the gospel truth." It was people's way of indicating that what they said or reported was as true as the New Testament's Gospels. Today the expression is often used without any awareness of its Christian connection.

"HARMLESS AS DOVES"

Jesus commanded his followers to be "as shrewd as snakes and as innocent as doves" (Matthew 10:16). It is from these words that the simile "harmless as doves" originated. The dove also gained symbolic significance among the early Christians in that at the baptism of Jesus the Holy Spirit descended on him like a dove (Mark 1:10). Thus, Christians have used the descending dove to symbolize the peaceful assurance of the Holy Spirit. Today even the secular world uses the dove as a symbol of peace, thereby showing its indebtedness to Jesus Christ. It would be interesting to speculate about what peace symbol would be used today had Jesus never referred to the harmlessness of a dove or had it not been used at his baptism, where it conveyed a message of peaceful assurance.

"A JUDAS"

Had Judas not betrayed Jesus the night before his crucifixion, this expression would not be in our vocabulary. As is well known, this term is often applied to an individual who is untrustworthy, someone who would betray or has betrayed his closest friend. So whenever this epithet is applied to a dishonest or conniving person, the tragic behavior of Judas Iscariot is recalled. Although the names of the other eleven disciples have for two thousand years been given to countless male children, the name of Judas has such an evil connotation that Christian parents in the West, since the time of Christ's betrayal, have tended not to give this name to a male child.

"Rob Peter to Pay Paul"

According to legend, the abbey church of St. Peter's in England's Westminster diocese became a cathedral in 1540. Ten years later St. Peter's became part of the London diocese, and many of its assets were used to pay for the repair of St. Paul's Cathedral that had been badly damaged by fire. Today "to rob Peter to pay Paul" often means taking money from one person or source and giving it to another, or especially to shift a debt—that is, pay off one by incurring another one. Thus, we have another expression that stems from Christian background.

"Thorn in the Flesh"

St. Paul told the Corinthian Christians that God had given him a "thorn in my flesh" that was difficult to bear, but it would keep him mindful of his dependency on God (2 Corinthians 12:7–10). What his "thorn" was no one knows. Today this expression is often used by many without any religious connotation to indicate that they have a perpetual problem or burden that is difficult to bear. Such a problem may refer to a physical condition, or situation, or even to a person. Moreover, it is interesting how St. Paul's problem, which God gave him to aid him in his spiritual life, is now often used in a nonspiritual sense.

"Turn the Other Cheek"

Everyone has heard this phrase. It comes from Jesus' Sermon on the Mount, where he said, "If someone strikes you on the right cheek, turn to him the other also" (Matthew 5:39). This advice, though well known, is not widely followed, even by the professed followers of Christ. Nevertheless, someone might counsel a friend not to fight back, but rather to "turn the other cheek." Such advice is meant to keep the situation calm and avoid painful conflict. It should be noted, however, that this expression refers only to interpersonal situations, for Jesus addressed it only to individuals. The context does not allow it to be applied to governmental authorities, as is sometimes done.

"When in Rome, do as the Romans do"

When St. Augustine (354–430) and his mother Monica moved from northern Africa to Milan, Italy, via Rome, she asked St. Ambrose (340–97),

CHRISTIAN DERIVATION
OF EXPRESSIONS AND SAYINGS

Expression/Saying	Source/Origin	Current Meaning
"Good Samaritan"	Jesus Christ's parable (Luke 10:30–37)	Someone who is kind and helpful, especially to strangers
"Avoid it like the plague"	St. Jerome, early 5th cent.	Avoid anything that might be harmful
"Brother"	A concept expressed by Jesus Christ (Mark 3:3)	Spiritual kinship with someone not biologically related
"Doubting Thomas"	Thomas doubting Christ's resurrection (John 20:24–28)	Someone who doubts valid evidence
"Filthy lucre"	St. Paul (Titus 1:11)	Often applied to all money
"The gospel truth"	The veracity of Jesus Christ's life and sayings in the four New Testament Gospels	A synonym for absolute truth
"Harmless as doves"	Jesus Christ (Matthew 10:16)	Someone who does no one any harm
"A Judas"	Betrayal of Jesus by Judas (New Testament Gospels)	An inside person who betrays a friend or group
"Rob Peter to pay Paul"	Assets of St. Peter's church in London being used to repair St. Paul's cathedral, 1540s	Taking money from one person or group to assist another
"Thorn in the flesh"	St. Paul's enduring personal ailment (2 Corinthians 12:7)	Any problem that continues to vex someone
"Turn the other cheek"	Jesus' Sermon on the Mount (Matthew 5:39)	Not getting even with one's enemy
"When in Rome, do as the Romans do"	St. Ambrose, ca. early 390s	Adopt the manners of the place one visits
"Wolf in sheep's clothing"	Jesus Christ (Matthew 7:15)	An appealing person can be deceptive

bishop of Milan, whether she should fast on Saturdays as the Christians did in Rome. Ambrose replied that in Milan he did not fast on Saturdays, but when he was in Rome, he fasted in concert with other Christians.[25] Thus, the saying "When in Rome, do as the Romans do" has a Christian origin that goes back to the latter part of the fourth century.

"Wolf in Sheep's Clothing"

Although the essence of this expression is in one of Aesop's fables, it apparently gained no currency until Jesus said, "Watch out for false prophets. They come to you in sheep's clothing, but inwardly they are ferocious wolves" (Matthew 7:15). Ever since Jesus uttered this warning, the expression has been used by Christians to indicate that false teachers, whose teachings may appear harmless or even appealing, are destructive to the Christian faith. The expression has, of course, spread beyond the circle of Christian usage. It is often used in nonreligious contexts to state that behind the veneer of a charismatic personality or ideology there might be catastrophic danger.

Christian Names

By the middle of the third century, the early Christians began to depart from giving their newly born children Roman names or names from pagan mythology such as Baachylus, Aphrodisius, or Daphne.[26] Eusebius, the early church historian, notes that Bishop Dionysius of Alexandria (d. 265) said that Christian parents preferred to give their children names of the apostles and other prominent Christian figures such as John, Peter, Timothy, Mark, or Paul (*Ecclesiastical History* 7.25.14–15). But this new practice did not become common until the latter part of the fourth century. On the other hand, Christians giving their children names of Old Testament characters did not occur until the age of Calvinism (sixteenth century), according to Adolf Harnack, the German historian of the early church.[27] Today, even among many nonreligious people, Christian names (names from the Judeo-Christian tradition) are given to men and women in the Western world. Names such as Andrew, Mark, Matthew, John, Paul, Timothy, Stephen, and Peter, all taken from the New Testament, are common among men. Men also have names derived from Jesus Christ. For instance, Christopher and Christian are among English-speaking males; Chretien is well known among the French; and the male name of Christiano is found in Italy and Spain. The name Jesu is quite common in Latin America. On the other hand, the names of Christine, Kirsten, Kristen, and Kristel are often given to women as well as the nicknames of Chrissy, Christie, and Tina.

The names of David, Aaron, Michael, Daniel, Adam, Joseph, Jacob, Benjamin, and Samuel that honor well-known individuals from the Old Testament are also common. Similarly, Christian names from the New Testament identify many women today—for example, Mary, Martha, Joanna, Priscilla, Eunice, Lydia, and Dorcas. And Sarah, Rebekah, Esther,

Ruth, Naomi, and Rachel are well-known names for women from the Old Testament. Giving names of biblical characters to one's children is another poignant illustration of Christianity's pervasive influence, an influence that has continued for almost two millennia.

CONCLUSION

Although Sunday, Christmas Day, Easter Day, and Pentecost often are no longer seen as Christian holy days by an increasing number of Westerners, these days have over the centuries nevertheless become an integral part of the culture in the Western hemisphere and in many other parts of the world. If these days were abolished and replaced with other days, most people, religious or not, would undoubtedly have their lives unfavorably altered, socially and psychologically. It is not likely that very many would opt for such a change. Even those who are of a nonreligious or secular orientation in the Western world have become creatures of habit with regard to these special Christian days in that culturally they are in many ways a part of their lives. In effect, they are beneficiaries of this Christian heritage.

Christian words and symbols have also become a part of the social and psychological fabric of countless individuals, whether or not they are Christian. Given their long-standing Christian history and etymology, it is hard to imagine that words such as *cathedral, chapel, cemetery, church, creed, heaven,* and *hell,* for example, could be replaced with other words and still convey the same meaning, because words both denote and connote rather specific information that cannot be conveyed by just any word or symbol. Thus, here too the Christian influence is very much present, even in a rapidly changing era.

Finally, whether it is the existence of holidays, vocabulary, symbols, verbal expressions, or personal names (derived from preceding Christians) that identify countless people today, the effects of Christianity have been immense and widespread. And when its many other contributions, cited in this book's pages, are considered, history and civilization owe Christianity a tremendous gratitude. The words of Carsten Thiede and Matthew D'Ancona seem appropriate when they say that "the [Christian] Gospels are the very building blocks of our civilization. Without them Giotto would not have painted his frescoes in the Arena Chapel at Padua; Dante would not have written the *Divine Comedy;* Mozart would not have composed his *Requiem;* and Wren would not have built St. Paul's Cathedral. The story and message of these four books—along with the Judaic tradition of the Old Testament—pervade not only the moral conventions of the West but also our systems of social organization, nomenclature, architecture, literature and education, as well as the rituals of marriage and death which shape our lives...Christians and non-Christians alike."[28]

NOTES

1. E. G. Richards, *Mapping Time: The Calendar and Its History* (New York: Oxford University Press, 1998), 210.

2. Tom Flynn, *The Trouble with Christmas* (Buffalo: Prometheus Books, 1993), 58.

3. Matthew Bunson, *Encyclopedia of the Roman Empire* (New York: Facts on File, 1992), 393.

4. Thomas Talley, *The Origins of the Liturgical Year* (Collegeville, Minn.: Liturgical Press, 1991), 90, 91.

5. J. Neil Alexander, *The Liturgical Meaning of Advent, Christmas, Epiphany: Waiting for the Coming* (Washington, D.C.: Pastoral Press, 1993), 51.

6. Bunson, *Encyclopedia of the Roman Empire,* 393.

7. Maxwell E. Johnson, "Let's Keep Advent Right Where It Is," *Lutheran Forum* (November 1994): 45–46.

8. E. Johnson, "Easter and Its Cycle," *New Catholic Encyclopedia* (San Francisco: McGraw-Hill, 1967), 5:6.

9. Elizabeth Hough Sechrist, "Halloween," *The World Book Encyclopedia* (Chicago: Field Enterprises Educational Corporation, 1958), 8:3245.

10. "Thanksgiving Proclamation," in *The Writings of George Washington* (Washington, D.C.: United States Government Printing Office, 1939), 30:427.

11. "Proclamation for Thanksgiving," in *The Writings of Abraham Lincoln* (New York: G. P. Putnam's Sons, 1906), 6:358.

12. Pierre Gaxotte, *The French Revolution* (New York: Charles Scribner's Sons, 1932), 329.

13. Richards, *Mapping Time,* 277.

14. Ibid., 160.

15. F. L. Cross and E. A. Livingstone, eds., *The Oxford Dictionary of the Christian Church* (New York: Oxford University Press, 1997), 312.

16. Marguerite Ickis, *The Book of Religious Holidays and Celebrations* (New York: Dodd, Mead, 1966), 51.

17. Ibid., 52.

18. Ibid.

19. Kevin D. Vogts, "Henry Schwann's Christmas Tree," *The Lutheran Witness* (December 1998): 8.

20. National Christmas Tree Association, 1999 data.

21. Robin Lane Fox, *Pagans and Christians* (New York: Knopf, 1986), 31.

22. Martin Luther, *Luther's Small Catechism* (St. Louis: Concordia Publishing House, 1986), 30–31.

23. Christine Ammer, *Have a Nice Day—No Problem* (New York: Penguin Books, 1992), 307.

24. See respectively Romans 15:30; 1 Thessalonians 5:25; and 1 John 3:13 NKJV.

25. Ammer, *Have a Nice Day,* 405.

26. Adolf Harnack, *The Mission and Expansion of Christianity in the First Three Centuries,* trans. James Moffat (New York: G. P. Putnam's Sons, 1908), 1:422.

27. Ibid., 1:430.

28. Carsten Peter Thiede and Matthew D'Ancona, *Eye Witness to Jesus: Amazing New Manuscript Evidence About the Origin of the Gospels* (New York: Doubleday, 1996), 153.

ACKNOWLEDGMENTS

Every author knows that one cannot write a book without the generous assistance of numerous people. This was also my good fortune. In particular, I first want to thank my wife, Carol, who not only tolerated my being holed up in my study for days and months in front of the computer, but also carefully read the entire manuscript, noting slips and errors.

Second on my list are the kind and helpful individuals in the library of Illinois College, Jacksonville, Illinois. I am especially grateful to Laura Sweatman, who obtained numerous books for me by means of interlibrary loan; she was always pleasant and eagerly searched to find many odd titles in libraries, far and near. Mike Westerbrook provided invaluable help in making numerous Internet searches for me. And Martin Gallas, head librarian, always tolerated my countless library visits with a spirit of professional demeanor. Also very helpful was the library staff of Concordia Seminary in

St. Louis, who gave me a few special privileges. The library at Washington University in St. Louis provided additional help in my research efforts. And not to be overlooked is the valuable assistance that Dan Malan provided in furnishing many illustrations, especially the biblical portraits from his vast collection of Gustave Doré and Julius Schnorr, two renowned artists of biblical art.

Given that my talents are not in the field of music, I took advantage of the expertise and generosity of two music professors, John Behnke of Concordia University in Milwaukee and Richard Resch of Concordia Theological Seminary in Fort Wayne, Indiana. I thank them for their professional comments regarding chapter 13, "The Sound of Music: Its Christian Resonance." Their comments were very helpful.

Last, but not least, I wish to thank at least four individuals at Zondervan, namely, Jim Ruark, Jonathan Petersen, Jack Kragt, and Curt Diepenhorst. As senior editor-at-large, Jim provided many helpful editorial comments and suggestions. Often the author is so close to his subject that he sometimes fails to see the need for an added detail or that a given thought might be expressed a better way. His kind, professional advice is highly appreciated. As marketing director, Jonathan did much to help establish the book's title. And I also wish to thank Curt, the graphic artist, for his efforts in designing the book's jacket. I also express my gratitude to all those at Zondervan with whom I did not interact directly but who nevertheless helped to launch this book.

Finally, I alone am responsible for any errors that might be found in this volume. As all authors know, the most meticulous proofreading rarely succeeds in producing a completely error-free book.

INDEX

Basilica churches, 296, 301, 310
"Battle Hymn of the Reformation," 322
"Battle Hymn of the Republic," 283
Bauer, Marion, 338
Bede, the Venerable, 214, 350, 369, 379, 382
Beecher, Catherine, 280
Beecher, Edward, 279, 280, 288
Beecher, Henry Ward, 280, 281
Beecher, Lyman, 279, 281
Beethoven, Ludwig van, 320, 328–29, 377
Before Christ (B.C.), 382, 390
Behnke, John, 343
Bell, Eric, 232
Benedict, St., 163, 186
Benedictine monasteries, 157
Benignus of Dijon, 53, 153
Berger, Peter L., 243
Ben-Hur, 366, 367, 369
Berea College, 282
Bernard, St., 197
Bestiality, 90, 92
Bible, The. *See* Holy Scriptures
Bill of Rights (American), 259
Bill of Rights (British), 259
Birney, James G., 283, 288
Bisexual Roman emperors, 87
Blackstone, William, 254
Blind education, 182, 183, 188
Bloom, Allan, 338
"Blue Laws," 376
Boer War, 333
Boettner, Loraine, 358
Bokris, Victor, 374
Bologna, University of, 187, 189
Bonaventure, St., 276
Bonhoeffer, Dietrich, 38, 59
Boniface, St., 175, 385
Bonzas, 131
Boorstin, Daniel, 213
Booth, William, 137
Bowen, James, 179
Bowers v. Hardwick, 89
Boyd, William, 172, 177
Boyle, Robert, 235, 241, 243
Boyle's Law, 235
Brace, Charles Loring, 134
Bradford, William, 137, 211, 381
Brahe, Tycho, 224, 227, 230, 231, 240

Brahms, Johannes, 330, 331, 335
Braille, Louis, 182–83, 188
Braille, reading method, 183
Braudel, Fernand, 13
Brephotophia, 132, 145
British Association for the Advancement of Science, 235
"Brother(s)," 385
Brothers Karamazov, The, 366, 369
Brown v. Board of Education, 287
Bruni, Leonardo, 174
Brunner, Emil, 197, 312
Brutus, Marcius and Decius, 60
Bugenhagen, Johannes, 179
Bunyan, John, 359, 369
Burdett, Henry, 154
Buridan, Jean, 221, 231, 240
Burtt, E. A., 232
Butterfield, Herbert, 232
Buxton, Thomas Fowell, 277
Byzantine churches, 300

C

Cadaver research, 189, 237
Caesar and God. *See* Church and State
Caecilius, 348
Caesarius of Arles, 58
Calendar, Gregorian, 382
Cahill, Thomas, 14
Caligula, 40, 52, 57, 75, 81
Callistus of Rome, 51, 53, 289
Calvin, John, 59, 177, 188, 199, 200, 204, 213, 261, 322, 358, 369
Calvinist Ethic. *See* Protestant Ethic; Christian Work Ethic
Calvinists (Calvinism), 200, 231, 261, 322, 358
Camille, Michael, 298
Canaanites, 66
Cannibalism, 58, 66–67, 76
"Canon" of Western literature, 356, 360
Canon Law, 187
Canons of St. Basil, 59
Cantatas, 320–21, 339
Canterbury Tales, The, 353–54, 369
Capitalism, 199, 200, 206–8, 367
Catamites, 82
Caracalla, 41
Carcopino, Jerome, 63, 82

DISCUSSION QUESTIONS

There are three kinds of questions for each chapter: information, interpretation, application. These can be used for either individual or group study.

CHAPTER 1: PEOPLE TRANSFORMED by JESUS CHRIST

LOOKING for FACTS

1. What town did Jesus use as his main base of operation during his ministry?

2. Most of the disciples were frightened and hid from Jesus' crucifixion, yet later endured persecution and even death in their desire to preach the Christian message. What event transformed them?

2. What did the Greek word *martyr* initially mean?

4. What young woman was martyred for her Christian faith in A.D. 202?

5. What does the Greek letter X (chi) superimposed on the Greek letter P (rho) represent?

6. What did the Edict of Milan in A.D. 313 do for the early Christians?

7. Who was first emperor to imprint the Christian cross on Roman coins?

8. What Roman emperor said "You Galileans have conquered"?

9. What did it mean to be a catechumen in the early Christian church?

10. Name at least three church fathers in the early church who were transformed by Jesus Christ.

INTERPRETING the FACTS

1. Why did the resurrected Christ have Thomas touch his crucifixion wounds?

2. Why do you think Emperor Constantine helped finance the building of so many Christian churches for his mother, Helena?

3. Explain why you think Emperor Constantine was a Christian or was not.

4. What role do you think Helena played in her son's legalizing Christianity in A.D. 313?

5. Does the Christian's faith validate Christ's resurrection, or does Christ's resurrection validate the Christian's faith?

APPLYING the FACTS

1. Show what Christians today can learn from the persecutions of the early Christians.

2. Explain how the message of Christ's physical resurrection from the dead can transform people today.

3. The pagan Greek physician Galen said the early Christians practiced "self-discipline and self-control." How can today's Christians learn from this posture of the early Christians?

4. Many Christians today are persecuted to varying degrees in many countries; others face discrimination. How can knowledge of the early Christians' persecution help Christians today cope with this?

CHAPTER 2: The SANCTIFICATION of HUMAN LIFE

LOOKING for FACTS

1. What countries or people in ancient times practiced infanticide?

2. In what manner did the pagan Greco-Romans abandon infants?

3. Name some Christian leaders who opposed infanticide or child abandonment.

4. What is the origin of the word *gladiators*?

5. What cruel behavioral practices of the Romans did Emperor Constantine and his son, Constantius, outlaw?

6. When and by whom were the Roman gladiatorial contests banned?

7. Name some groups of people who sacrificed human beings besides the Romans.

8. Name some early Christian leaders and church councils that opposed suicide.

9. Christian opposition to cremation influenced the pagan Romans to abandon the practice in what century?

INTERPRETING the FACTS

1. Why did the early Christians oppose child abandonment, infanticide, and abortion?

2. What significance does the Greek word *pharmakeia* have in regard to the abortion practices of the Greco-Romans?

3. Why did the early Christians refuse to attend the Roman gladiatorial contests?

4. What arguments did the early Christian theologians use to oppose suicide?

5. Why did the early Christians reject and oppose cremating their dead?

APPLYING the FACTS

1. Explain what modern Christians can learn from their early Christian ancestors with regard to abortion today.

2. Show what today's Christians can learn from the early Christians in opposing assisted suicide.

3. Early Christianity stood for the sanctity of human life. Show how some of that sanctity is present in the world today.

CHAPTER 3: CHRISTIANITY ELEVATES SEXUAL MORALITY

LOOKING for FACTS

1. What kind of picture did the Greco-Roman writers portray regarding their culture's heterosexual life?

2. What does the Roman phrase *"Qualis rex, talis grex"* mean?

3. Which sinful sexual behaviors did the early Christians and their descendants condemn?

4. Which Roman emperor's efforts helped bring dignity to marriage?

5. Homosexual behavior among Greco-Roman men was primarily confined to what kind of partners or consorts?

6. The letters of NAMBLA are the abbreviation for the name of what organization?

7. What kinds of biblically condemned sexual behaviors were common and legal in Roman society?

INTERPRETING the FACTS

1. In what ways might the Roman phrase *"Qualis rex, talis grex"* describe or not describe American culture today?

2. Which New Testament passages specifically condemn homosexual behavior?

3. What role did the Christian women in the early church play in bringing dignity to marriage?

4. How did Roman life in their households contribute to sexually deviant behavior?

5. What effect can sexually deviant behavior have on society?

APPLYING the FACTS

1. Discuss the biblical principles behind the Christian teaching that sexual behavior is to be confined to marriage between a man and a woman.

2. Explain how today's secular norm of "consenting adults" conflicts with what the early Christians believed and practiced in regard to sexual behavior.

3. Using the early Christians as examples, how might people today counter sexually deviant behavior?

CHAPTER 4: WOMEN RECEIVE FREEDOM and DIGNITY

LOOKING for FACTS

1. What specific behaviors were not permitted to Greek women in ancient Athens?

2. What specific behaviors were not permitted to ancient Hebrew women?

3. What ancient Roman law gave the father virtually absolute power over any member of his family?

4. Who was unhappy with how Jesus interacted with the Samaritan woman?

5. What Judaic or rabbinic law did Jesus violate by teaching Mary theology?

6. Name some active, leading women mentioned in the New Testament.

7. Name several specific freedoms Christianity gave to women that the Greco-Roman society did not allow.

INTERPRETING the FACTS

1. How do Jesus' words "There are those who are last who will be first, and first who will be last" relate to his appearing first to women after his resurrection?

2. How did the early church's acceptance of women conflict with the Greco-Roman view of women?

3. Why did some of the church fathers (early church leaders) ignore or forget the way Jesus viewed women?

4. For several centuries Christian women were required to wear a veil of some kind. Why did this practice eventually disappear?

5. Some people say that "all cultures are essentially equal." If this is true, can the practice of clitoridectomy or widow burning logically be condemned?

6. Discuss why Jesus did not start a women's movement.

APPLYING the FACTS

1. Show what relevance Jesus' view of women has for life among Christians today.

2. Explain what relevance Jesus' view of women has to radical feminism.

3. Show how Jesus' view of marriage is relevant to monogamy.

4. Explain what relevance Ephesians 5:21 has for Christian marriages today.

CHAPTER 5: CHARITY and COMPASSION: THEIR CHRISTIAN CONNECTION

LOOKING for FACTS

1. What methods of charity did the Hebrews practice in the Old Testament era?
2. What directions for charity did Jesus give?
3. What were the two types of charity the ancient Romans practiced? Which of these did the early Christians employ?
4. What three components are necessary in order for charity to be Christian?
5. Which ancient pagan philosophers argued against charity?
6. Cite some examples in history that show compassion was not part of the pagan past.
7. Name three institutions of charity in early Christianity.
8. Which two European scholars-writers saw America as charity-oriented?
9. When and where were child labor laws first enacted?
10. Name some American service clubs that practice charity.

INTERPRETING the FACTS

1. Show how compassion is a Christian innovation.
2. Show the difference between state welfare programs and Christian charity.
3. Discuss why Christian charity has become secularized.
4. What role does volunteerism play in Christian charity versus state welfare?
5. In what way was the early YMCA a charity-oriented organization?
6. In what way do American fraternal benefit organizations function as charity organizations?
7. How did Jesus' view of charity differ from that of the pagan philosophers?

APPLYING the FACTS

1. Show how Christians, in the context of Christian charity, can practice the Golden Rule.

2. Show how and why helping the poor and needy in our society today is not necessarily an example of Christian charity.

3. Give an example or two in our society today of what this chapter calls *liberalitas*.

CHAPTER 6: HOSPITALS and HEALTH CARE: THEIR CHRISTIAN ROOTS

LOOKING for FACTS

1. What else did Jesus command his disciples to do besides preach the Word of God?

2. What does this chapter mean by "the pagan void"?

3. In what year was the first Christian hospital built?

4. At what well-known church council were bishops urged to establish hospices?

5. For what is Dorothy Dix noted in America?

6. When and where was the Red Cross founded?

7. How do the names of many hospitals today remind us of their Christian origin?

INTERPRETING the FACTS

1. Discuss why the Greco-Romans had no hospitals.

2. Why do you think Florence Nightingale ignored her parents' wish not to be a nurse?

3. Why were hospitals in medieval England often called "God's Houses"?

4. Economically, what was different about the early Christian hospitals from those in our society today?

APPLYING the FACTS

1. How can Christians make it known that hospitals originated in the context of Christian charity?

2. Show how Christian charity can be preempted by the way hospitals are supported financially.

3. In light of 1 Timothy 3:2 and Titus 1:8, how might American Christians today be more hospitable?

CHAPTER 7: CHRISTIANITY'S IMPRINT on EDUCATION

LOOKING for FACTS

1. An early theological manual in the early church was formally known by what name?

2. Those receiving catechetical instruction in early church were commonly known by what name?

3. What were the seven subjects and the two divisions of an ancient liberal arts education?

4. Who was the first modern advocate of compulsory education?

5. Which Christian thinker in the Reformation era first proposed graded education?

6. Who was the Christian layman to first introduce the philosophy of kindergarten education?

7. What biblical passage prompted the founding of the first Sunday school?

INTERPRETING the FACTS

1. How did the first Sunday schools differ from Sunday schools today?

2. Why did the early Christians catechize (instruct) both men and women?

3. Show the origin of the concept of providing education for everyone.

4. Explain why universities originated in the context of monasteries.

APPLYING the FACTS

1. What is a relatively easy way to show that colleges and universities had Christian origins?
2. Explain how the concept of graded education influenced modern education.
3. Some critics contend that Christianity is anti-intellectual. What evidence does this chapter provide to counter this criticism?

CHAPTER 8: LABOR and ECONOMIC FREEDOM DIGNIFIED

LOOKING for FACTS

1. The ancient Greeks saw manual labor only fitting for what kind of people?
2. The dignity Christianity gave to work and labor undermined what ancient social institution?
3. Who said, "If a man will not work, he shall not eat"?
4. Who said, "The laborer is worthy of his wages"?
5. Who saw work as the "mask of God" (*larvae Dei*), meaning God is in it?
6. Which Protestant theologian approved the taking of interest money (usury)?
7. Which political ideology (movement) opposes private property?
8. Which one of Jesus' parables condones or approves the profit motive?
9. Name two early American sites where socialism was tried and failed.
10. Give some examples that show Columbus was a sincere Christian.

INTERPRETING the FACTS

1. Explain why "Christian socialism" may be viewed as an oxymoron.
2. Fyodor Dostoyevsky said, "The socialist who is a Christian is more to be dreaded than a socialist who is an atheist." What did he mean?
3. Why has capitalism been called a by-product of Christianity?
4. Why has communism or socialism been called a "Christian heresy"?
5. Why did socialism fail in early New England?
6. What motives did Columbus have besides economics?

APPLYING the FACTS

1. Explain how Christians can rightfully use economic profits.

2. Explain how profits are necessary in order to pay laborers their wages.

3. Show how Christianity operates with a lineal concept of time.

4. Show why and how property rights are vital to people's freedom.

CHAPTER 9: SCIENCE: ITS CHRISTIAN CONNECTIONS

LOOKING for FACTS

1. What non-Christian philosopher argued that it was Christianity's "insistence on the rationality of God" that made science possible?

2. Which pagan religious belief sees the divine in nature and nature in the divine?

3. Which theory about the sun—heliostatic or heliocentric—did Copernicus teach? Which system did Johannes Kepler teach?

4. What pioneering Christian astronomer gave science its first three "natural laws"?

5. What famous scientist said, "We know God only through Jesus Christ"?

6. Who was the scientist known as *Lutherus medicorum* (the Luther of medicine), and what was his contribution to the field?

7. According to this chapter, when did "methodological atheism" become an operating assumption for many scientists?

INTERPRETING the FACTS

1. Why is Christianity's insistence on the rationality of God necessary for science?

2. Christianity teaches that God is separate from his creation. Why is this concept important for science?

3. What evidence is there that none of the pioneering scientists from the thirteenth to eighteenth centuries operated with "methodological atheism"?

4. Kepler showed that planets orbited elliptically (his first law). Show how this finding contradicted Aristotle's theory.

APPLYING the FACTS

1. How can Christians counter today's widely held belief that science and Christianity are enemies, or at least incompatible?

2. Show how the findings of science can be seen as a gift of God.

3. Explain how science can be seen as consistent with God's command that man is to have "dominion . . . over all the earth" (Genesis 1:26 NKJV).

CHAPTER 10: LIBERTY and JUSTICE for ALL

LOOKING for FACTS

1. When and where did the concept of "due process of law" first appear?

2. What Christian bishop first applied the concept of "no one is above the law" to a Roman emperor?

3. Who in the New Testament clearly states the concept of natural law?

4. Who said the Ten Commandments are a reflection of the natural law?

5. When and by whom was the concept of natural law applied to natural rights?

6. The words "the Law of Nature and Nature's God" are found in what document?

7. The words "We hold these truths to be self-evident" in the Declaration of Independence of the United States are a reflection of what words in the New Testament?

8. What non-American is known as "the godfather of the American Constitution"?

9. Who were some advocates of religious freedom in early Christianity?

10. Who was the Christian bishop to first apply the principle of the separation of church and state?

11. When and where did the phrase "wall of separation" in the context of the relationship between church and state in the United States first appear?

INTERPRETING the FACTS

1. How is the concept of "no one is above the law" revealed in the Magna Carta?

2. Why does the Bible in Deuteronomy 19 require two or more witnesses in order to convict someone of a crime?

3. What is the significance of Emperor Theodosius's public repentance?

4. How did Montesquieu's book *The Spirit of Laws* (1748) shape United States government?

5. What evidence supports the concept that Christianity influenced the formation of the Constitution of the United States?

6. How does Christianity's emphasis on the equality of individuals differ from the secular understanding of equality of individuals?

7. Which words of Jesus Christ are commonly cited in support of the separation of church and state?

APPLYING the FACTS

1. Show how Christians can and should defend the concept of "no one is above the law."

2. Give an example from your knowledge when the principle of "no one is above the law" was clearly violated in history.

3. Discuss whether freedom of religion in the United States means a religious group may practice any of its values (such as barring vaccination or allowing polygamy).

4. Give an example of how group rights and individual rights can be in conflict.

5. Show how the Christian principle of equality can be misunderstood.

6. Discuss the idea that deleting the phrase "under God" in the American Pledge of Allegiance is promoting freedom *from* religion rather than *of* religion.

CHAPTER II: SLAVERY ABOLISHED: a CHRISTIAN ACHIEVEMENT

LOOKING for FACTS

1. Where was slavery first practiced before it made its way to Western Europe?

2. Which New Testament book shows that slavery is not compatible with Christianity?

3. Which Christian Roman emperor imposed the death penalty in A.D. 315 on those who stole children in order to bring them up as slaves?

4. Who was the most prominent Christian abolitionist in Great Britain in the nineteenth century?

5. What percentage of Americans in the South owned slaves before the Civil War?

6. Who is often known as the first martyr of the American Abolition Movement?

7. In what year did Harriet Beecher Stowe pen *Uncle Tom's Cabin*?

8. Where was the first American anti-slavery proclamation issued in America, and who drafted it?

9. In what present-day Islamic countries is slavery still practiced?

INTERPRETING the FACTS

1. What prompted and motivated William Wilberforce to work so fervently to abolish slavery in the British Empire?

2. How did many of the early Christians show they were opposed to slavery?

3. What prompted and motivated Harriet Beecher Stowe to write her book *Uncle Tom's Cabin*?

4. In what ways is the book *Uncle Tom's Cabin* congruent with New Testament teaching?

5. Why do you think slavery is still practiced today in some African Islamic countries?

APPLYING the FACTS

1. How can Christians make it better known that it was Christianity that prompted the outlawing of slavery?

2. Explain how the term "Uncle Tom" is frequently misused and misunderstood as being subservient to values of white people.

3. Show how and why slavery was first outlawed in countries where Christianity has had a major presence.

CHAPTER 12: CHRISTIANITY'S STAMP on ART and ARCHITECTURE

LOOKING for FACTS

1. The earliest Christian art was commonly found in what places?

2. How did early Christian art depict Jesus Christ?

3. Gothic architecture of church buildings began in 1144 with the construction of which cathedral?

4. Byzantine church art and architecture began with the construction of what church in about A.D. 526?

5. Gothic architecture was based on the Latin cross, whereas the Byzantine church architecture was based on which other type of Christian cross?

6. Hagia Sophia is located in what European city that since 1453 has been under the control of Muslim Turks?

7. Why can the term *renaissance* (meaning reborn) be construed as a misnomer in regard to the arts?

INTERPRETING the FACTS

1. How did early Christian art and architecture differ from Greek art and architecture?

2. Why was there so little art before Christianity was legalized in A.D. 313?

3. Why has Gothic architecture been described as the style that best exemplifies Christian theology?

4. How did the Gothic architecture of the churches often compensate in part for people not being permitted to read the Bible?

5. Amid a diversity of features in Gothic cathedrals, what features did they have in common?

6. Discuss why the term *renaissance* did not become popular until several centuries after the era to which it refers.

APPLYING the FACTS

1. Explain how Christians today can show appreciation for Christian art in their homes.

2. Discuss the use or lack of use of Christian symbols in contemporary church architecture.

3. Discuss how Christian art forms of the past, such as mosaics, the Latin Christian cross, and the crucifix, are used or not used in churches today.

CHAPTER 13: The SOUND of MUSIC: ITS CHRISTIAN RESONANCE

LOOKING for FACTS

1. Who was the Roman governmental official who reported to the emperor that Christians sang hymns "to Christ as to a god"?

2. Christian songs, sung monophonically, in the early church were commonly called by what name?

3. Who introduced polyphonic music, which combines two or more melodies in harmony?

4. Who first recorded music notes on a staff of four lines, and when?

5. Who was the famous musician who set Christian theology and its gospel to polyphonic music in the eighteenth century?

6. What two world-famous musicians were German and Lutheran and born in the same year?

7. Who was the Austrian musical genius who died at the young age of thirty-five?

8. What musician brought the inspiring Christian music of Johann Sebastian Bach to light a century after Bach died?

9. Martin Luther wrote 37 Christian hymns. Of these, which one is the best known among Christians?

INTERPRETING the FACTS

1. Why is it not an overstatement to say the Christian church was born in song?

2. Why is polyphonic music said to be more beautiful than monophonic music?

3. In your opinion, why has the monophonic music once advocated by Calvin and by the Puritans in America been replaced by and large by polyphonic music?

4. Why has Bach been called "the fifth evangelist"?

APPLYING the FACTS

1. How can it be argued that Handel's *Messiah* was the product of divine inspiration?

2. Discuss the fact that some esteemed church music has been written by people who did not claim to be Christians.

3. How might Christians today be taught greater appreciation of historic Christian hymns?

CHAPTER 14: HALLMARKS of LITERATURE: THEIR CHRISTIAN IMPRINT

LOOKING FOR FACTS

1. Christian writings written to defend the gospel of Jesus Christ are formally called by what name?

2. Christian writings that argue against adversarial teachings are formally called by what name?

3. Who is known as "the Christian Herodotus"?

4. What renowned Christian bishop and theologian wrote *The City of God* in the fifth century?

5. Who introduced the expression of *anno ab incarnatione Domini* (abbreviated as A.D.) in England in the eighth century?

6. Who do historians say laid the egg that Luther hatched in the Reformation?

7. What document ushered in the birthdate of the Lutheran church in 1530?

8. What is the name of John Calvin's classical work in theology?

INTERPRETING the FACTS

1. How has Thomas More's *Utopia* often been misunderstood?

2. What is meant by "Pascal's *Wager*"?

3. What contribution did Edward Gibbon's *The Decline and Fall of the Roman Empire* make to our understanding of Christianity's influence in the world?

4. How did Charles Dickens's book *A Christmas Carol* change the Puritan way of observing Christmas in New England?

5. What motivated Lewis Wallace to write his book *Ben-Hur*?

APPLYING the FACTS

1. How can John Bunyan's *The Pilgrim's Progress* serve as inspiration for Christians?

2. Explain how Pascal's *Wager* can be used to strengthen a Christian's faith.

3. Show how C. S. Lewis's *Mere Christianity* refutes the belief that Jesus Christ was a great teacher but not God.

4. Discuss what Christians today can learn from early Christian apologetic writings.

CHAPTER 15: ADDITIONAL INFLUENCE: HOLIDAYS, WORDS, SYMBOLS, and EXPRESSIONS

LOOKING for FACTS

1. The *Didache*, an early Christian manual of theology, referred to Sunday by what name?

2. What early church father said that Christians attending divine services on Sunday had nothing to do with the pagan sun god?

3. What Christian Roman emperor in the early fourth century made certain activities illegal on Sunday?

4. The expression "Before Christ" (B.C.) originated in what century?

5. What does the word *cemetery* mean?

6. Who first said, "When in Rome, do as the Romans do"?

INTERPRETING the FACTS

1. Discuss the belief that Christians in the third-century chose to celebrate Christmas Day on a pagan festival day.

2. Discuss the belief that Christians chose for worship the first day of the week to preempt the day that honored the Roman sun god.

3. Why is the expression "Doubting Thomas" not beneficial to Christianity?

4. In what way does the expression "Good Samaritan" reflect positively on Christianity?

5. Explain why the early Christians chose the word *pagan* to refer to non-Christians.

APPLYING THE FACTS

1. Discuss how and why Christians should or should not celebrate common Western holidays.

2. Explain how Christians today can benefit from using Christian names and symbols.

3. Show how the Doubting Thomas incident in the Bible can be used to defend and argue for the historicity of Christ's physical resurrection.

We want to hear from you. Please send your comments about this
book to us in care of zreview@zondervan.com. Thank you.

ZONDERVAN.com/
AUTHORTRACKER
follow your favorite authors